STEPHEN KING

THE DARK TOWER

TREACHERY

CREATIVE DIRECTOR AND EXECUTIVE DIRECTOR
STEPHEN KING

PLOTTING AND CONSULTATION
ROBIN FURTH

SCRIPT
PETER DAVID

ART
JAE LEE, AND RICHARD ISANOVE

LETTERING
CHRIS ELIOPOULOS

ASSISTANT EDITORS
LAUREN SANKOVITCH, LAUREN HENRY,
NATHAN COSBY AND MICHAEL HORWITZ

CONSULTING EDITOR
NICOLE BOOSE

EDITOR
RALPH MACCHIO

COVER ART
JAE LEE

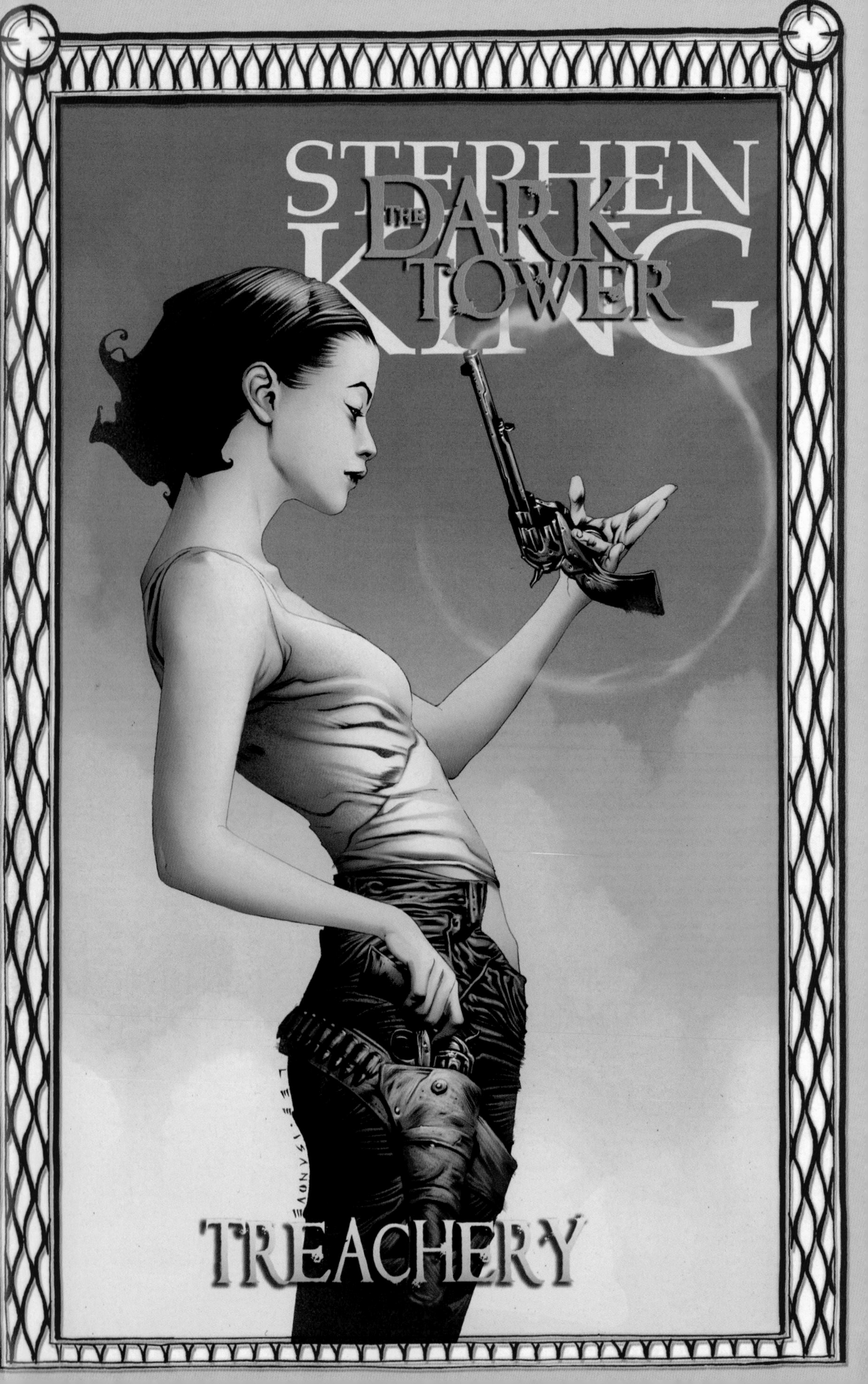
STEPHEN KING
THE DARK TOWER
TREACHERY

THE RIGHT STUFF

What does it really take to become a gunslinger? Roland Deschain, our protagonist, at the tender age of fourteen, became the youngest aspirant to get his guns. He was secretly goaded into challenging his mentor Cortland Andrus by the evil wizard Marten Broadcloak, who'd hoped for his failure. But Roland succeeded, defeating the wily Cort and winning four years too early, earning entry into this elite fighting force. He is the son of Steven Deschain, ruler of the barony of Gilead. This makes him the direct descendant of Arthur Eld, who was the king of All-World. The spirit of his hawk who was slain in the struggle with Cort, joined with Roland's own, bolstering his already formidable courage and resourcefulness.

Thus Roland stands as a singular figure in the Dark Tower mythos through both lineage and accomplishment. But what of the others who seek the coveted role of gunslinger? What of their qualities? Two of Roland's ka-tet, Cuthbert Allgood and Alain Johns are in the running. Both have stood alongside Roland in life-and-death struggles, proving their mettle. And in this story arc collected herein, we introduce a brand new entry into the gunslinger trials, Aileen Ritter, the niece of Cortland Andrus himself. This markedly ambitious young lady plans to achieve what no woman before her has ever attempted—to break the glass ceiling and surmount the gender barrier. We thought it would be intriguing to bring onstage such a character into the rigid society of Gilead to shake up the status quo.

Still, let's recall that Ms. Ritter isn't the only member of the distaff out to make a difference in Mid-World. There is the women's sect known as the Sisters of Oriza. Although they are primarily known as cooks and healers, the Sisters have honed their martial skills, as well. Because no woman may carry a gun, they specialize in throwing a weapon, which resembles both a dinner plate and a discus, whose edges are sharpened like a razor's. It has been said that the Sisters' accuracy with their weapons surpasses that of gunslingers themselves.

Aileen does not intend to enter the cult of the goddess Oriza. She has her sights set on becoming a gunslinger, beating the boys at their own game. The obstacles before her are formidable. The attrition rate among such warriors is almost necessarily high. And failure in this quest means banishment from Gilead, from one's own family. So, the price is very steep.

COLLECTION EDITOR
MARK D. BEAZLEY

ASSISTANT EDITORS
JOHN DENNING AND CORY LEVINE

EDITOR, SPECIAL PROJECTS
JENNIFER GRUNWALD

SENIOR EDITOR, SPECIAL PROJECTS
JEFF YOUNGQUIST

SENIOR VICE PRESIDENT OF SALES
DAVID GABRIEL

SENIOR VICE PRESIDENT OF STRATEGIC DEVELOPMENT
RUWAN JAYATILLEKE

BOOK DESIGN
SPRING HOTELING AND PATRICK MCGRATH

EDITOR IN CHIEF
JOE QUESADA

PUBLISHER
DAN BUCKLEY

SPECIAL THANKS TO CHUCK VERRILL, MARSHA DEFILLIPO,
RALPH VICINANZA, BARBARA ANN MCINTYRE, BRIAN STARK,
JIM NAUSEDAS, JIM MCCANN, ARUNE SINGH, CHRIS ALLO,
JEFF SUTER, JOHN BARBER JIM CALAFIORE

FOR MORE INFORMATION ON DARK TOWER COMICS, VISIT MARVEL.COM/DARKTOWER.
TO FIND MARVEL COMICS AT A LOCAL COMIC SHOP, CALL 1-888-COMICBOOK.

DARK TOWER: TREACHERY. Contains material originally published in magazine form as DARK TOWER: TREACHERY #1-6. First printing 2008. ISBN# 978-0-7851-3574-6. Published by MARVEL PUBLISHING, INC., a subsidiary of MARVEL ENTERTAINMENT, INC. OFFICE OF PUBLICATION: 417 5th Avenue, New York, NY 10016. © 2009 Stephen King. All rights reserved. $24.99 per copy in the U.S. (GST #R127032852); Canadian Agreement #40668537. All characters featured in this issue and the distinctive names and likenesses thereof, and all related indicia are trademarks of Stephen King. No similarity between any of the names, characters, persons, and/or institutions in this magazine with those of any living or dead person or institution is intended, and any such similarity which may exist is purely coincidental. Printed in the U.S.A. ALAN FINE, CEO Marvel Toys & Publishing Divisions and CMO Marvel Characters, Inc.; JIM SOKOLOWSKI, Chief Operating Officer; DAVID GABRIEL, SVP of Publishing Sales & Circulation; DAVID BOGART, SVP of Business Affairs & Talent Management; MICHAEL PASCIULLO, VP Merchandising & Communications; JIM O'KEEFE, VP of Operations & Logistics; DAN CARR, Executive Director of Publishing Technology; JUSTIN F. GABRIE, Director of Publishing & Editorial Operations; SUSAN CRESPI, Editorial Operations Manager; ALEX MORALES, Publishing Operations Manager; STAN LEE, Chairman Emeritus. For information regarding advertising in Marvel Comics or on Marvel.com, please contact Mitch Dane, Advertising Director, at mdane@marvel.com. For Marvel subscription inquiries, please call 800-217-9158.

10 9 8 7 6 5 4 3 2 1

But the reward for success in Aileen's instance is extraordinarily high. She will not simply become a member of this elite assemblage; she will become the first of her sex to have penetrated these exalted and exclusive ranks. And she's willing to risk all in the trying. Her Uncle Cort and Gilead ruler Steven Deschain have other plans for Aileen. Plans that involve Roland Deschain. Does she have the fortitude to remain true to her self-styled calling, or will the burdens and expectations placed upon her be too much? Only Gan knows, and he isn't talking.

This voyage to storied Mid-World will reveal some of the workings of the society within Gilead's walls. While it is truly a place of other-worldly wonder and fears, you may find striking parallels to our own troubled times. Do ya kennit?

Enjoy the ride!

Ralph Macchio

--Ralph Macchio

IN A WORLD THAT HAS MOVED ON...

Earning the title of Gunslinger at the unheard-of age of fourteen, young Roland Deschain quickly became a target for his father's enemies, namely the "Good Man" John Farson, and was forced to flee his home of Gilead or face death.

Accompanied by his ka-tet mates, Cuthbert and Alain, Roland journeyed to the seaside town of Hambry and fell in love with Susan Delgado. When Susan was killed by the townspeople, who were revealed to be under the control of Farson and his evil master, the Crimson King, the ka-tet fled, with the Hambry posse in hot pursuit.

Having secured Farson's greatest prize, the seeing sphere known as Maerlyn's Grapefruit, during their escape, the ka-tet were caught unawares as the sphere sucked Roland's consciousness deep into the demonic realm known as End-World, where he was confronted by the diabolical Crimson King.

Despite being rescued from the Crimson King's clutches by his young friend, Sheemie, Roland, now safe in Gilead with the rest of his ka-tet, is still secretly under the Grapefruit's spell which could mean certain doom for the unsuspecting people of Gilead.

STEPHEN KING

THE DARK TOWER

TREACHERY

CHAPTER ONE

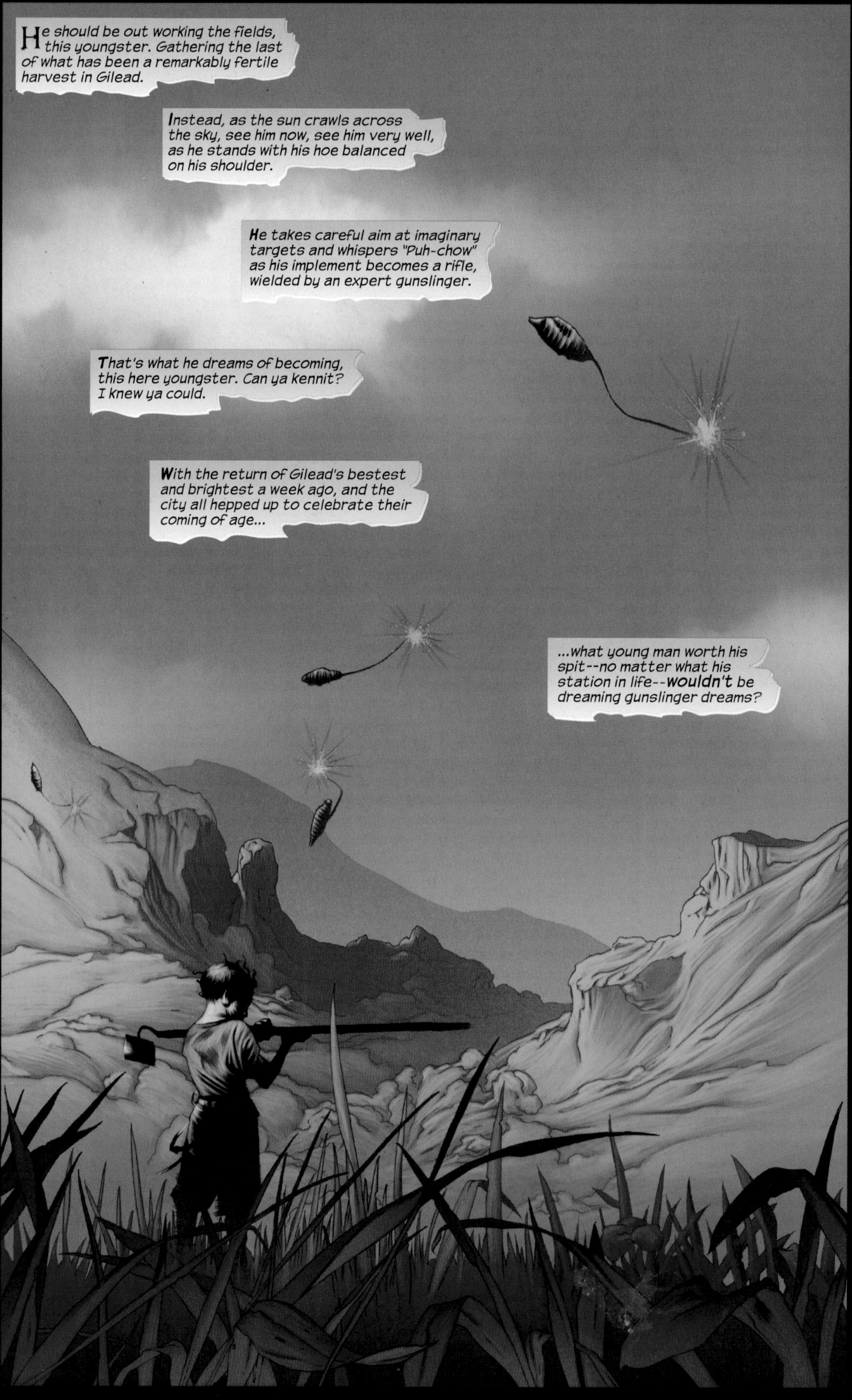
He should be out working the fields, this youngster. Gathering the last of what has been a remarkably fertile harvest in Gilead.
Instead, as the sun crawls across the sky, see him now, see him very well, as he stands with his hoe balanced on his shoulder.
He takes careful aim at imaginary targets and whispers "Puh-chow" as his implement becomes a rifle, wielded by an expert gunslinger.
That's what he dreams of becoming, this here youngster. Can ya kennit? I knew ya could.
With the return of Gilead's bestest and brightest a week ago, and the city all hepped up to celebrate their coming of age...
...what young man worth his spit--no matter what his station in life--wouldn't be dreaming gunslinger dreams?

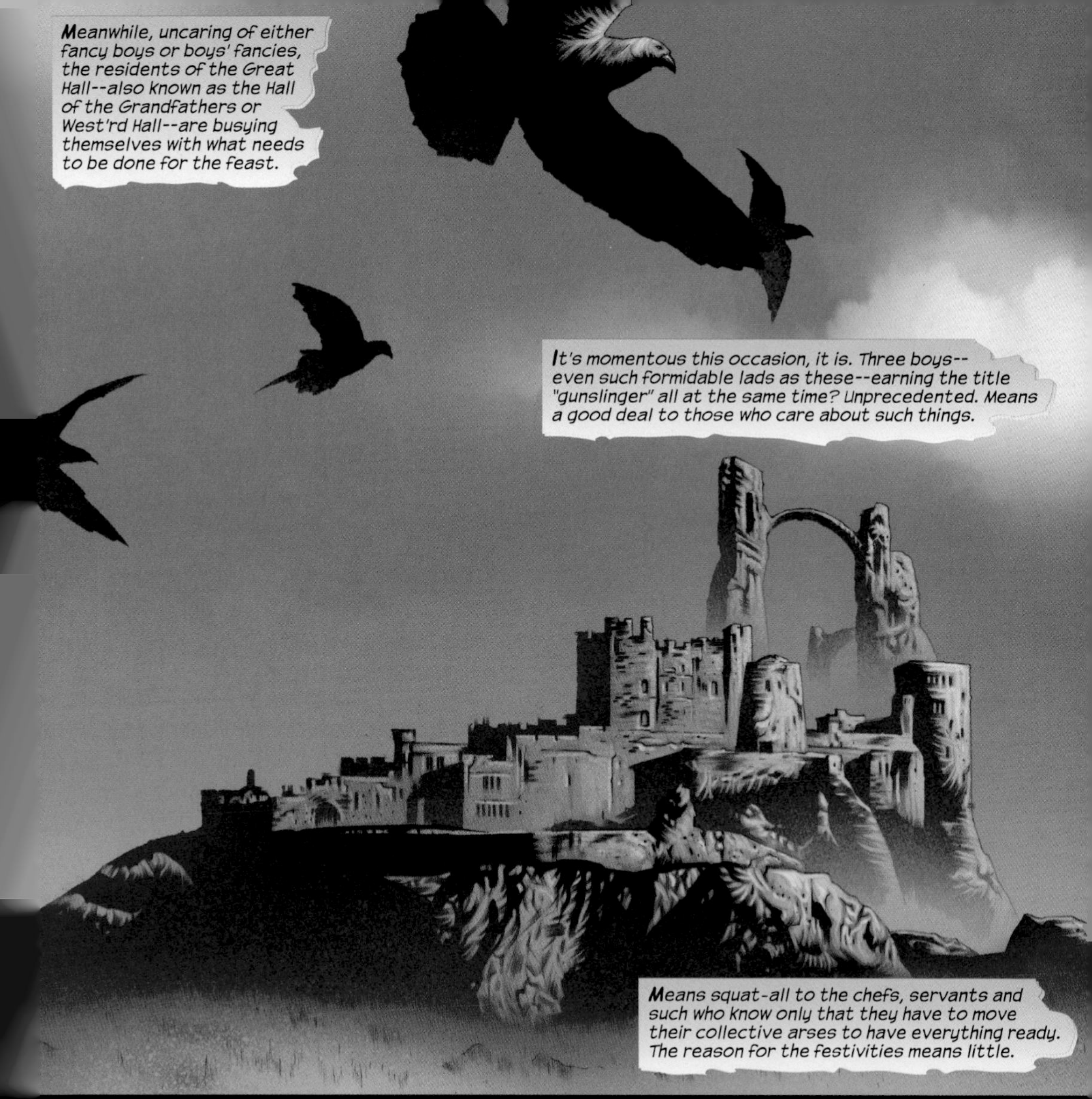
Meanwhile, uncaring of either fancy boys or boys' fancies, the residents of the Great Hall--also known as the Hall of the Grandfathers or West'rd Hall--are busying themselves with what needs to be done for the feast.
It's momentous this occasion, it is. Three boys--even such formidable lads as these--earning the title "gunslinger" all at the same time? Unprecedented. Means a good deal to those who care about such things.
Means squat-all to the chefs, servants and such who know only that they have to move their collective arses to have everything ready. The reason for the festivities means little.

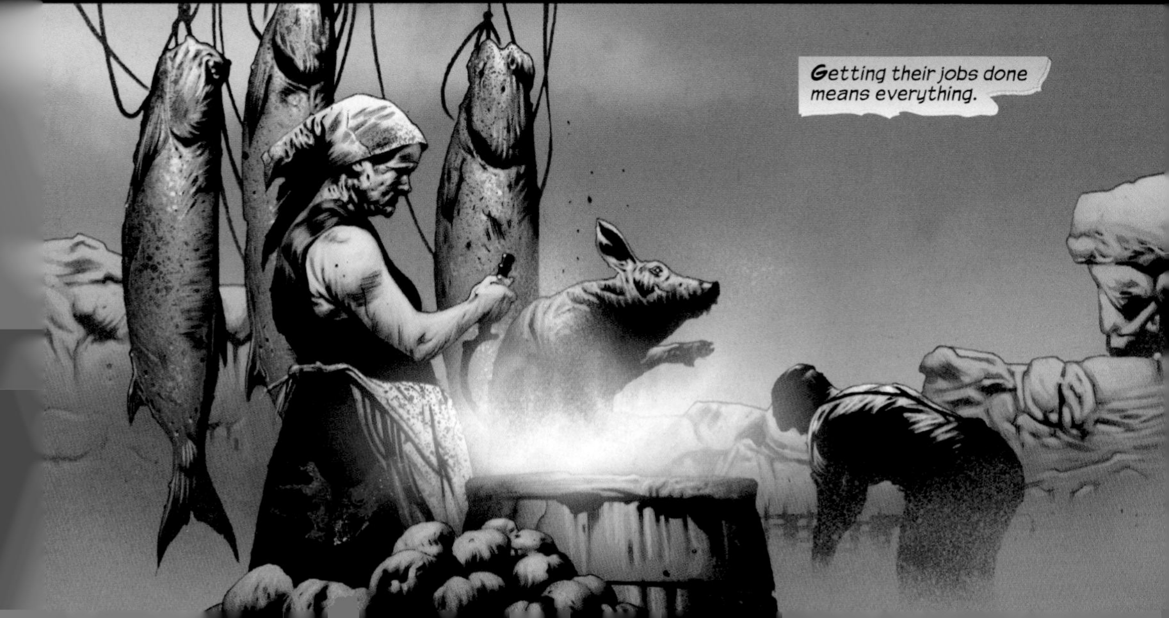
Getting their jobs done means everything.

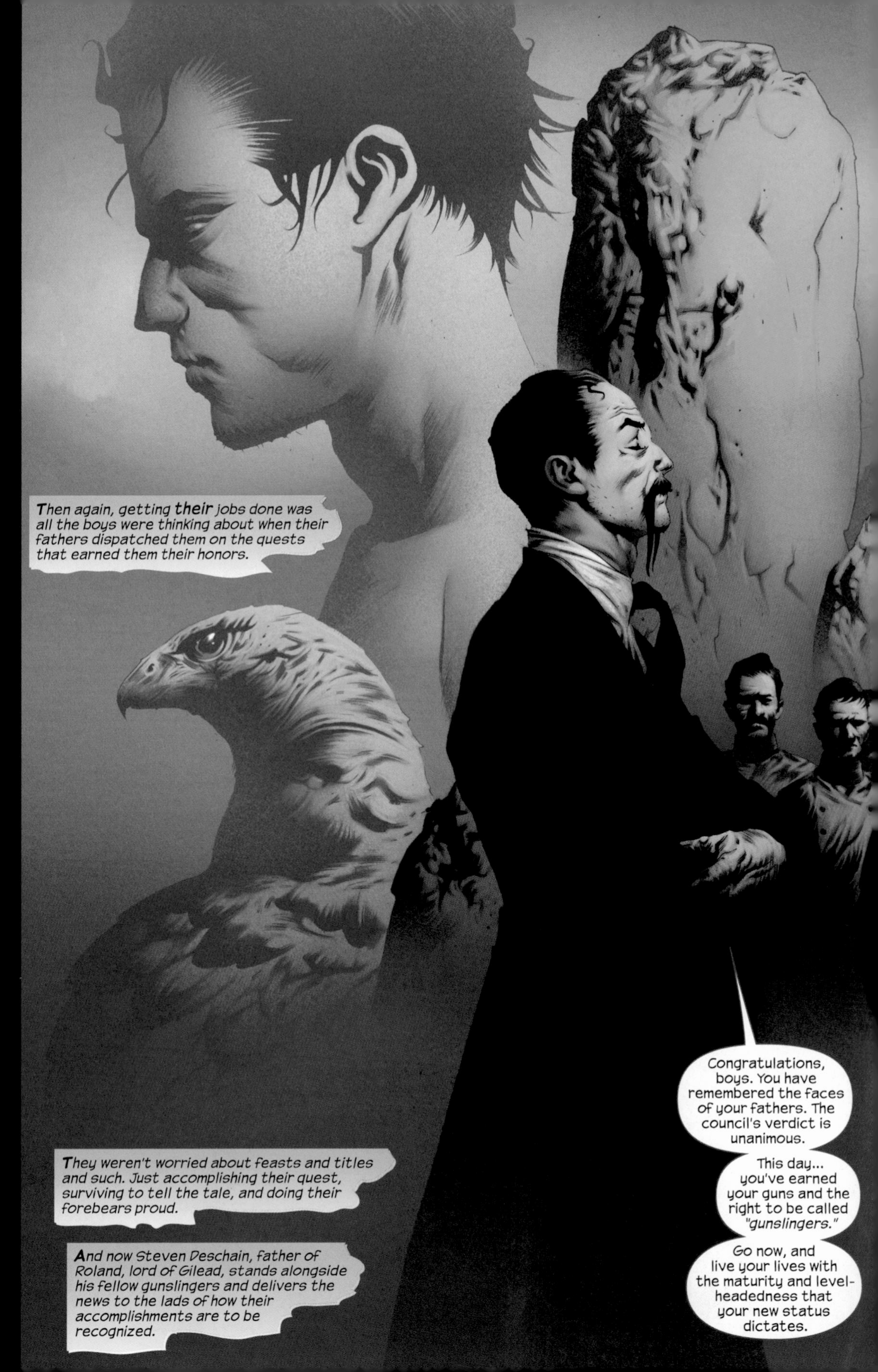
Then again, getting their jobs done was all the boys were thinking about when their fathers dispatched them on the quests that earned them their honors.
They weren't worried about feasts and titles and such. Just accomplishing their quest, surviving to tell the tale, and doing their forebears proud.
And now Steven Deschain, father of Roland, lord of Gilead, stands alongside his fellow gunslingers and delivers the news to the lads of how their accomplishments are to be recognized.
Congratulations, boys. You have remembered the faces of your fathers. The council's verdict is unanimous.
This day... you've earned your guns and the right to be called "gunslingers."
Go now, and live your lives with the maturity and level-headedness that your new status dictates.

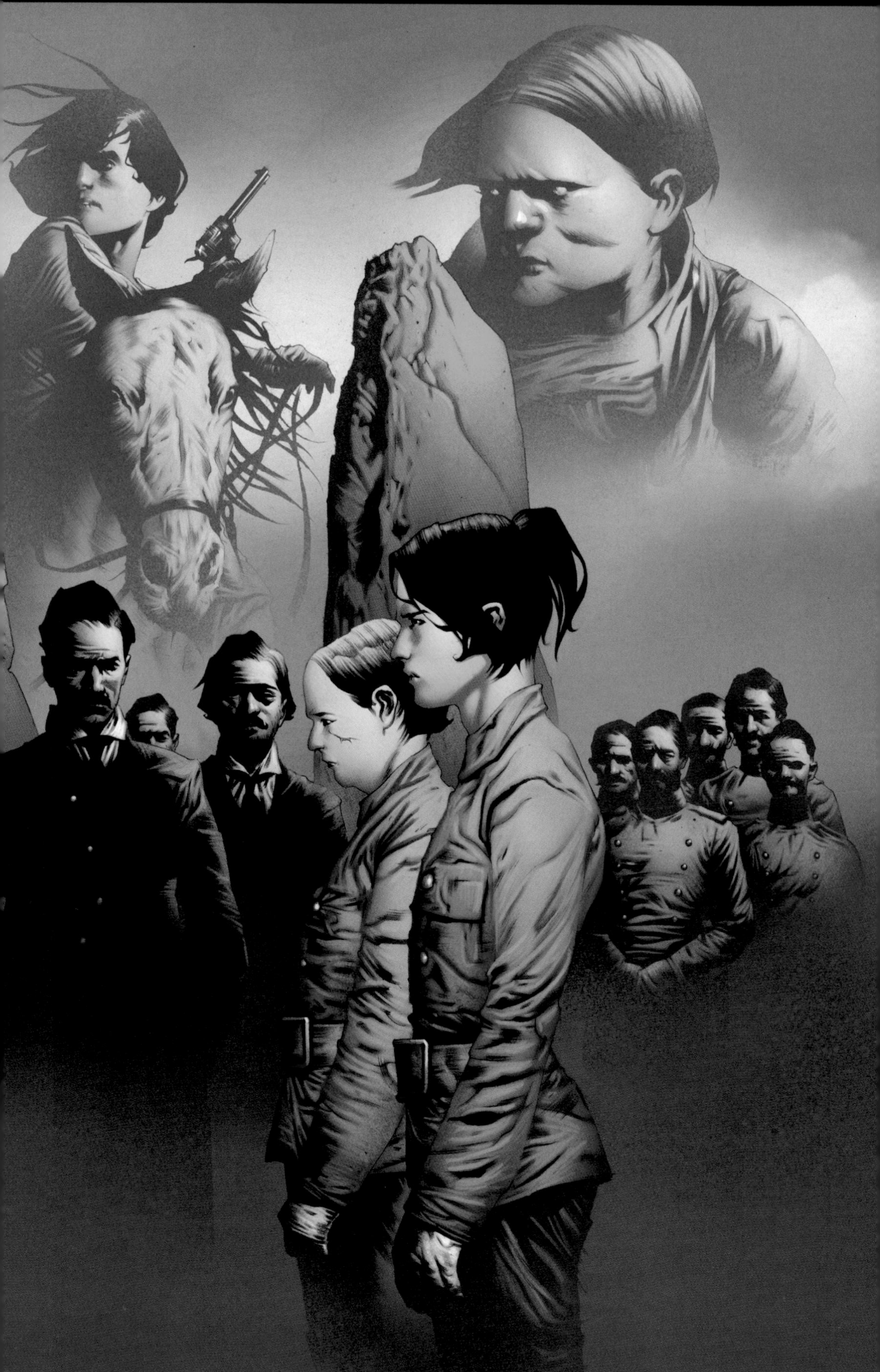

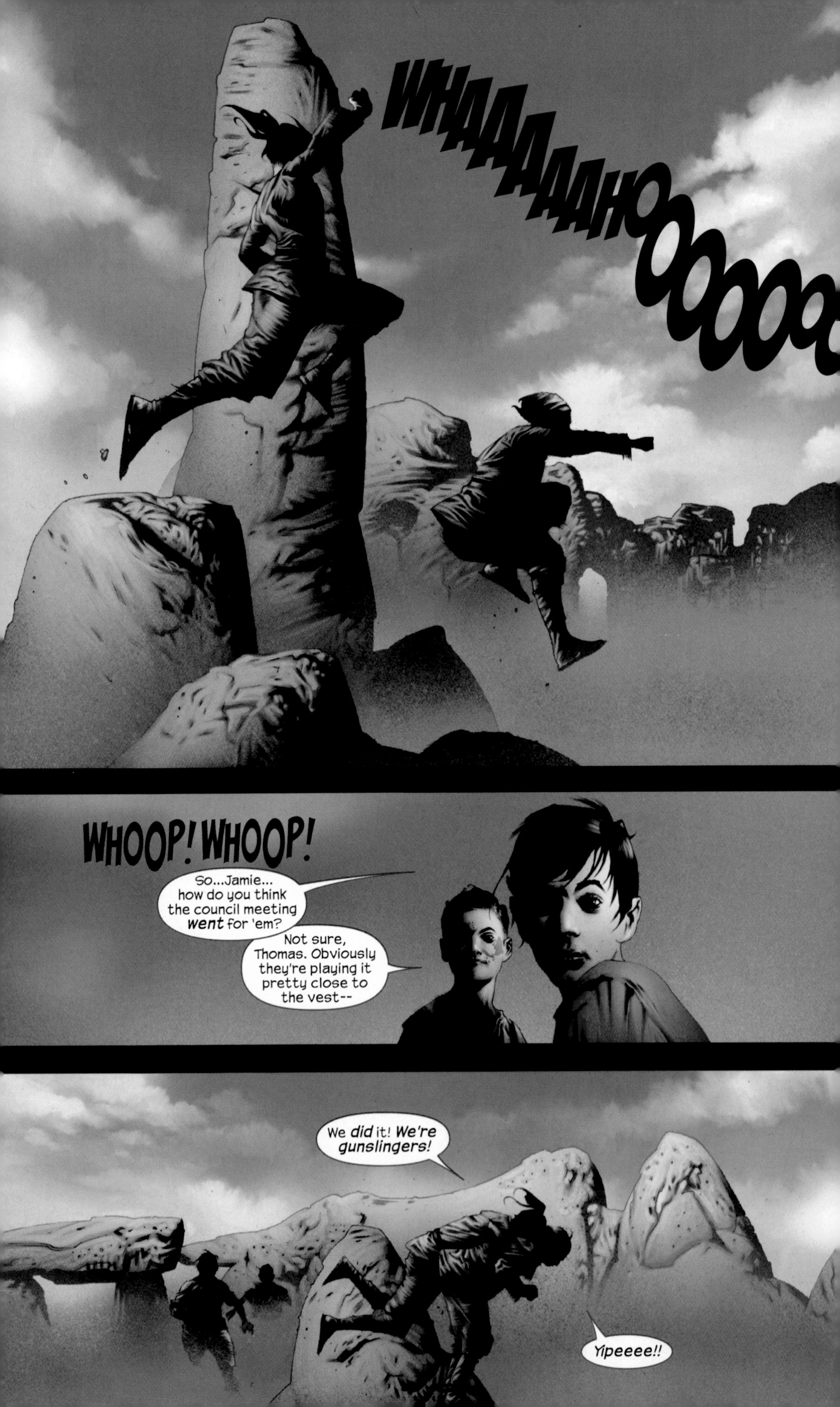
WHAAAAAAHOOOOOO
WHOOP! WHOOP!
So...Jamie... how do you think the council meeting went for 'em?
Not sure, Thomas. Obviously they're playing it pretty close to the vest--
We did it! We're gunslingers!
Yipeeee!!

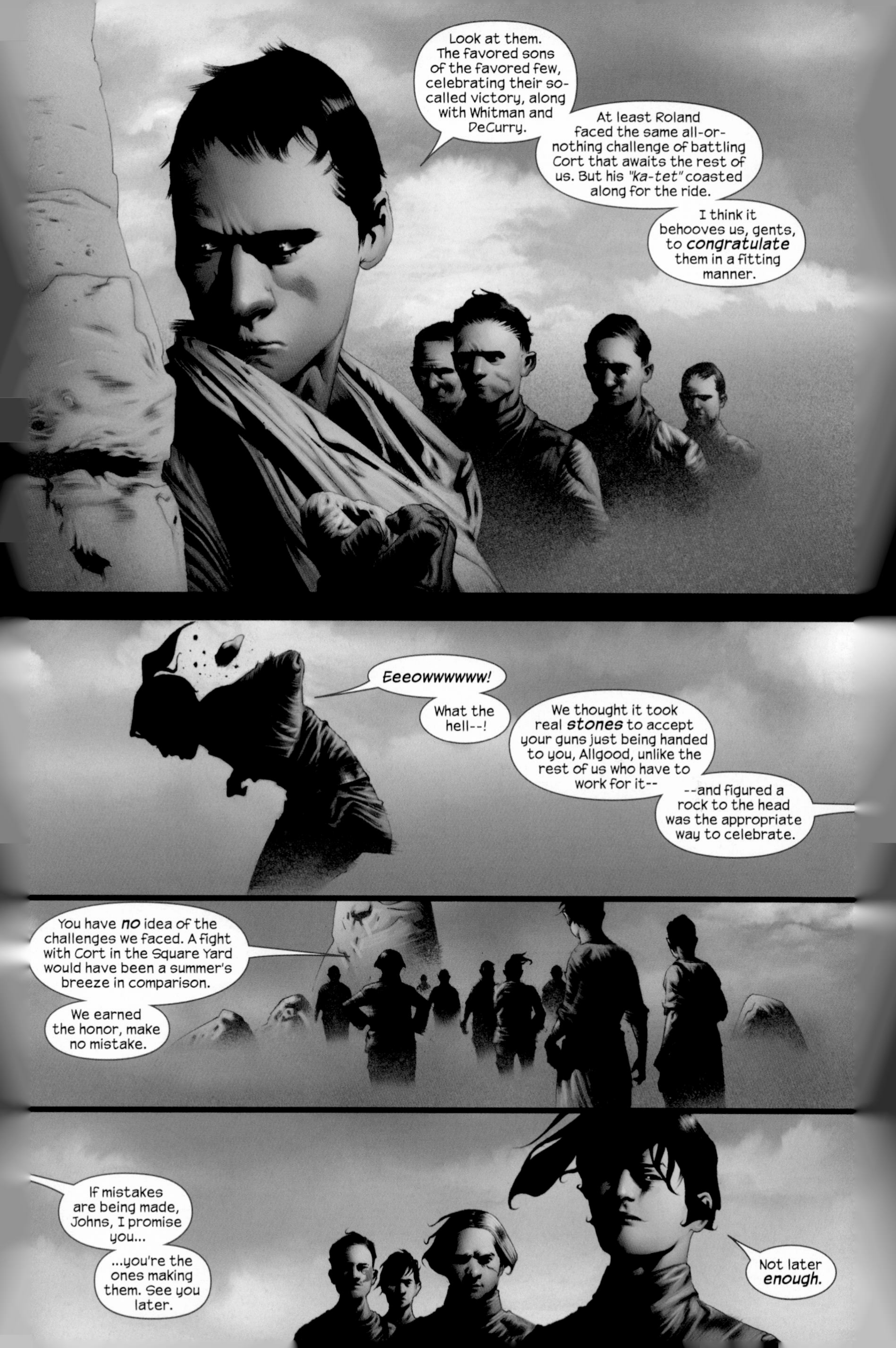
Look at them. The favored sons of the favored few, celebrating their so-called victory, along with Whitman and DeCurry.
At least Roland faced the same all-or-nothing challenge of battling Cort that awaits the rest of us. But his "ka-tet" coasted along for the ride.
I think it behooves us, gents, to congratulate them in a fitting manner.
Eeeowwwwww!
What the hell--!
We thought it took real stones to accept your guns just being handed to you, Allgood, unlike the rest of us who have to work for it--
--and figured a rock to the head was the appropriate way to celebrate.
You have no idea of the challenges we faced. A fight with Cort in the Square Yard would have been a summer's breeze in comparison.
We earned the honor, make no mistake.
If mistakes are being made, Johns, I promise you...
...you're the ones making them. See you later.
Not later enough.

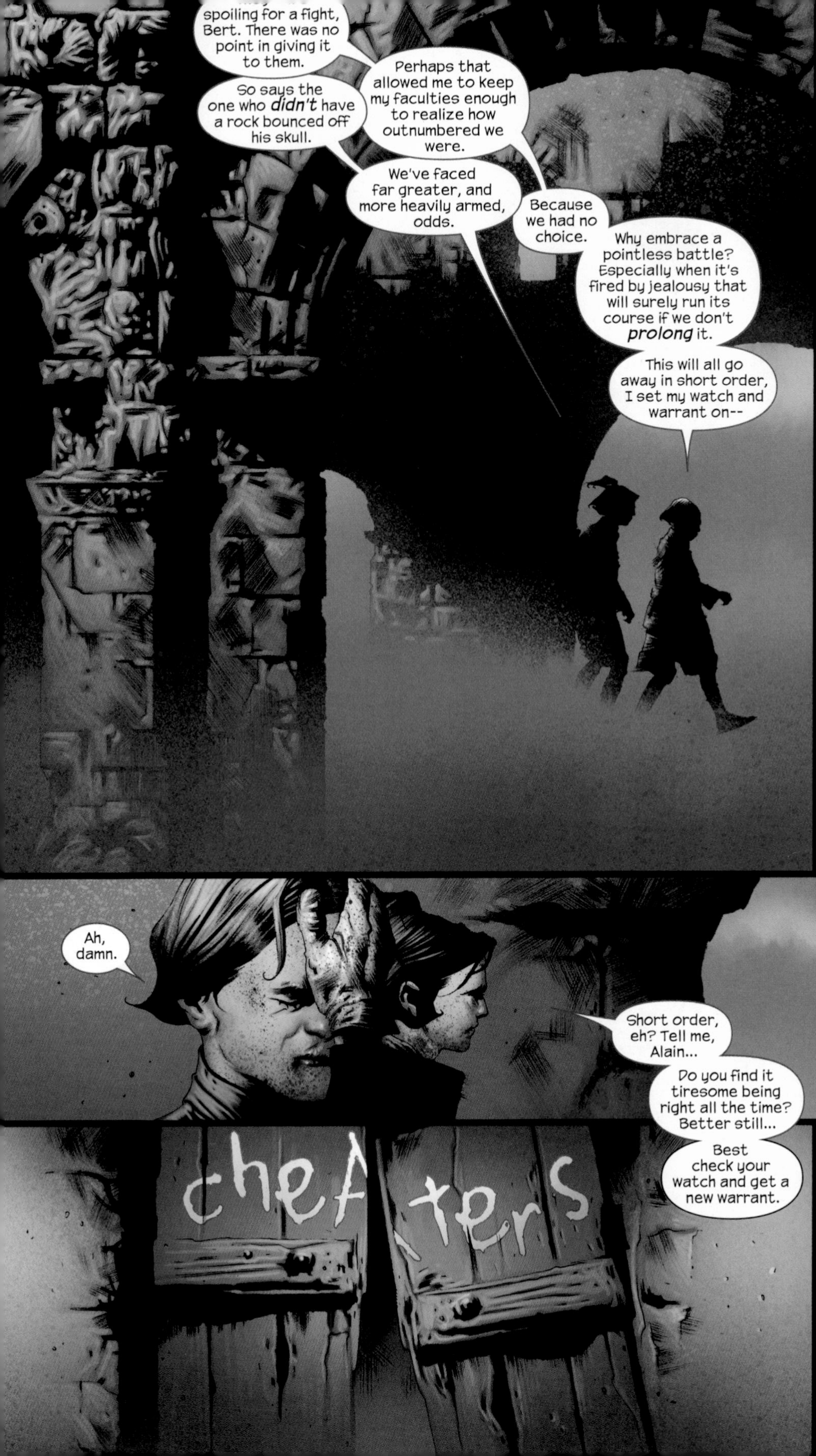

spoiling for a fight, Bert. There was no point in giving it to them.
So says the one who *didn't* have a rock bounced off his skull.
Perhaps that allowed me to keep my faculties enough to realize how outnumbered we were.
We've faced far greater, and more heavily armed, odds.
Because we had no choice.
Why embrace a pointless battle? Especially when it's fired by jealousy that will surely run its course if we don't *prolong* it.
This will all go away in short order, I set my watch and warrant on--
Ah, damn.
Short order, eh? Tell me, Alain...
Do you find it tiresome being right all the time? Better still...
Best check your watch and get a new warrant.
cheaters

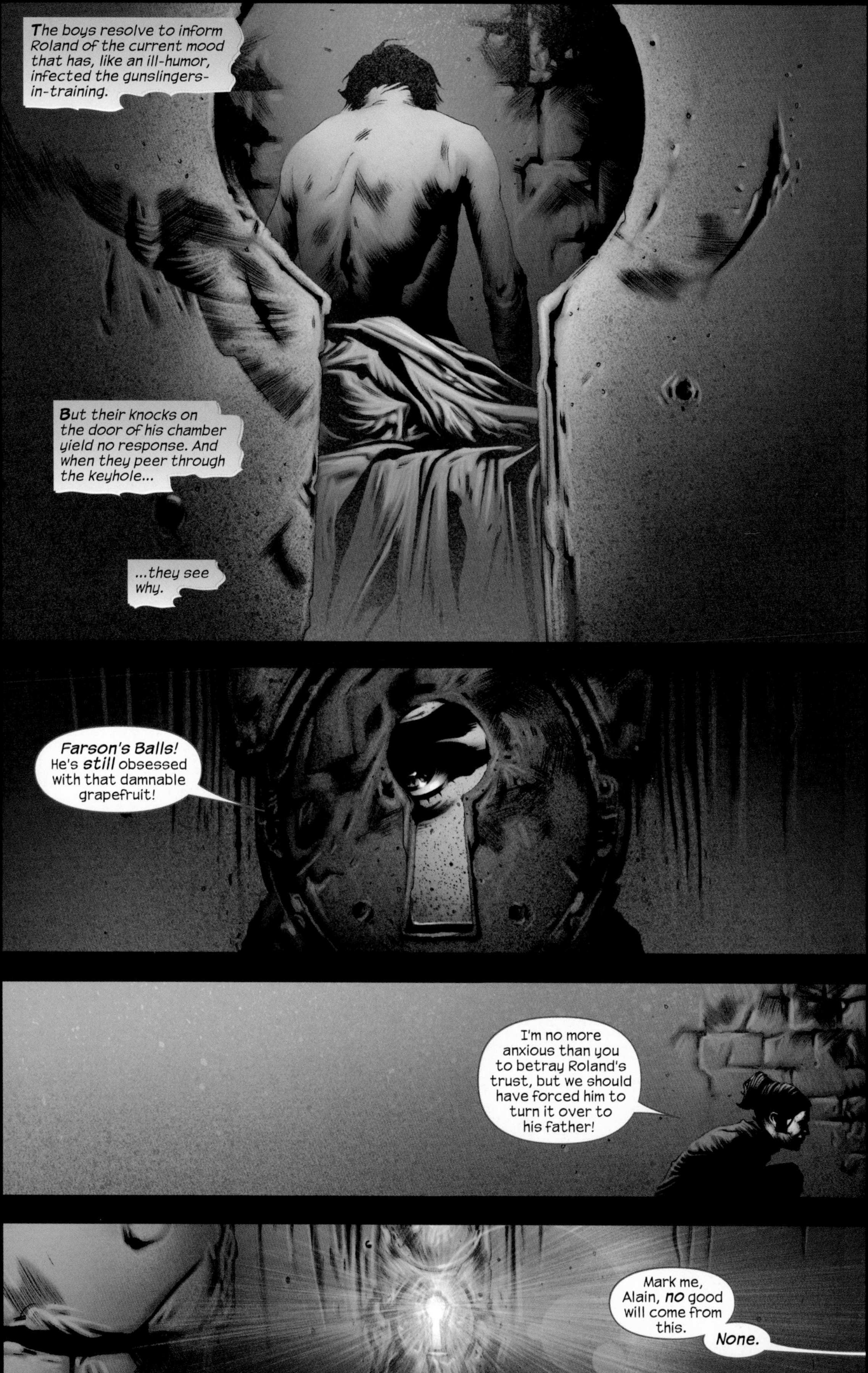
The boys resolve to inform Roland of the current mood that has, like an ill-humor, infected the gunslingers-in-training.
But their knocks on the door of his chamber yield no response. And when they peer through the keyhole...
...they see why.
Farson's Balls! He's still obsessed with that damnable grapefruit!
I'm no more anxious than you to betray Roland's trust, but we should have forced him to turn it over to his father!
Mark me, Alain, no good will come from this.
None.

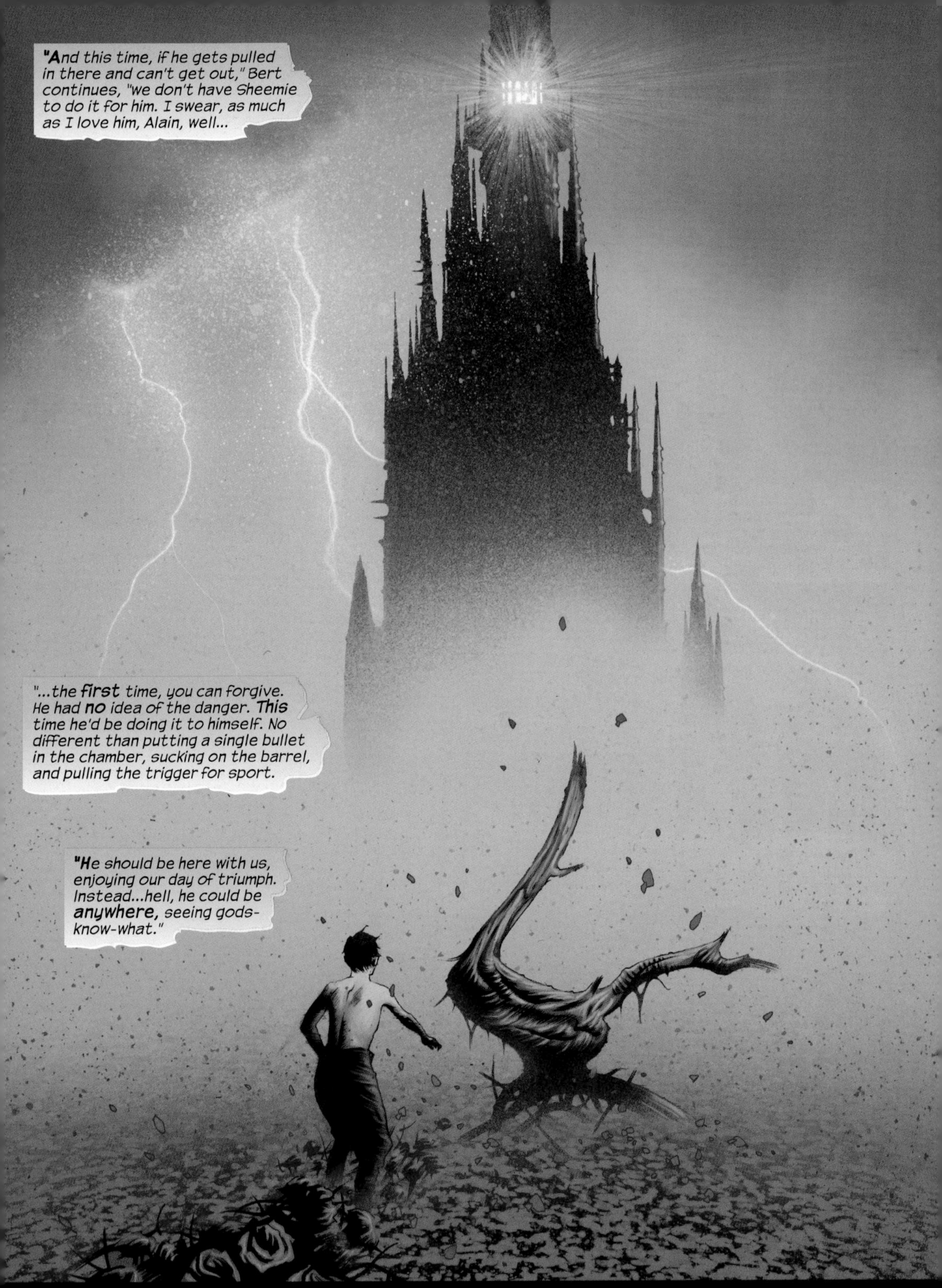
"And this time, if he gets pulled in there and can't get out," Bert continues, "we don't have Sheemie to do it for him. I swear, as much as I love him, Alain, well...
"...the first time, you can forgive. He had no idea of the danger. This time he'd be doing it to himself. No different than putting a single bullet in the chamber, sucking on the barrel, and pulling the trigger for sport.
"He should be here with us, enjoying our day of triumph. Instead...hell, he could be anywhere, seeing gods-know-what."

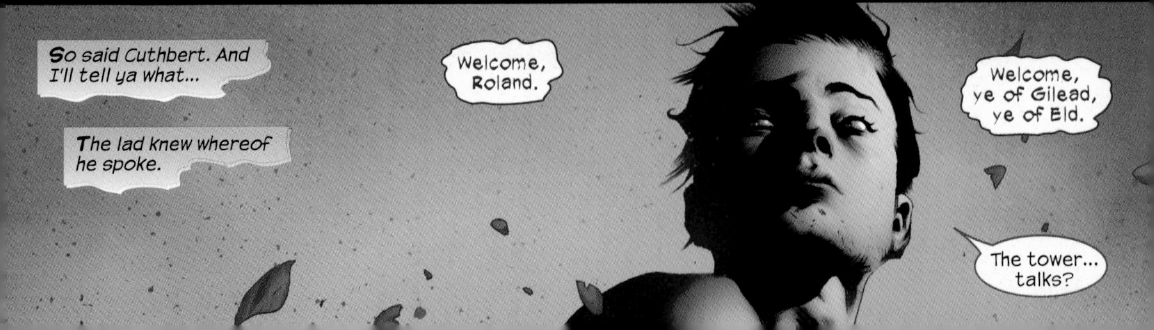
So said Cuthbert. And I'll tell ya what...
The lad knew whereof he spoke.
Welcome, Roland.
Welcome, ye of Gilead, ye of Eld.
The tower... talks?

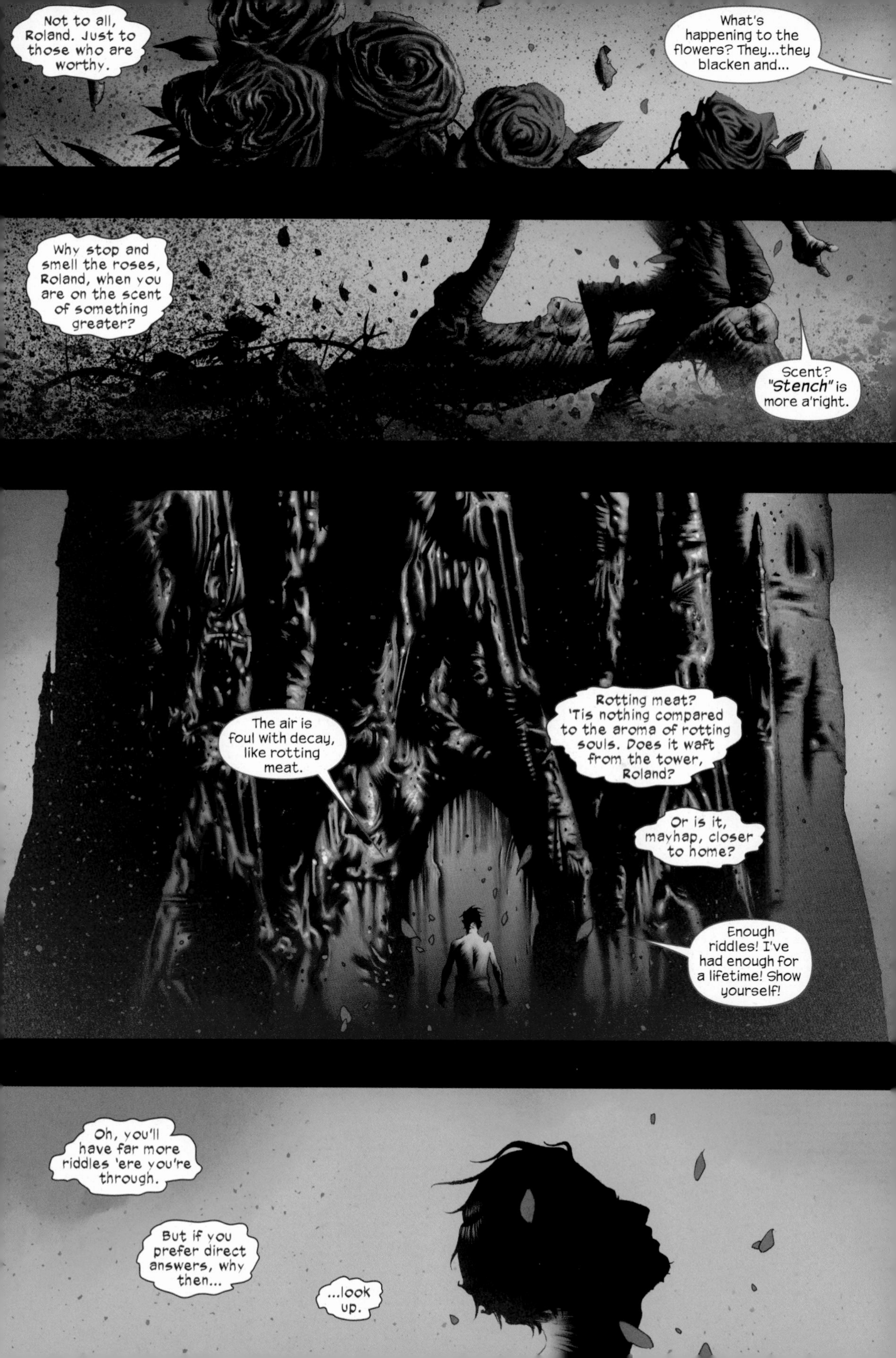
Not to all, Roland. Just to those who are worthy.
What's happening to the flowers? They...they blacken and...
Why stop and smell the roses, Roland, when you are on the scent of something greater?
Scent? "Stench" is more a'right.
The air is foul with decay, like rotting meat.
Rotting meat? 'Tis nothing compared to the aroma of rotting souls. Does it waft from the tower, Roland?
Or is it, mayhap, closer to home?
Enough riddles! I've had enough for a lifetime! Show yourself!
Oh, you'll have far more riddles 'ere you're through.
But if you prefer direct answers, why then...
...look up.

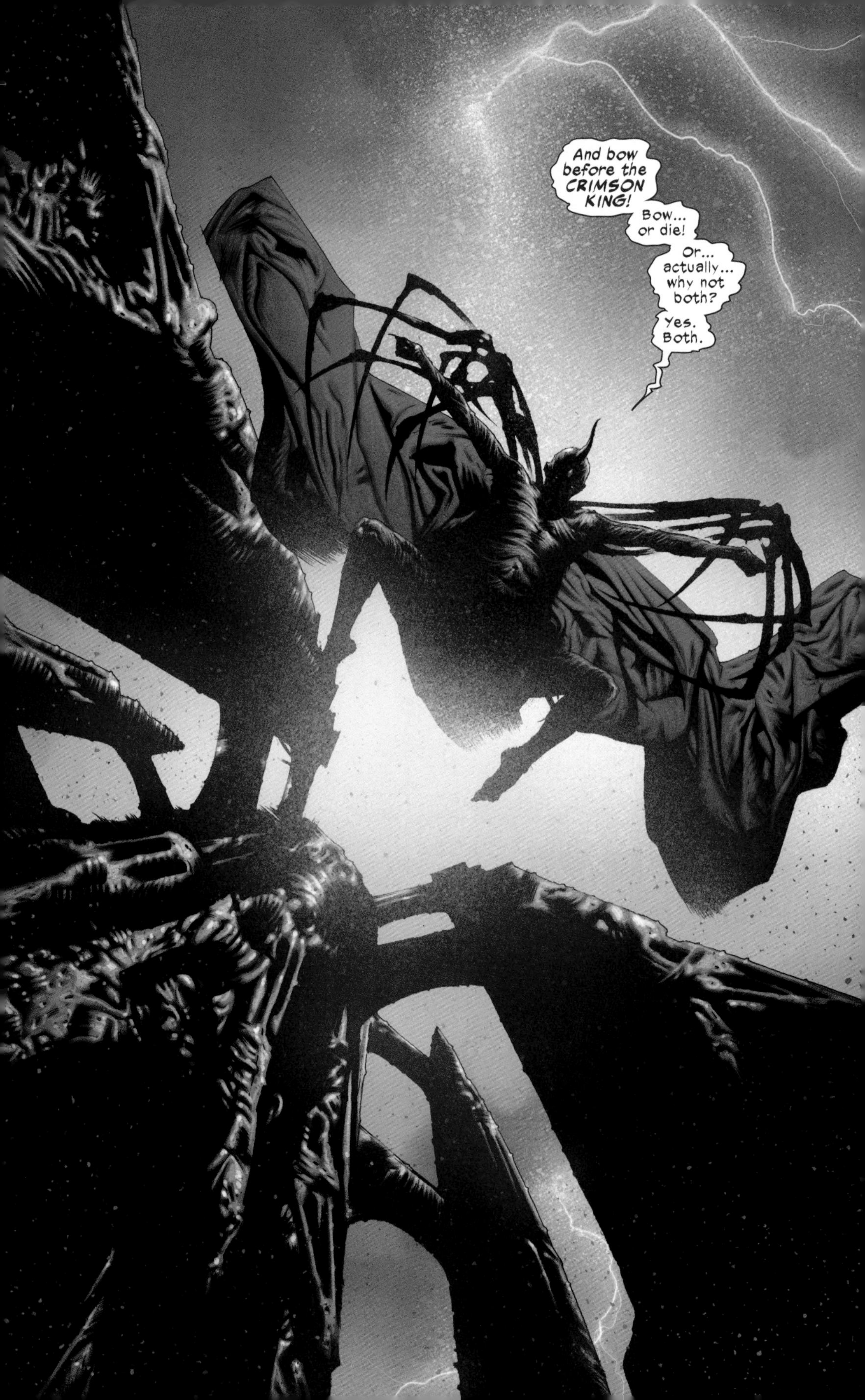
And bow before the CRIMSON KING!
Bow... or die!
Or... actually... why not both?
Yes. Both.

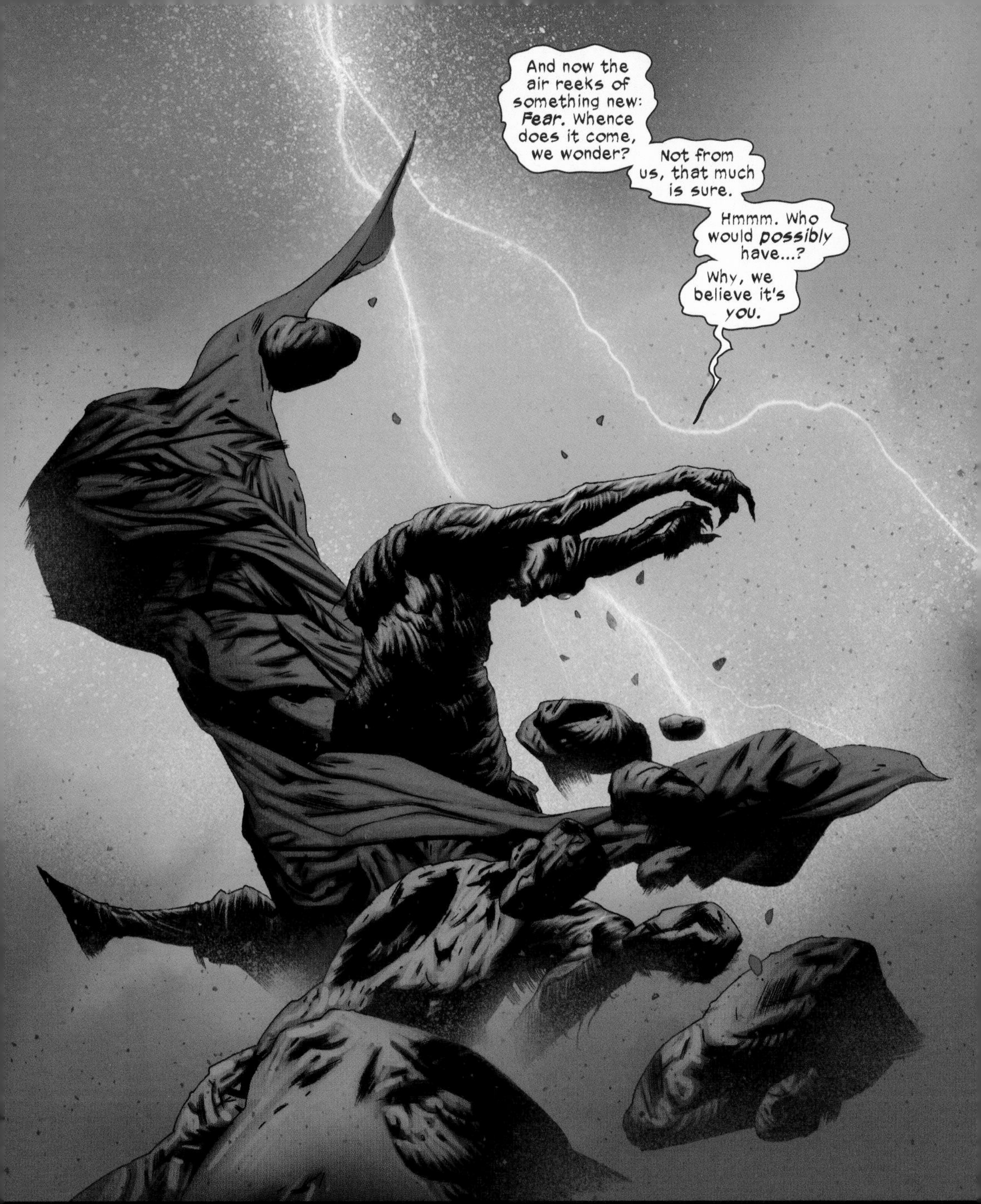

And now the air reeks of something new: *Fear.* Whence does it come, we wonder?
Not from us, that much is sure.
Hmmm. Who would *possibly* have...?
Why, we believe it's *you.*

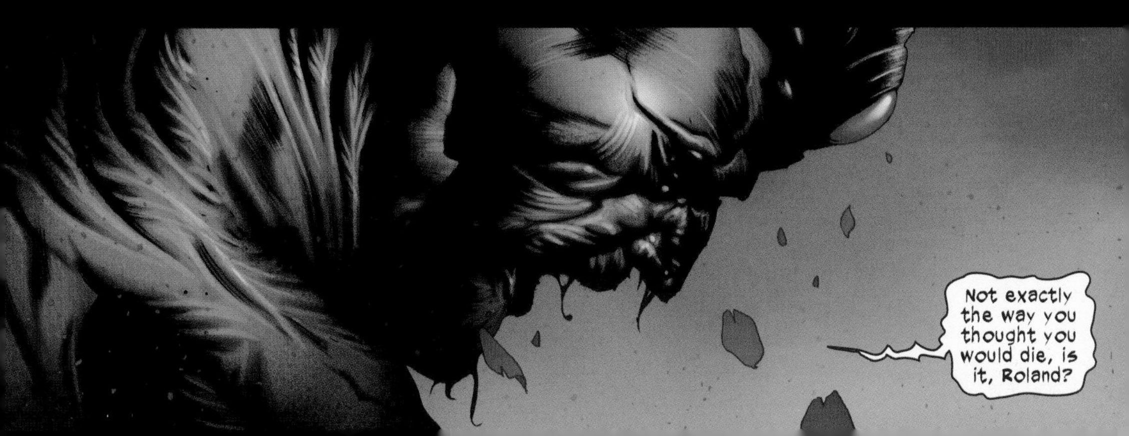

Not exactly the way you thought you would die, is it, Roland?

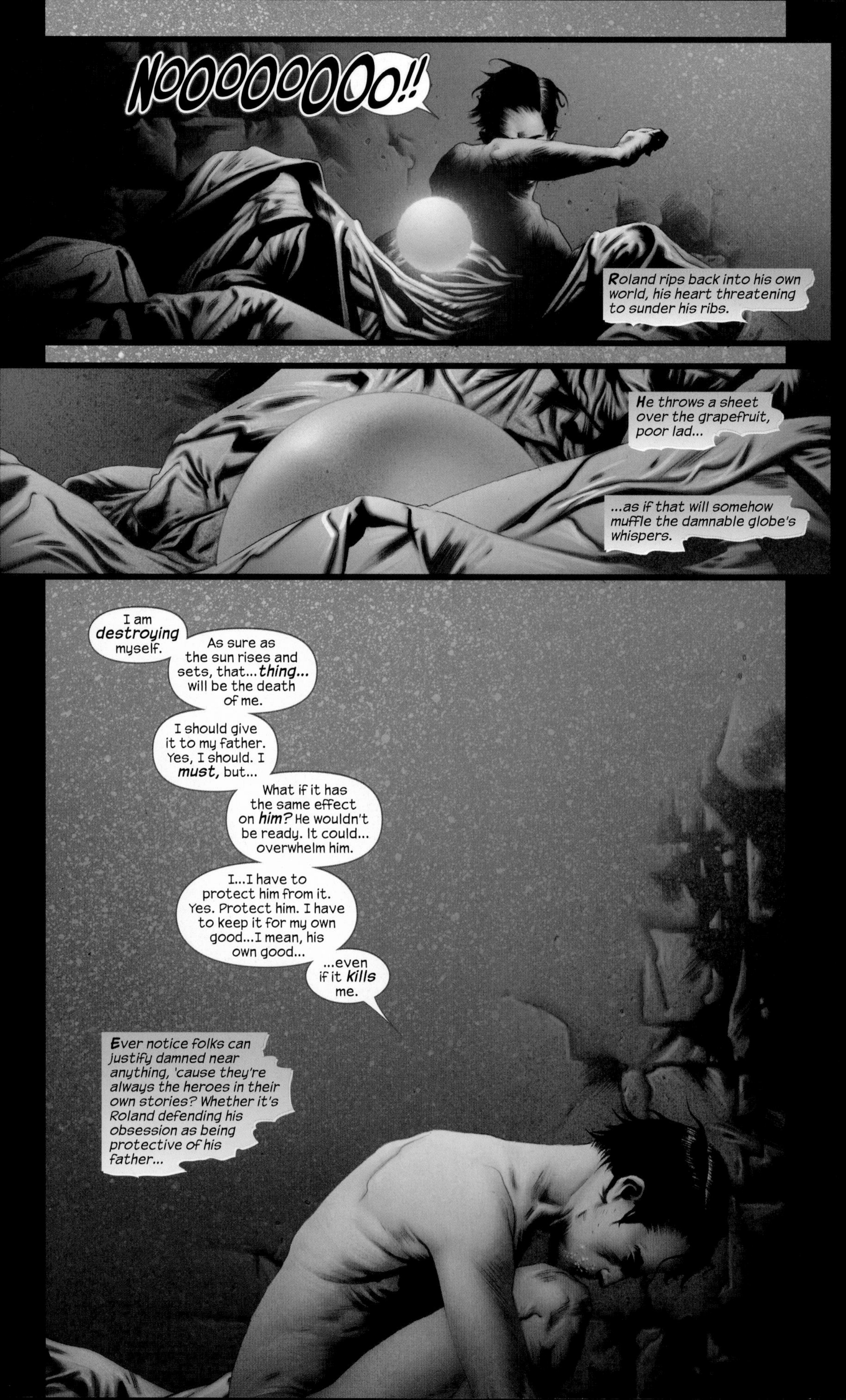

NOOOOOOOO!!
Roland rips back into his own world, his heart threatening to sunder his ribs.
He throws a sheet over the grapefruit, poor lad...
...as if that will somehow muffle the damnable globe's whispers.
I am destroying myself.
As sure as the sun rises and sets, that...thing... will be the death of me.
I should give it to my father. Yes, I should. I must, but...
What if it has the same effect on him? He wouldn't be ready. It could... overwhelm him.
I...I have to protect him from it. Yes. Protect him. I have to keep it for my own good...I mean, his own good...
...even if it kills me.
Ever notice folks can justify damned near anything, 'cause they're always the heroes in their own stories? Whether it's Roland defending his obsession as being protective of his father...

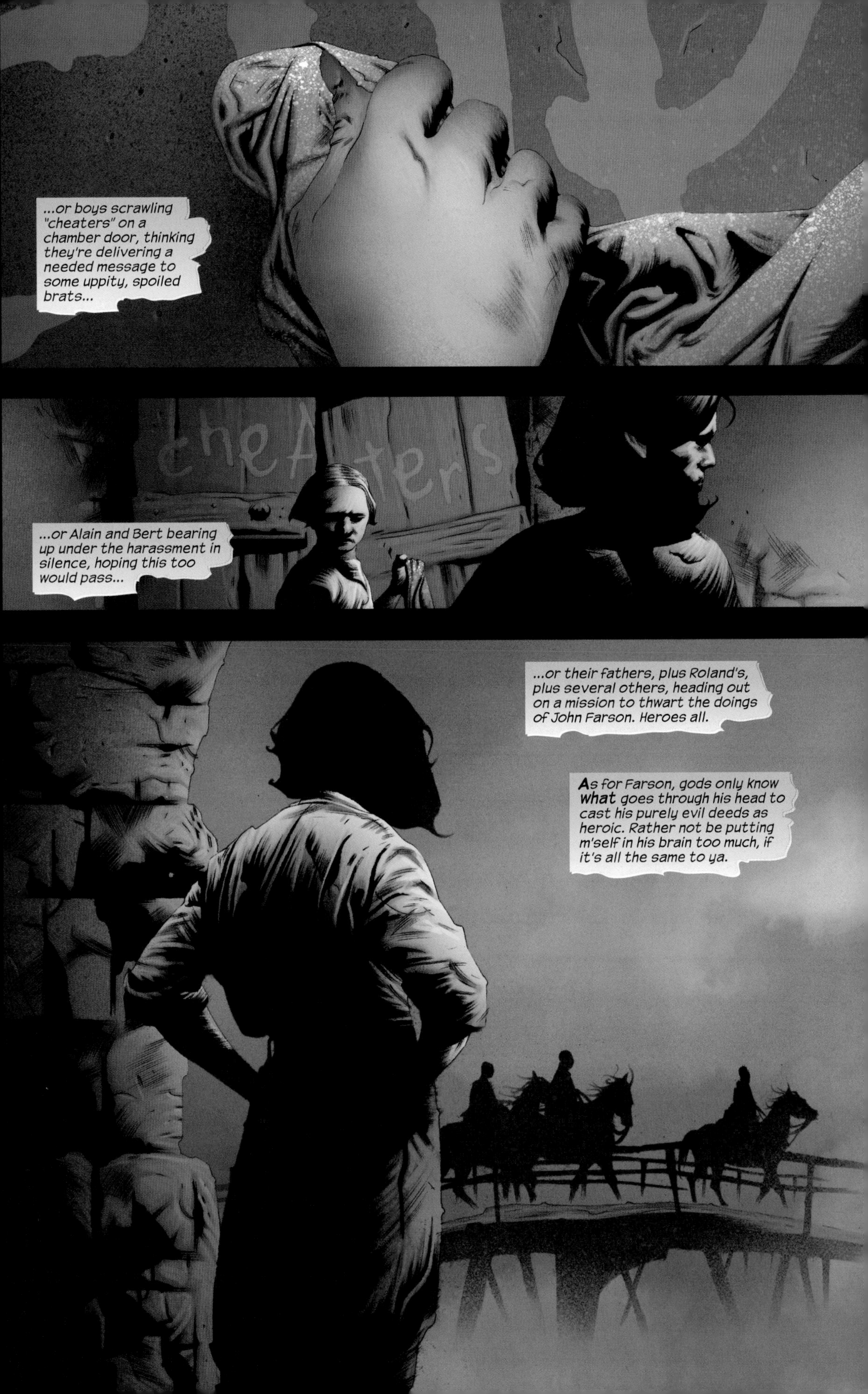
...or boys scrawling "cheaters" on a chamber door, thinking they're delivering a needed message to some uppity, spoiled brats...
cheAters
...or Alain and Bert bearing up under the harassment in silence, hoping this too would pass...
...or their fathers, plus Roland's, plus several others, heading out on a mission to thwart the doings of John Farson. Heroes all.
As for Farson, gods only know what goes through his head to cast his purely evil deeds as heroic. Rather not be putting m'self in his brain too much, if it's all the same to ya.

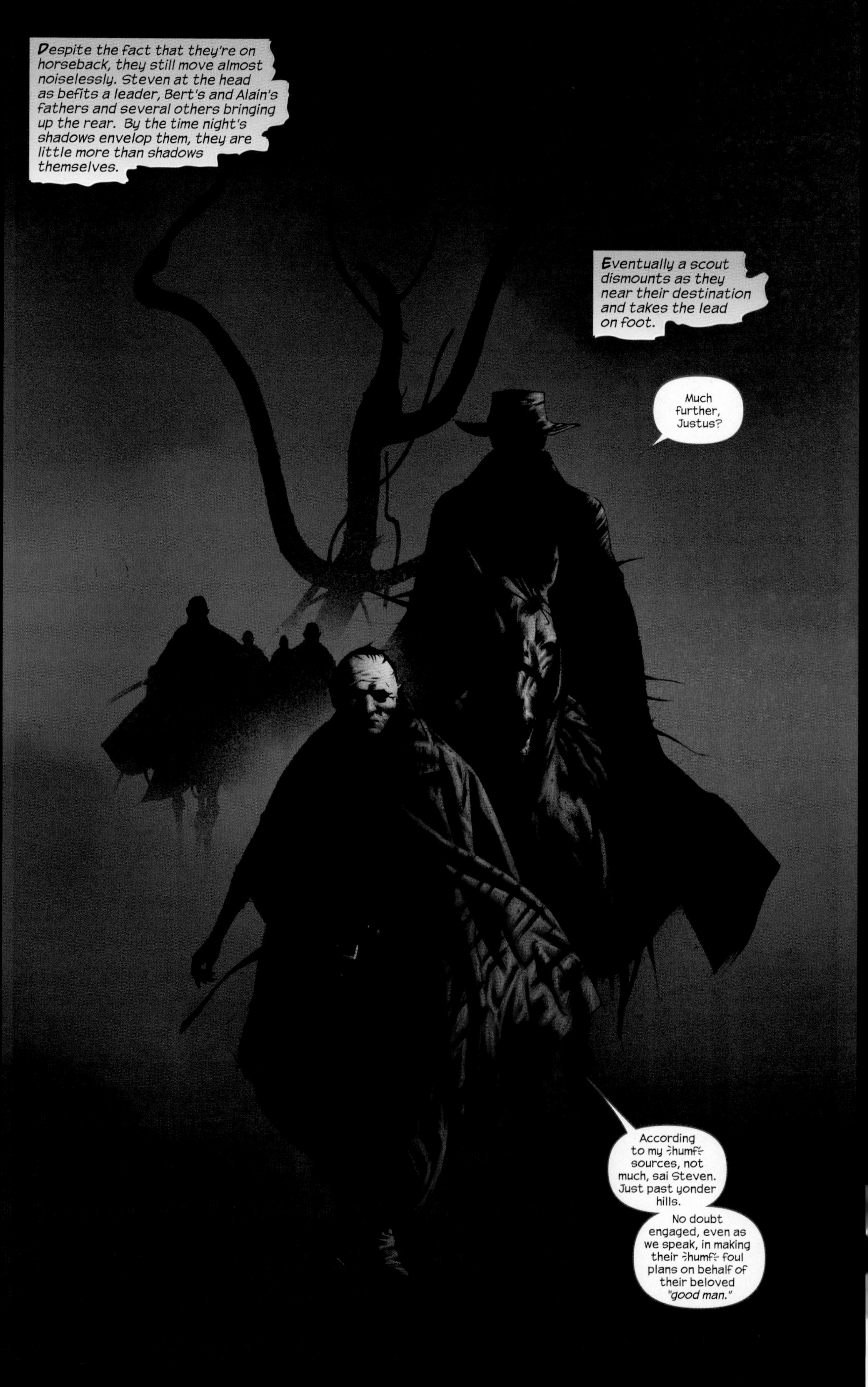
Despite the fact that they're on horseback, they still move almost noiselessly. Steven at the head as befits a leader, Bert's and Alain's fathers and several others bringing up the rear. By the time night's shadows envelop them, they are little more than shadows themselves.
Eventually a scout dismounts as they near their destination and takes the lead on foot.
Much further, Justus?
According to my =humf= sources, not much, sai Steven. Just past yonder hills.
No doubt engaged, even as we speak, in making their =humf= foul plans on behalf of their beloved "good man."

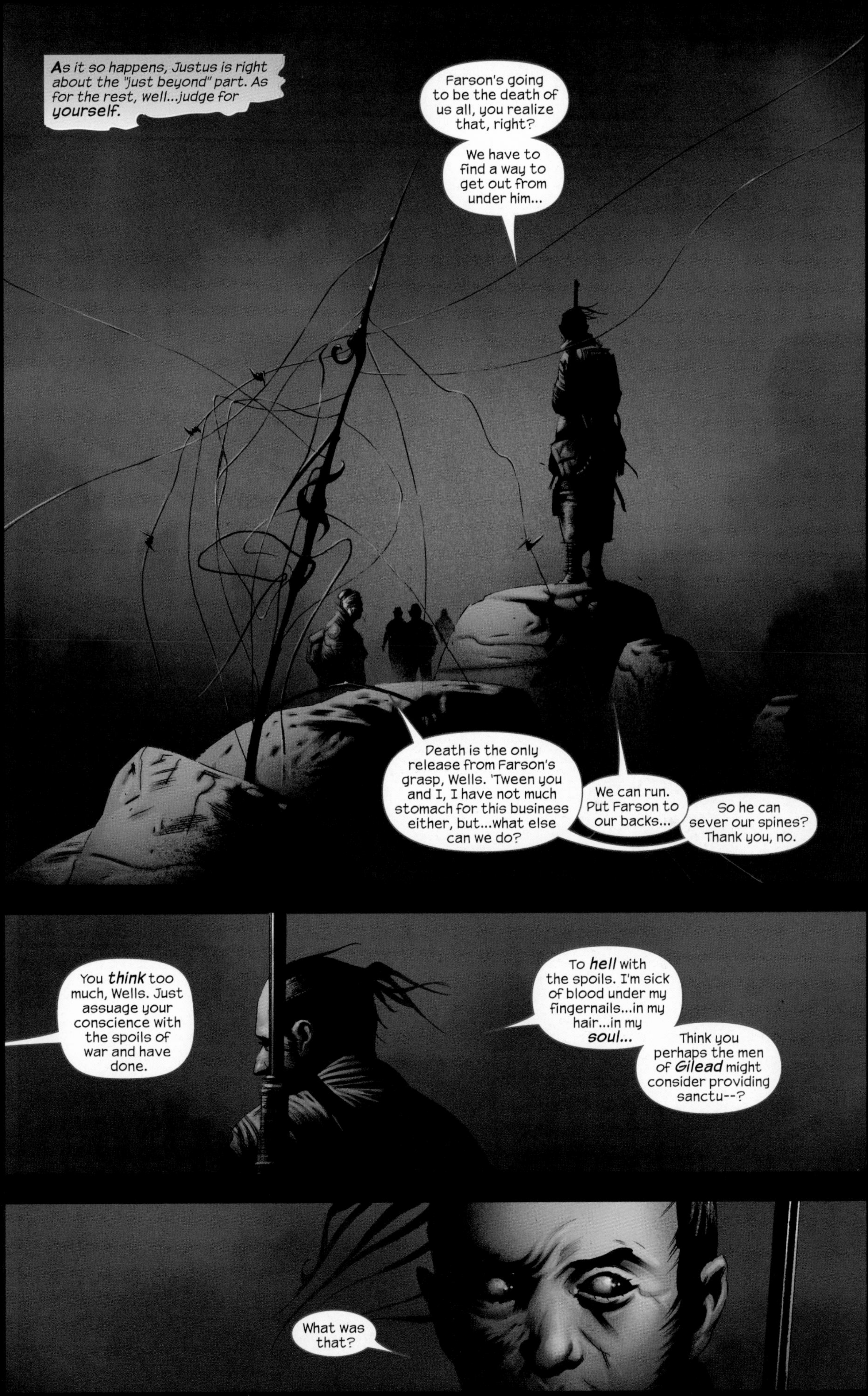
As it so happens, Justus is right about the "just beyond" part. As for the rest, well...judge for yourself.
Farson's going to be the death of us all, you realize that, right?
We have to find a way to get out from under him...
Death is the only release from Farson's grasp, Wells. 'Tween you and I, I have not much stomach for this business either, but...what else can we do?
We can run. Put Farson to our backs...
So he can sever our spines? Thank you, no.
You think too much, Wells. Just assuage your conscience with the spoils of war and have done.
To hell with the spoils. I'm sick of blood under my fingernails...in my hair...in my soul...
Think you perhaps the men of Gilead might consider providing sanctu--?
What was that?

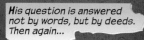
His question is answered not by words, but by deeds. Then again...

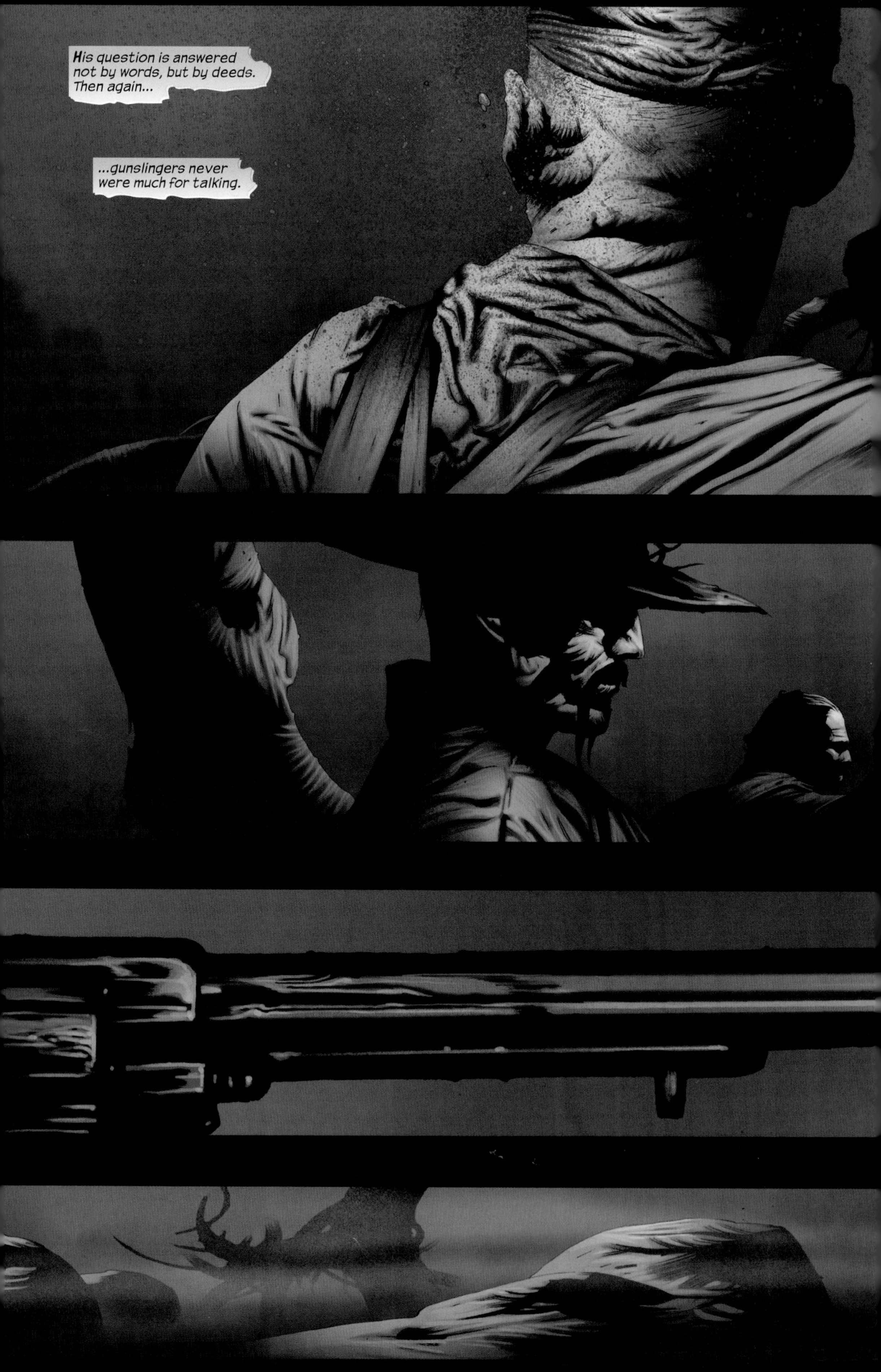

...gunslingers never were much for talking.

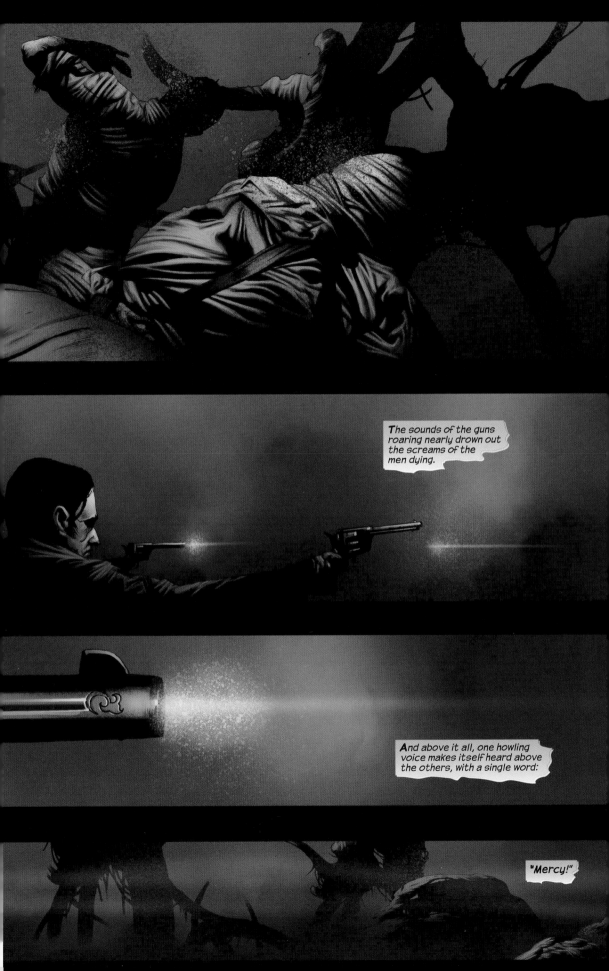

The sounds of the guns roaring nearly drown out the screams of the men dying.

And above it all, one howling voice makes itself heard above the others, with a single word:

"Mercy!"

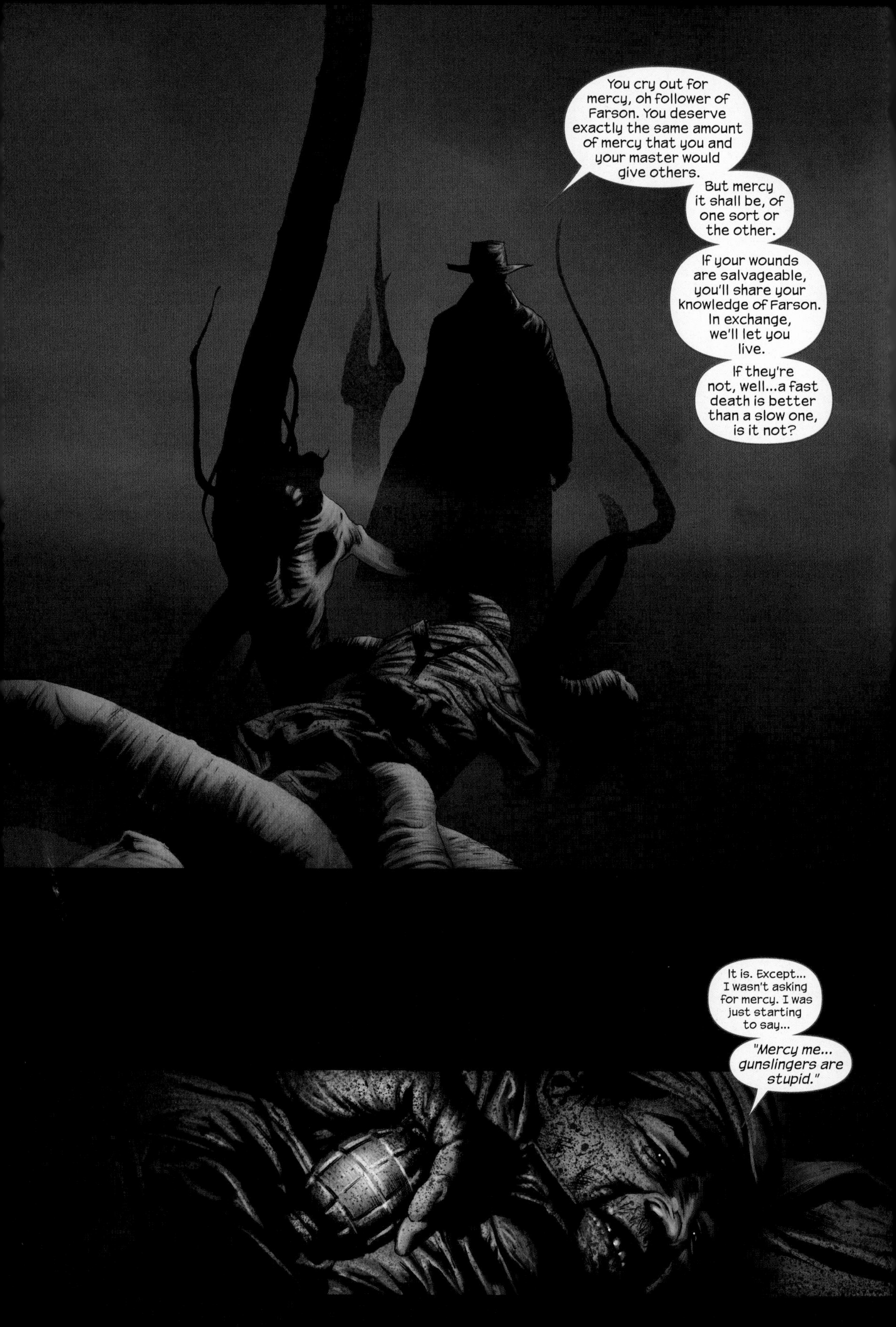
You cry out for mercy, oh follower of Farson. You deserve exactly the same amount of mercy that you and your master would give others.
But mercy it shall be, of one sort or the other.
If your wounds are salvageable, you'll share your knowledge of Farson. In exchange, we'll let you live.
If they're not, well...a fast death is better than a slow one, is it not?
It is. Except... I wasn't asking for mercy. I was just starting to say...
"Mercy me... gunslingers are stupid."

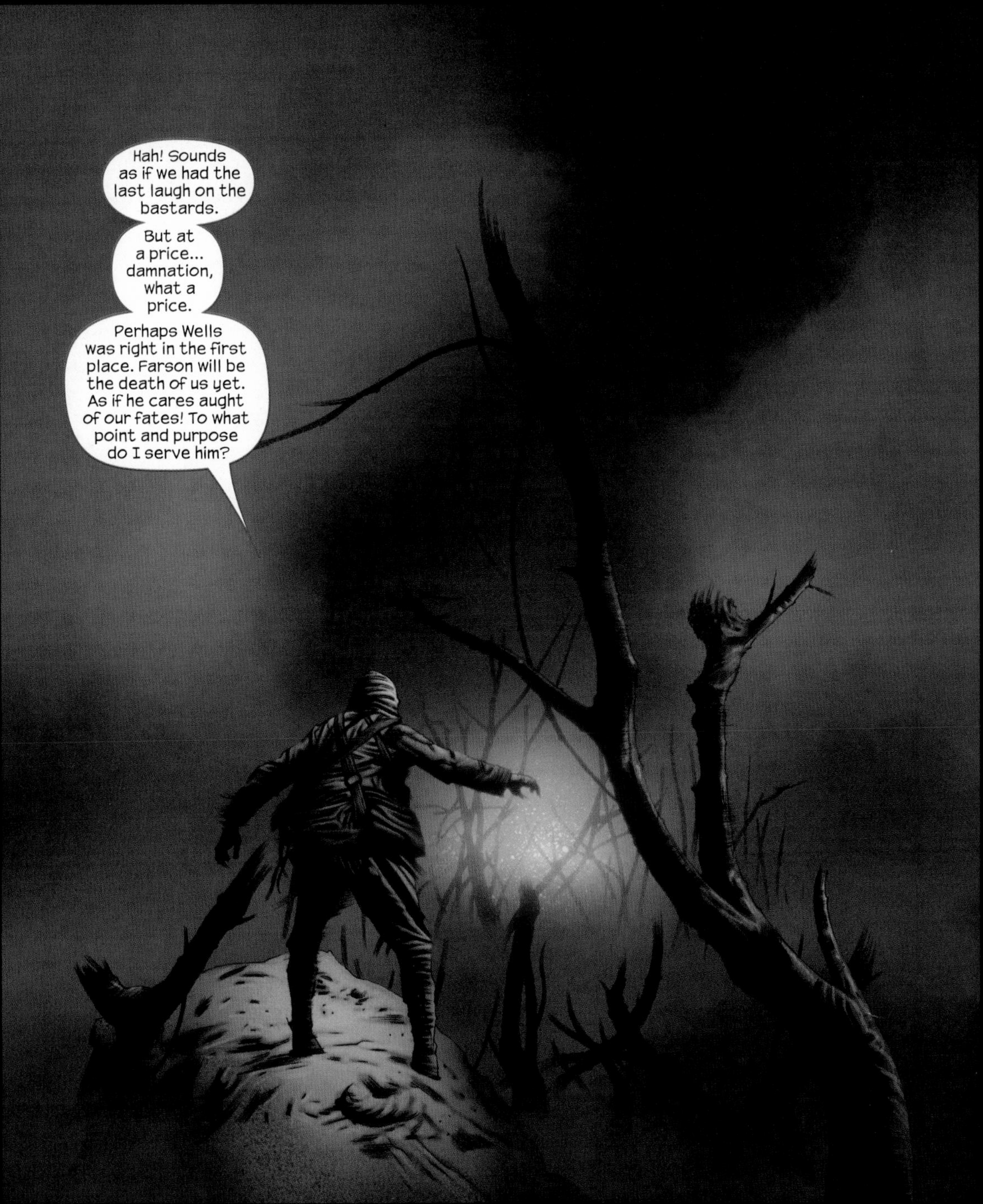
Hah! Sounds as if we had the last laugh on the bastards.
But at a price... damnation, what a price.
Perhaps Wells was right in the first place. Farson will be the death of us yet. As if he cares aught of our fates! To what point and purpose do I serve him?

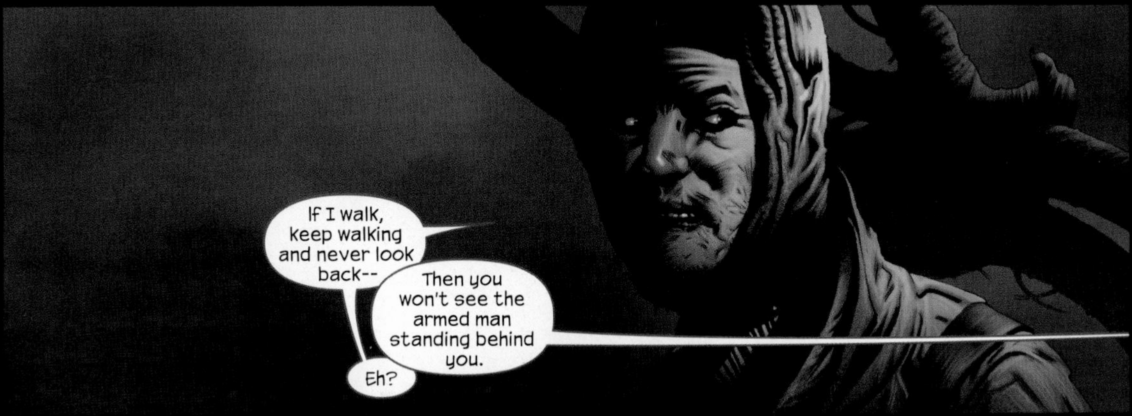
If I walk, keep walking and never look back--
Then you won't see the armed man standing behind you.
Eh?

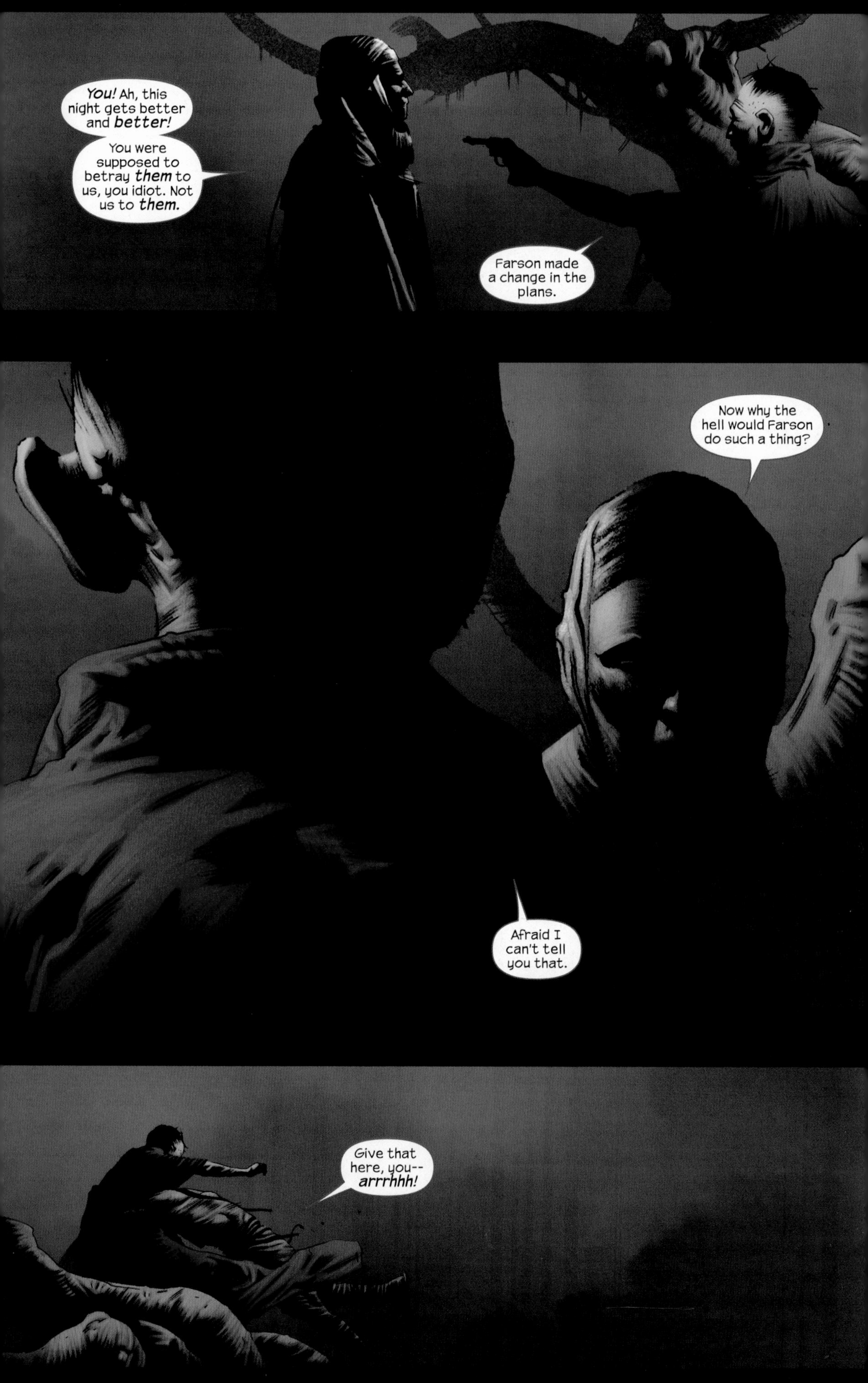
You! Ah, this night gets better and better!
You were supposed to betray them to us, you idiot. Not us to them.
Farson made a change in the plans.
Now why the hell would Farson do such a thing?
Afraid I can't tell you that.
Give that here, you-- arrrhhh!

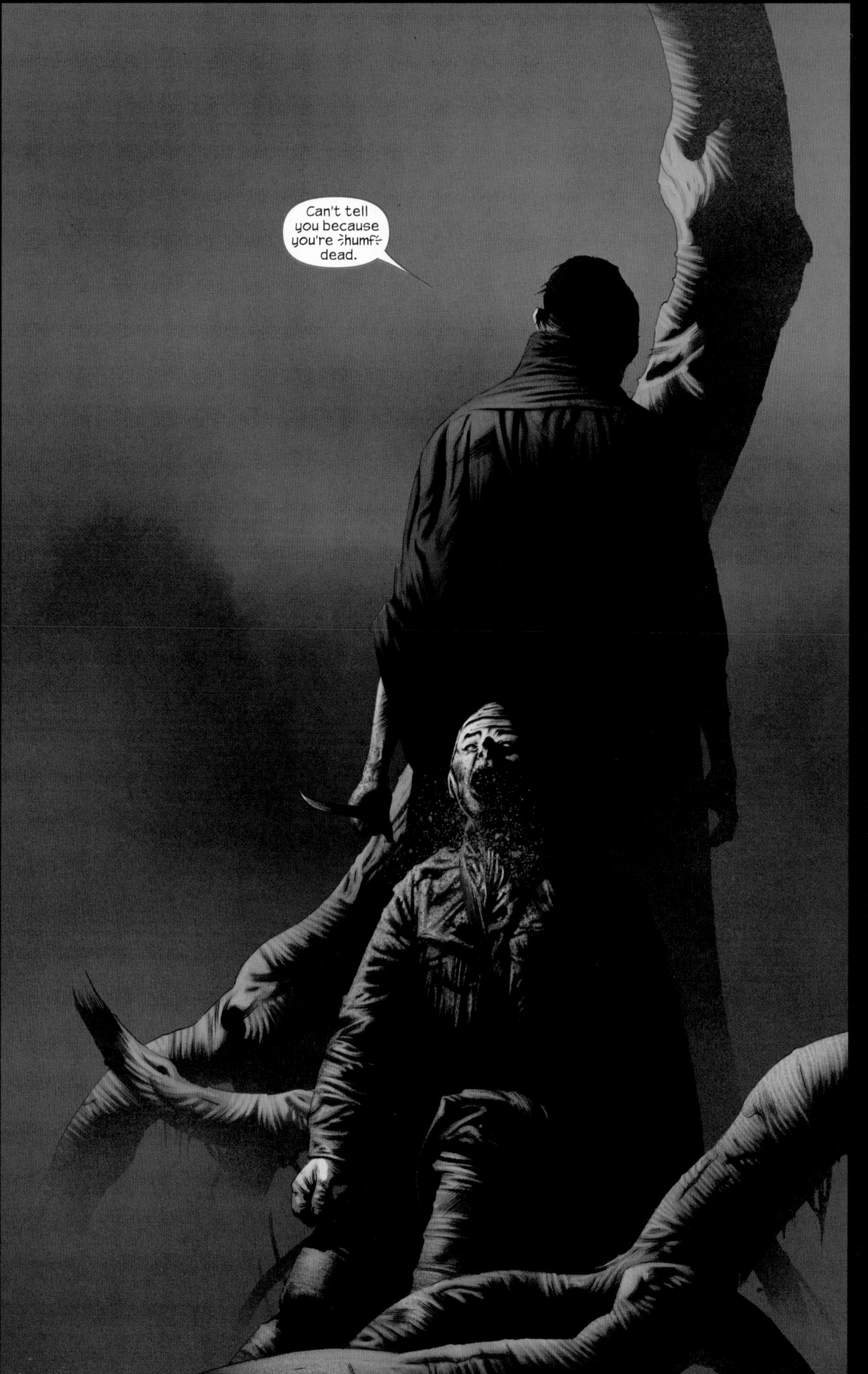
Can't tell you because you're ~humf~ dead.

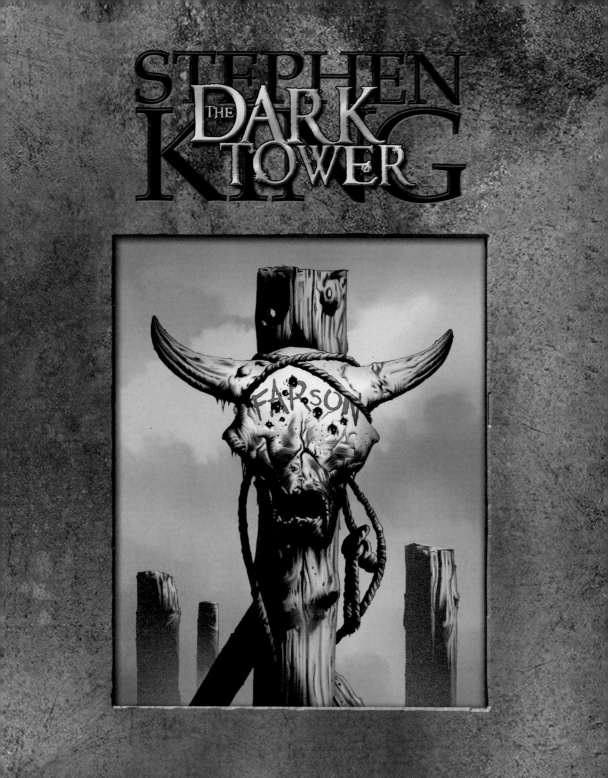

STEPHEN KING

THE DARK TOWER

TREACHERY

CHAPTER TWO

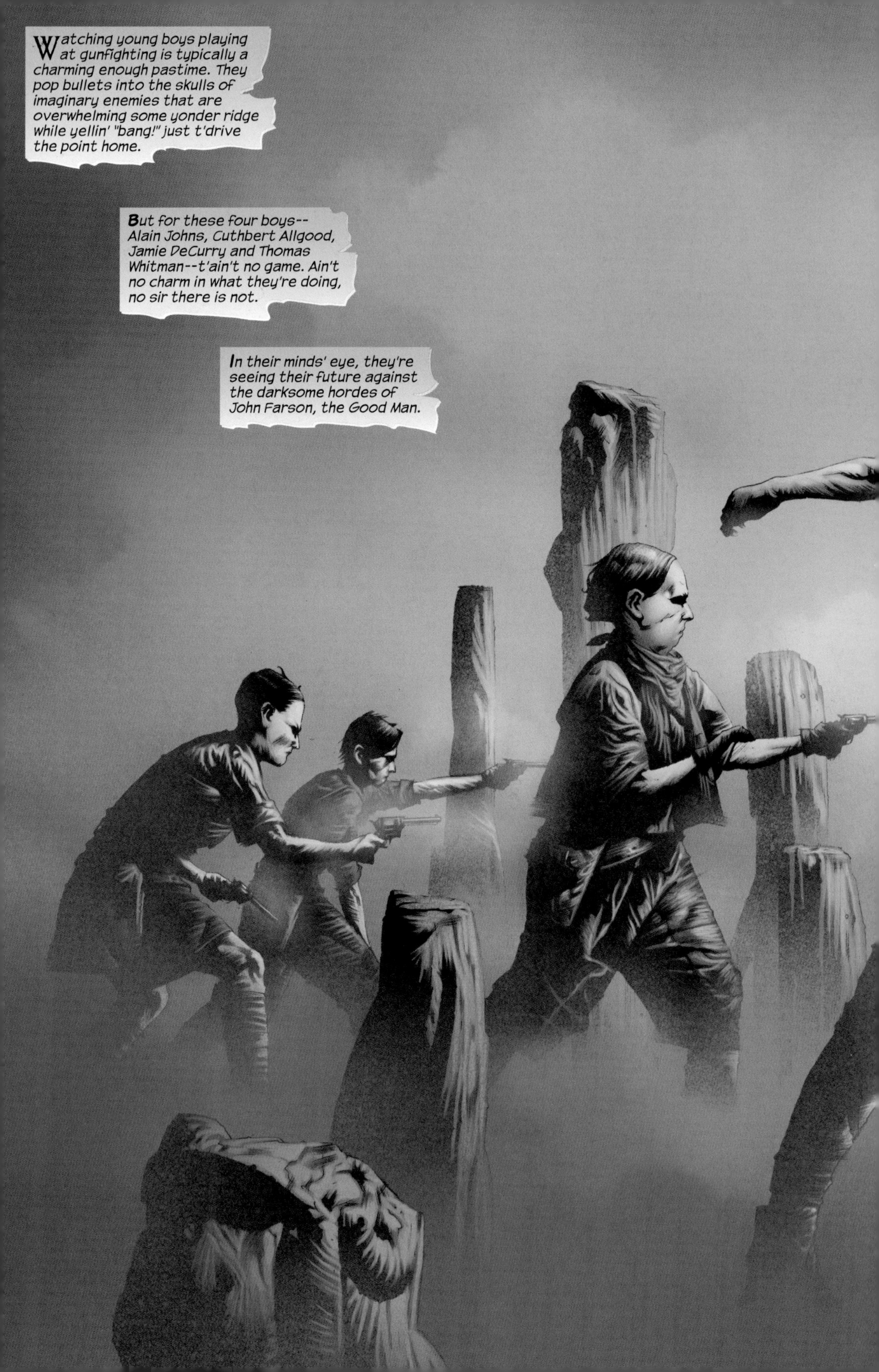
Watching young boys playing at gunfighting is typically a charming enough pastime. They pop bullets into the skulls of imaginary enemies that are overwhelming some yonder ridge while yellin' "bang!" just t'drive the point home.
But for these four boys-- Alain Johns, Cuthbert Allgood, Jamie DeCurry and Thomas Whitman--t'ain't no game. Ain't no charm in what they're doing, no sir there is not.
In their minds' eye, they're seeing their future against the darksome hordes of John Farson, the Good Man.

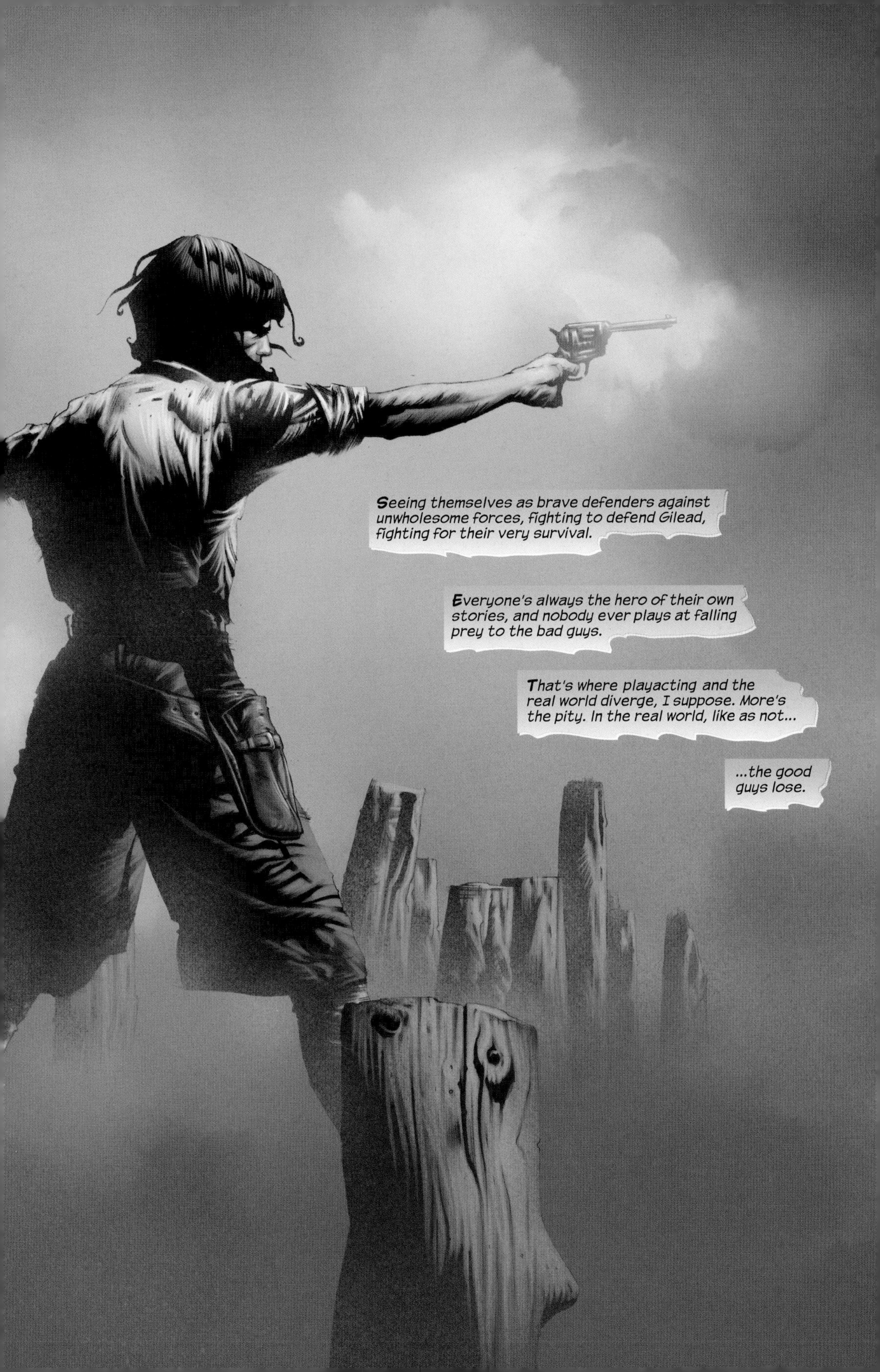
Seeing themselves as brave defenders against unwholesome forces, fighting to defend Gilead, fighting for their very survival.
Everyone's always the hero of their own stories, and nobody ever plays at falling prey to the bad guys.
That's where playacting and the real world diverge, I suppose. More's the pity. In the real world, like as not...
...the good guys lose.

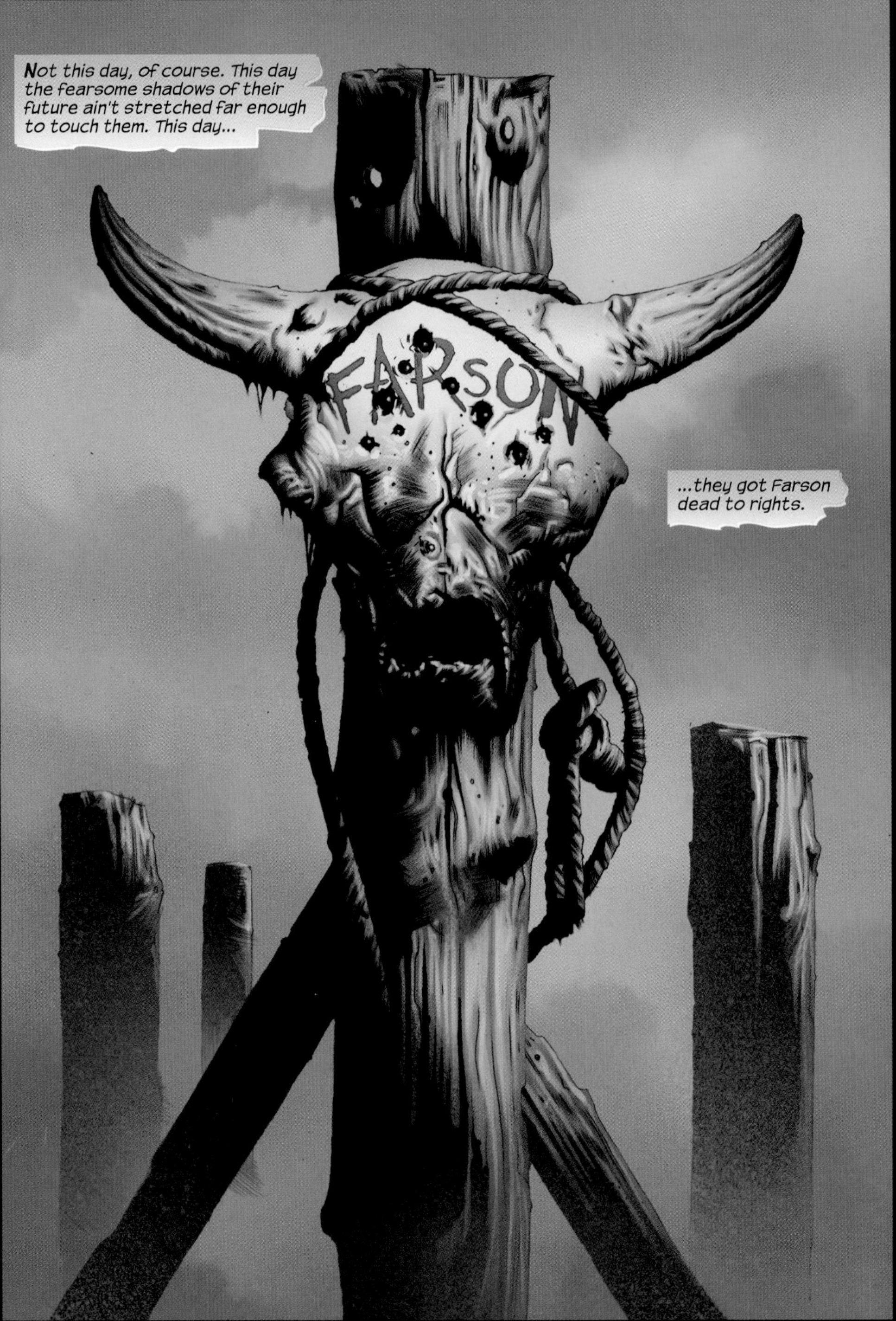
Not this day, of course. This day the fearsome shadows of their future ain't stretched far enough to touch them. This day...
FARSON
...they got Farson dead to rights.

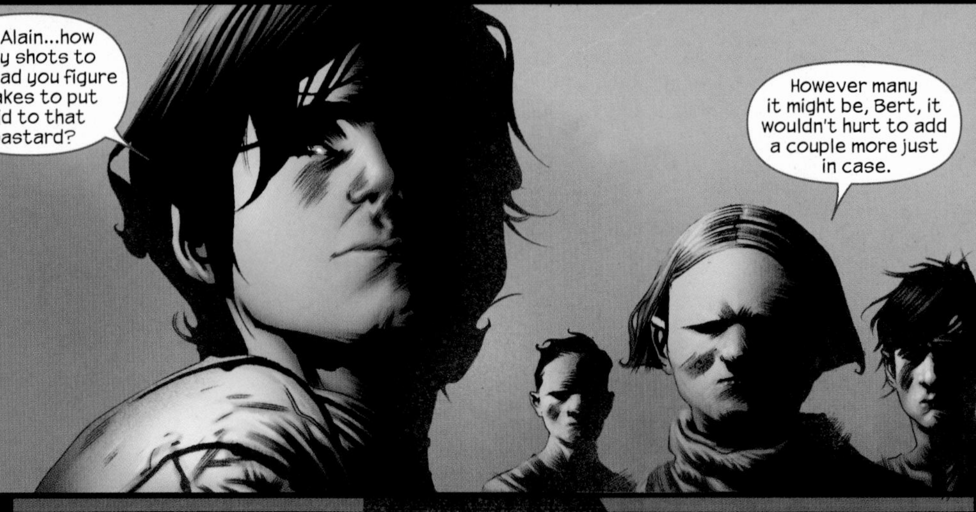
So, Alain...how many shots to the head you figure it takes to put paid to that bastard?
However many it might be, Bert, it wouldn't hurt to add a couple more just in case.

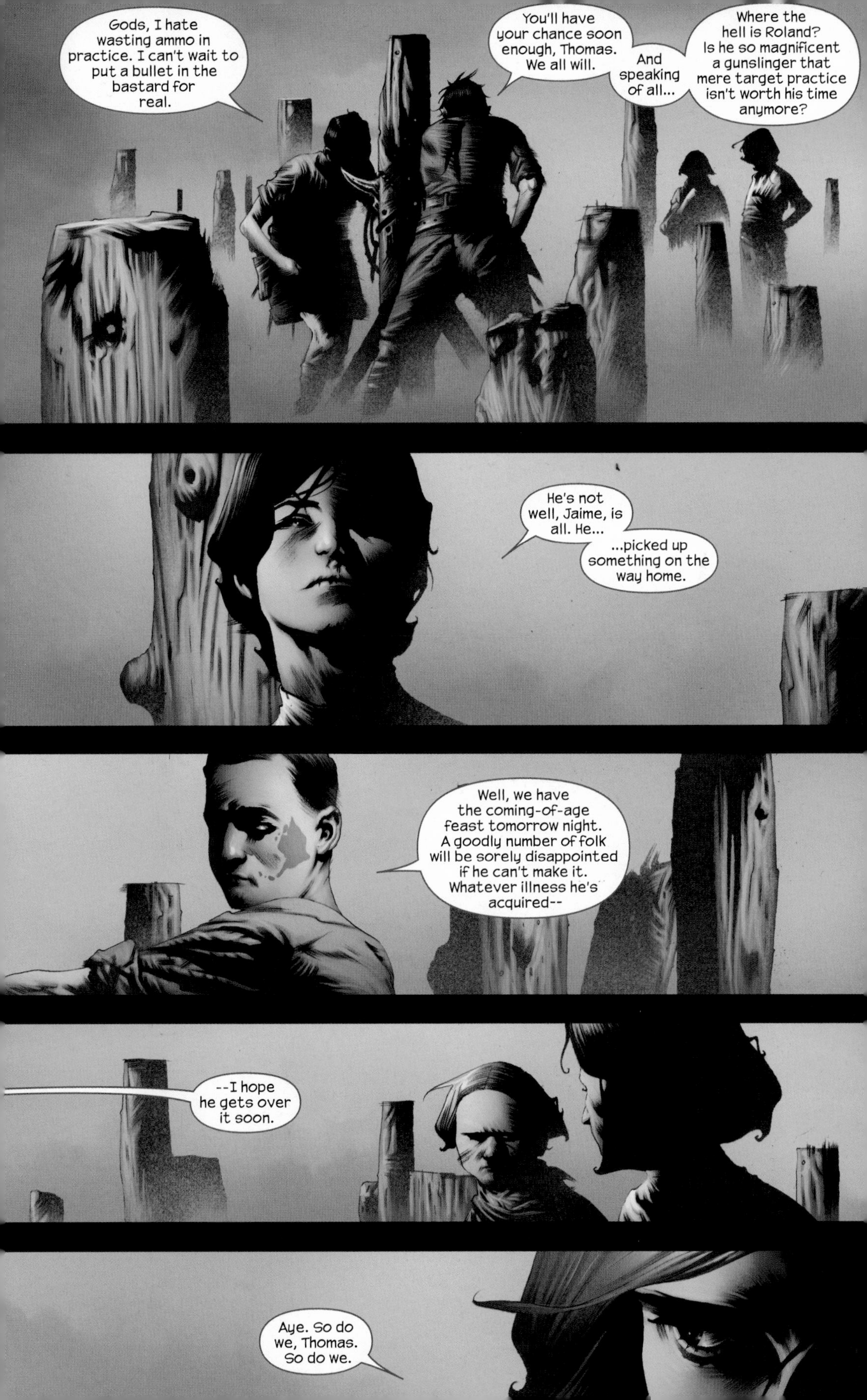

Gods, I hate wasting ammo in practice. I can't wait to put a bullet in the bastard for real.
You'll have your chance soon enough, Thomas. We all will.
And speaking of all...
Where the hell is Roland? Is he so magnificent a gunslinger that mere target practice isn't worth his time anymore?
He's not well, Jaime, is all. He...
...picked up something on the way home.
Well, we have the coming-of-age feast tomorrow night. A goodly number of folk will be sorely disappointed if he can't make it. Whatever illness he's acquired--
--I hope he gets over it soon.
Aye. So do we, Thomas. So do we.

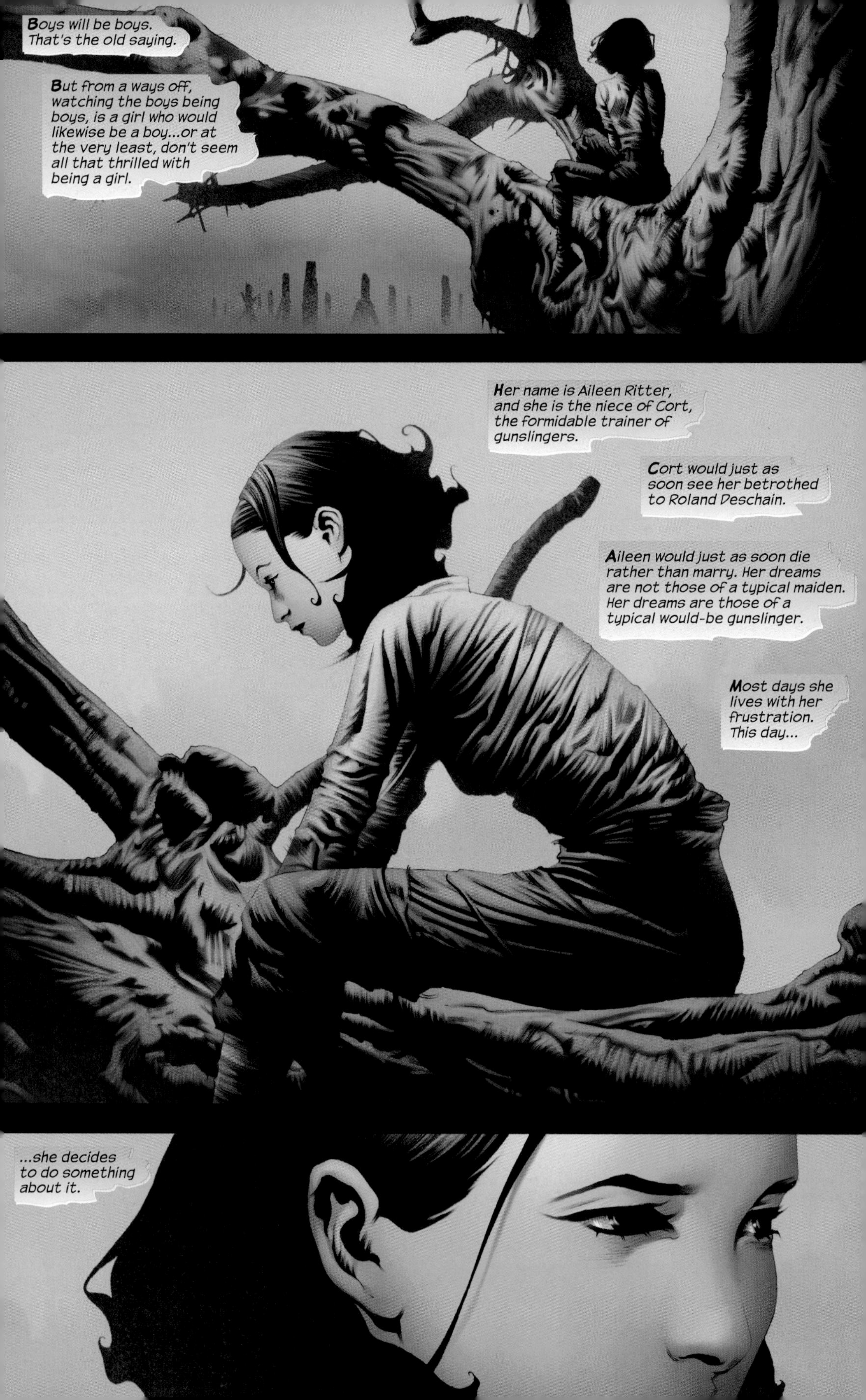
Boys will be boys. That's the old saying.
But from a ways off, watching the boys being boys, is a girl who would likewise be a boy...or at the very least, don't seem all that thrilled with being a girl.
Her name is Aileen Ritter, and she is the niece of Cort, the formidable trainer of gunslingers.
Cort would just as soon see her betrothed to Roland Deschain.
Aileen would just as soon die rather than marry. Her dreams are not those of a typical maiden. Her dreams are those of a typical would-be gunslinger.
Most days she lives with her frustration. This day...
...she decides to do something about it.

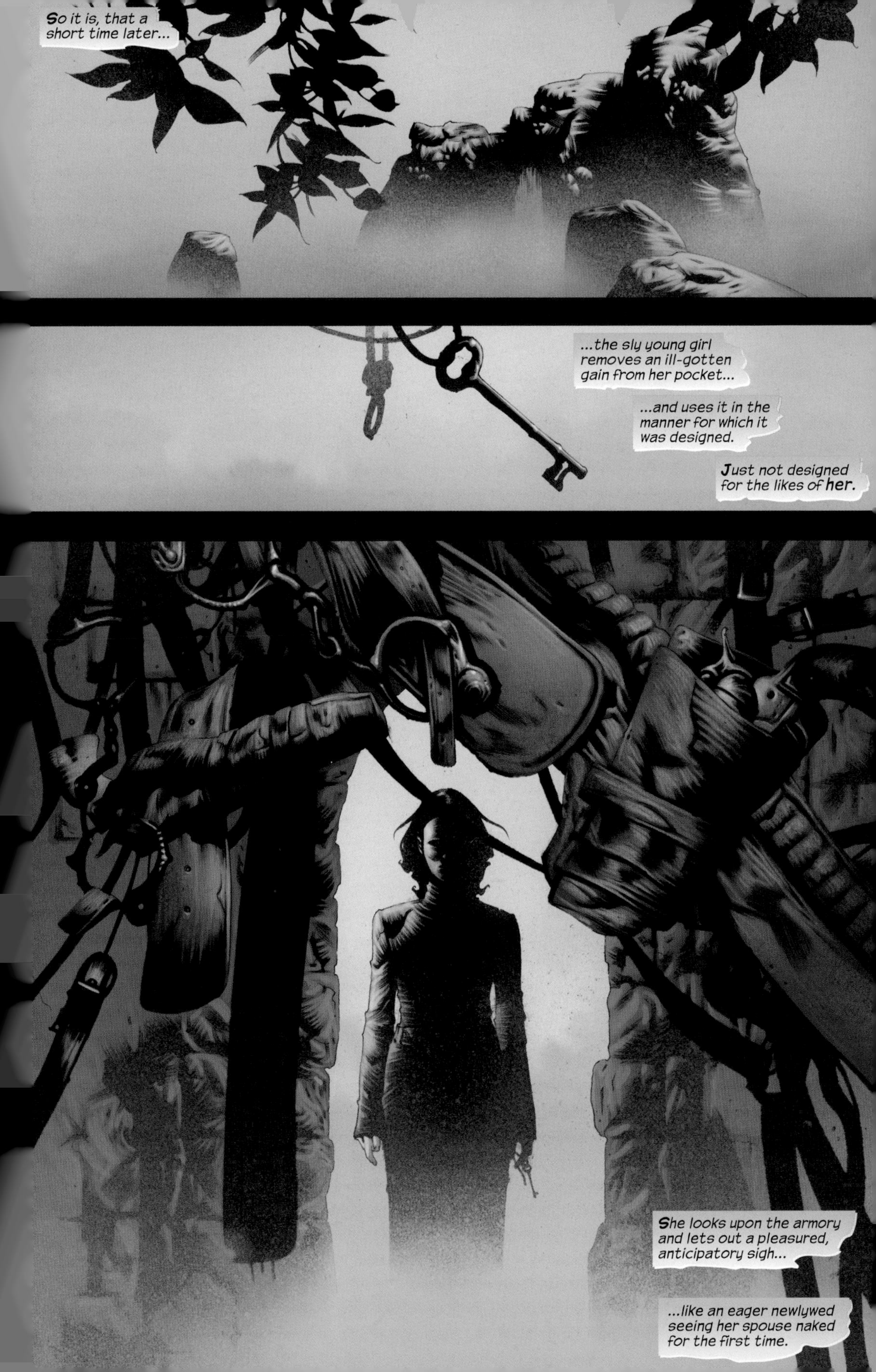
So it is, that a short time later...
...the sly young girl removes an ill-gotten gain from her pocket...
...and uses it in the manner for which it was designed.
Just not designed for the likes of **her**.
She looks upon the armory and lets out a pleasured, anticipatory sigh...
...like an eager newlywed seeing her spouse naked for the first time.

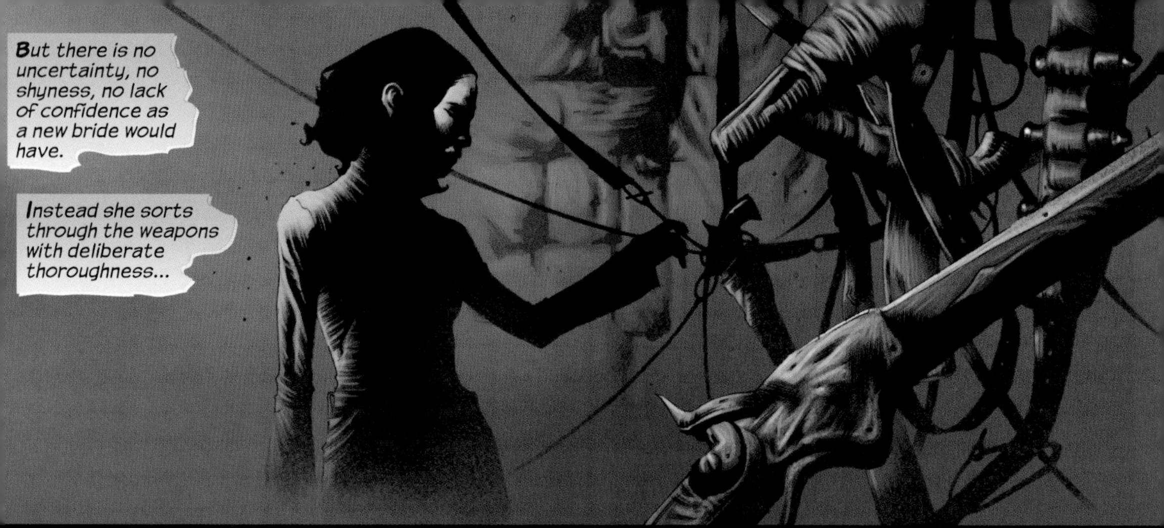

But there is no uncertainty, no shyness, no lack of confidence as a new bride would have.
Instead she sorts through the weapons with deliberate thoroughness...

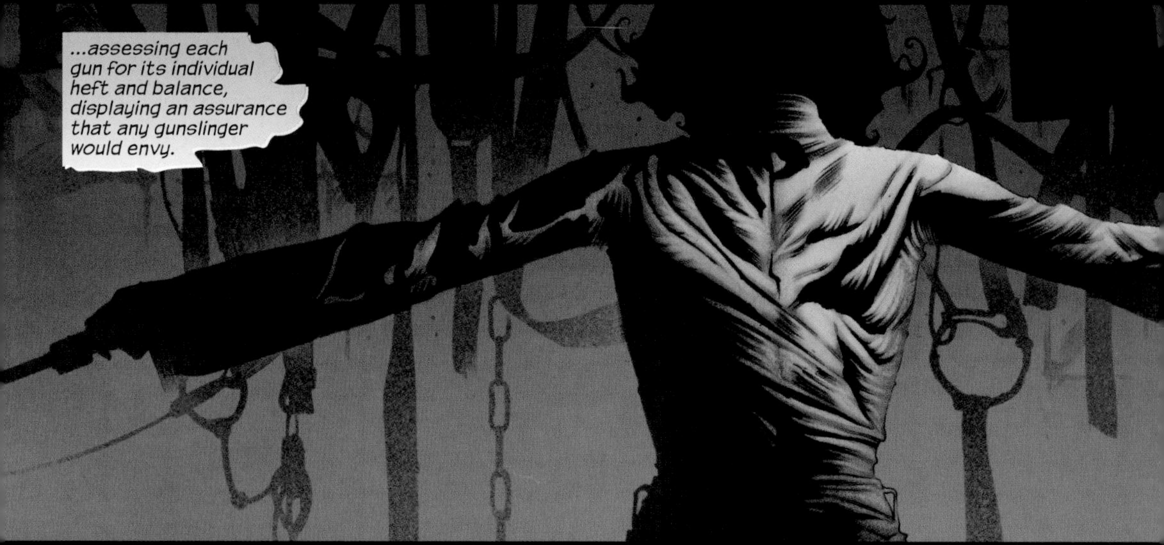

...assessing each gun for its individual heft and balance, displaying an assurance that any gunslinger would envy.

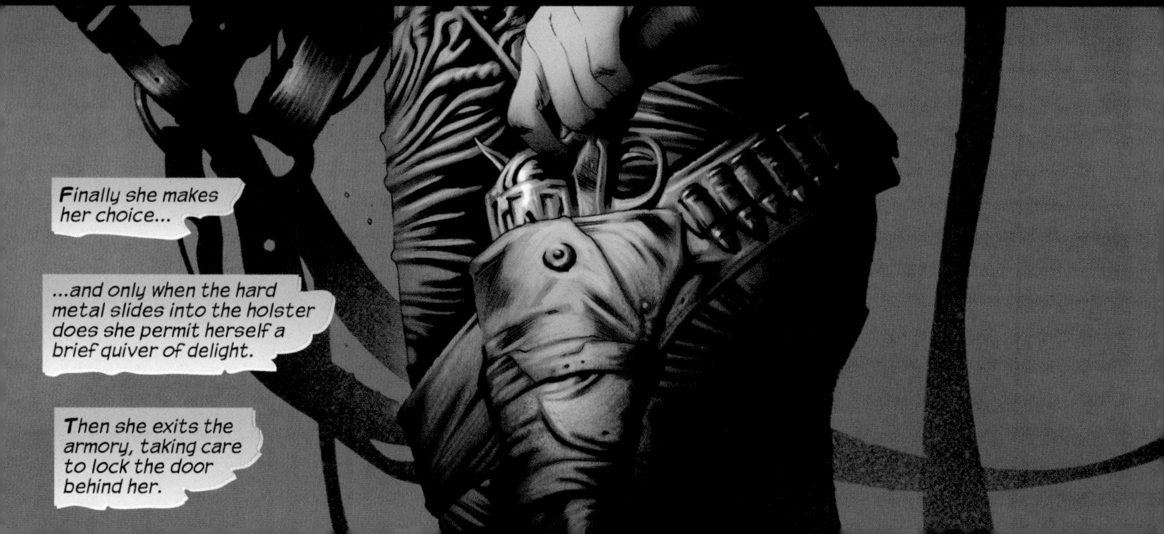

Finally she makes her choice...
...and only when the hard metal slides into the holster does she permit herself a brief quiver of delight.
Then she exits the armory, taking care to lock the door behind her.

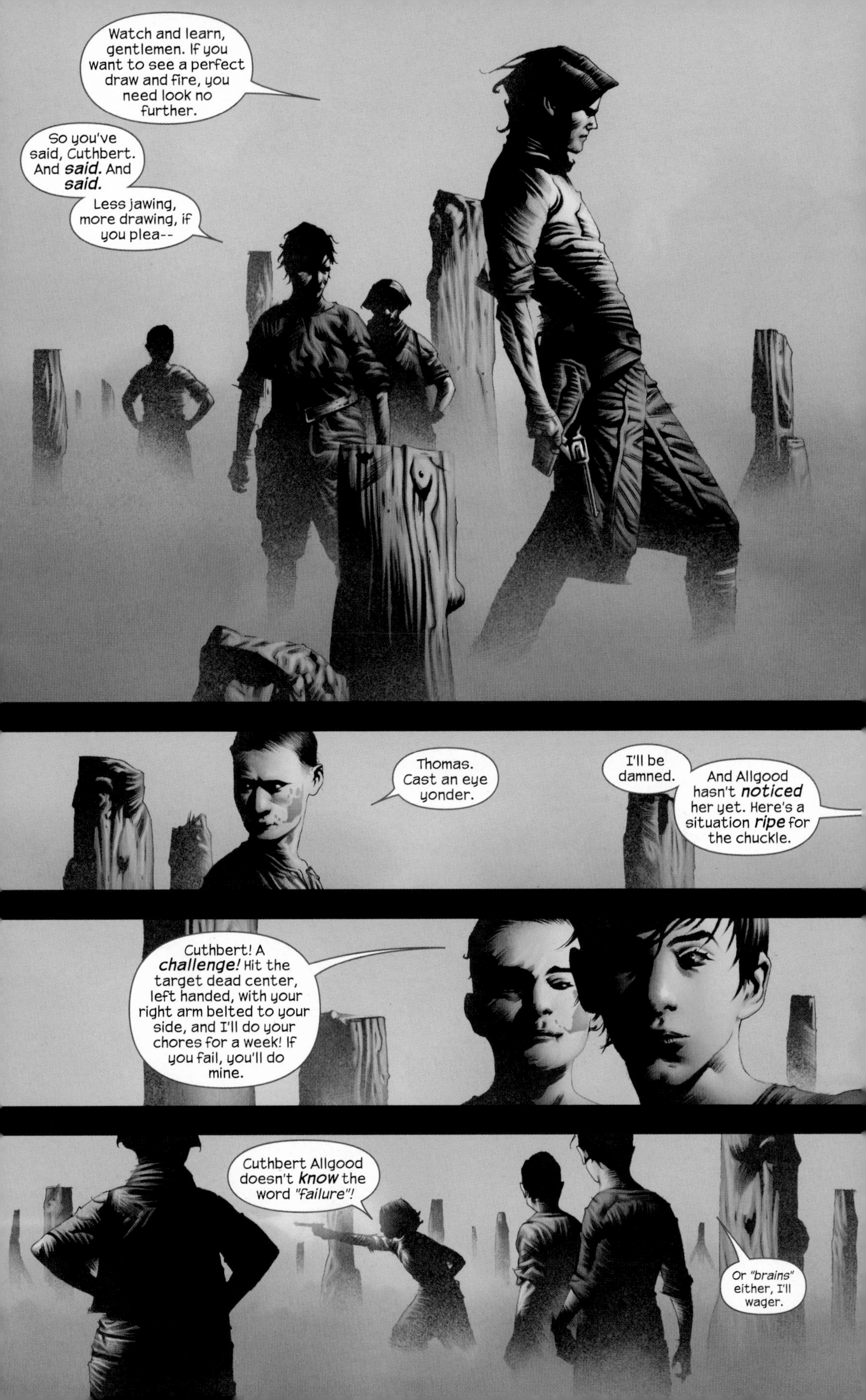

Watch and learn, gentlemen. If you want to see a perfect draw and fire, you need look no further.
So you've said, Cuthbert. And ***said.*** And ***said.***
Less jawing, more drawing, if you plea--
Thomas. Cast an eye yonder.
I'll be damned.
And Allgood hasn't ***noticed*** her yet. Here's a situation ***ripe*** for the chuckle.
Cuthbert! A ***challenge!*** Hit the target dead center, left handed, with your right arm belted to your side, and I'll do your chores for a week! If you fail, you'll do mine.
Cuthbert Allgood doesn't ***know*** the word *"failure"*!
Or *"brains"* either, I'll wager.

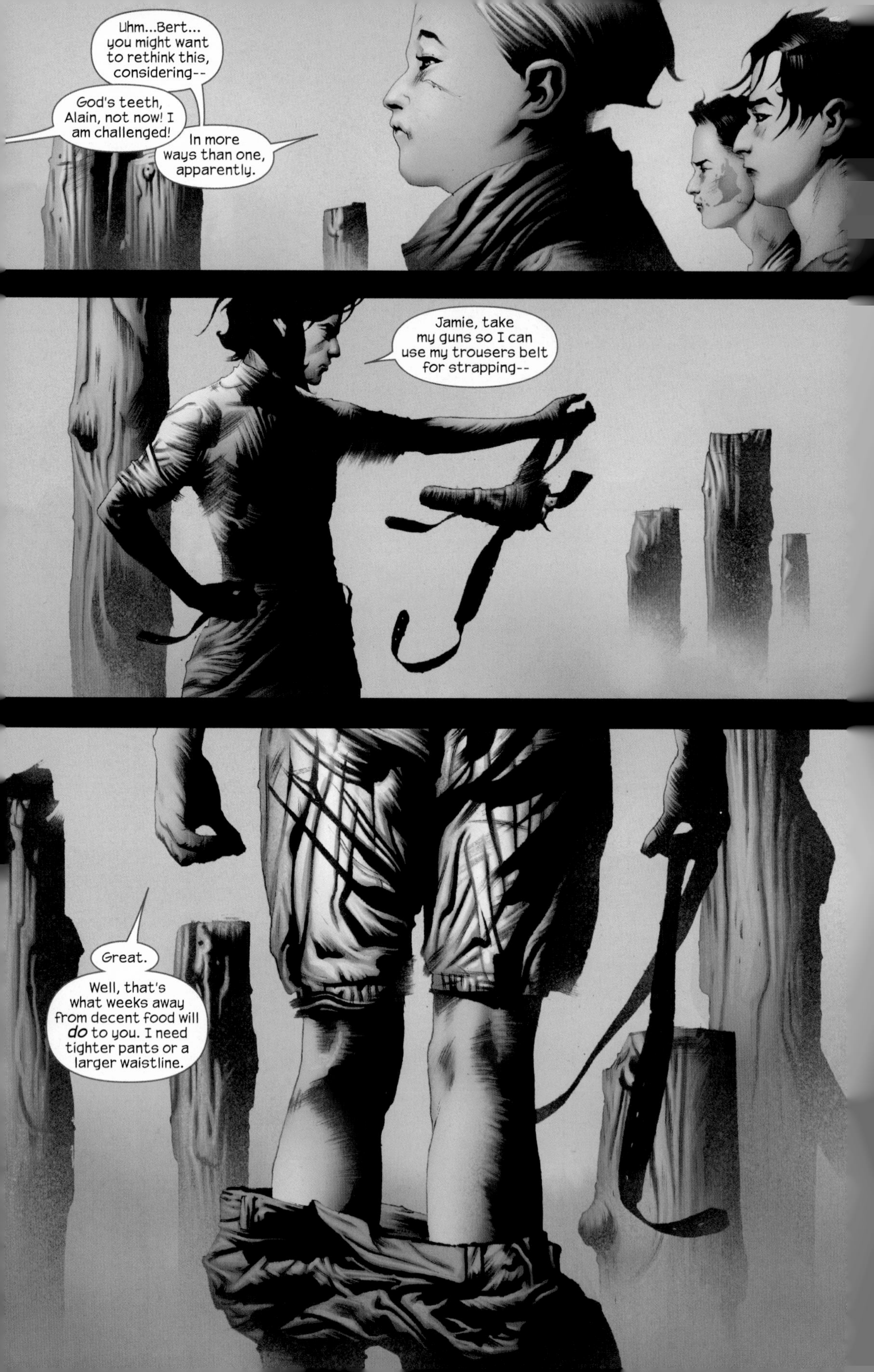
Uhm...Bert... you might want to rethink this, considering--
God's teeth, Alain, not now! I am challenged!
In more ways than one, apparently.
Jamie, take my guns so I can use my trousers belt for strapping--
Great.
Well, that's what weeks away from decent food will *do* to you. I need tighter pants or a larger waistline.

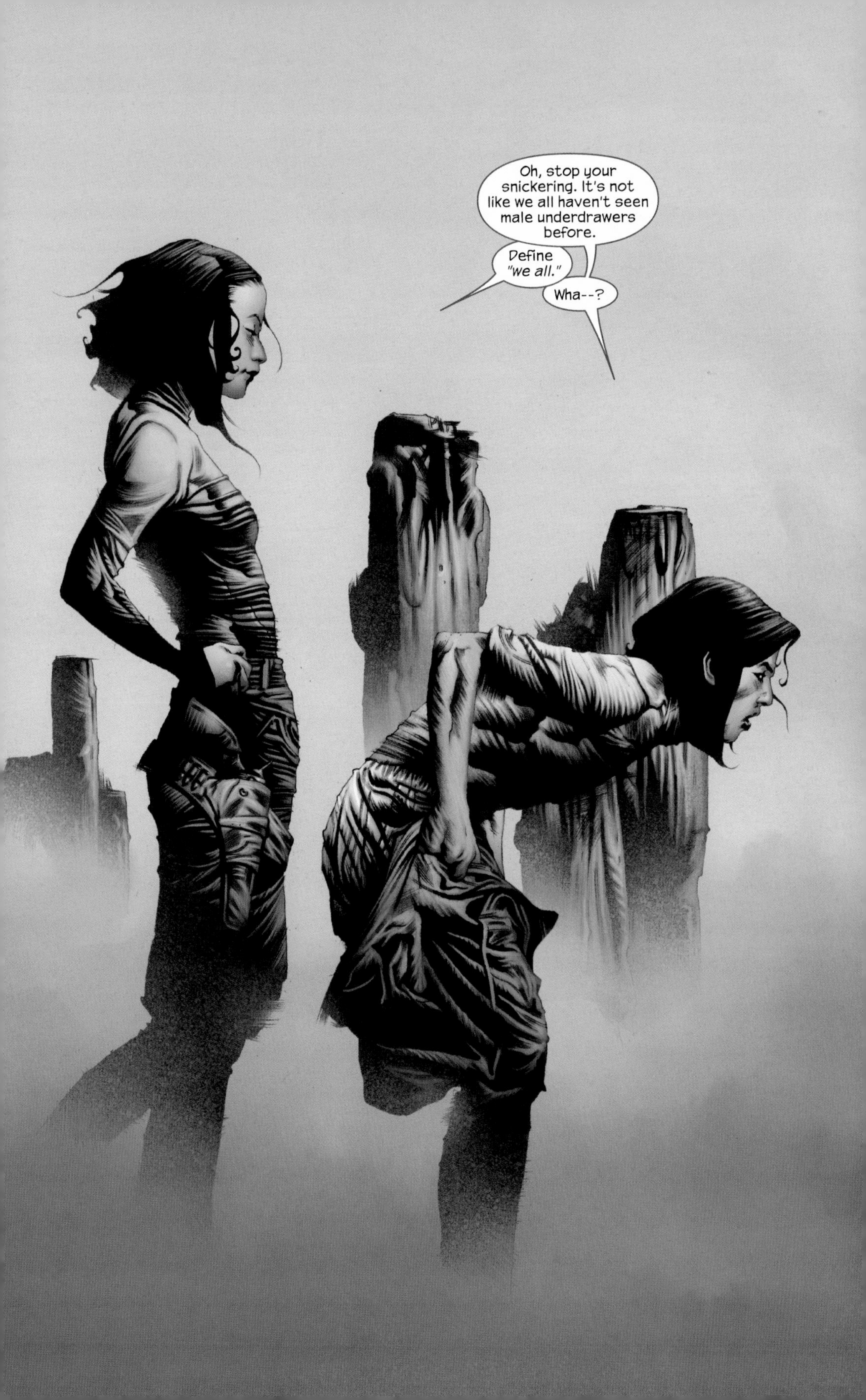
Oh, stop your snickering. It's not like we all haven't seen male underdrawers before.
Define "we all."
Wha--?

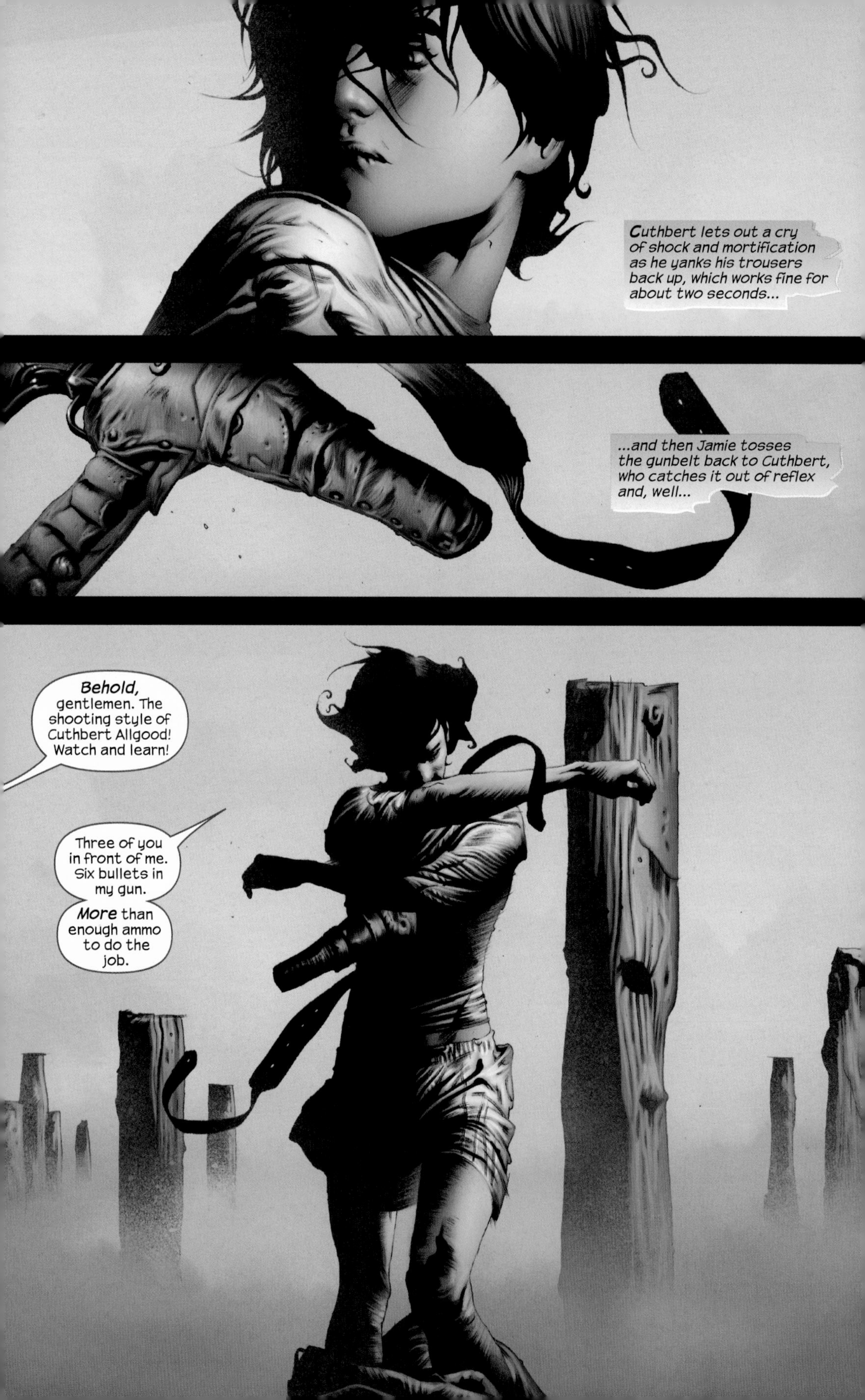
Cuthbert lets out a cry of shock and mortification as he yanks his trousers back up, which works fine for about two seconds...
...and then Jamie tosses the gunbelt back to Cuthbert, who catches it out of reflex and, well...
Behold, gentlemen. The shooting style of Cuthbert Allgood! Watch and learn!
Three of you in front of me. Six bullets in my gun.
More than enough ammo to do the job.

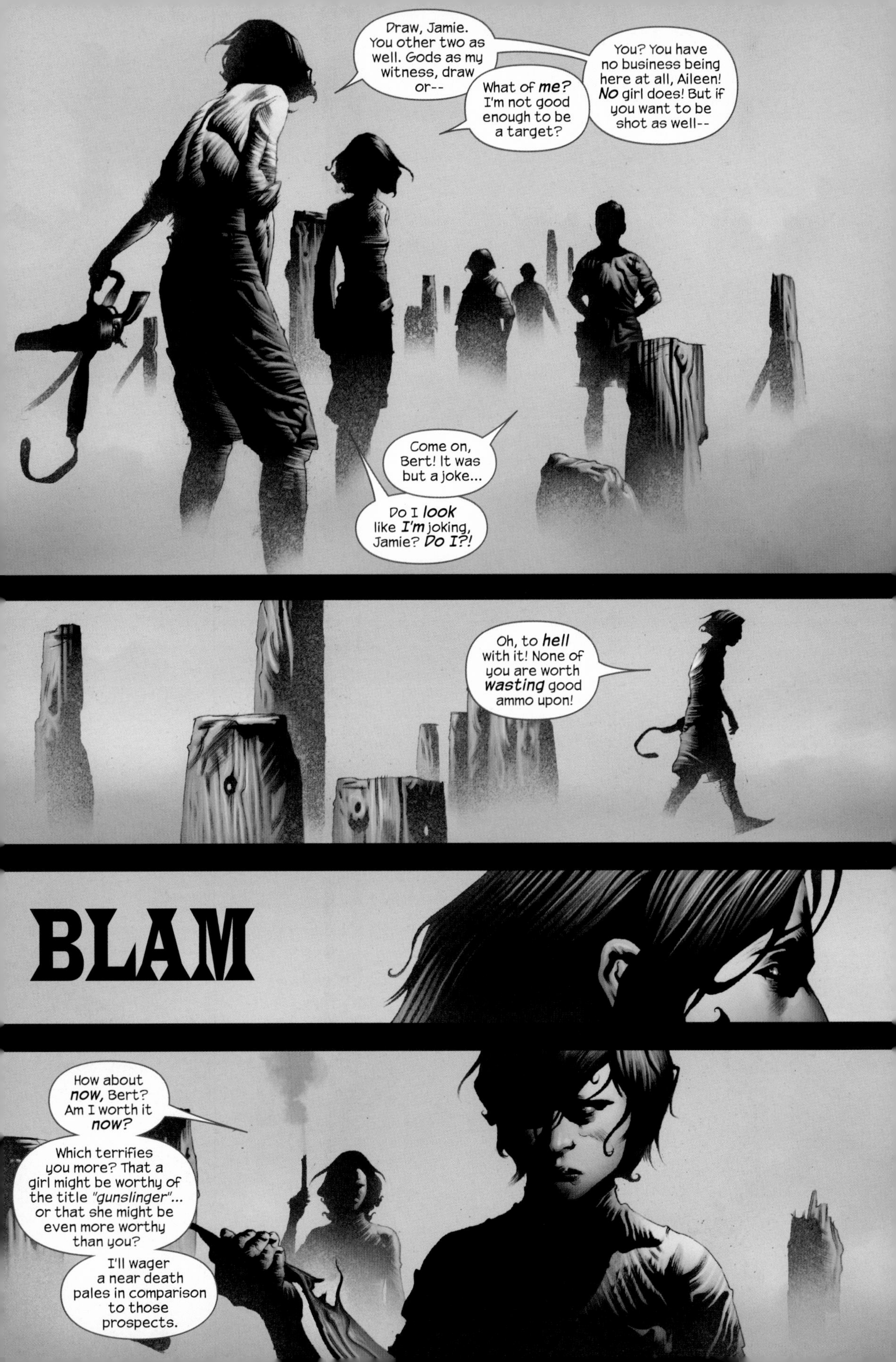
Draw, Jamie. You other two as well. Gods as my witness, draw or--
What of *me?* I'm not good enough to be a target?
You? You have no business being here at all, Aileen! *No* girl does! But if you want to be shot as well--
Come on, Bert! It was but a joke...
Do I *look* like *I'm* joking, Jamie? *Do I?!*
Oh, to *hell* with it! None of you are worth *wasting* good ammo upon!
BLAM
How about *now,* Bert? Am I worth it *now?*
Which terrifies you more? That a girl might be worthy of the title *"gunslinger"*... or that she might be even more worthy than you?
I'll wager a near death pales in comparison to those prospects.

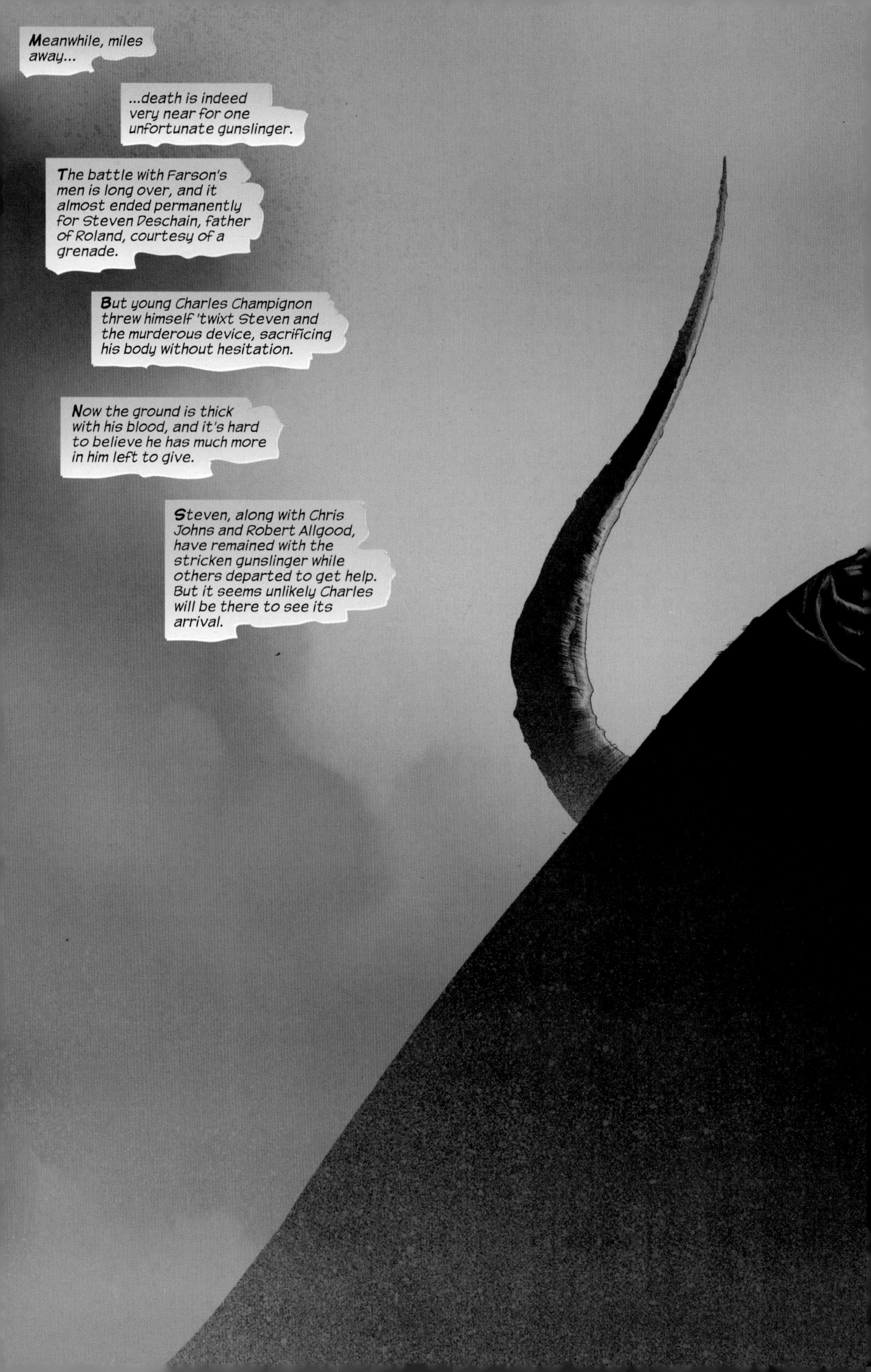
Meanwhile, miles away...
...death is indeed very near for one unfortunate gunslinger.
The battle with Farson's men is long over, and it almost ended permanently for Steven Deschain, father of Roland, courtesy of a grenade.
But young Charles Champignon threw himself 'twixt Steven and the murderous device, sacrificing his body without hesitation.
Now the ground is thick with his blood, and it's hard to believe he has much more in him left to give.
Steven, along with Chris Johns and Robert Allgood, have remained with the stricken gunslinger while others departed to get help. But it seems unlikely Charles will be there to see its arrival.

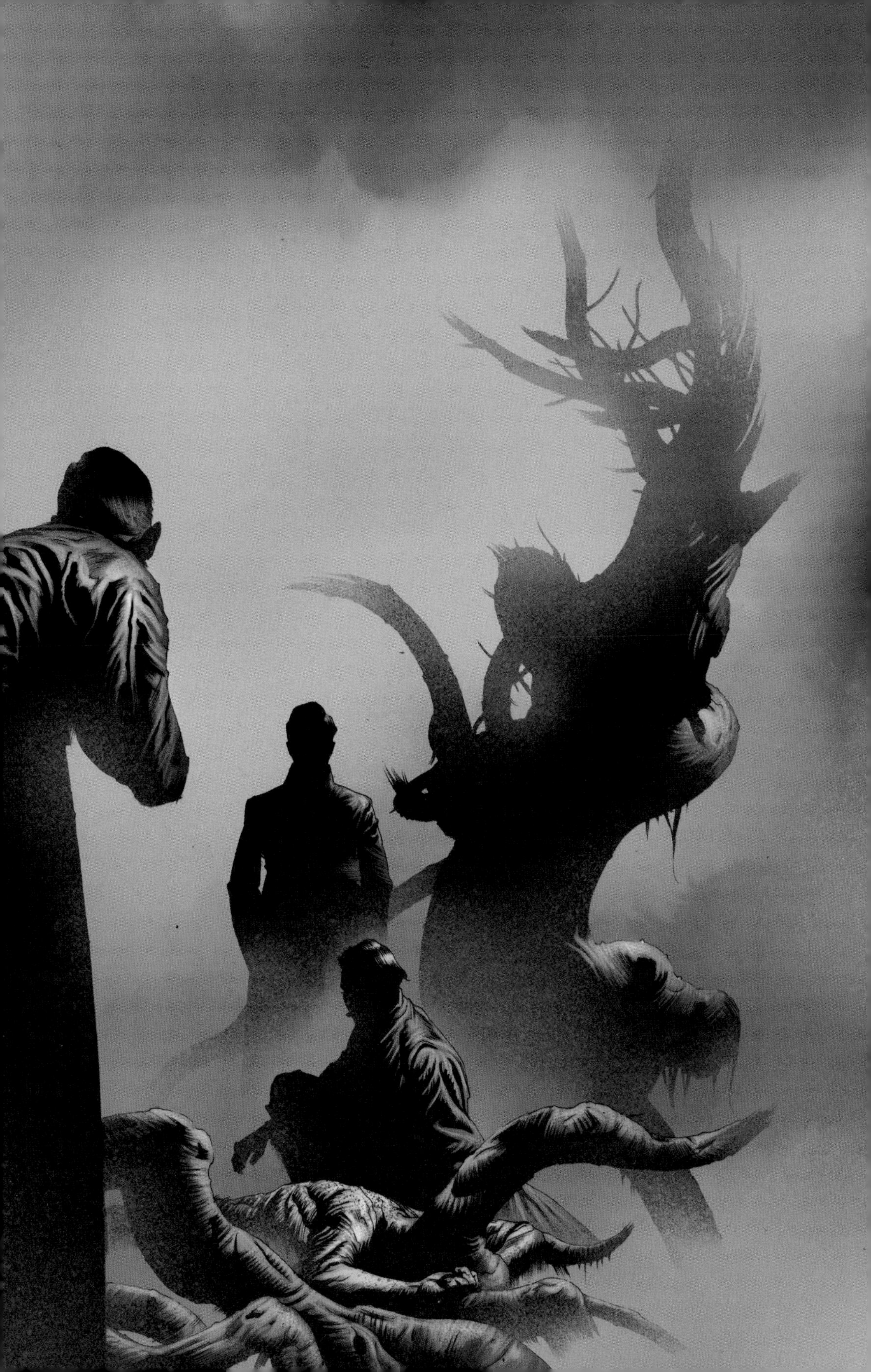

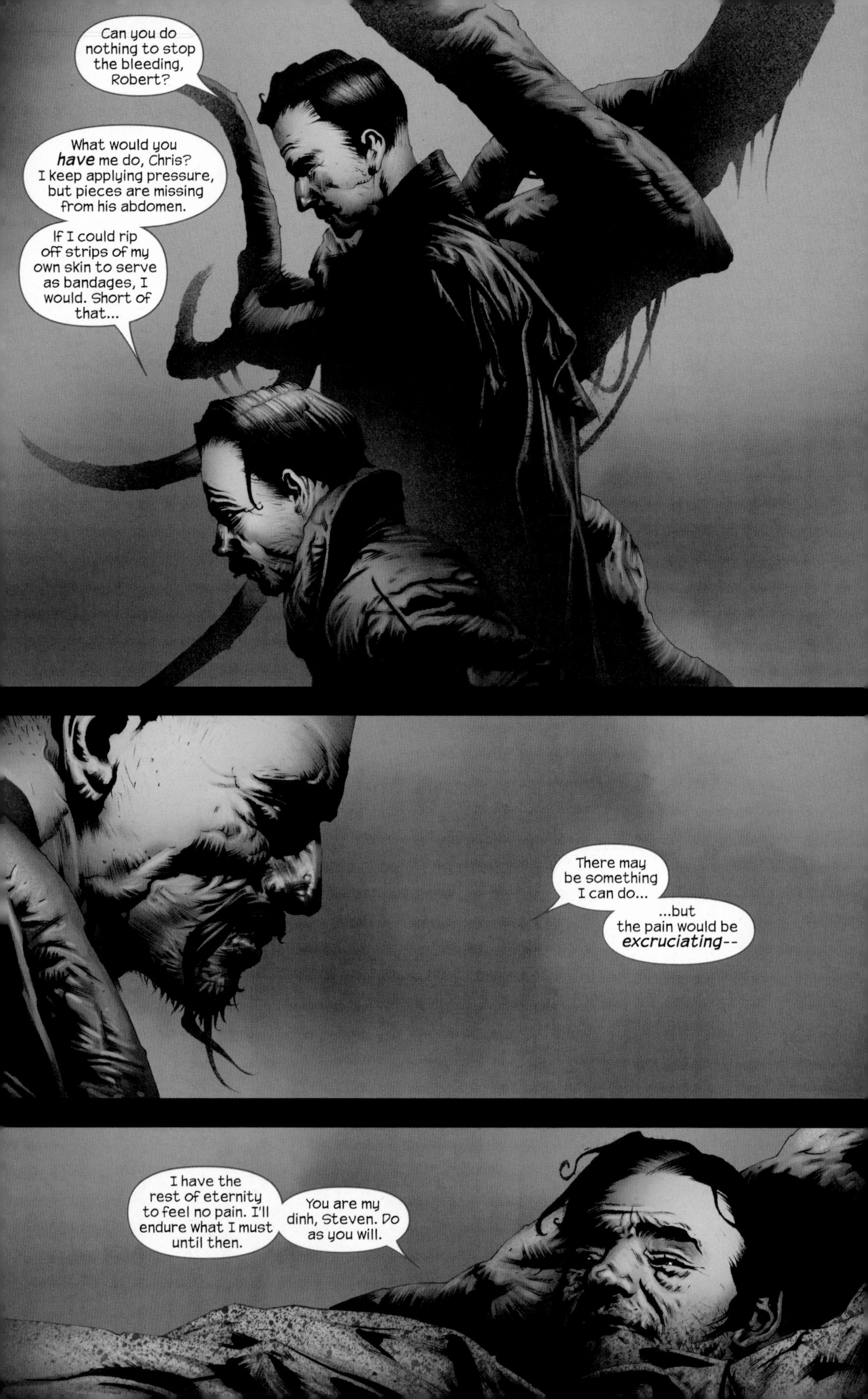
Can you do nothing to stop the bleeding, Robert?
What would you *have* me do, Chris? I keep applying pressure, but pieces are missing from his abdomen.
If I could rip off strips of my own skin to serve as bandages, I would. Short of that...
There may be something I can do...
...but the pain would be *excruciating*--
I have the rest of eternity to feel no pain. I'll endure what I must until then.
You are my dinh, Steven. Do as you will.

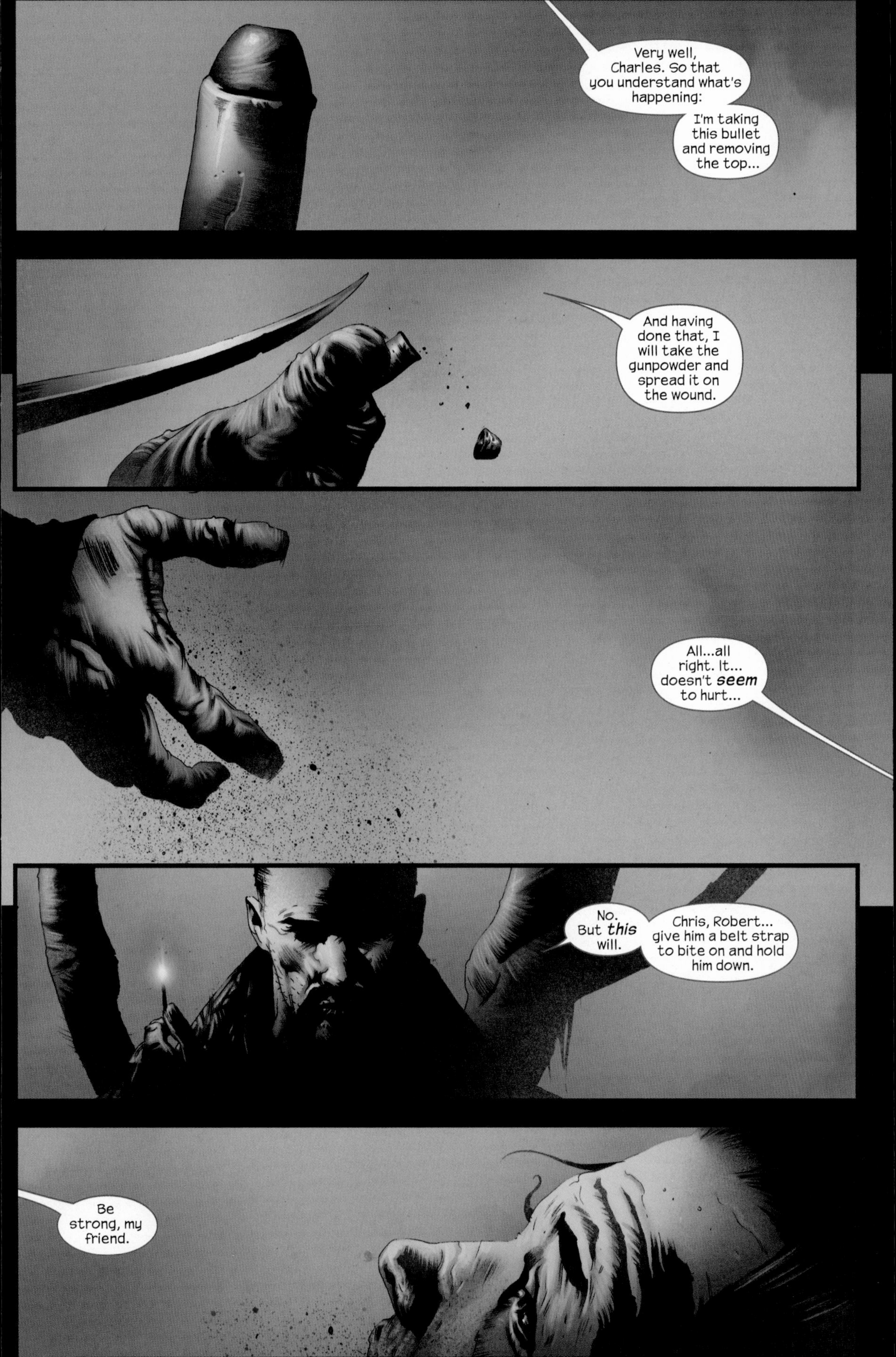
Very well, Charles. So that you understand what's happening:
I'm taking this bullet and removing the top...
And having done that, I will take the gunpowder and spread it on the wound.
All...all right. It... doesn't *seem* to hurt...
No. But *this* will.
Chris, Robert... give him a belt strap to bite on and hold him down.
Be strong, my friend.

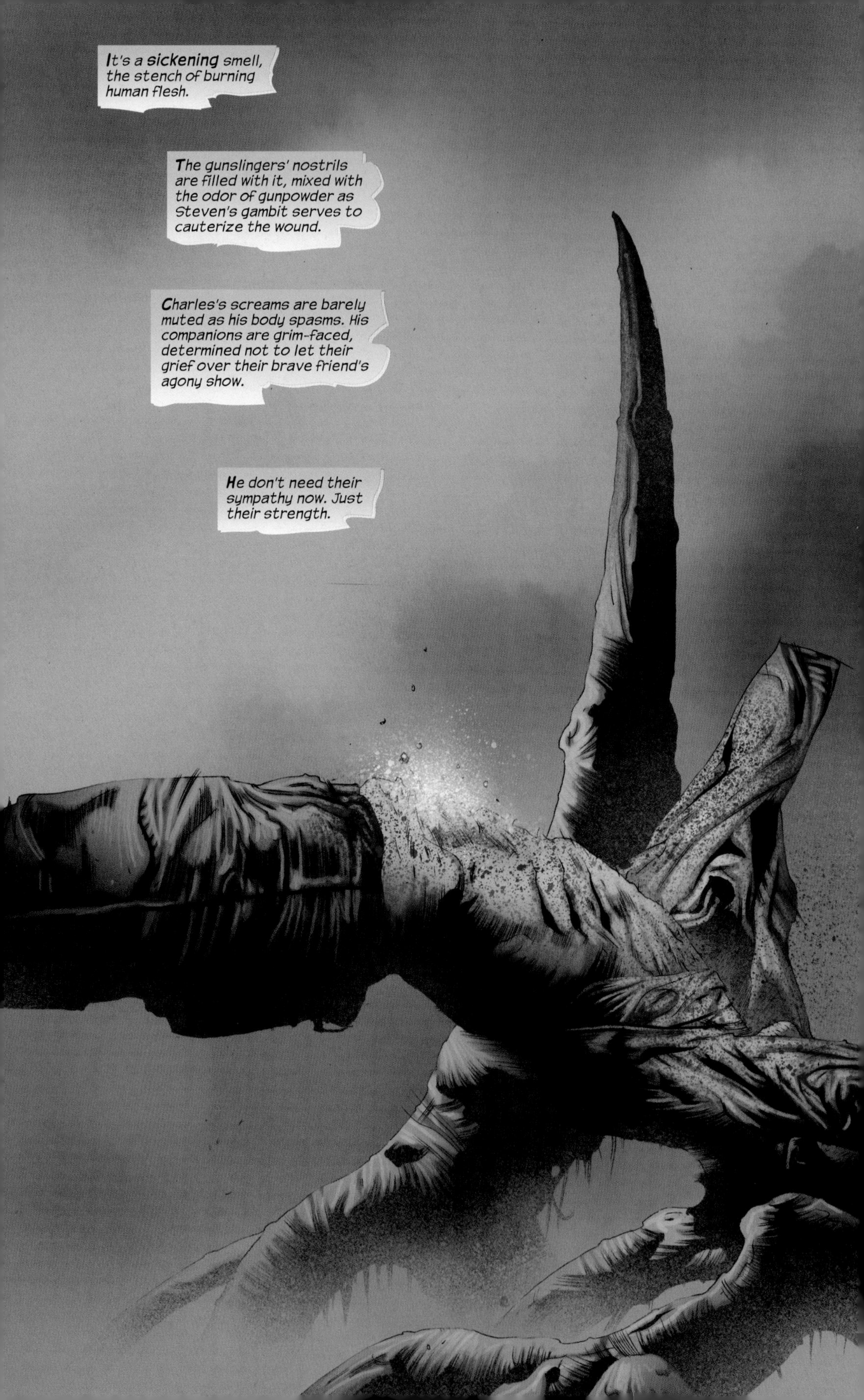

It's a sickening smell, the stench of burning human flesh.
The gunslingers' nostrils are filled with it, mixed with the odor of gunpowder as Steven's gambit serves to cauterize the wound.
Charles's screams are barely muted as his body spasms. His companions are grim-faced, determined not to let their grief over their brave friend's agony show.
He don't need their sympathy now. Just their strength.

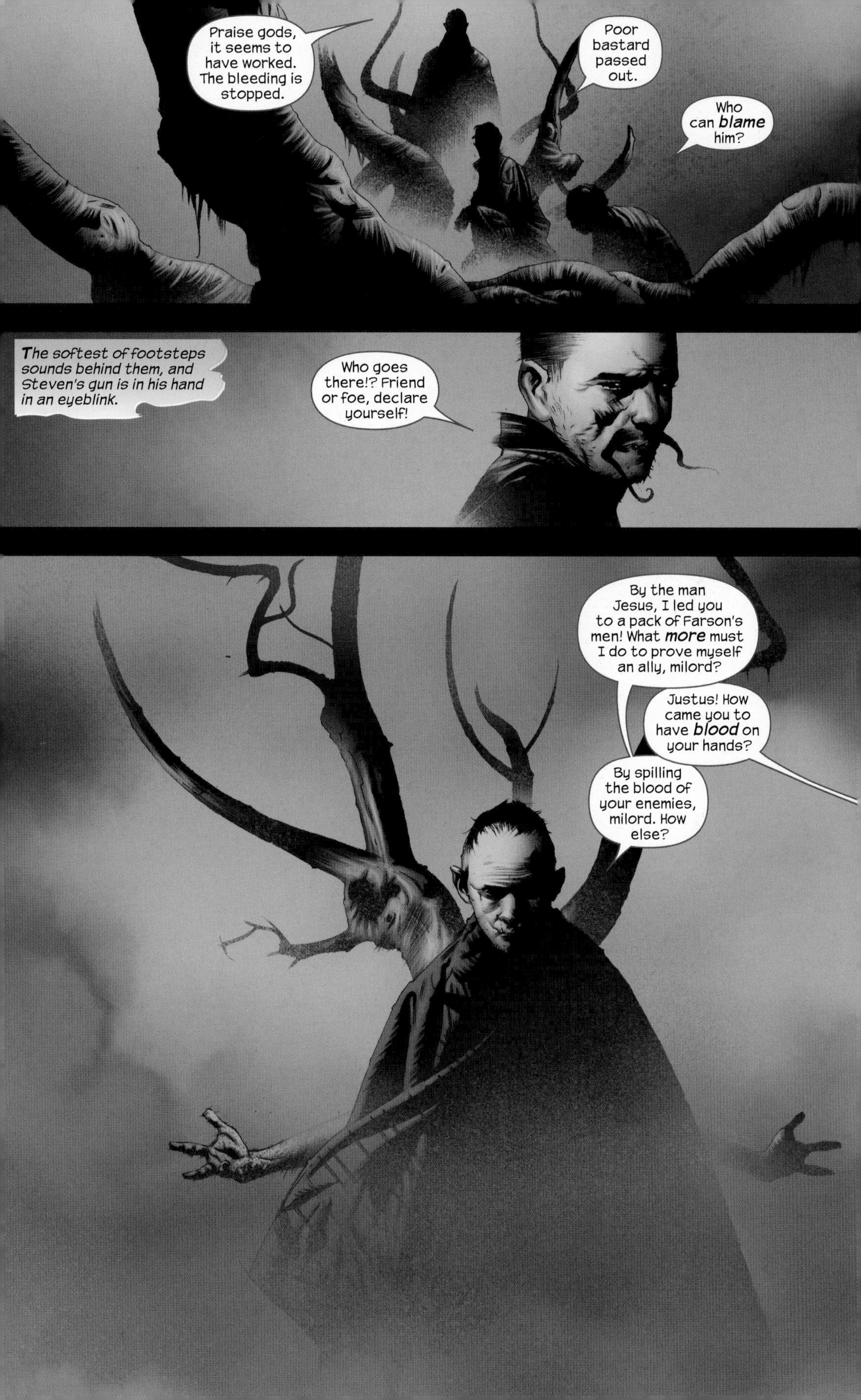
Praise gods, it seems to have worked. The bleeding is stopped.
Poor bastard passed out.
Who can *blame* him?
*T*he softest of footsteps sounds behind them, and Steven's gun is in his hand in an eyeblink.
Who goes there!? Friend or foe, declare yourself!
By the man Jesus, I led you to a pack of Farson's men! What *more* must I do to prove myself an ally, milord?
Justus! How came you to have *blood* on your hands?
By spilling the blood of your enemies, milord. How else?

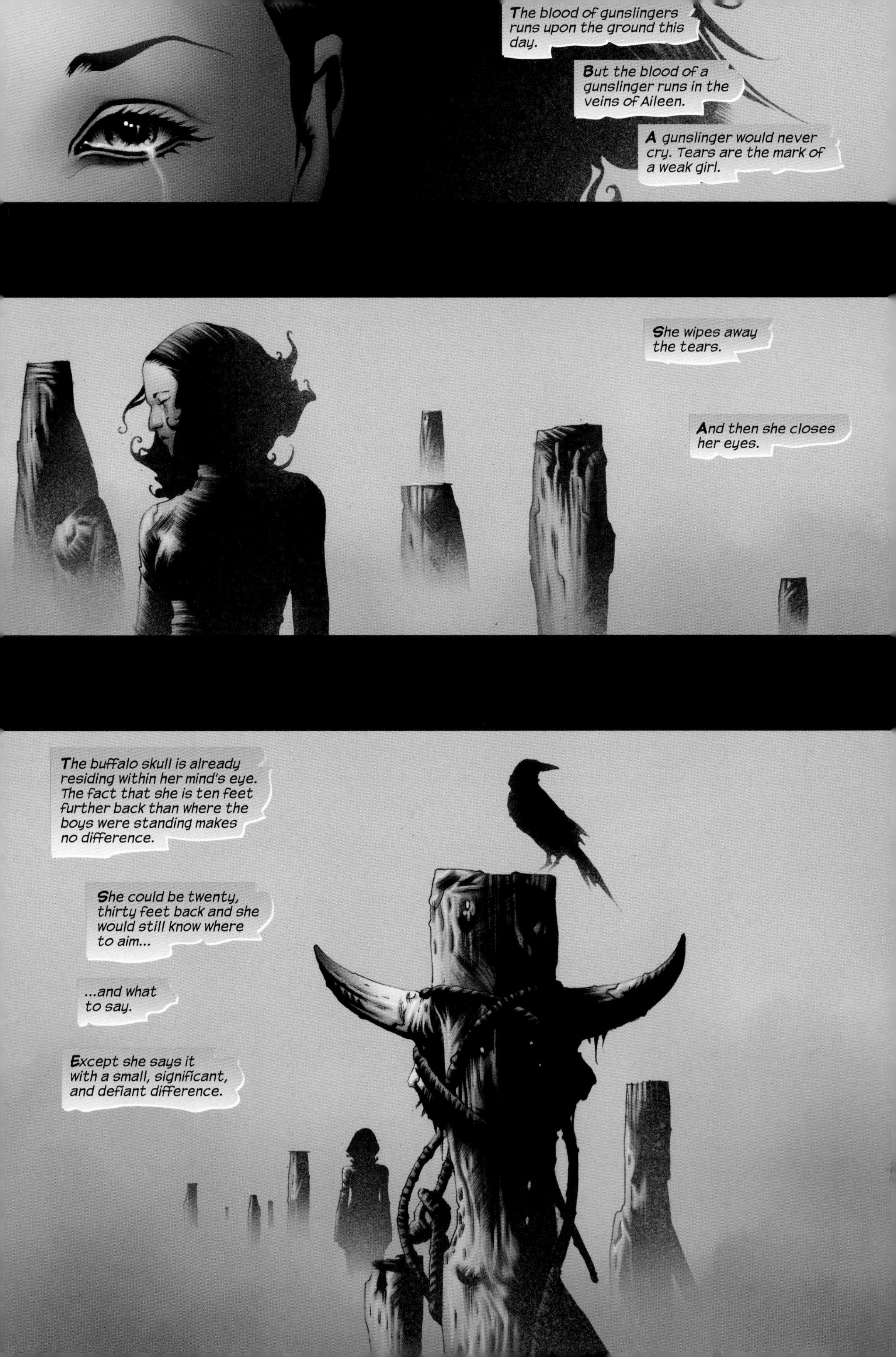
The blood of gunslingers runs upon the ground this day.
But the blood of a gunslinger runs in the veins of Aileen.
A gunslinger would never cry. Tears are the mark of a weak girl.
She wipes away the tears.
And then she closes her eyes.
The buffalo skull is already residing within her mind's eye. The fact that she is ten feet further back than where the boys were standing makes no difference.
She could be twenty, thirty feet back and she would still know where to aim...
...and what to say.
Except she says it with a small, significant, and defiant difference.

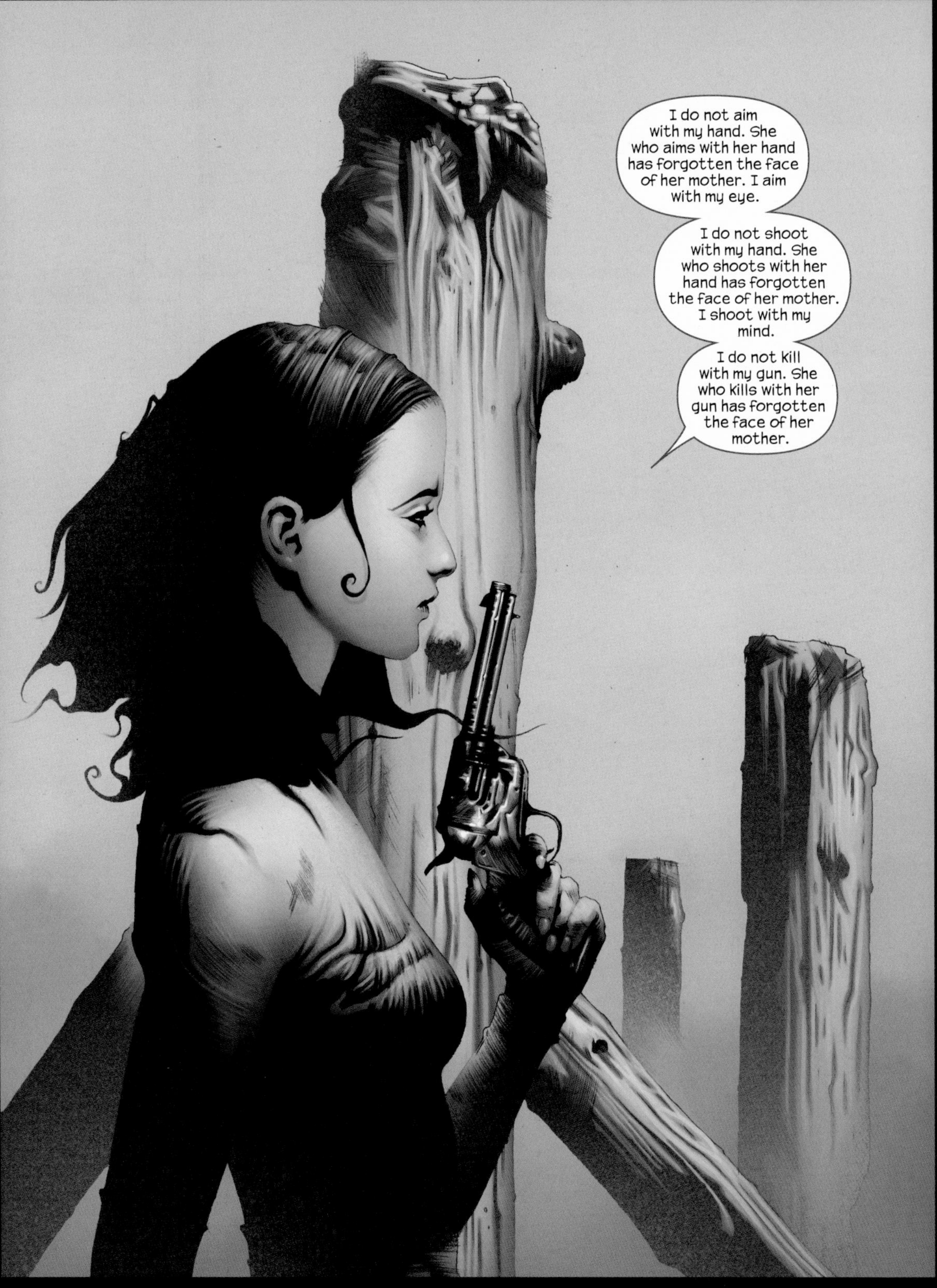

I do not aim with my hand. She who aims with her hand has forgotten the face of her mother. I aim with my eye.
I do not shoot with my hand. She who shoots with her hand has forgotten the face of her mother. I shoot with my mind.
I do not kill with my gun. She who kills with her gun has forgotten the face of her mother.

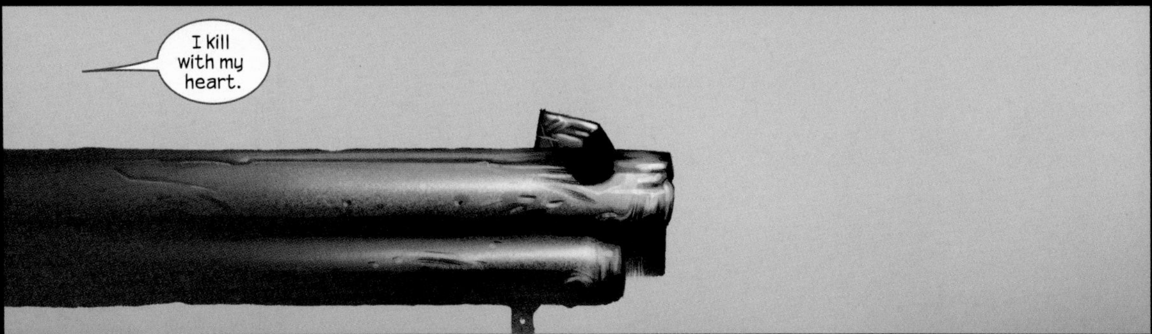

I kill with my heart.

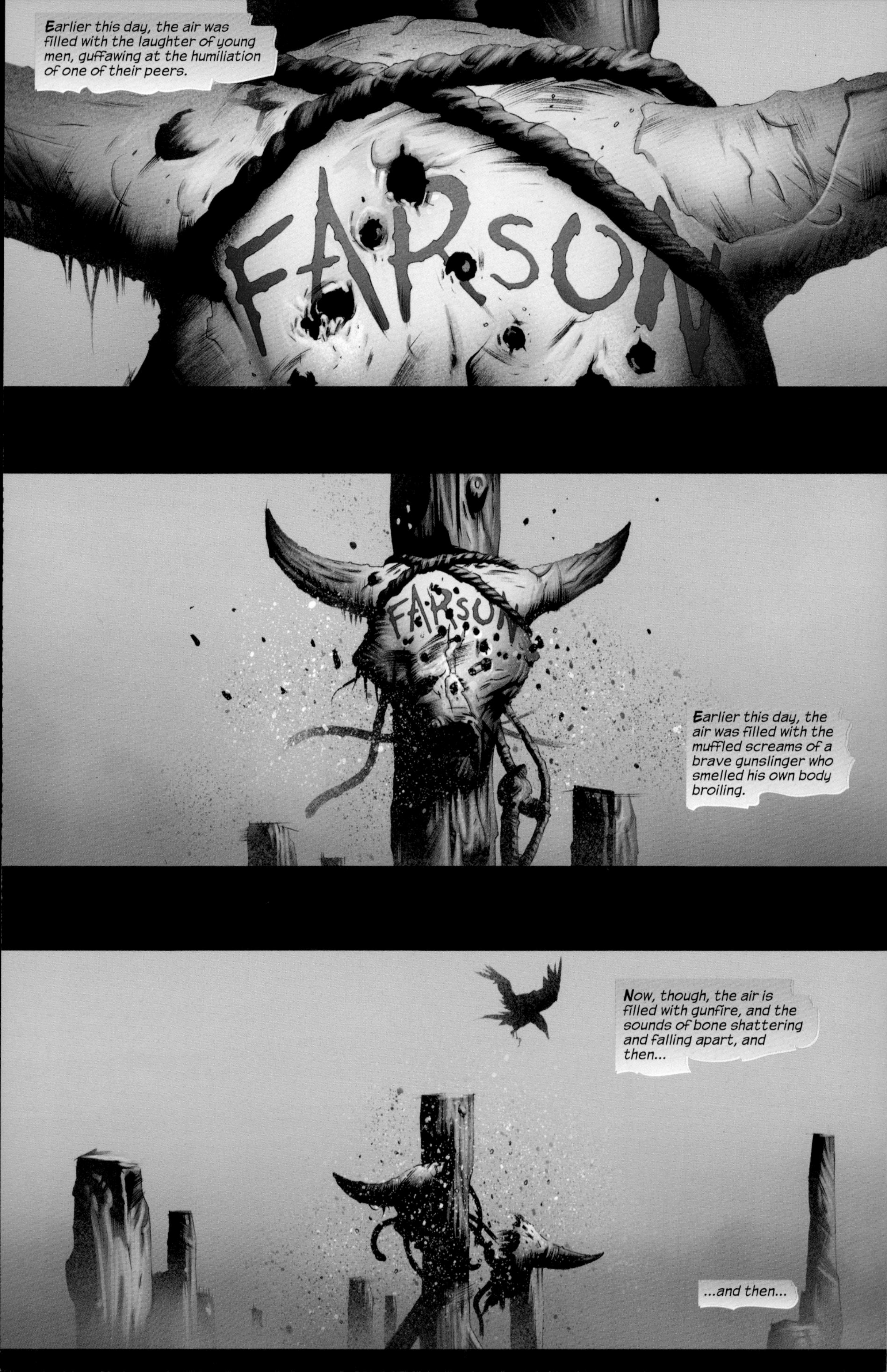
Earlier this day, the air was filled with the laughter of young men, guffawing at the humiliation of one of their peers.
FARSON
FARSON
Earlier this day, the air was filled with the muffled screams of a brave gunslinger who smelled his own body broiling.
Now, though, the air is filled with gunfire, and the sounds of bone shattering and falling apart, and then...
...and then...

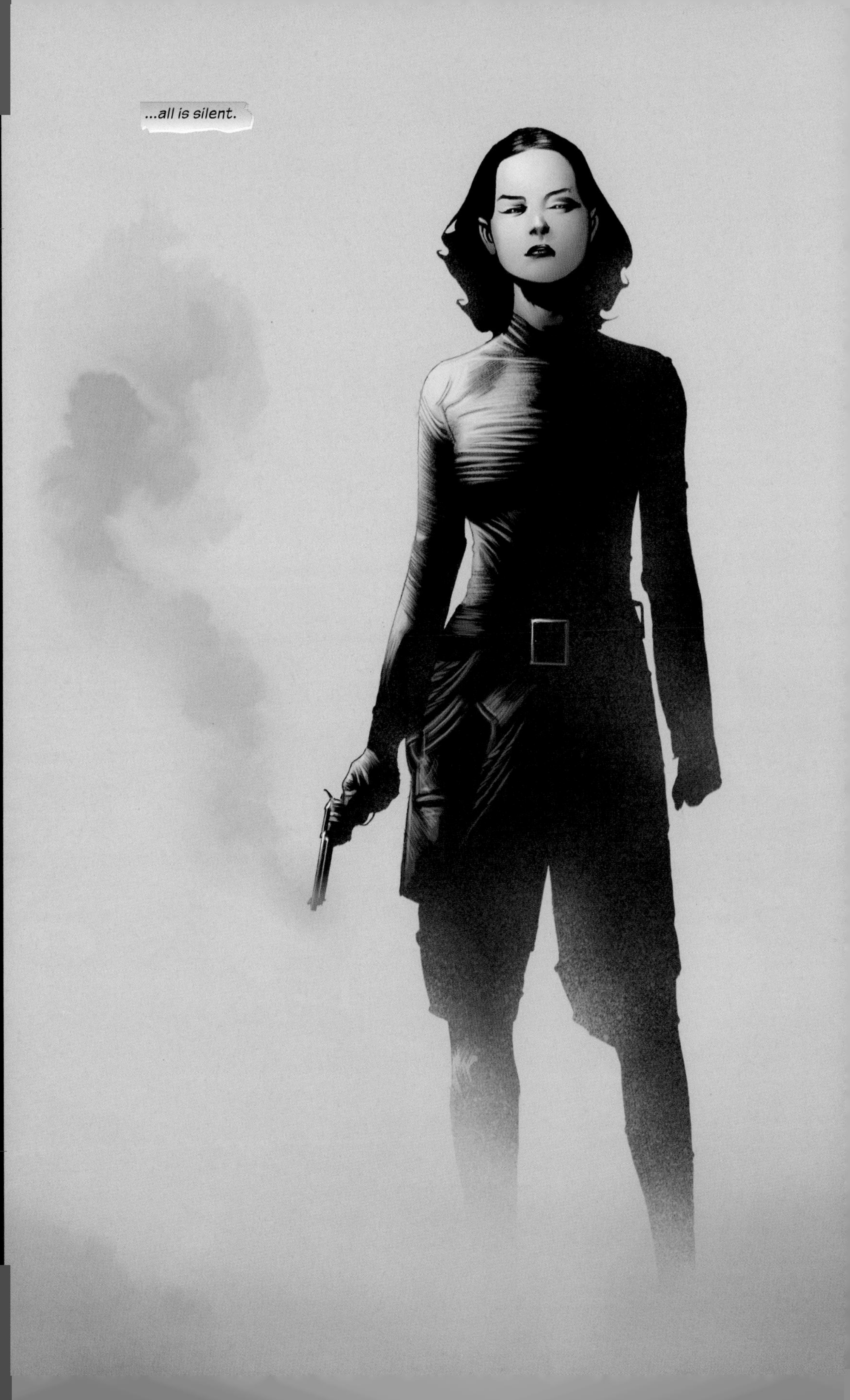
...all is silent.

STEPHEN KING

THE DARK TOWER

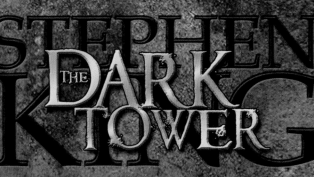

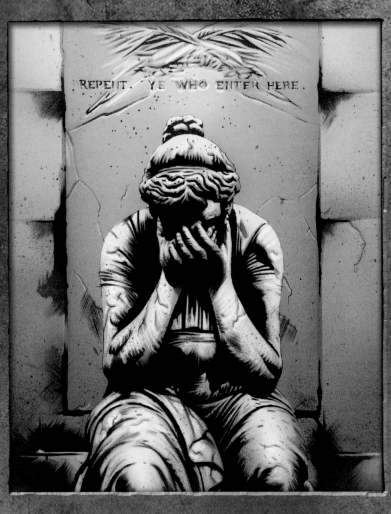

REPENT. YE WHO ENTER HERE.

TREACHERY

CHAPTER THREE

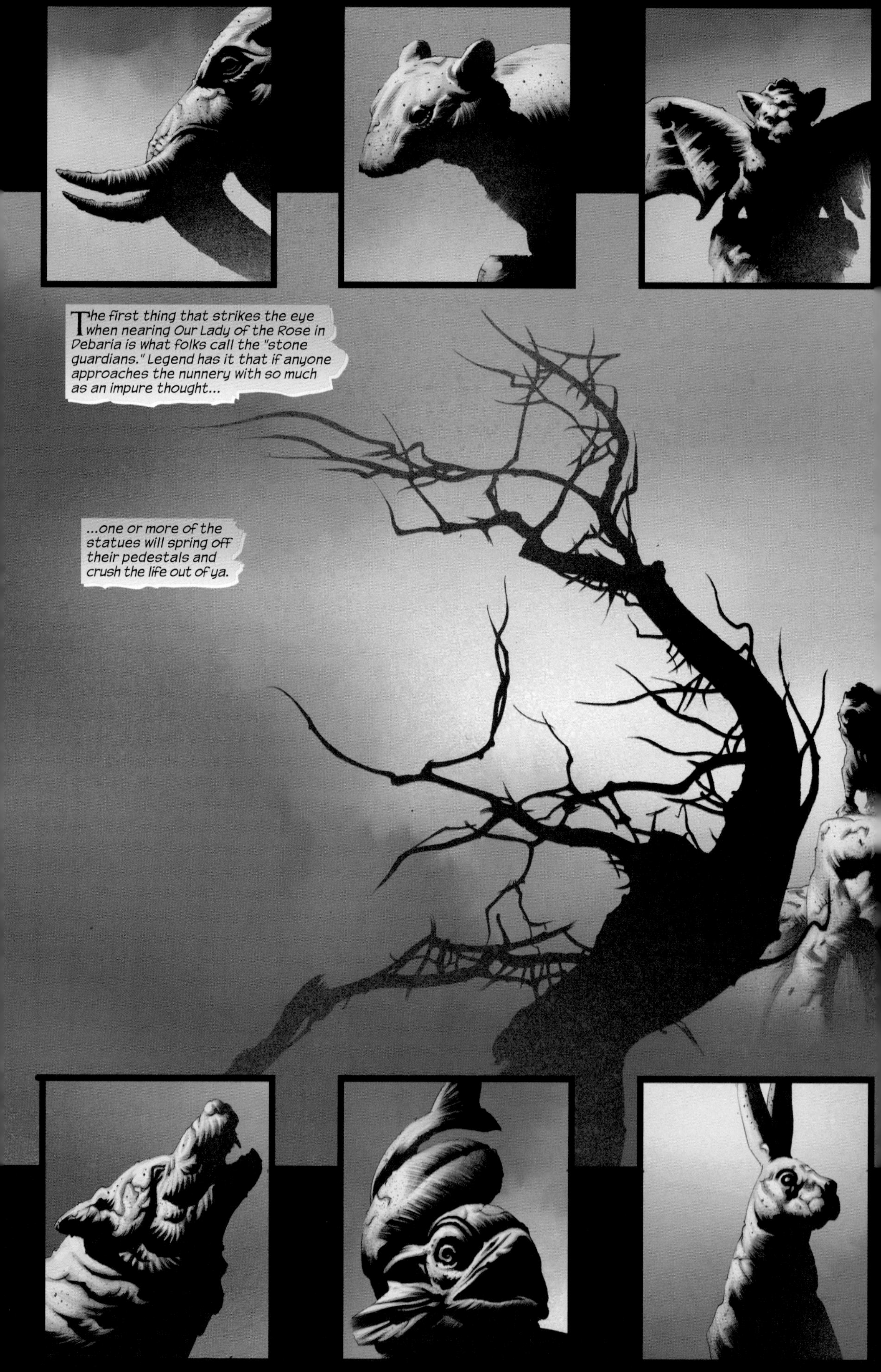
The first thing that strikes the eye when nearing Our Lady of the Rose in Debaria is what folks call the "stone guardians." Legend has it that if anyone approaches the nunnery with so much as an impure thought...
...one or more of the statues will spring off their pedestals and crush the life out of ya.

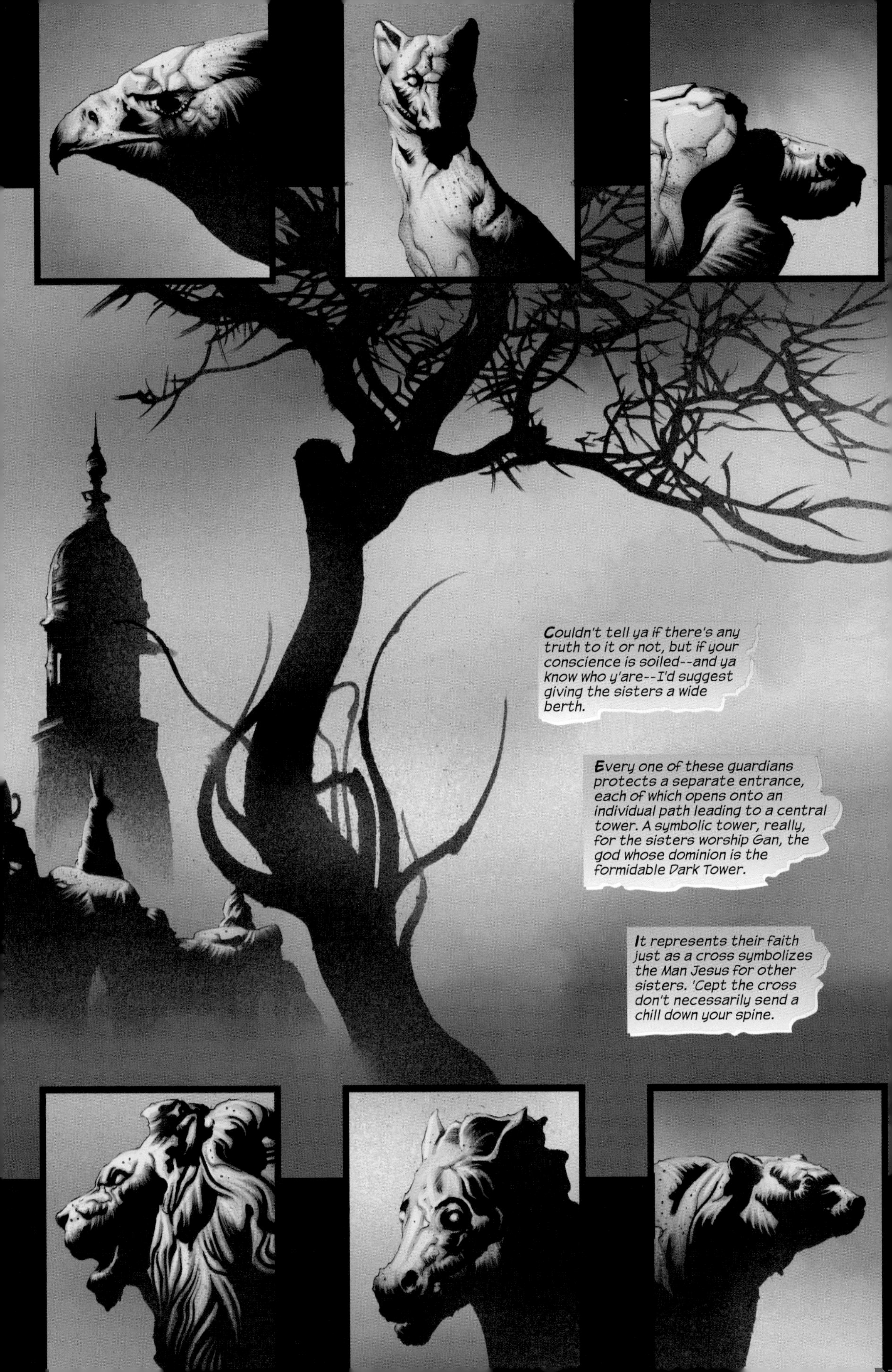
Couldn't tell ya if there's any truth to it or not, but if your conscience is soiled--and ya know who y'are--I'd suggest giving the sisters a wide berth.
Every one of these guardians protects a separate entrance, each of which opens onto an individual path leading to a central tower. A symbolic tower, really, for the sisters worship Gan, the god whose dominion is the formidable Dark Tower.
It represents their faith just as a cross symbolizes the Man Jesus for other sisters. 'Cept the cross don't necessarily send a chill down your spine.

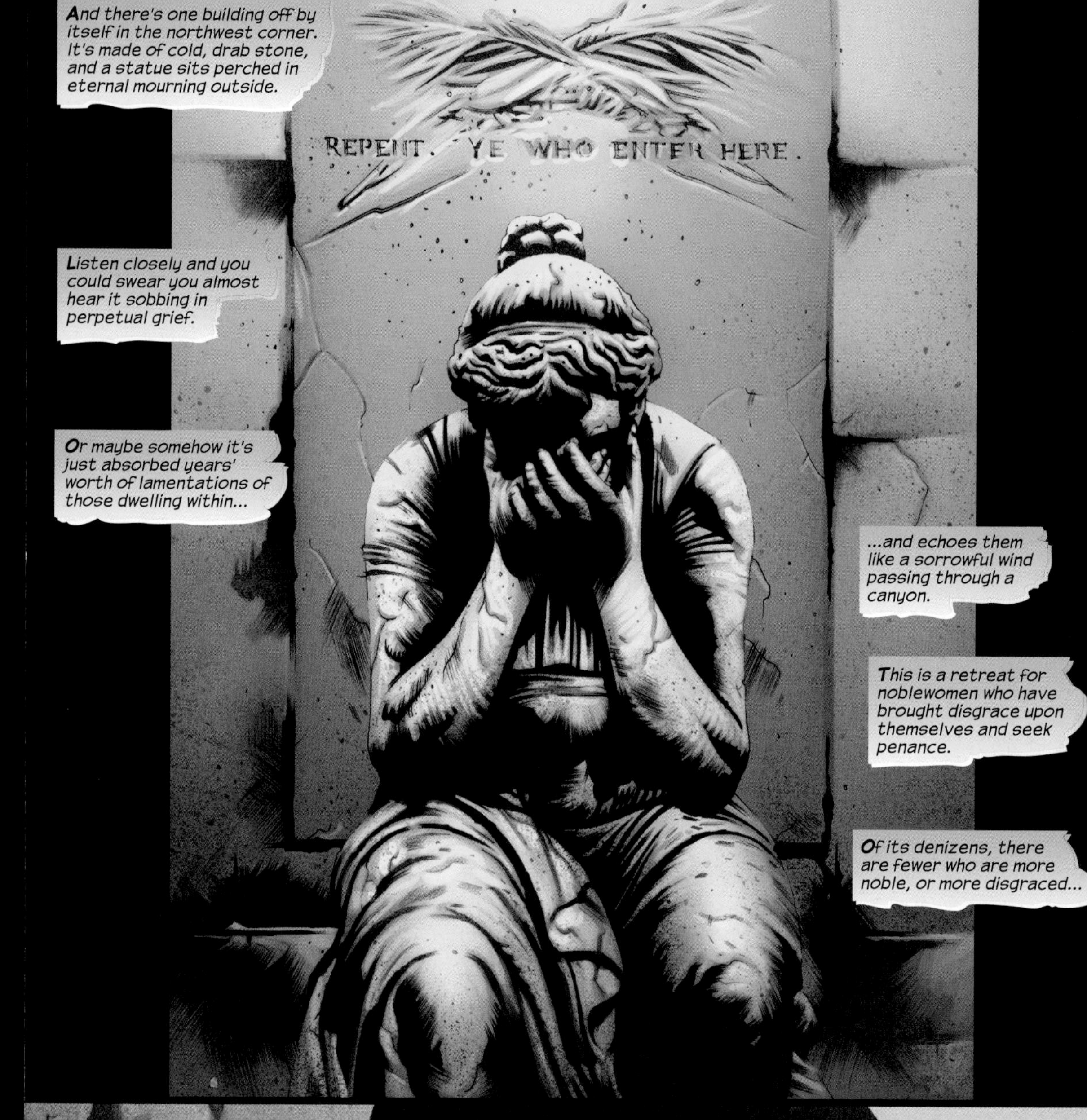
And there's one building off by itself in the northwest corner. It's made of cold, drab stone, and a statue sits perched in eternal mourning outside.
REPENT. YE WHO ENTER HERE.
Listen closely and you could swear you almost hear it sobbing in perpetual grief.
Or maybe somehow it's just absorbed years' worth of lamentations of those dwelling within...
...and echoes them like a sorrowful wind passing through a canyon.
This is a retreat for noblewomen who have brought disgrace upon themselves and seek penance.
Of its denizens, there are fewer who are more noble, or more disgraced...

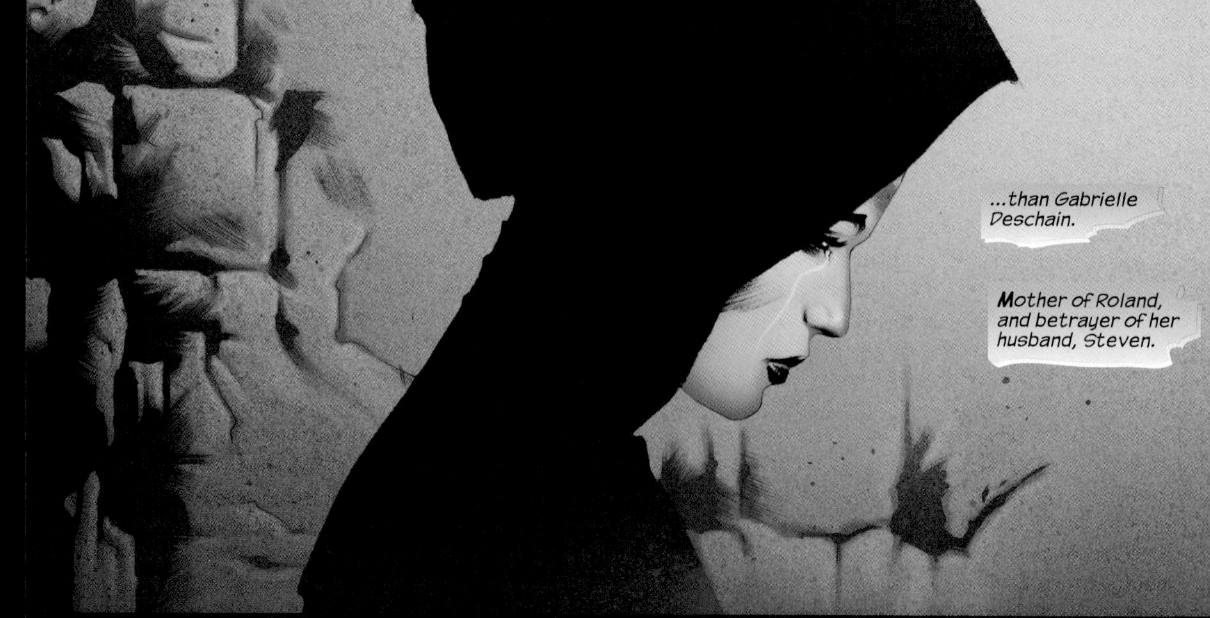
...than Gabrielle Deschain.
Mother of Roland, and betrayer of her husband, Steven.

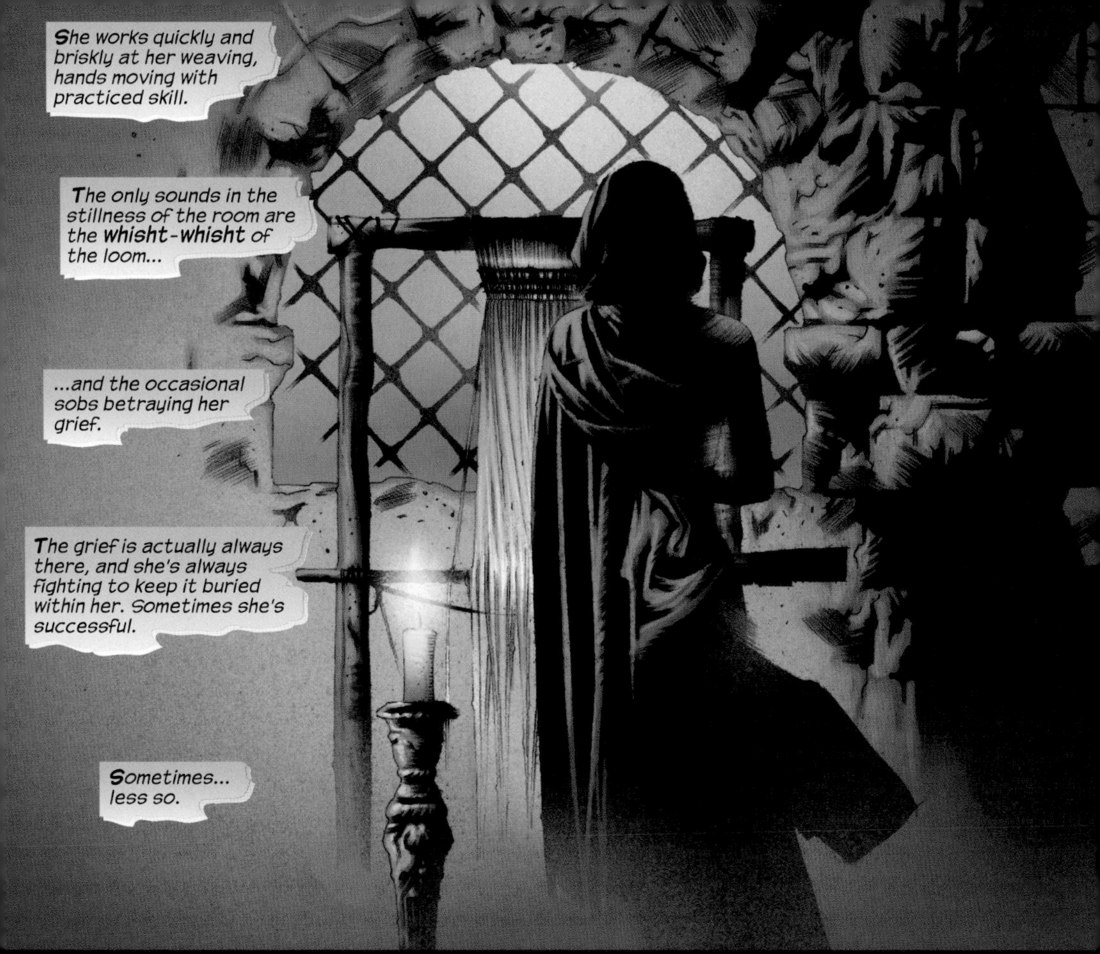
She works quickly and briskly at her weaving, hands moving with practiced skill.
The only sounds in the stillness of the room are the whisht-whisht of the loom...
...and the occasional sobs betraying her grief.
The grief is actually always there, and she's always fighting to keep it buried within her. Sometimes she's successful.
Sometimes... less so.

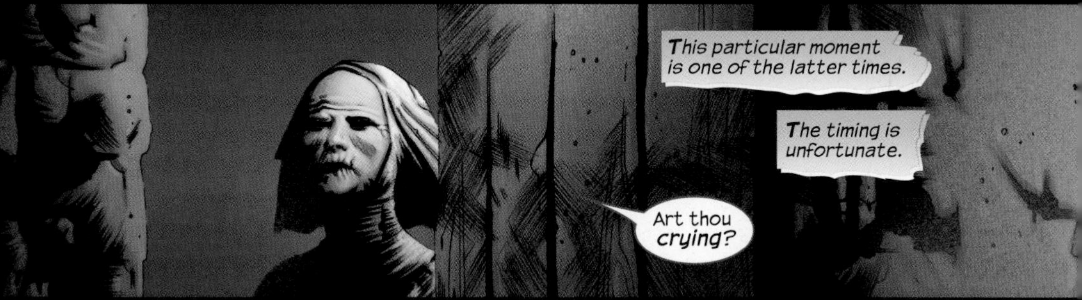
This particular moment is one of the latter times.
The timing is unfortunate.
Art thou crying?

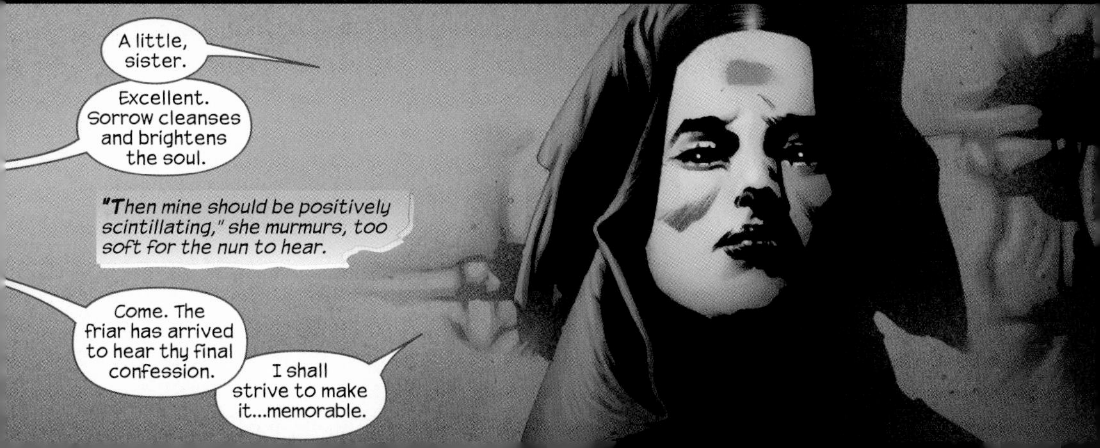
A little, sister.
Excellent. Sorrow cleanses and brightens the soul.
"Then mine should be positively scintillating," she murmurs, too soft for the nun to hear.
Come. The friar has arrived to hear thy final confession.
I shall strive to make it...memorable.

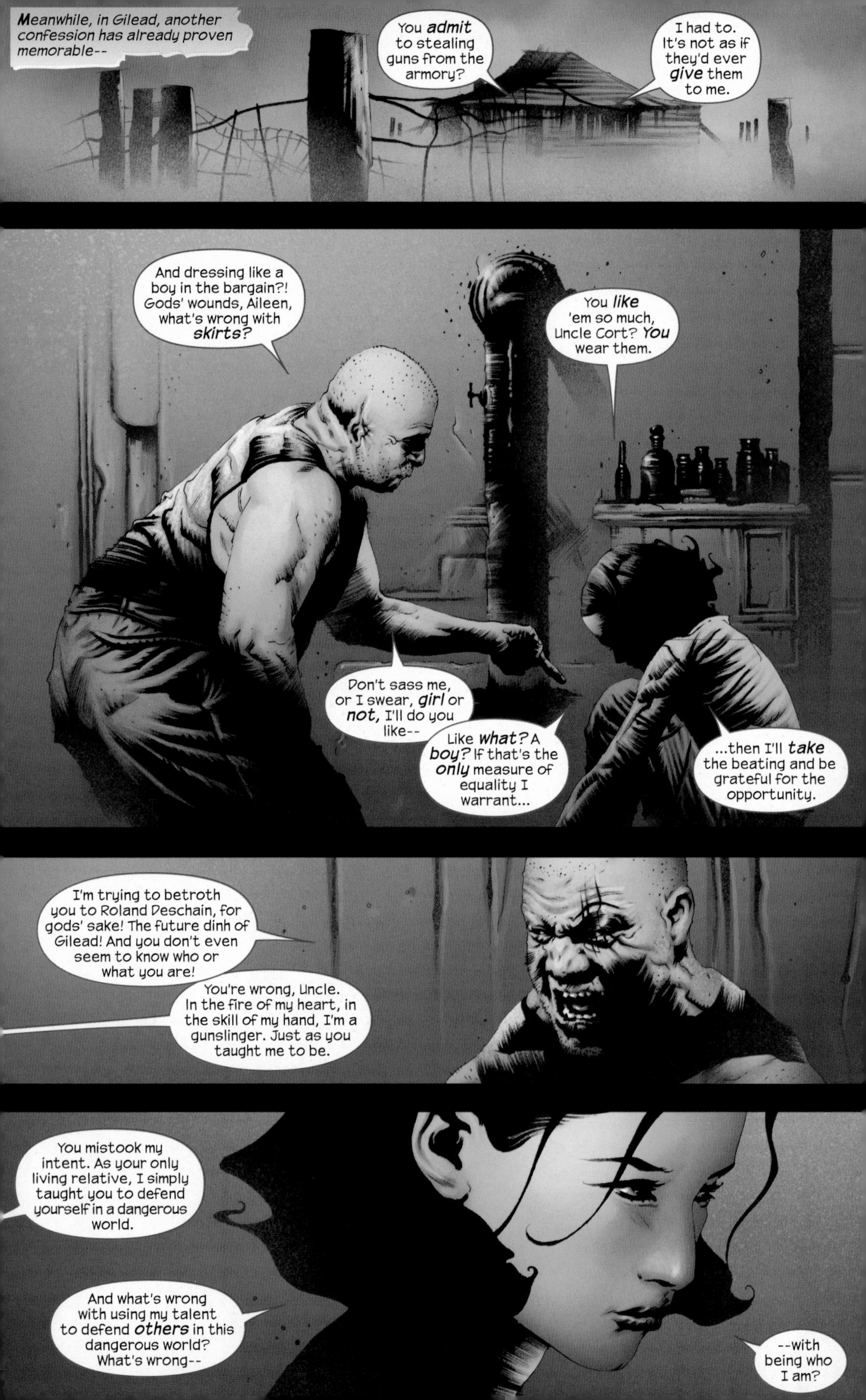
Meanwhile, in Gilead, another confession has already proven memorable--
You admit to stealing guns from the armory?
I had to. It's not as if they'd ever give them to me.
And dressing like a boy in the bargain?! Gods' wounds, Aileen, what's wrong with skirts?
You like 'em so much, Uncle Cort? You wear them.
Don't sass me, or I swear, girl or not, I'll do you like--
Like what? A boy? If that's the only measure of equality I warrant...
...then I'll take the beating and be grateful for the opportunity.
I'm trying to betroth you to Roland Deschain, for gods' sake! The future dinh of Gilead! And you don't even seem to know who or what you are!
You're wrong, Uncle. In the fire of my heart, in the skill of my hand, I'm a gunslinger. Just as you taught me to be.
You mistook my intent. As your only living relative, I simply taught you to defend yourself in a dangerous world.
And what's wrong with using my talent to defend others in this dangerous world? What's wrong--
--with being who I am?

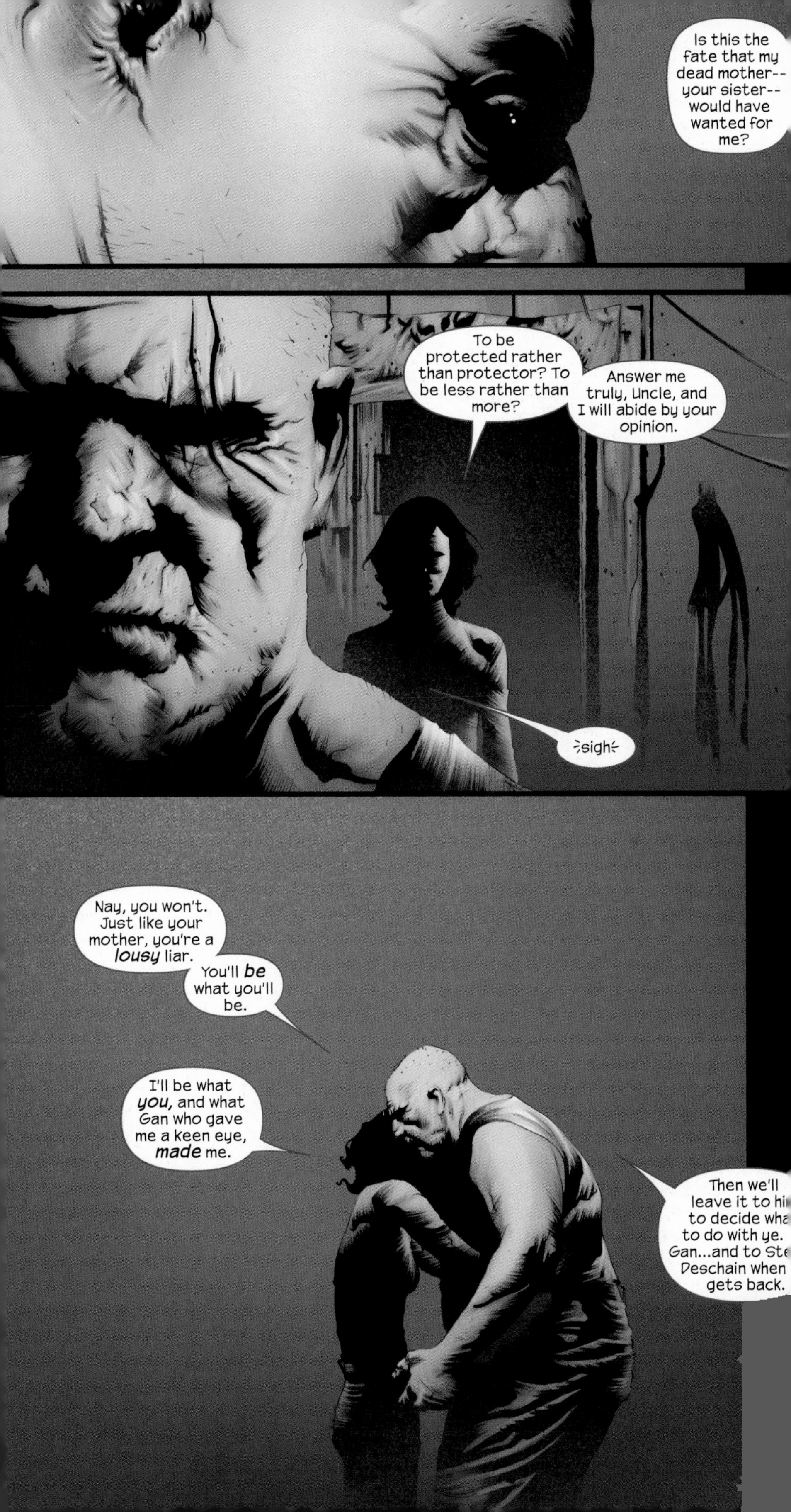

Is this the fate that my dead mother-- your sister-- would have wanted for me?
To be protected rather than protector? To be less rather than more?
Answer me truly, Uncle, and I will abide by your opinion.
⁼sigh⁼
Nay, you won't. Just like your mother, you're a *lousy* liar.
You'll *be* what you'll be.
I'll be what *you,* and what Gan who gave me a keen eye, *made* me.
Then we'll leave it to hi to decide wha to do with ye. Gan...and to Ste Deschain when gets back.

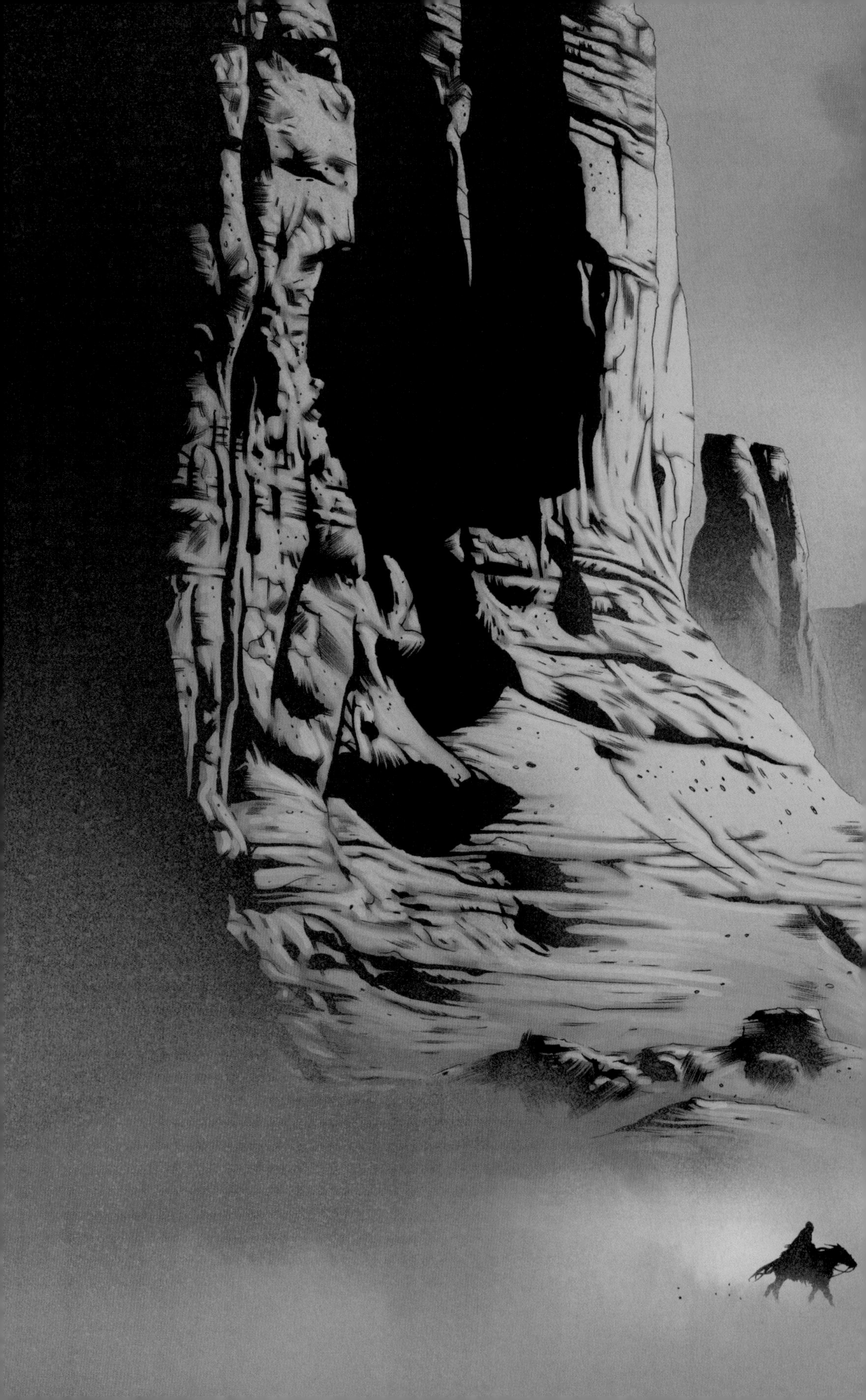

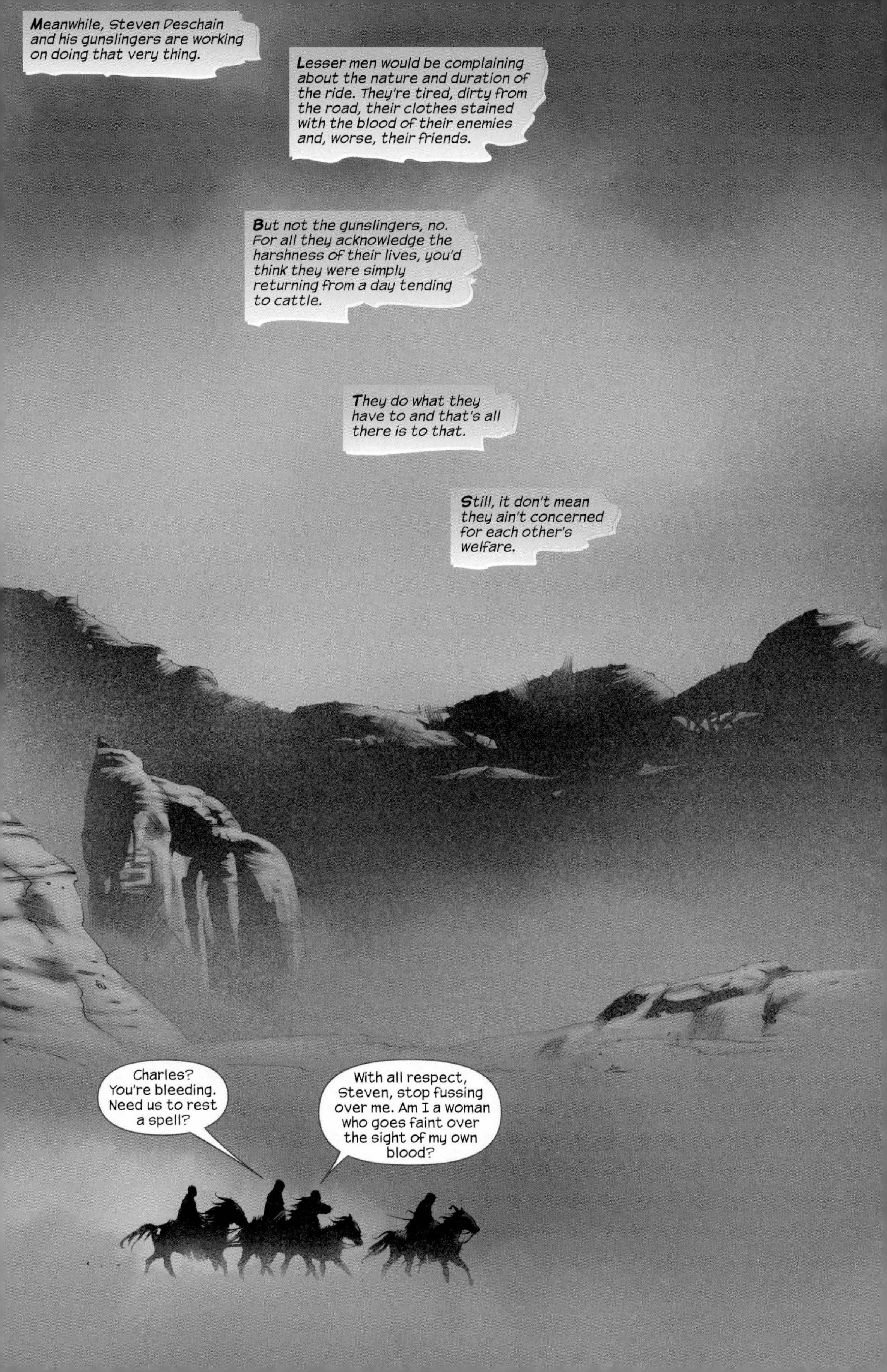
Meanwhile, Steven Deschain and his gunslingers are working on doing that very thing.
Lesser men would be complaining about the nature and duration of the ride. They're tired, dirty from the road, their clothes stained with the blood of their enemies and, worse, their friends.
But not the gunslingers, no. For all they acknowledge the harshness of their lives, you'd think they were simply returning from a day tending to cattle.
They do what they have to and that's all there is to that.
Still, it don't mean they ain't concerned for each other's welfare.
Charles? You're bleeding. Need us to rest a spell?
With all respect, Steven, stop fussing over me. Am I a woman who goes faint over the sight of my own blood?

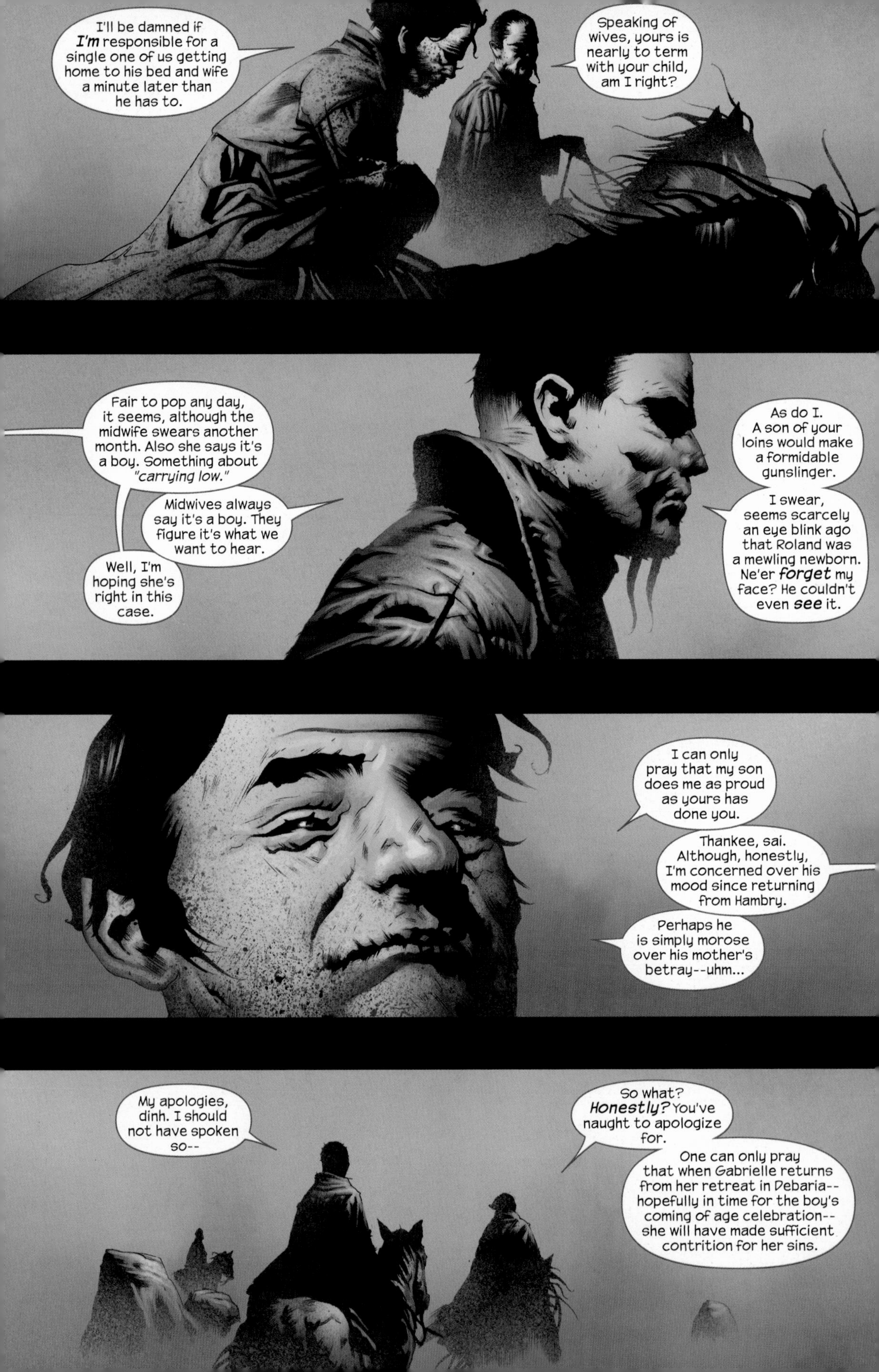
I'll be damned if *I'm* responsible for a single one of us getting home to his bed and wife a minute later than he has to.
Speaking of wives, yours is nearly to term with your child, am I right?
Fair to pop any day, it seems, although the midwife swears another month. Also she says it's a boy. Something about *"carrying low."*
Midwives always say it's a boy. They figure it's what we want to hear.
Well, I'm hoping she's right in this case.
As do I. A son of your loins would make a formidable gunslinger.
I swear, seems scarcely an eye blink ago that Roland was a mewling newborn. Ne'er **forget** my face? He couldn't even **see** it.
I can only pray that my son does me as proud as yours has done you.
Thankee, sai. Although, honestly, I'm concerned over his mood since returning from Hambry.
Perhaps he is simply morose over his mother's betray--uhm...
My apologies, dinh. I should not have spoken so--
So what? **Honestly?** You've naught to apologize for.
One can only pray that when Gabrielle returns from her retreat in Debaria--hopefully in time for the boy's coming of age celebration--she will have made sufficient contrition for her sins.

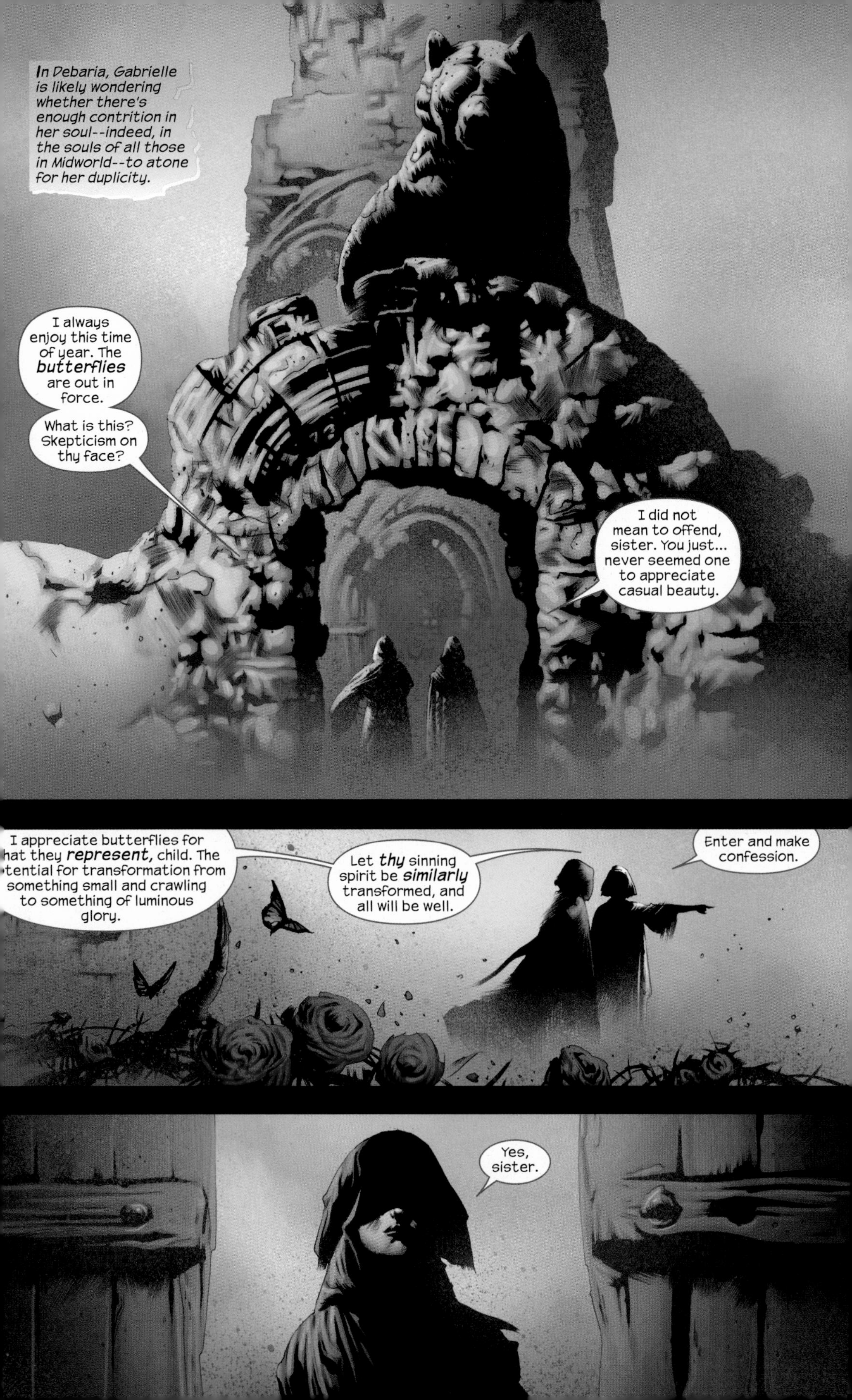
In Debaria, Gabrielle is likely wondering whether there's enough contrition in her soul--indeed, in the souls of all those in Midworld--to atone for her duplicity.
I always enjoy this time of year. The butterflies are out in force.
What is this? Skepticism on thy face?
I did not mean to offend, sister. You just... never seemed one to appreciate casual beauty.
I appreciate butterflies for hat they represent, child. The tential for transformation from something small and crawling to something of luminous glory.
Let thy sinning spirit be similarly transformed, and all will be well.
Enter and make confession.
Yes, sister.

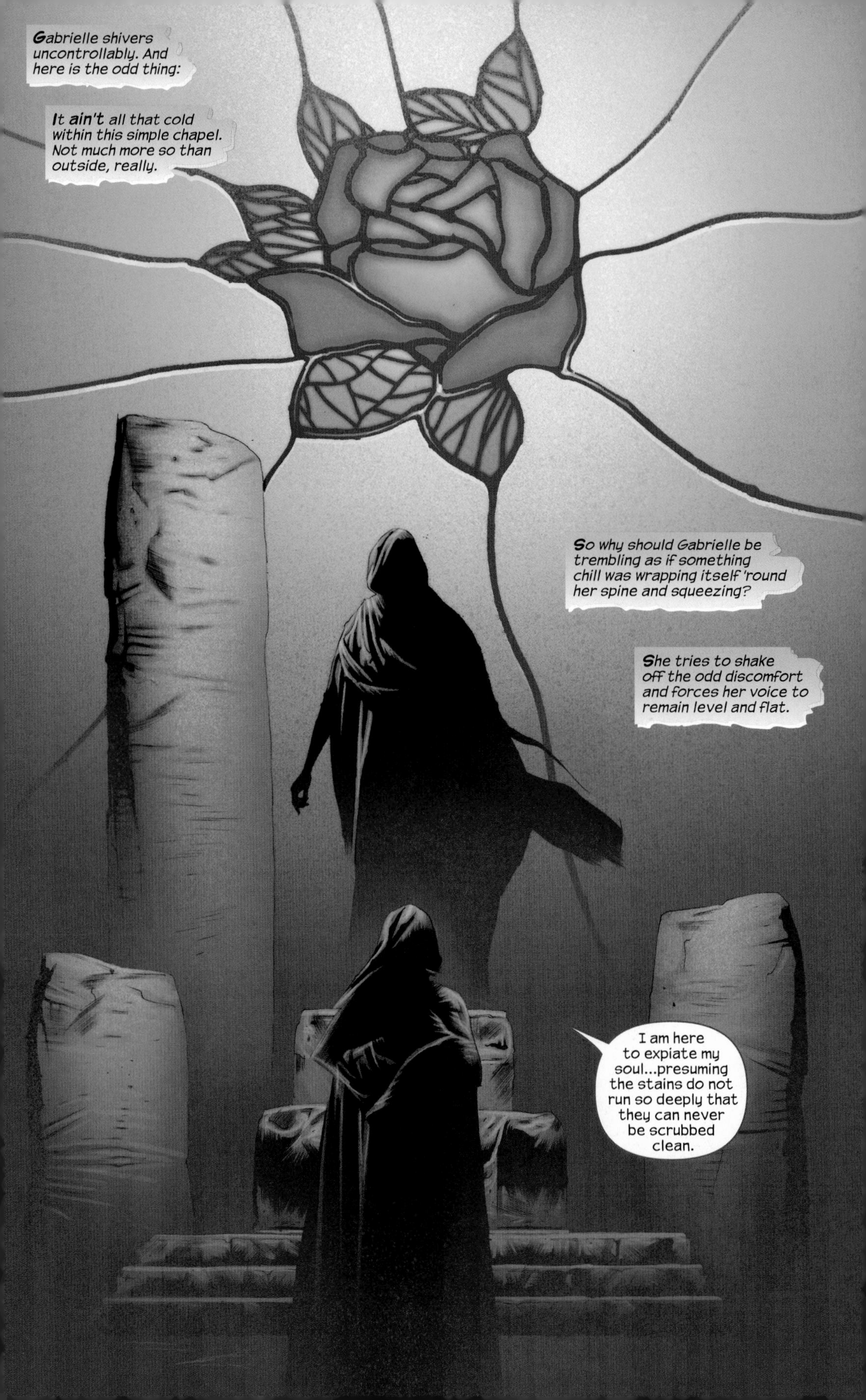
Gabrielle shivers uncontrollably. And here is the odd thing:
It ain't all that cold within this simple chapel. Not much more so than outside, really.
So why should Gabrielle be trembling as if something chill was wrapping itself 'round her spine and squeezing?
She tries to shake off the odd discomfort and forces her voice to remain level and flat.
I am here to expiate my soul...presuming the stains do not run so deeply that they can never be scrubbed clean.

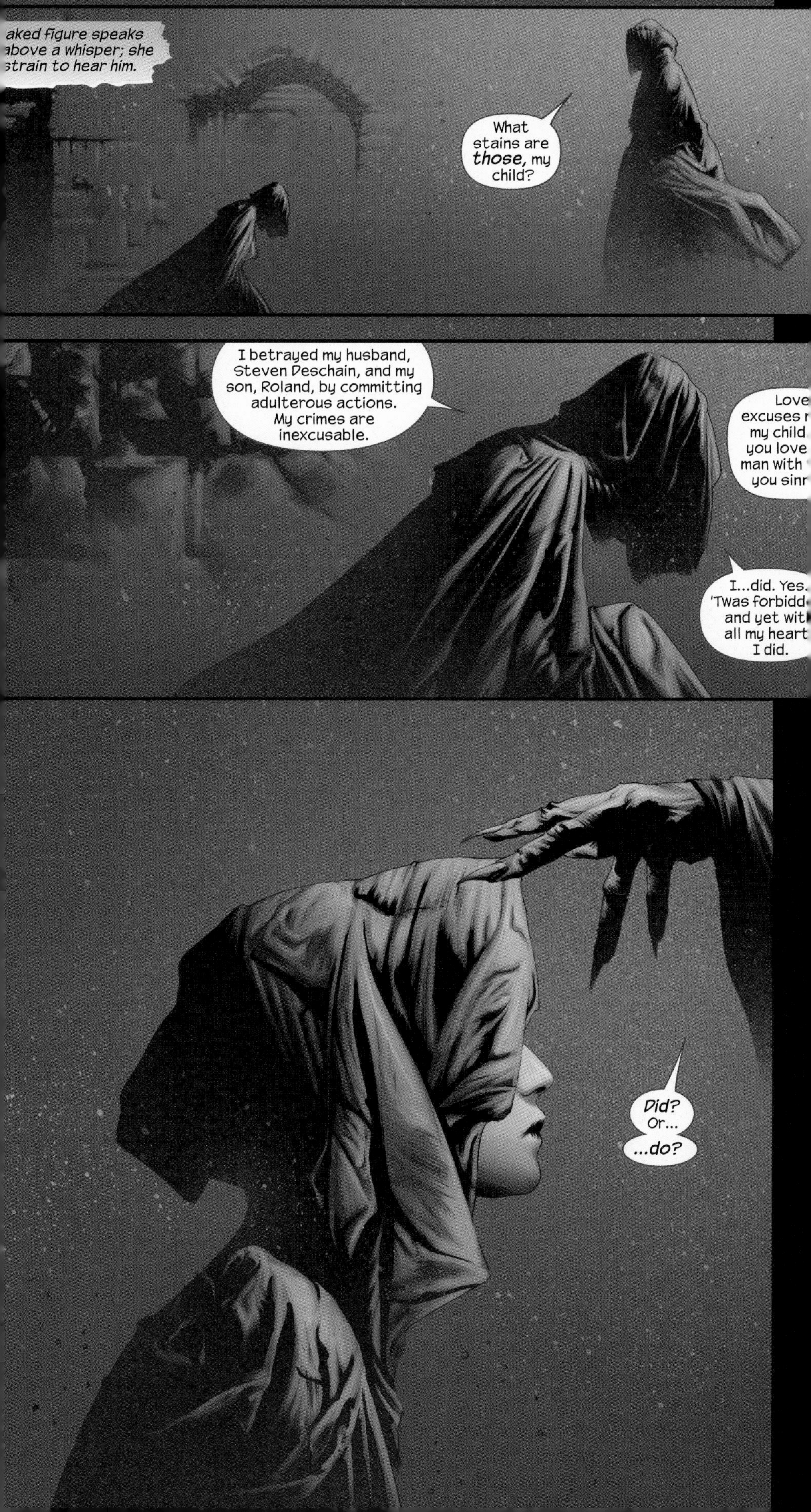
aked figure speaks above a whisper; she strain to hear him.
What stains are *those*, my child?
I betrayed my husband, Steven Deschain, and my son, Roland, by committing adulterous actions. My crimes are inexcusable.
Love excuses my child you love man with you sinr
I...did. Yes. 'Twas forbidd and yet with all my heart I did.
Did? Or... ...*do?*

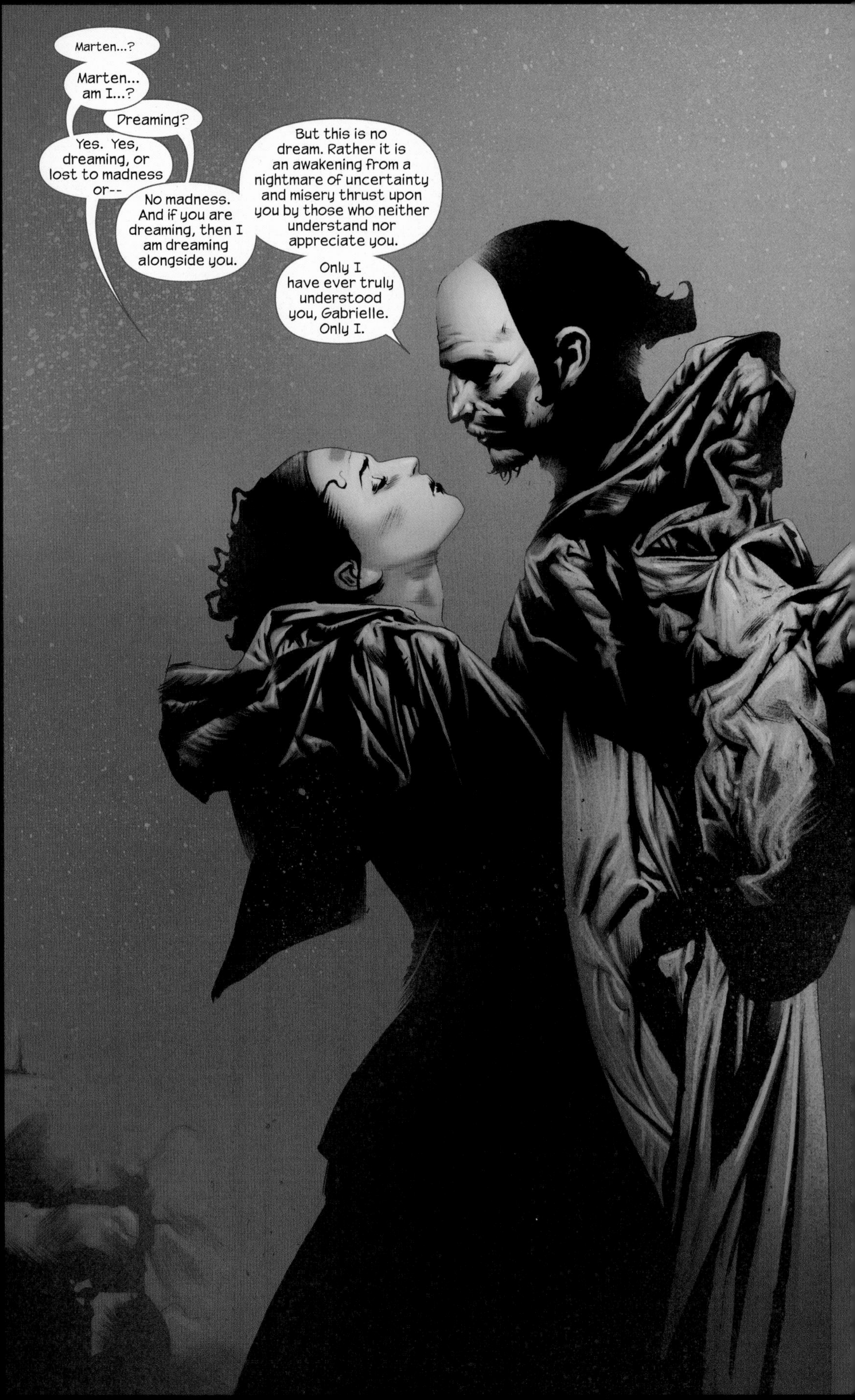

Marten...?
Marten... am I...?
Dreaming?
Yes. Yes, dreaming, or lost to madness or--
No madness. And if you are dreaming, then I am dreaming alongside you.
But this is no dream. Rather it is an awakening from a nightmare of uncertainty and misery thrust upon you by those who neither understand nor appreciate you.
Only I have ever truly understood you, Gabrielle. Only I.

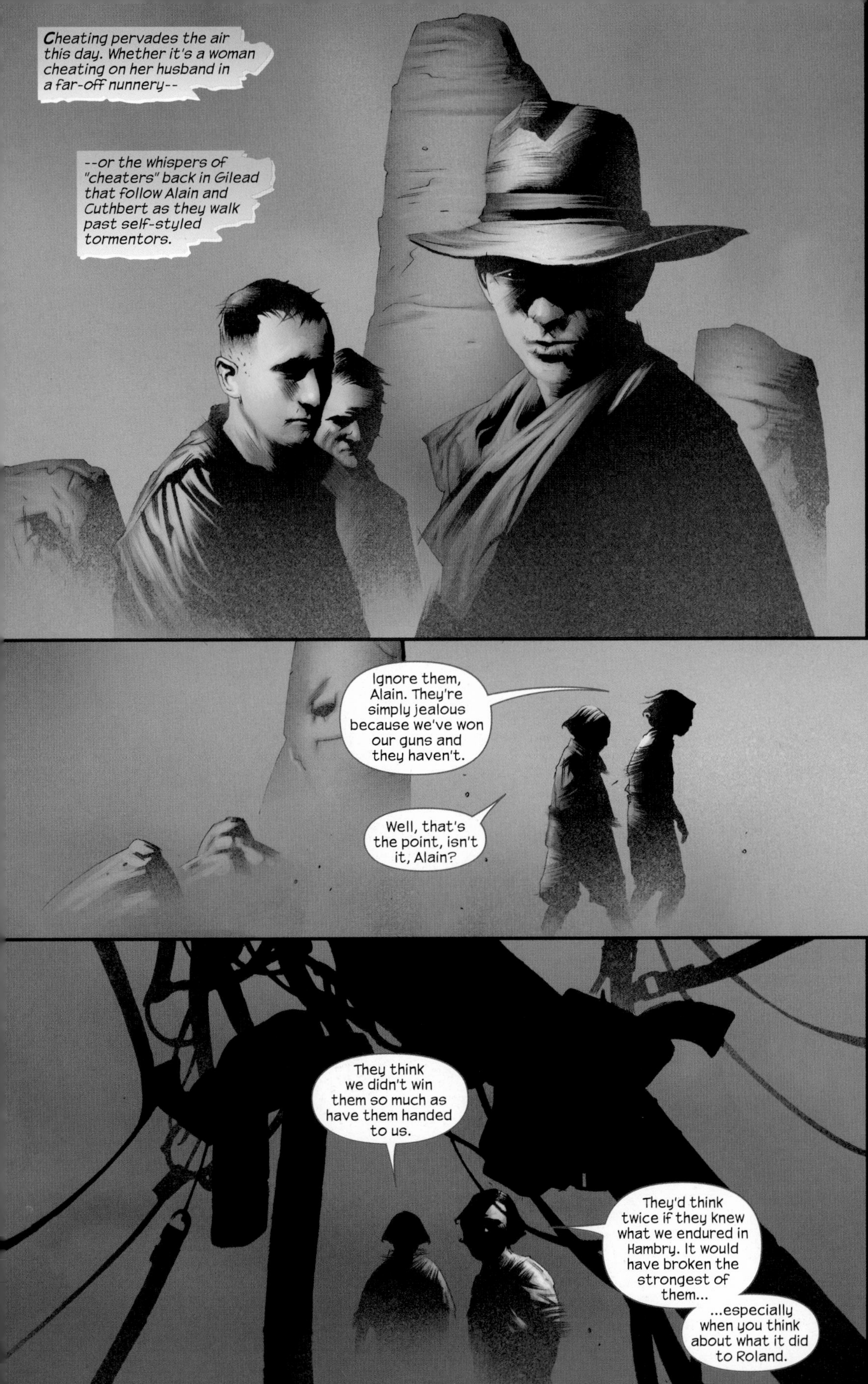
Cheating pervades the air this day. Whether it's a woman cheating on her husband in a far-off nunnery--
--or the whispers of "cheaters" back in Gilead that follow Alain and Cuthbert as they walk past self-styled tormentors.
Ignore them, Alain. They're simply jealous because we've won our guns and they haven't.
Well, that's the point, isn't it, Alain?
They think we didn't win them so much as have them handed to us.
They'd think twice if they knew what we endured in Hambry. It would have broken the strongest of them...
...especially when you think about what it did to Roland.

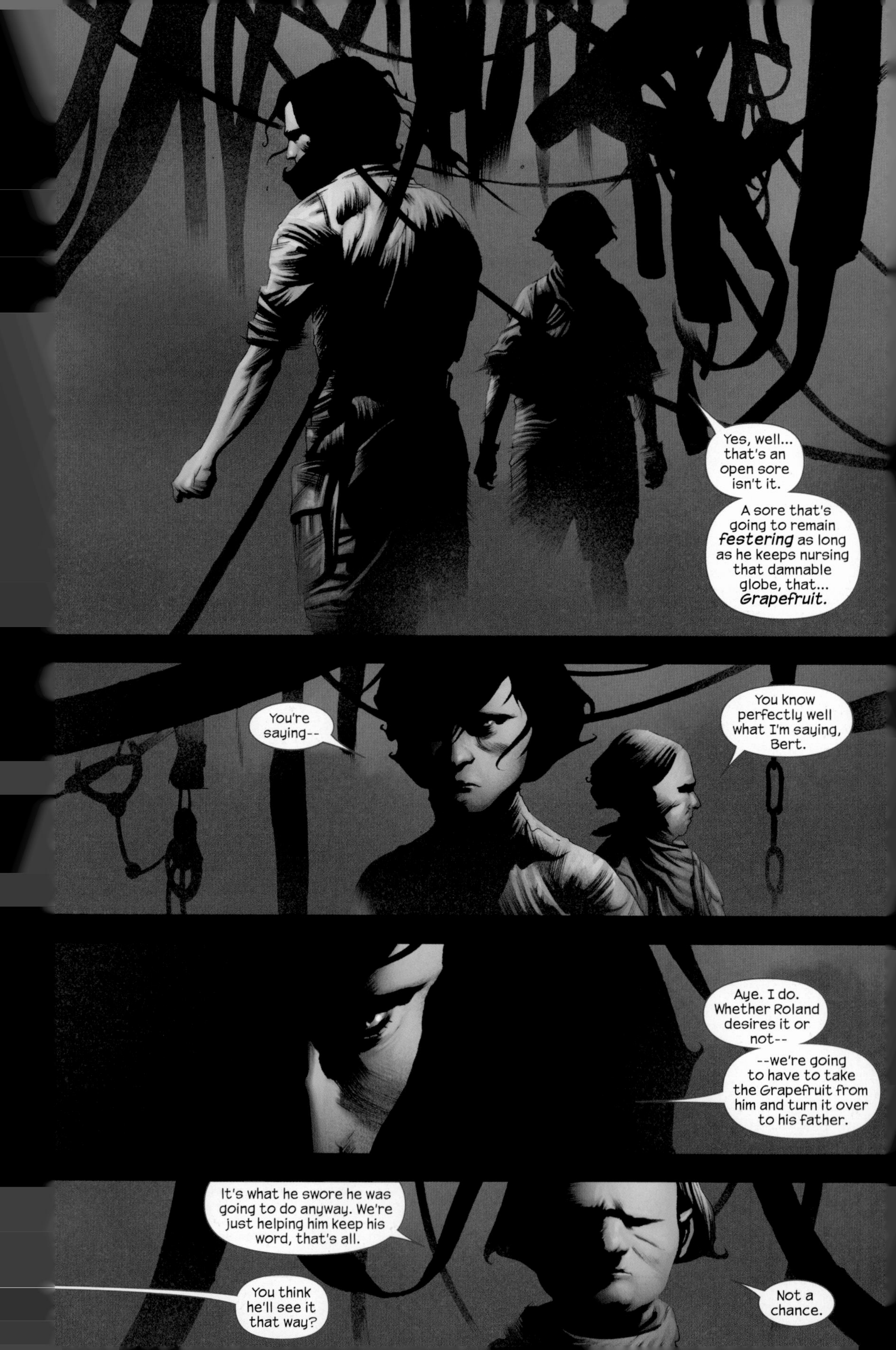
Yes, well... that's an open sore isn't it.
A sore that's going to remain *festering* as long as he keeps nursing that damnable globe, that... *Grapefruit.*
You're saying--
You know perfectly well what I'm saying, Bert.
Aye. I do. Whether Roland desires it or not--
--we're going to have to take the Grapefruit from him and turn it over to his father.
It's what he swore he was going to do anyway. We're just helping him keep his word, that's all.
You think he'll see it that way?
Not a chance.

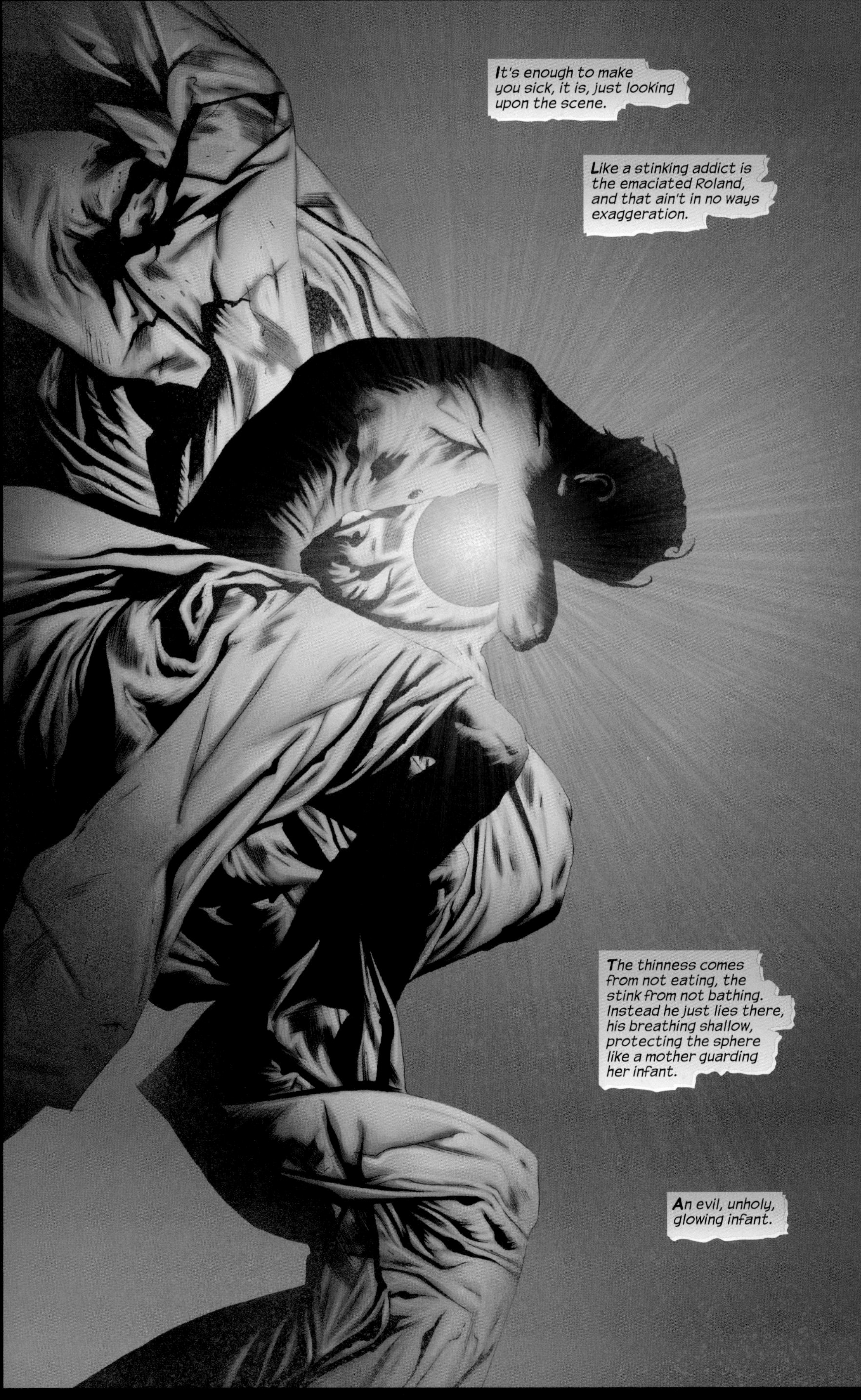
It's enough to make you sick, it is, just looking upon the scene.
Like a stinking addict is the emaciated Roland, and that ain't in no ways exaggeration.
The thinness comes from not eating, the stink from not bathing. Instead he just lies there, his breathing shallow, protecting the sphere like a mother guarding her infant.
An evil, unholy, glowing infant.

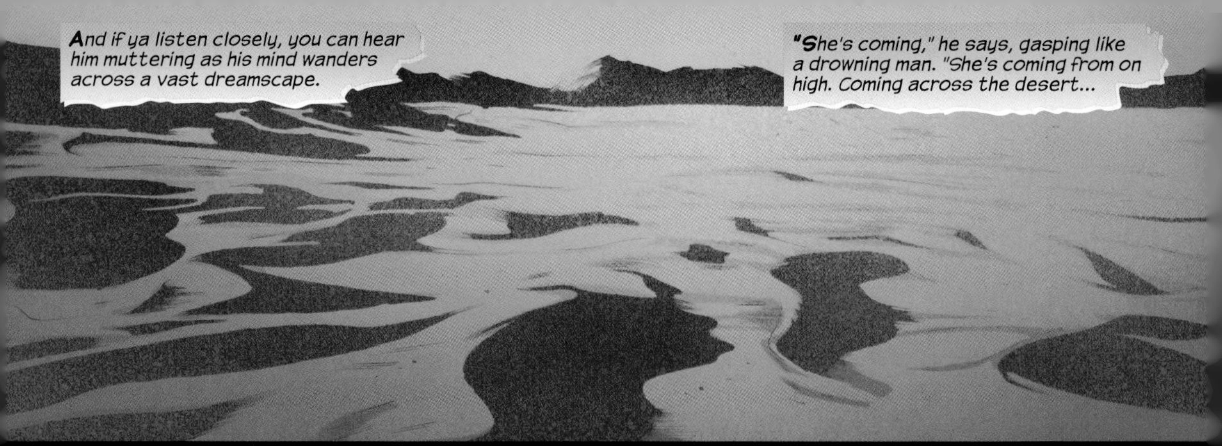
And if ya listen closely, you can hear him muttering as his mind wanders across a vast dreamscape.
"She's coming," he says, gasping like a drowning man. "She's coming from on high. Coming across the desert...

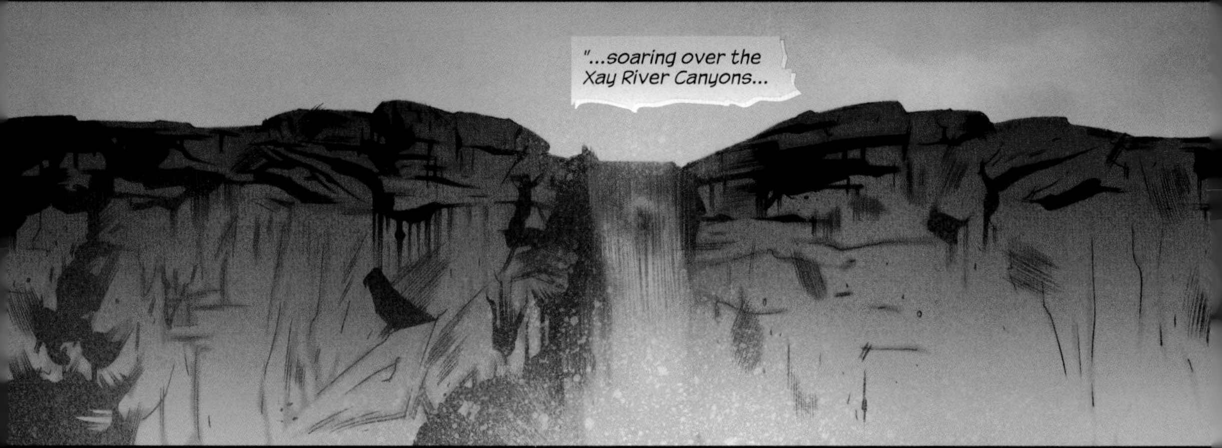
"...soaring over the Xay River Canyons...

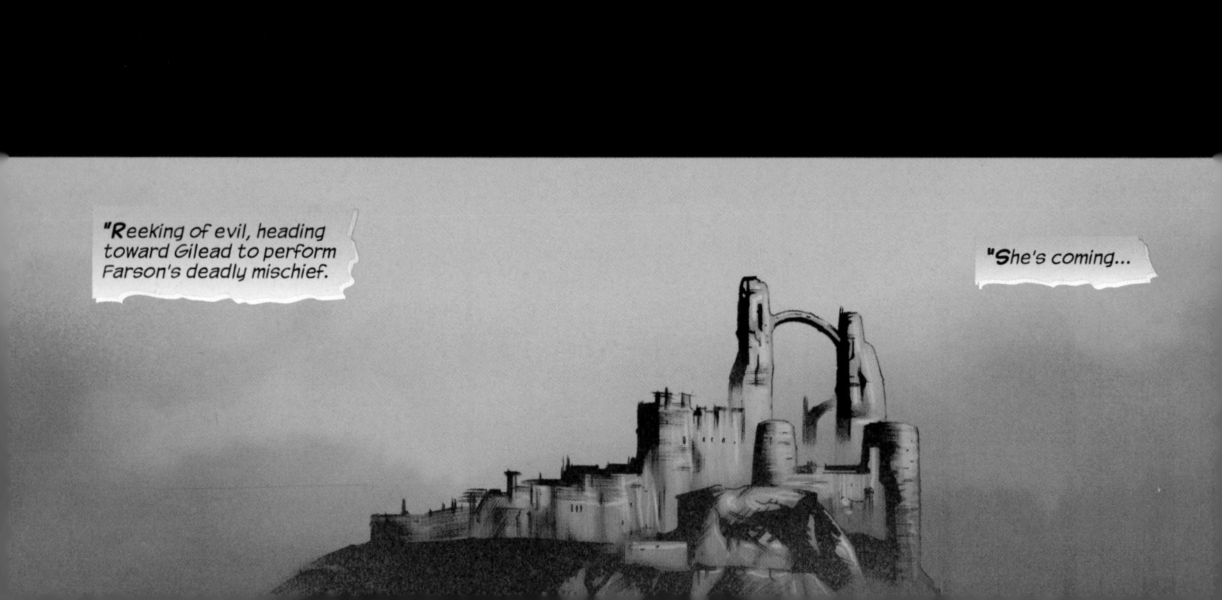
"Reeking of evil, heading toward Gilead to perform Farson's deadly mischief.
"She's coming...

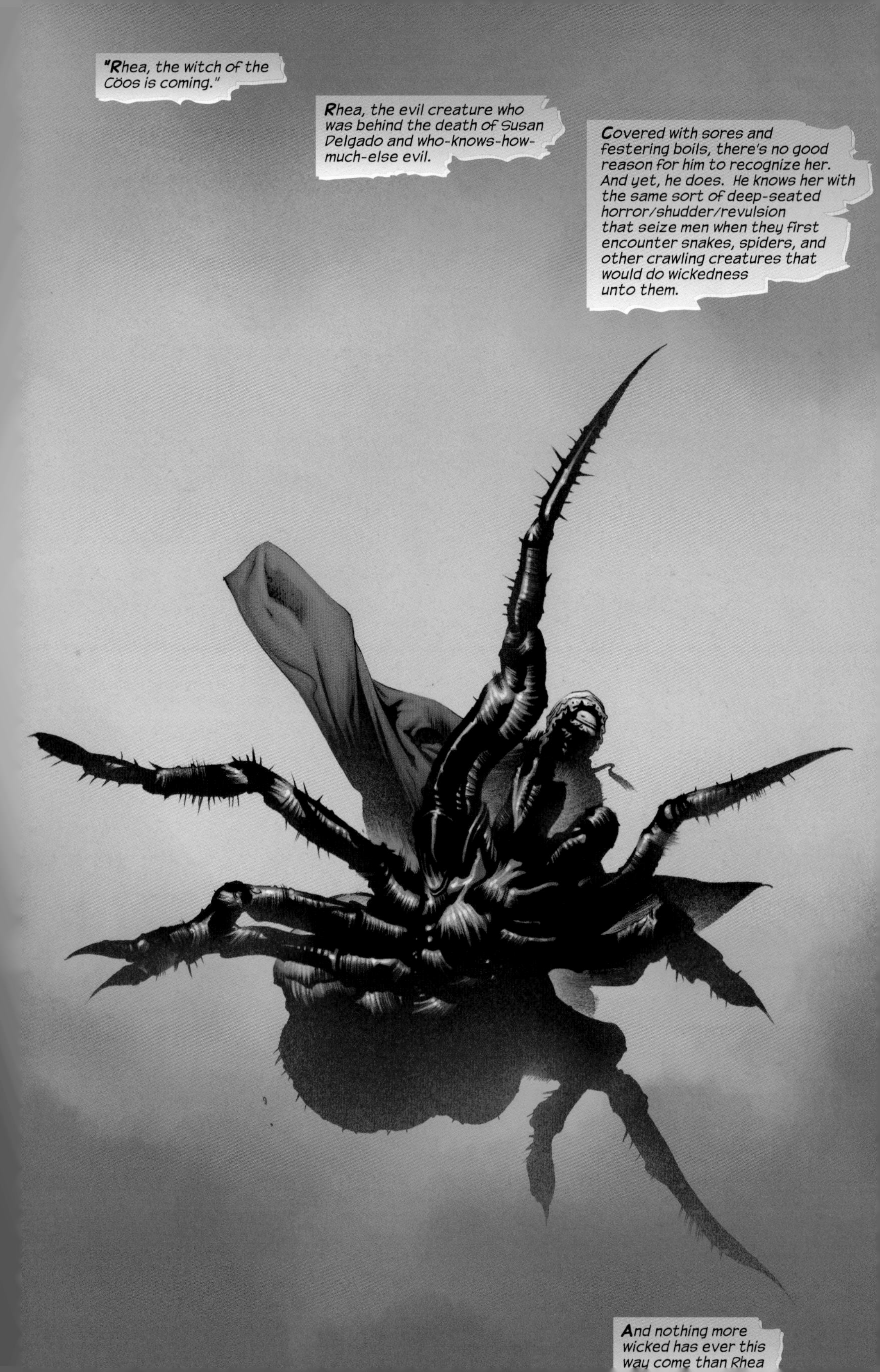
"Rhea, the witch of the Cöos is coming."
Rhea, the evil creature who was behind the death of Susan Delgado and who-knows-how-much-else evil.
Covered with sores and festering boils, there's no good reason for him to recognize her. And yet, he does. He knows her with the same sort of deep-seated horror/shudder/revulsion that seize men when they first encounter snakes, spiders, and other crawling creatures that would do wickedness unto them.
And nothing more wicked has ever this way come than Rhea

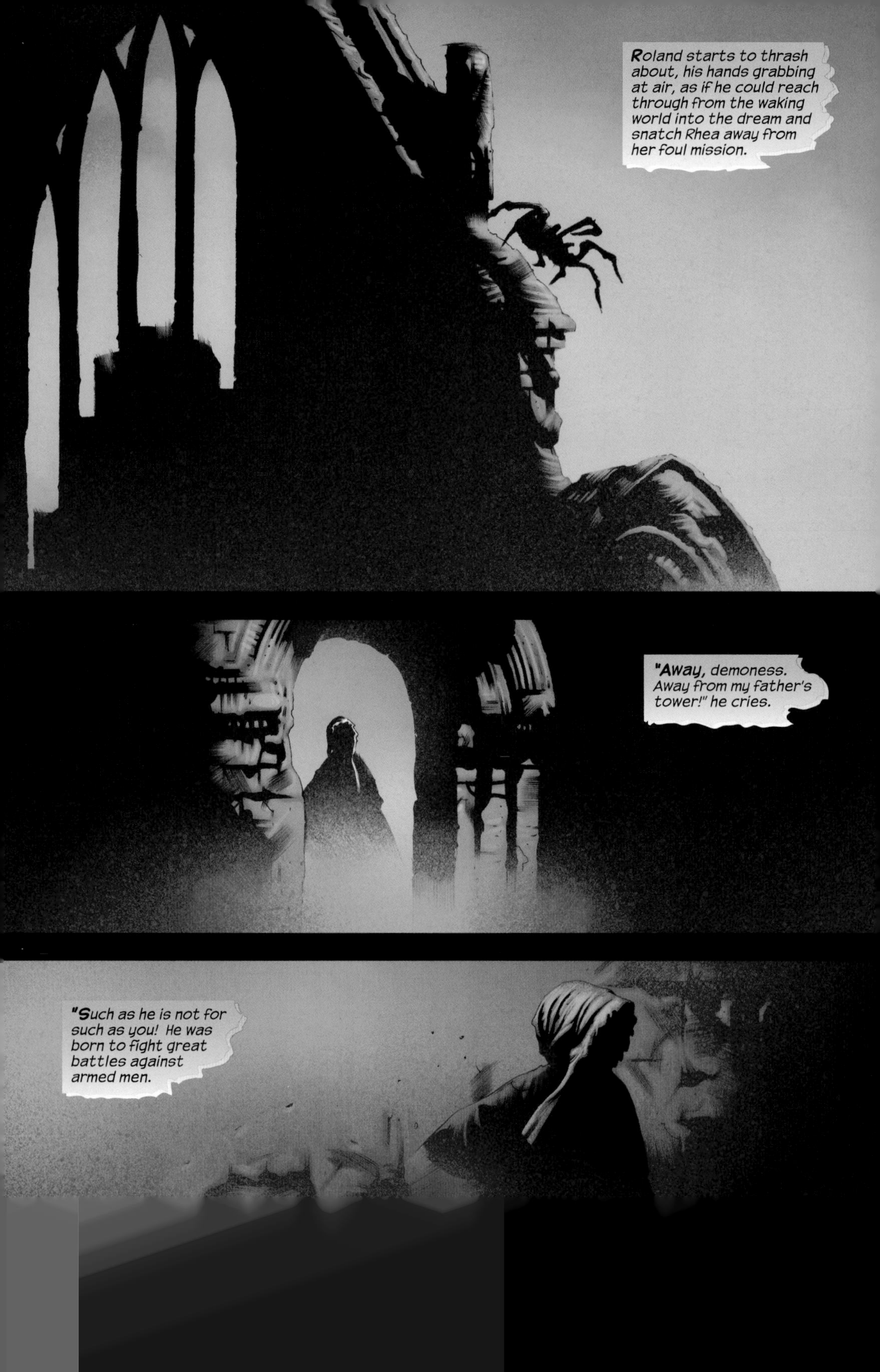
Roland starts to thrash about, his hands grabbing at air, as if he could reach through from the waking world into the dream and snatch Rhea away from her foul mission.
"Away, demoness. Away from my father's tower!" he cries.
"Such as he is not for such as you! He was born to fight great battles against armed men.

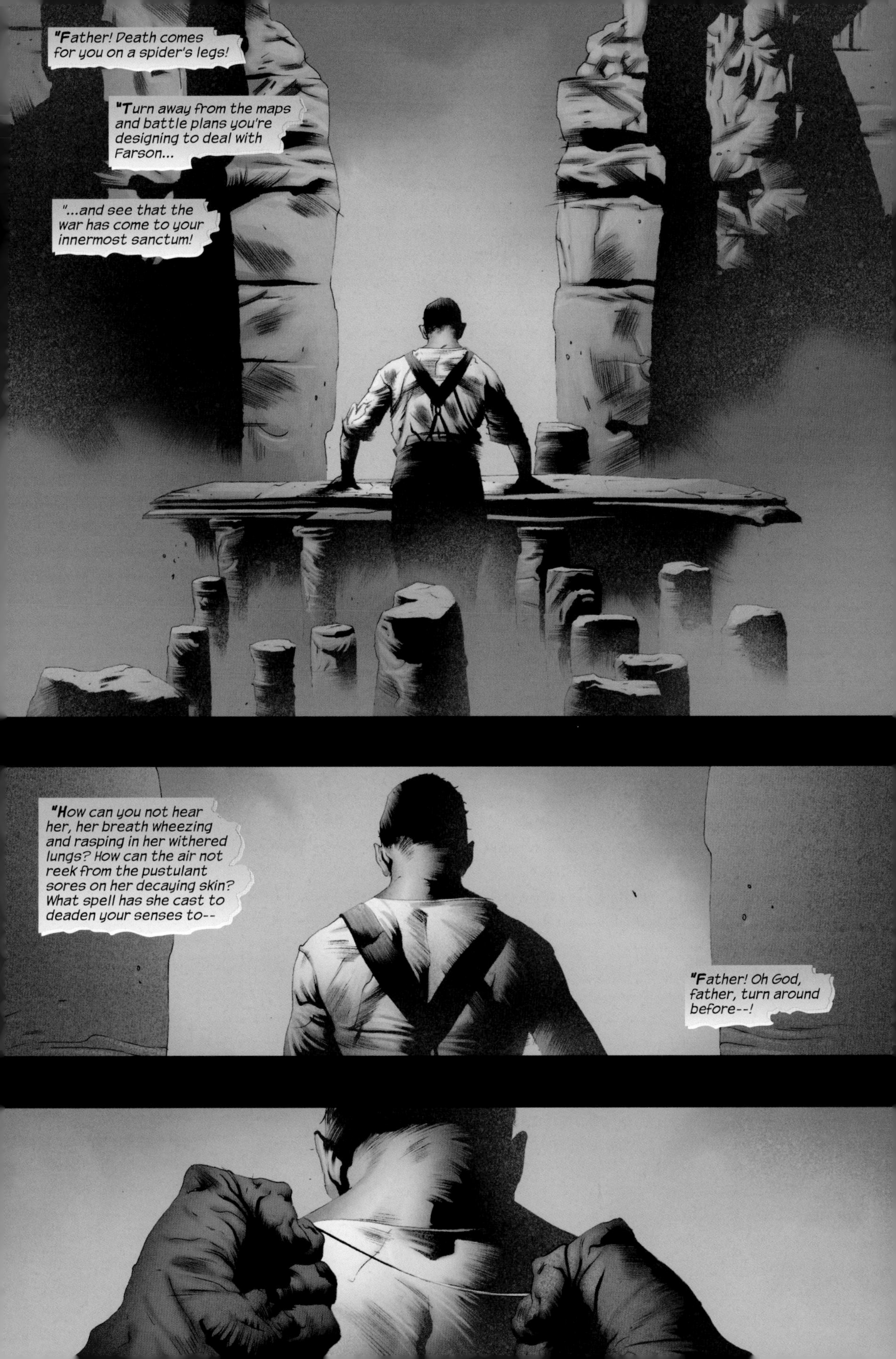
"Father! Death comes for you on a spider's legs!
"Turn away from the maps and battle plans you're designing to deal with Farson...
"...and see that the war has come to your innermost sanctum!
"How can you not hear her, her breath wheezing and rasping in her withered lungs? How can the air not reek from the pustulant sores on her decaying skin? What spell has she cast to deaden your senses to--
"Father! Oh God, father, turn around before--!

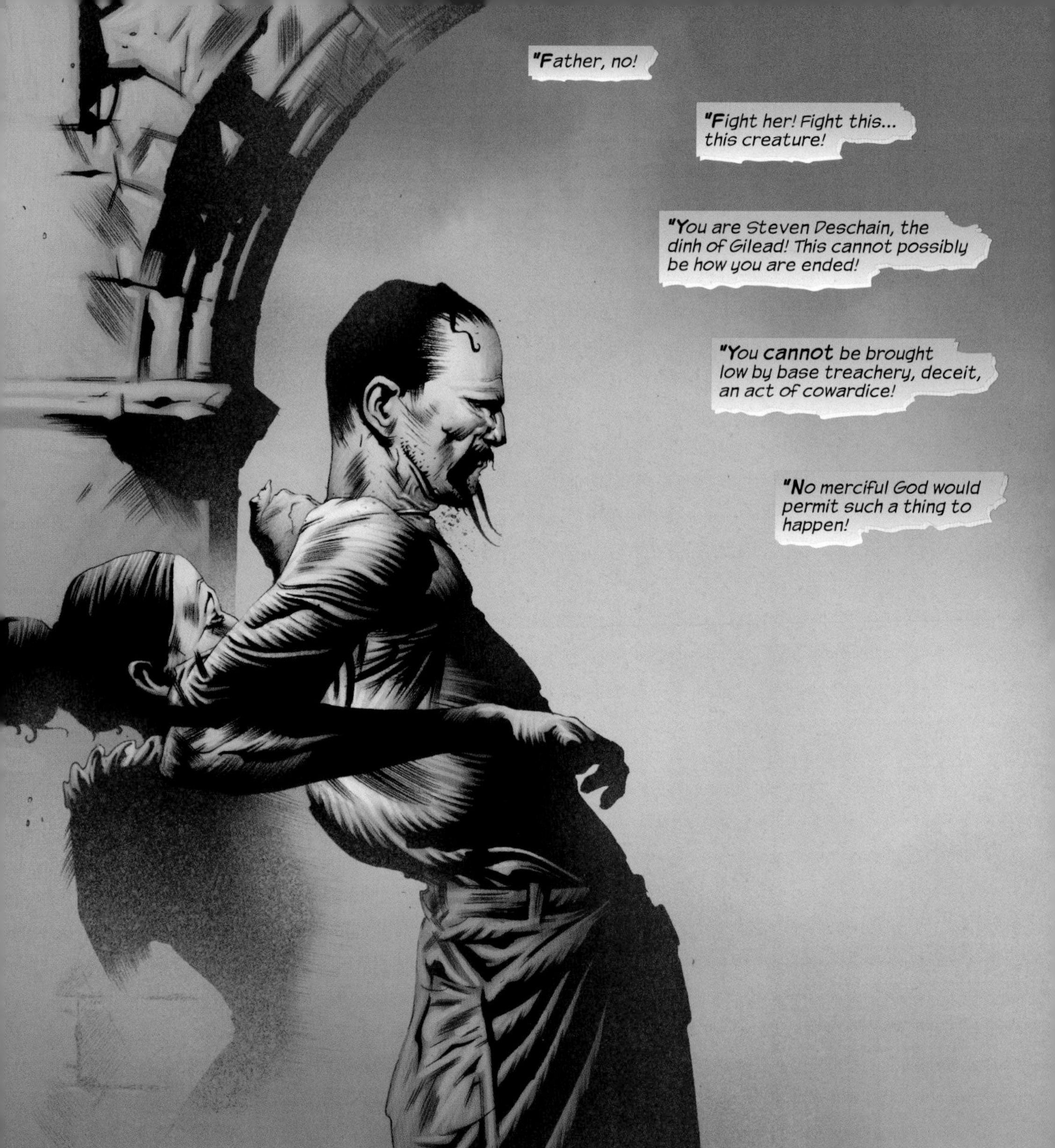
"Father, no!
"Fight her! Fight this... this creature!
"You are Steven Deschain, the dinh of Gilead! This cannot possibly be how you are ended!
"You cannot be brought low by base treachery, deceit, an act of cowardice!
"No merciful God would permit such a thing to happen!

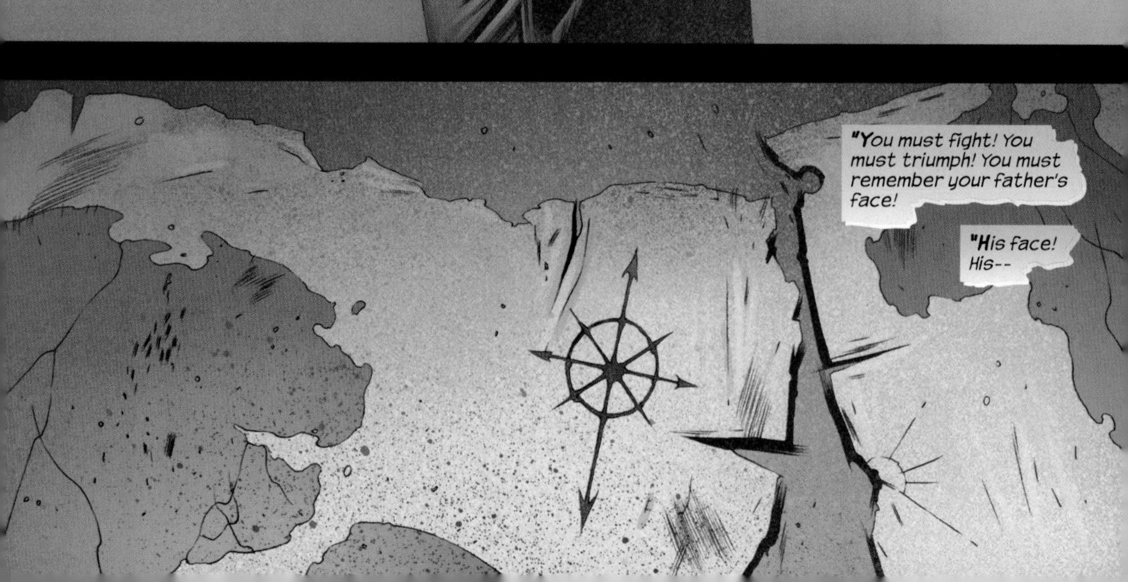
"You must fight! You must triumph! You must remember your father's face!
"His face! His--

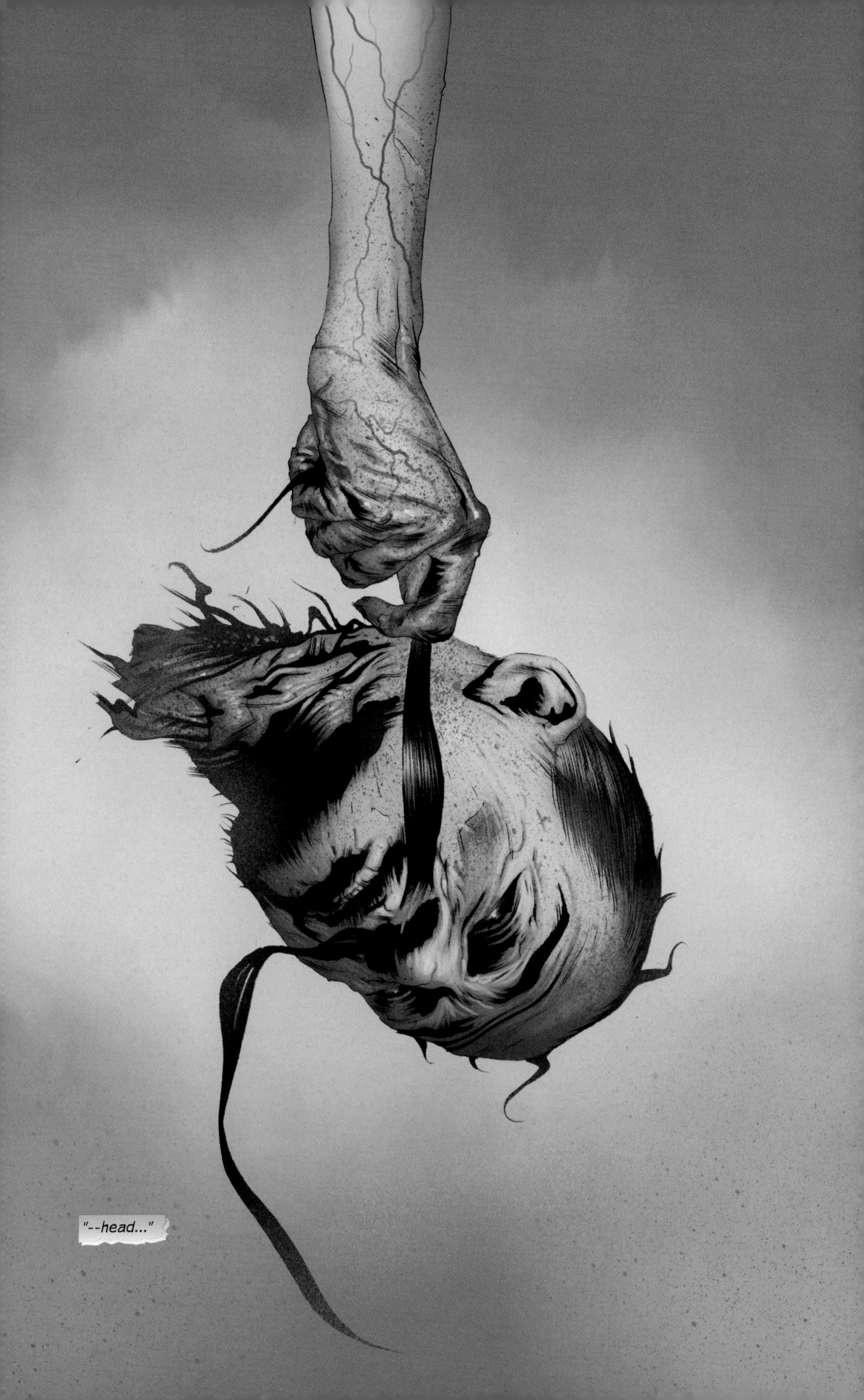
"--head..."

STEPHEN KING

THE DARK TOWER

TREACHERY

CHAPTER FOUR

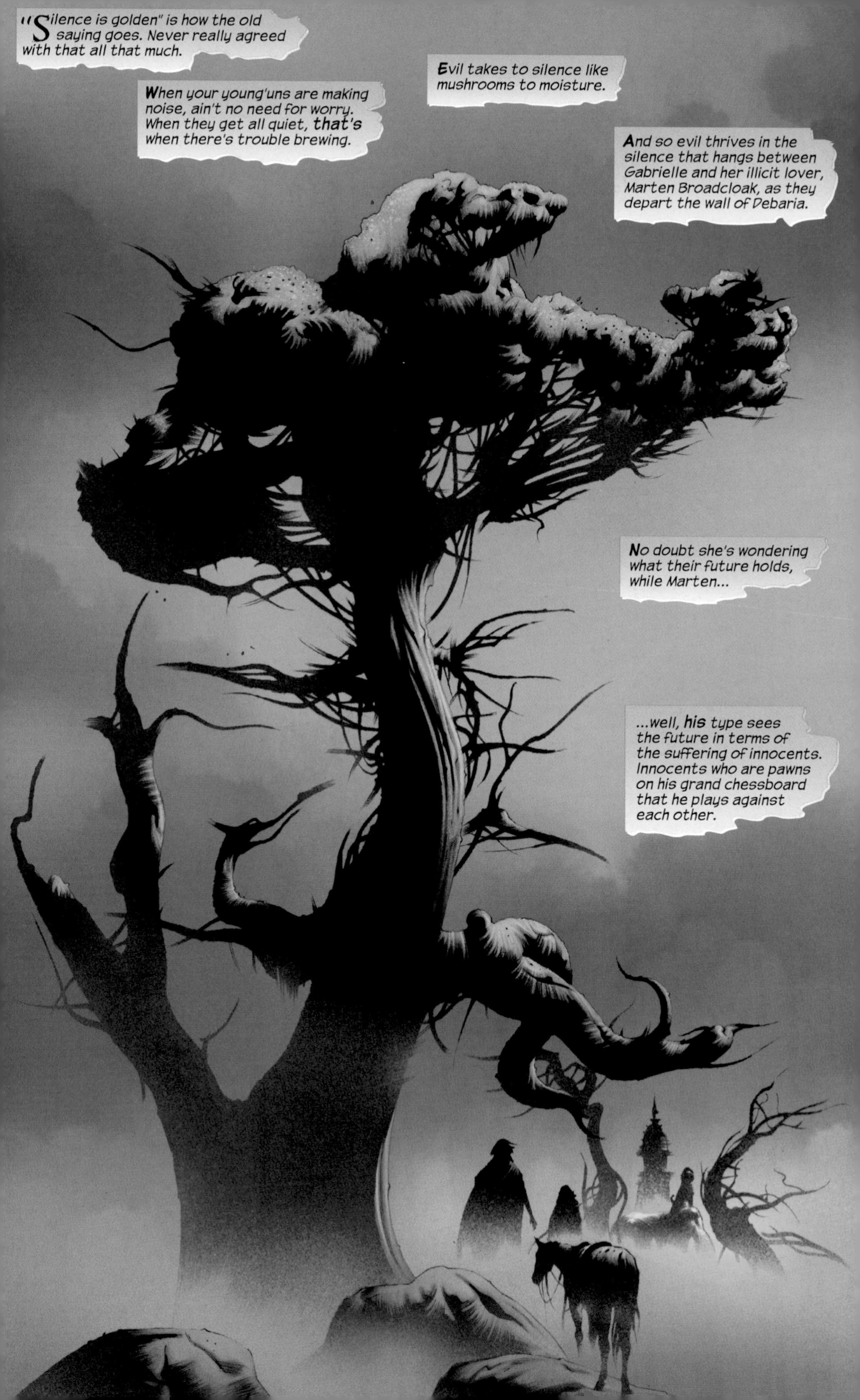
"Silence is golden" is how the old saying goes. Never really agreed with that all that much.
When your young'uns are making noise, ain't no need for worry. When they get all quiet, **that's** when there's trouble brewing.
Evil takes to silence like mushrooms to moisture.
And so evil thrives in the silence that hangs between Gabrielle and her illicit lover, Marten Broadcloak, as they depart the wall of Debaria.
No doubt she's wondering what their future holds, while Marten...
...well, **his** type sees the future in terms of the suffering of innocents. Innocents who are pawns on his grand chessboard that he plays against each other.

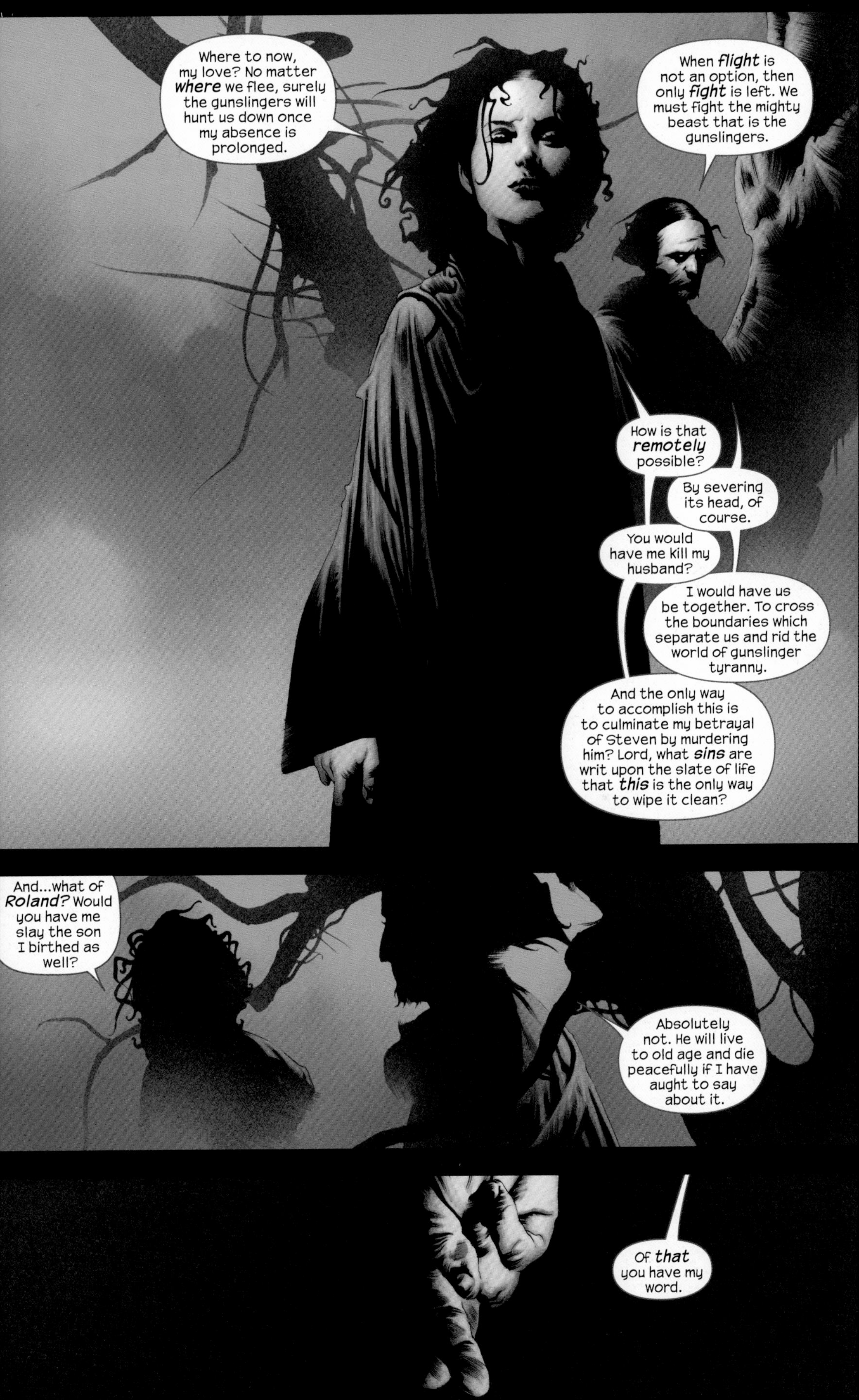
Where to now, my love? No matter *where* we flee, surely the gunslingers will hunt us down once my absence is prolonged.
When *flight* is not an option, then only *fight* is left. We must fight the mighty beast that is the gunslingers.
How is that *remotely* possible?
By severing its head, of course.
You would have me kill my husband?
I would have us be together. To cross the boundaries which separate us and rid the world of gunslinger tyranny.
And the only way to accomplish this is to culminate my betrayal of Steven by murdering him? Lord, what *sins* are writ upon the slate of life that *this* is the only way to wipe it clean?
And...what of *Roland?* Would you have me slay the son I birthed as well?
Absolutely not. He will live to old age and die peacefully if I have aught to say about it.
Of *that* you have my word.

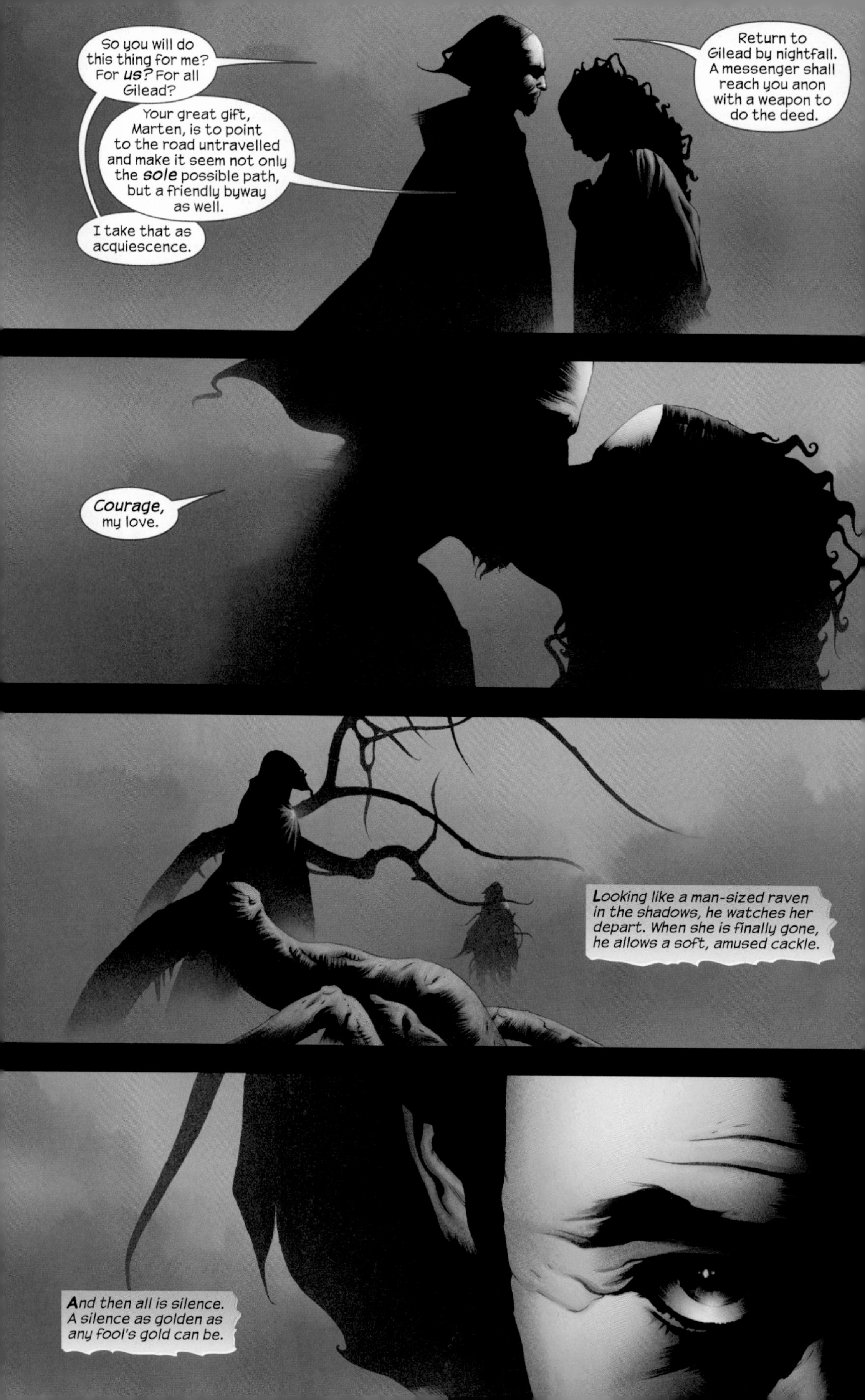

So you will do this thing for me? For *us?* For all Gilead?
Return to Gilead by nightfall. A messenger shall reach you anon with a weapon to do the deed.
Your great gift, Marten, is to point to the road untravelled and make it seem not only the *sole* possible path, but a friendly byway as well.
I take that as acquiescence.
Courage, my love.
Looking like a man-sized raven in the shadows, he watches her depart. When she is finally gone, he allows a soft, amused cackle.
And then all is silence. A silence as golden as any fool's gold can be.

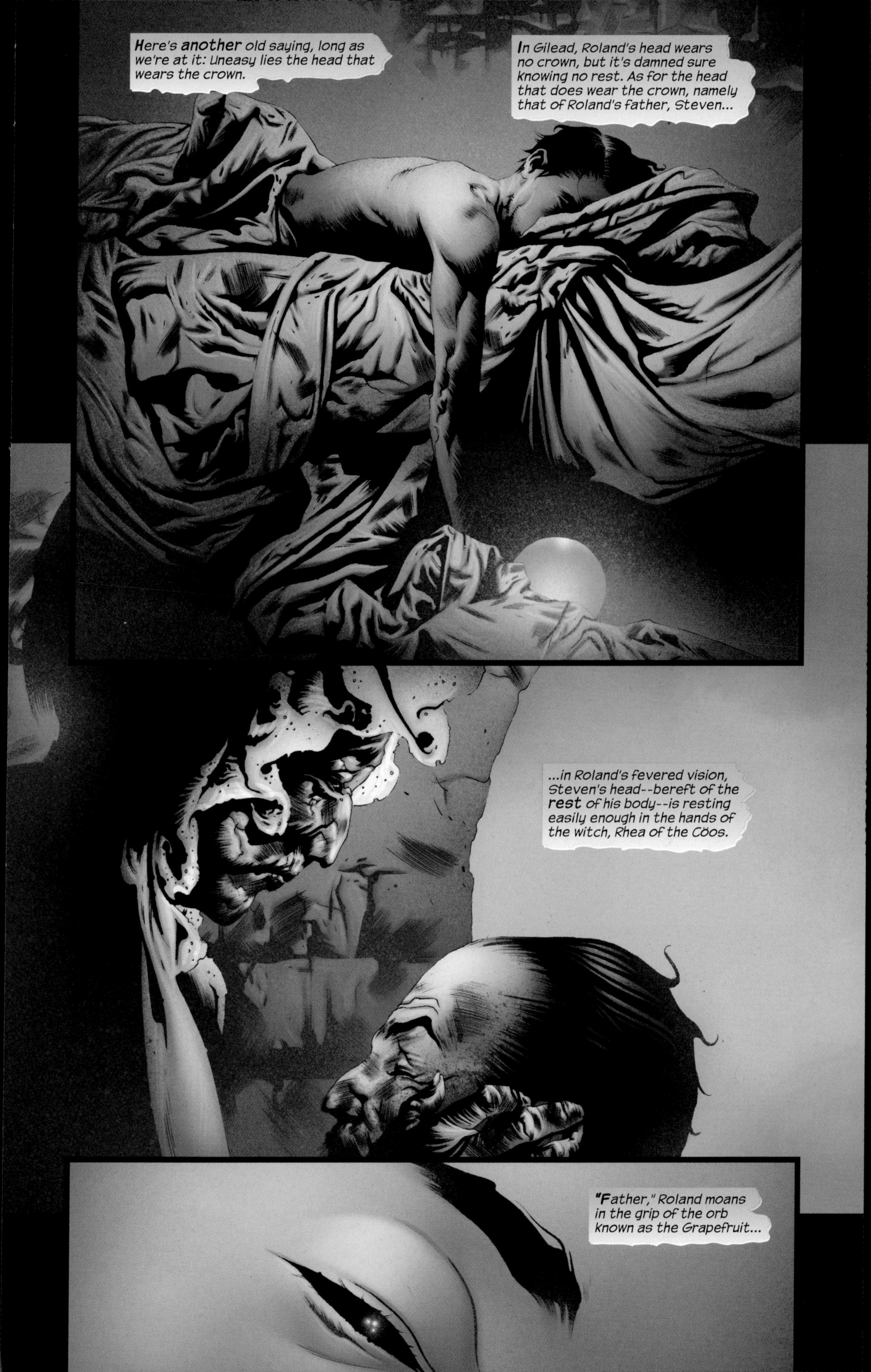
Here's another old saying, long as we're at it: Uneasy lies the head that wears the crown.
In Gilead, Roland's head wears no crown, but it's damned sure knowing no rest. As for the head that does wear the crown, namely that of Roland's father, Steven...
...in Roland's fevered vision, Steven's head--bereft of the rest of his body--is resting easily enough in the hands of the witch, Rhea of the Cöos.
"Father," Roland moans in the grip of the orb known as the Grapefruit...

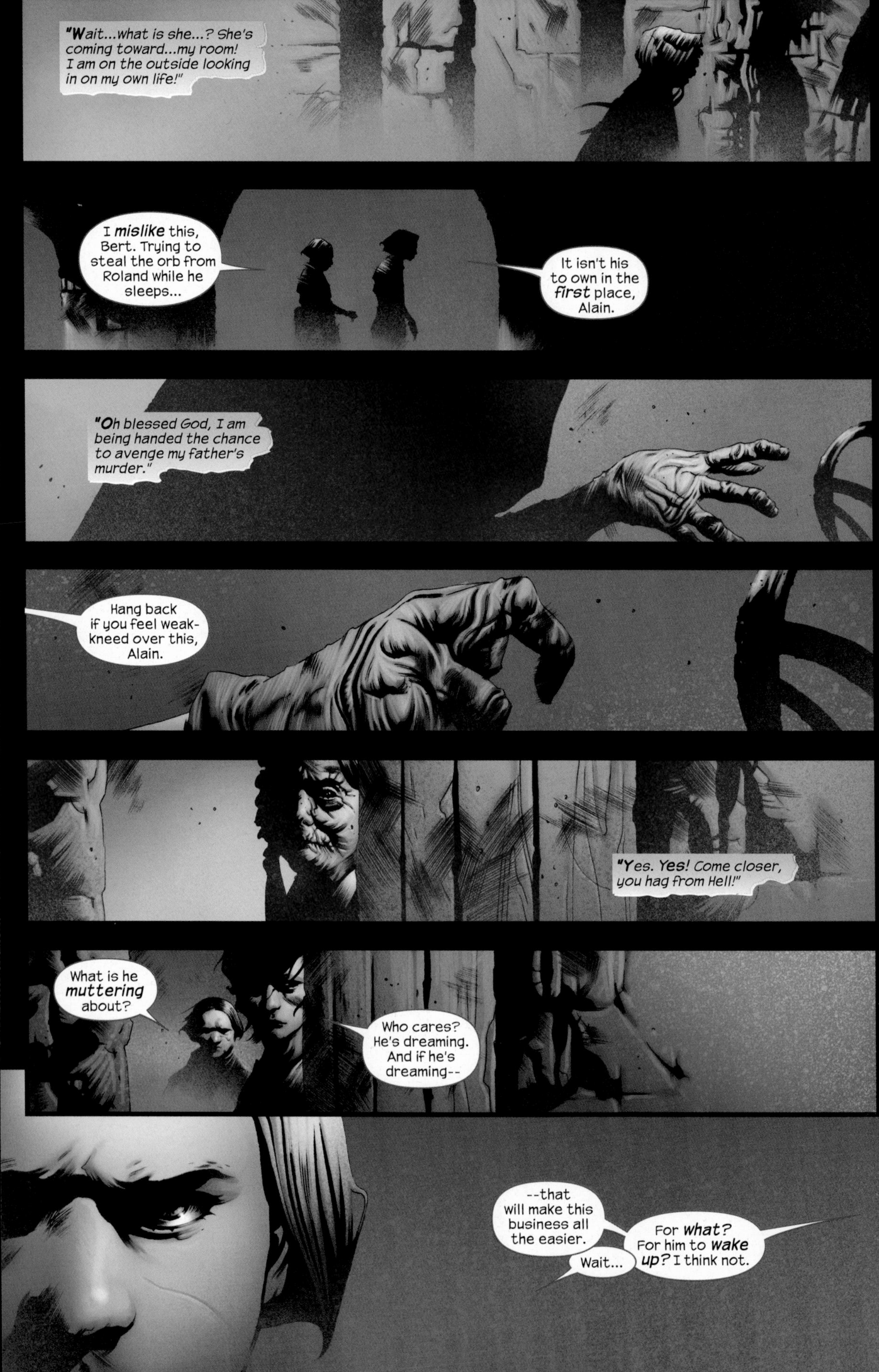
"Wait...what is she...? She's coming toward...my room! I am on the outside looking in on my own life!"
I mislike this, Bert. Trying to steal the orb from Roland while he sleeps...
It isn't his to own in the first place, Alain.
"Oh blessed God, I am being handed the chance to avenge my father's murder."
Hang back if you feel weak-kneed over this, Alain.
"Yes. Yes! Come closer, you hag from Hell!"
What is he muttering about?
Who cares? He's dreaming. And if he's dreaming--
--that will make this business all the easier.
Wait...
For what? For him to wake up? I think not.

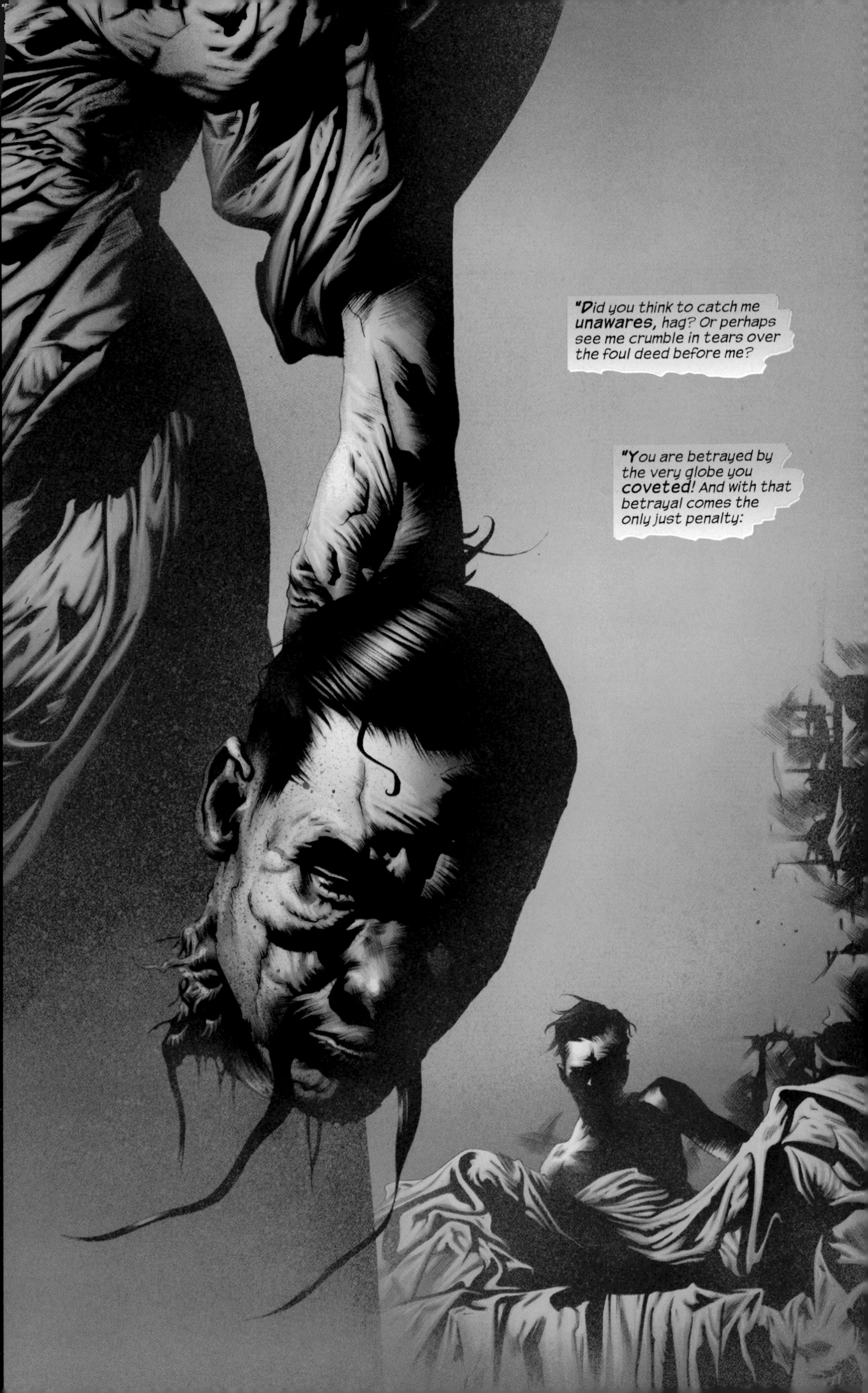
"Did you think to catch me unawares, hag? Or perhaps see me crumble in tears over the foul deed before me?
"You are betrayed by the very globe you coveted! And with that betrayal comes the only just penalty:

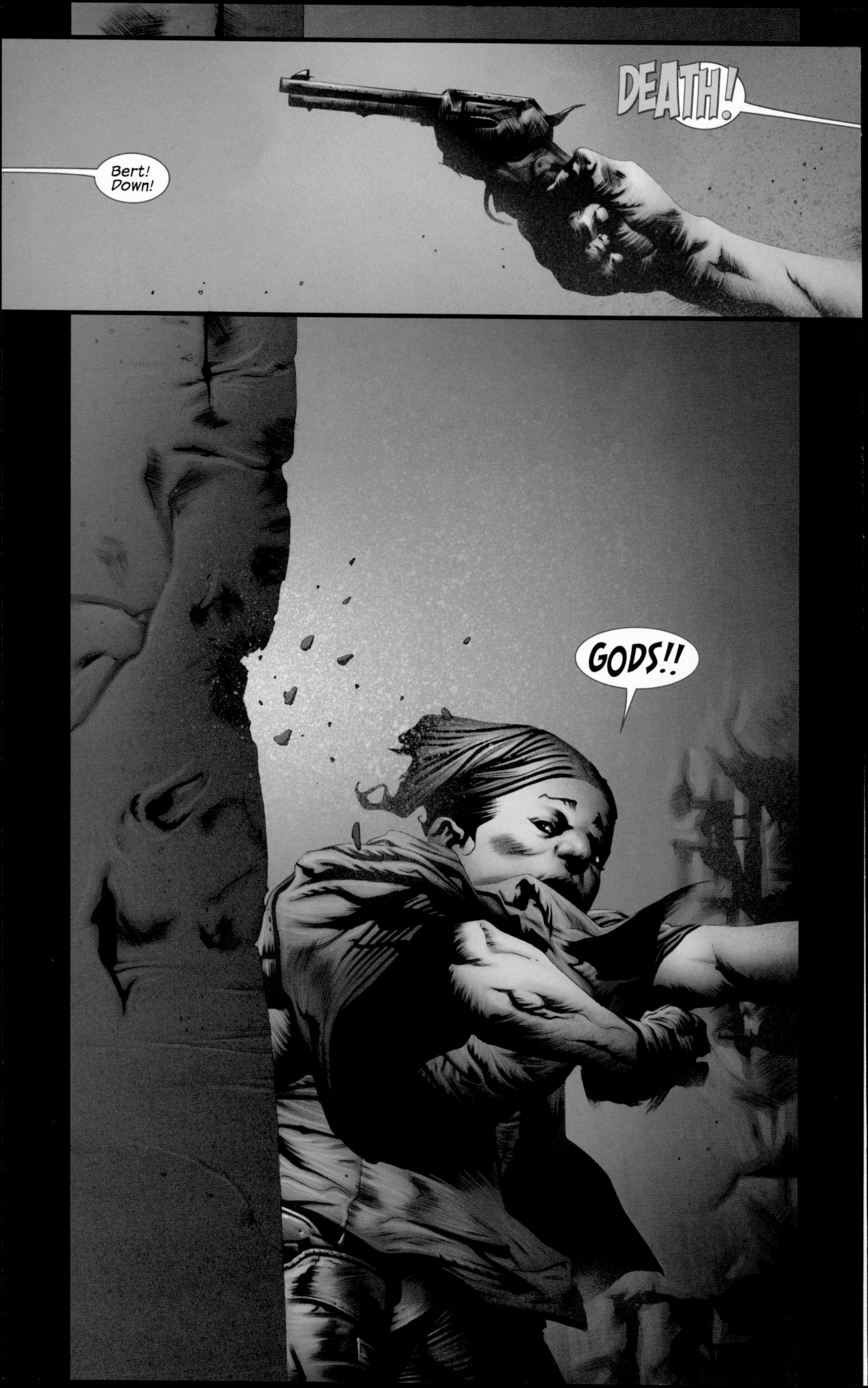
Bert!
Down!
DEATH!
GODS!!

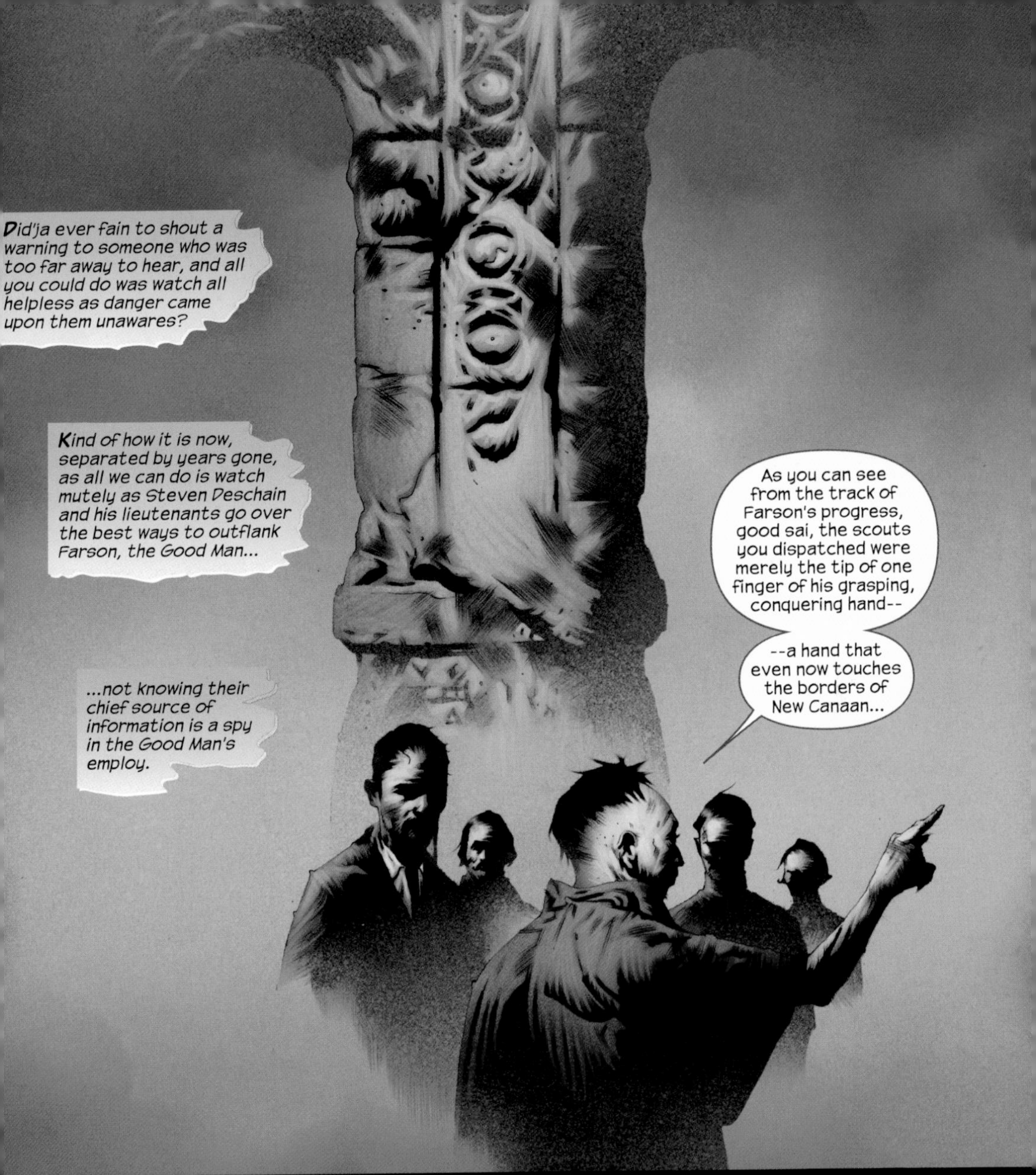
Did'ja ever fain to shout a warning to someone who was too far away to hear, and all you could do was watch all helpless as danger came upon them unawares?
Kind of how it is now, separated by years gone, as all we can do is watch mutely as Steven Deschain and his lieutenants go over the best ways to outflank Farson, the Good Man...
...not knowing their chief source of information is a spy in the Good Man's employ.
As you can see from the track of Farson's progress, good sai, the scouts you dispatched were merely the tip of one finger of his grasping, conquering hand--
--a hand that even now touches the borders of New Canaan...

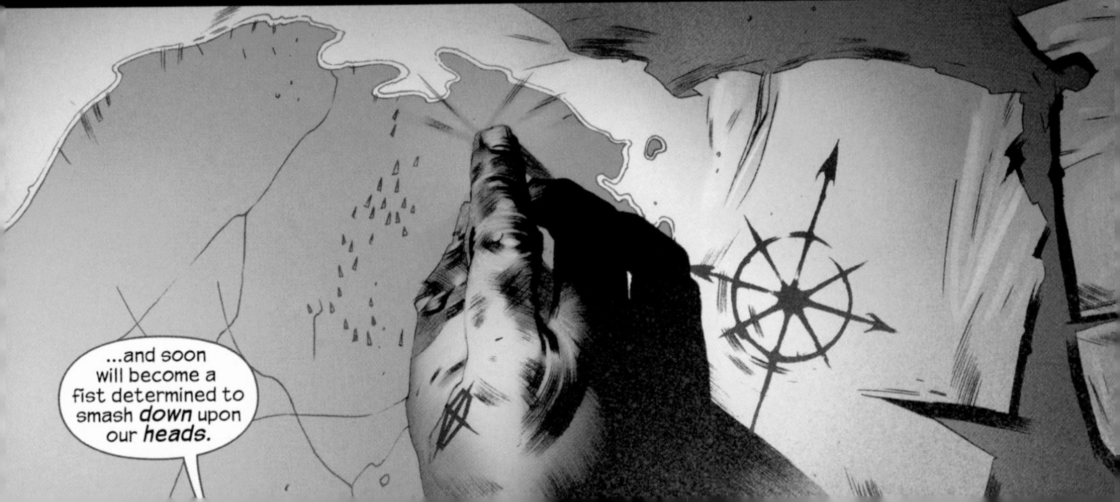
...and soon will become a fist determined to smash *down* upon our *heads.*

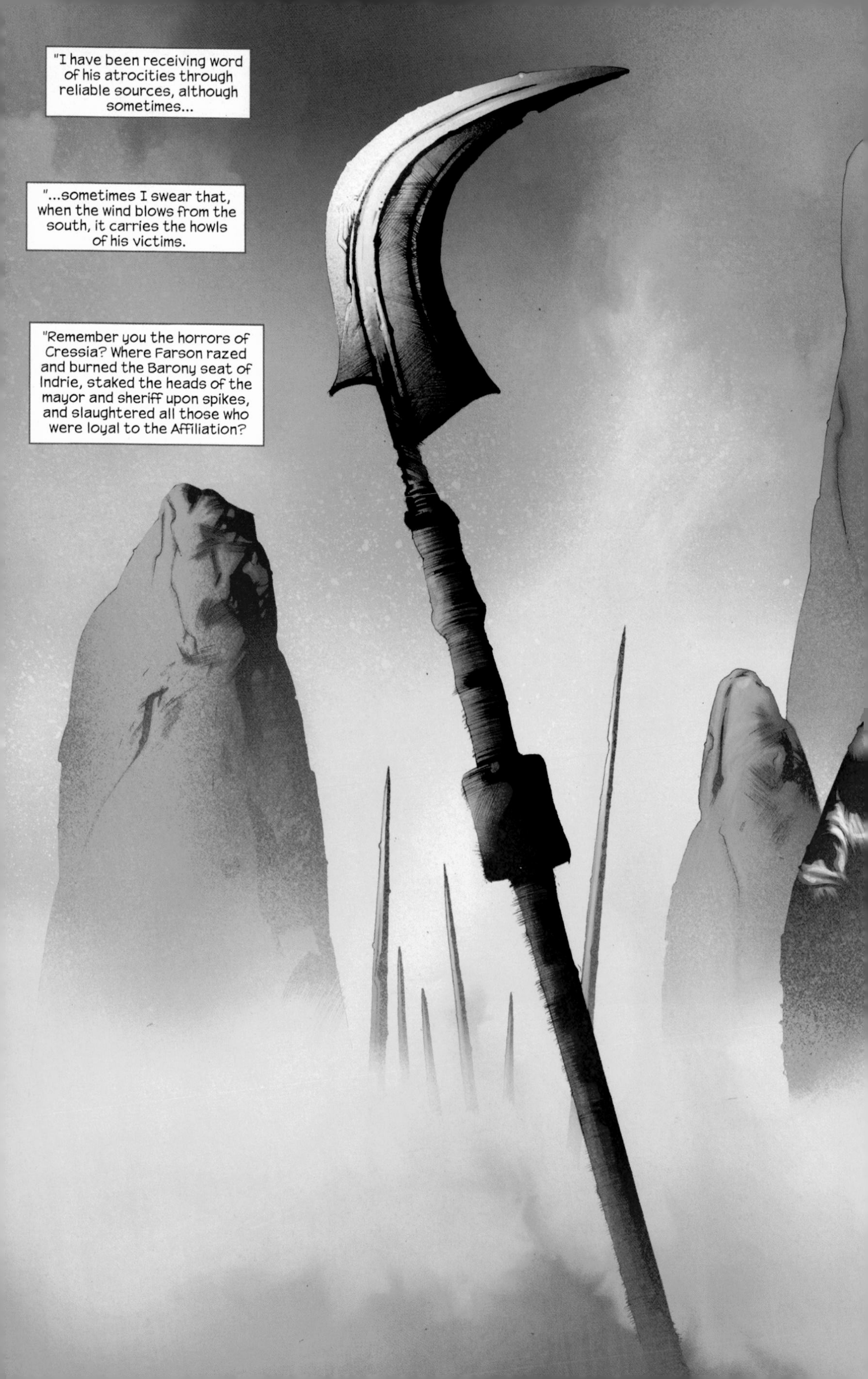
"I have been receiving word of his atrocities through reliable sources, although sometimes...
"...sometimes I swear that, when the wind blows from the south, it carries the howls of his victims.
"Remember you the horrors of Cressia? Where Farson razed and burned the Barony seat of Indrie, staked the heads of the mayor and sheriff upon spikes, and slaughtered all those who were loyal to the Affiliation?

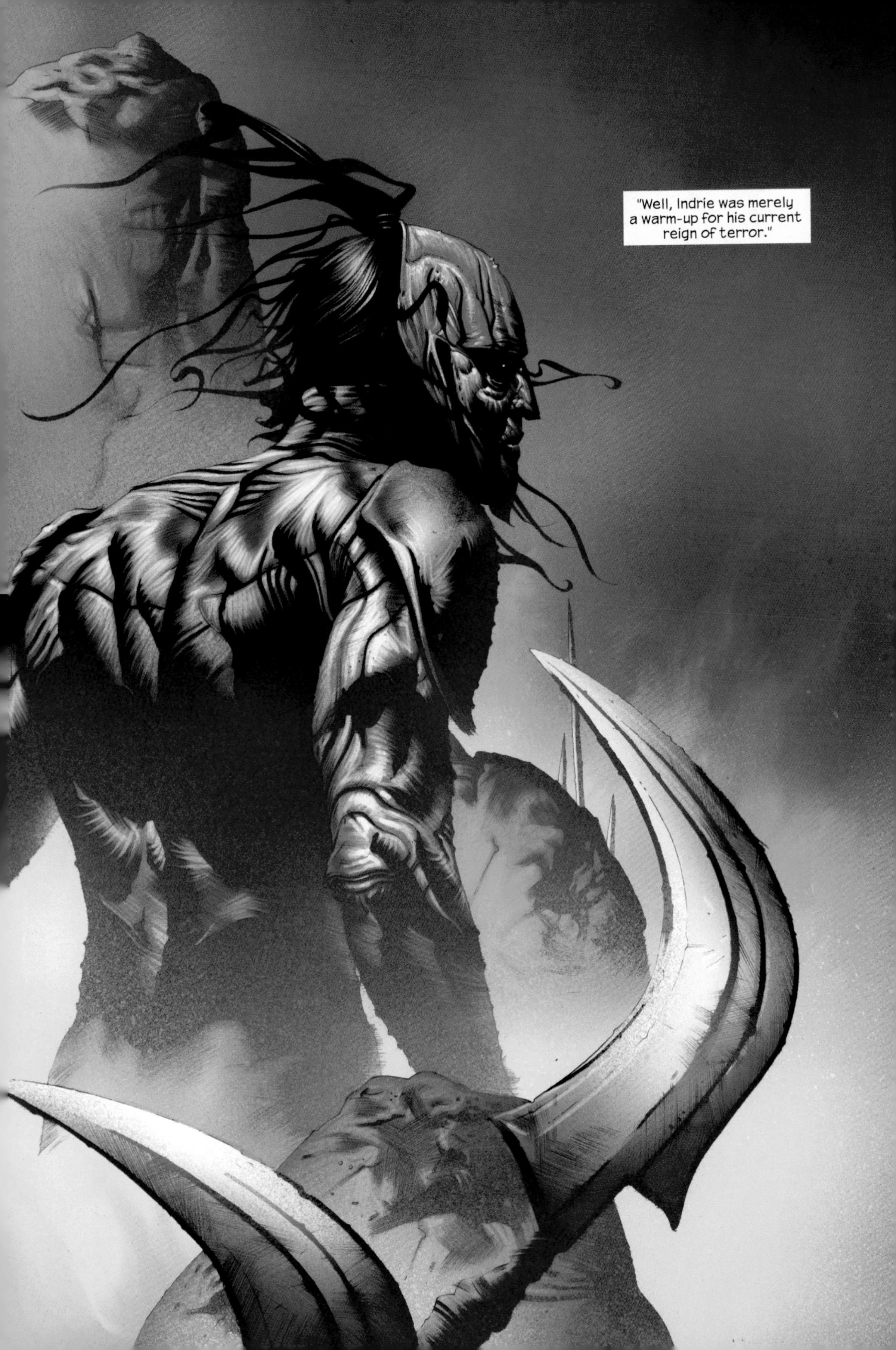
"Well, Indrie was merely a warm-up for his current reign of terror."

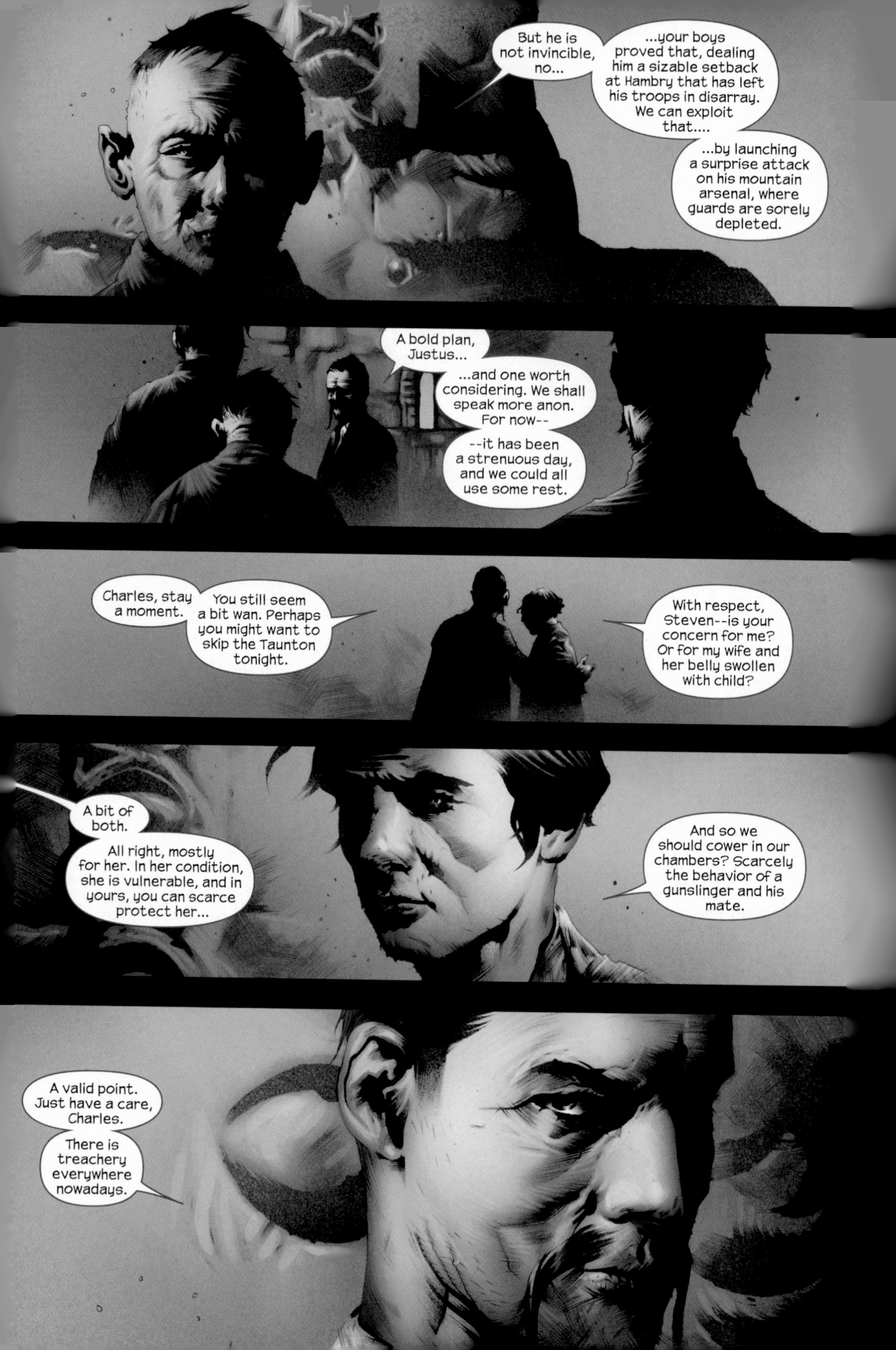

But he is not invincible, no...
...your boys proved that, dealing him a sizable setback at Hambry that has left his troops in disarray. We can exploit that....
...by launching a surprise attack on his mountain arsenal, where guards are sorely depleted.
A bold plan, Justus...
...and one worth considering. We shall speak more anon. For now--
--it has been a strenuous day, and we could all use some rest.
Charles, stay a moment.
You still seem a bit wan. Perhaps you might want to skip the Taunton tonight.
With respect, Steven--is your concern for me? Or for my wife and her belly swollen with child?
A bit of both.
All right, mostly for her. In her condition, she is vulnerable, and in yours, you can scarce protect her...
And so we should cower in our chambers? Scarcely the behavior of a gunslinger and his mate.
A valid point. Just have a care, Charles.
There is treachery everywhere nowadays.

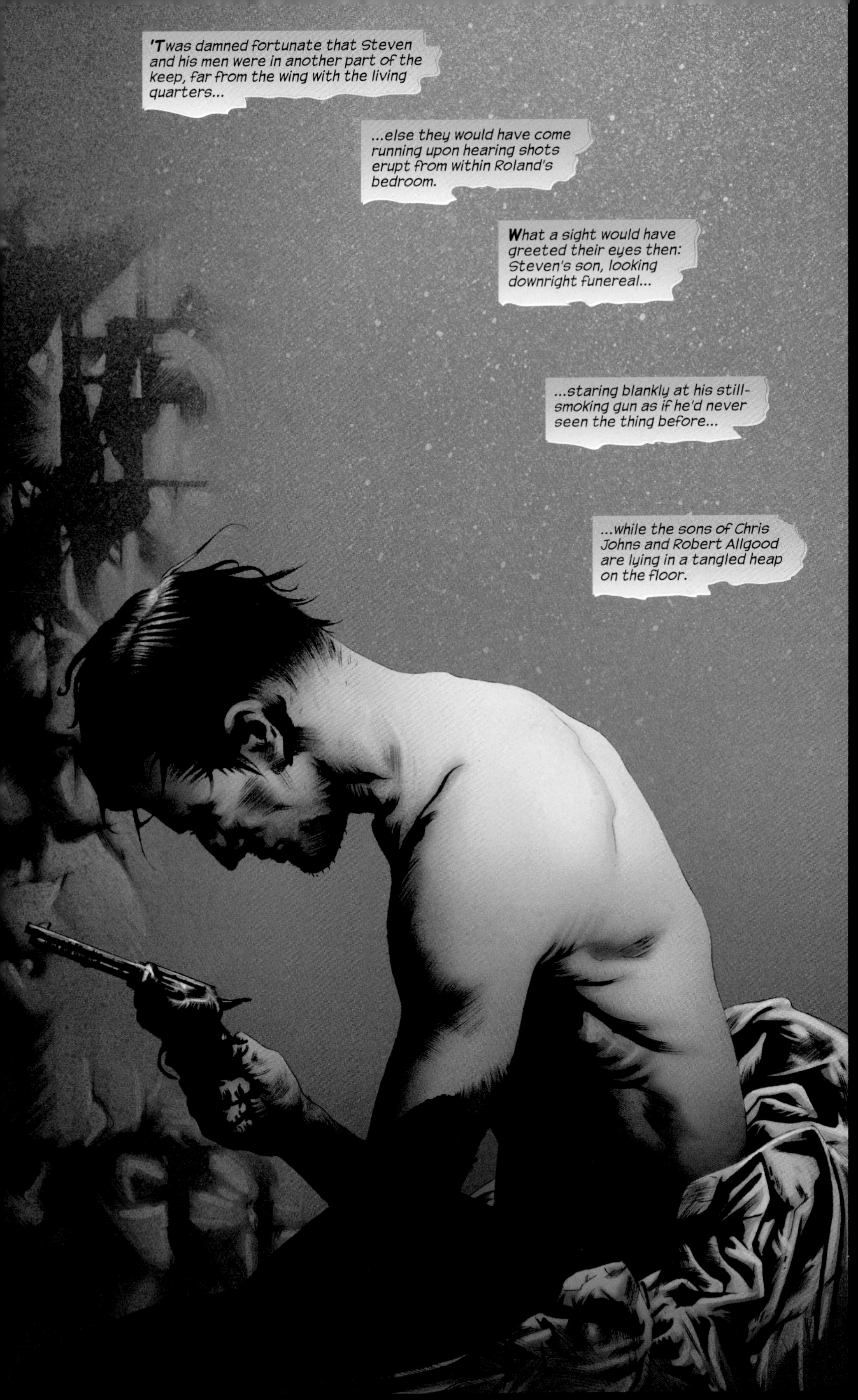
'Twas damned fortunate that Steven and his men were in another part of the keep, far from the wing with the living quarters...
...else they would have come running upon hearing shots erupt from within Roland's bedroom.
What a sight would have greeted their eyes then: Steven's son, looking downright funereal...
...staring blankly at his still-smoking gun as if he'd never seen the thing before...
...while the sons of Chris Johns and Robert Allgood are lying in a tangled heap on the floor.

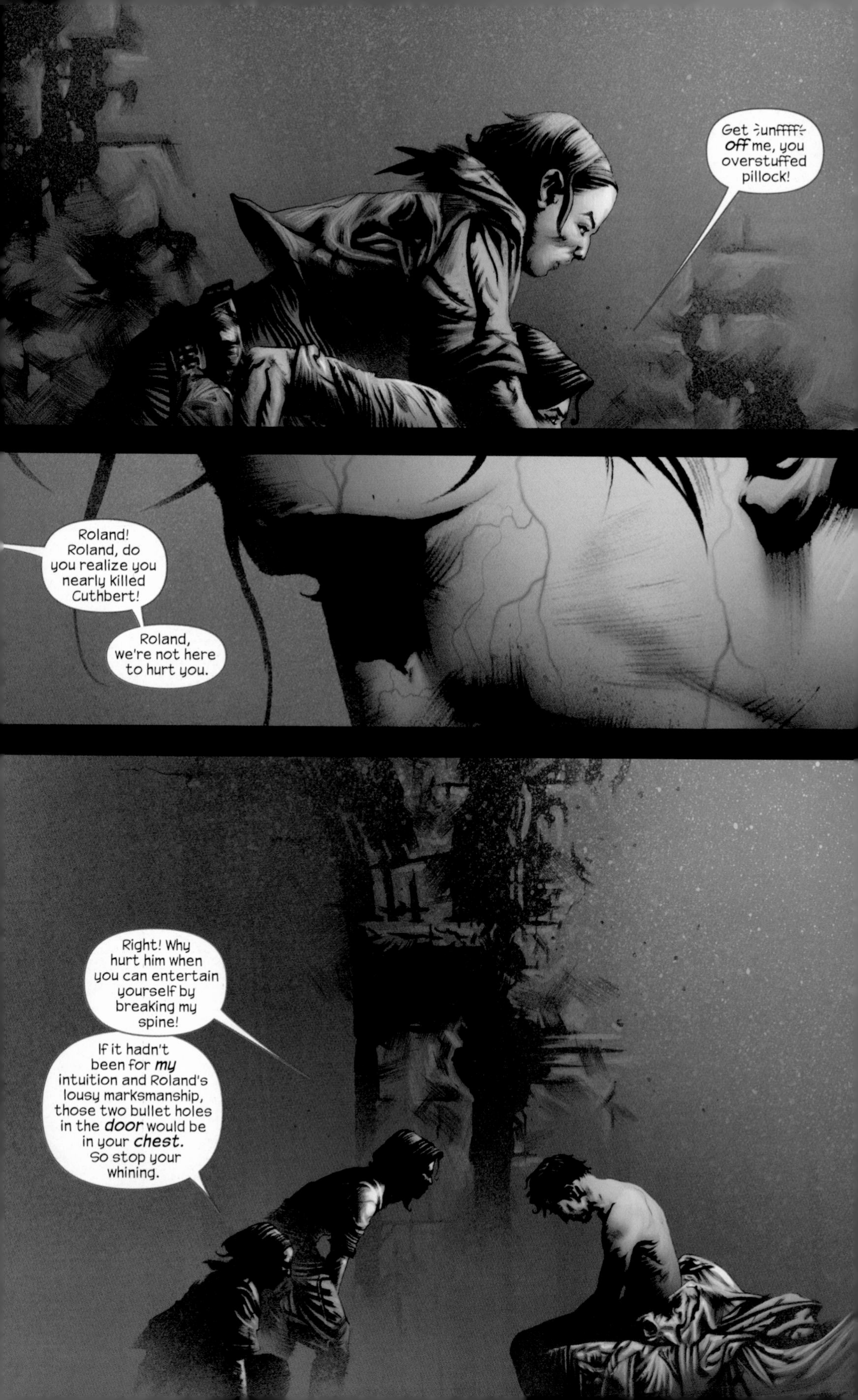

Get ~unffff~ *off* me, you overstuffed pillock!
Roland! Roland, do you realize you nearly killed Cuthbert!
Roland, we're not here to hurt you.
Right! Why hurt him when you can entertain yourself by breaking my spine!
If it hadn't been for *my* intuition and Roland's lousy marksmanship, those two bullet holes in the *door* would be in your *chest*. So stop your whining.

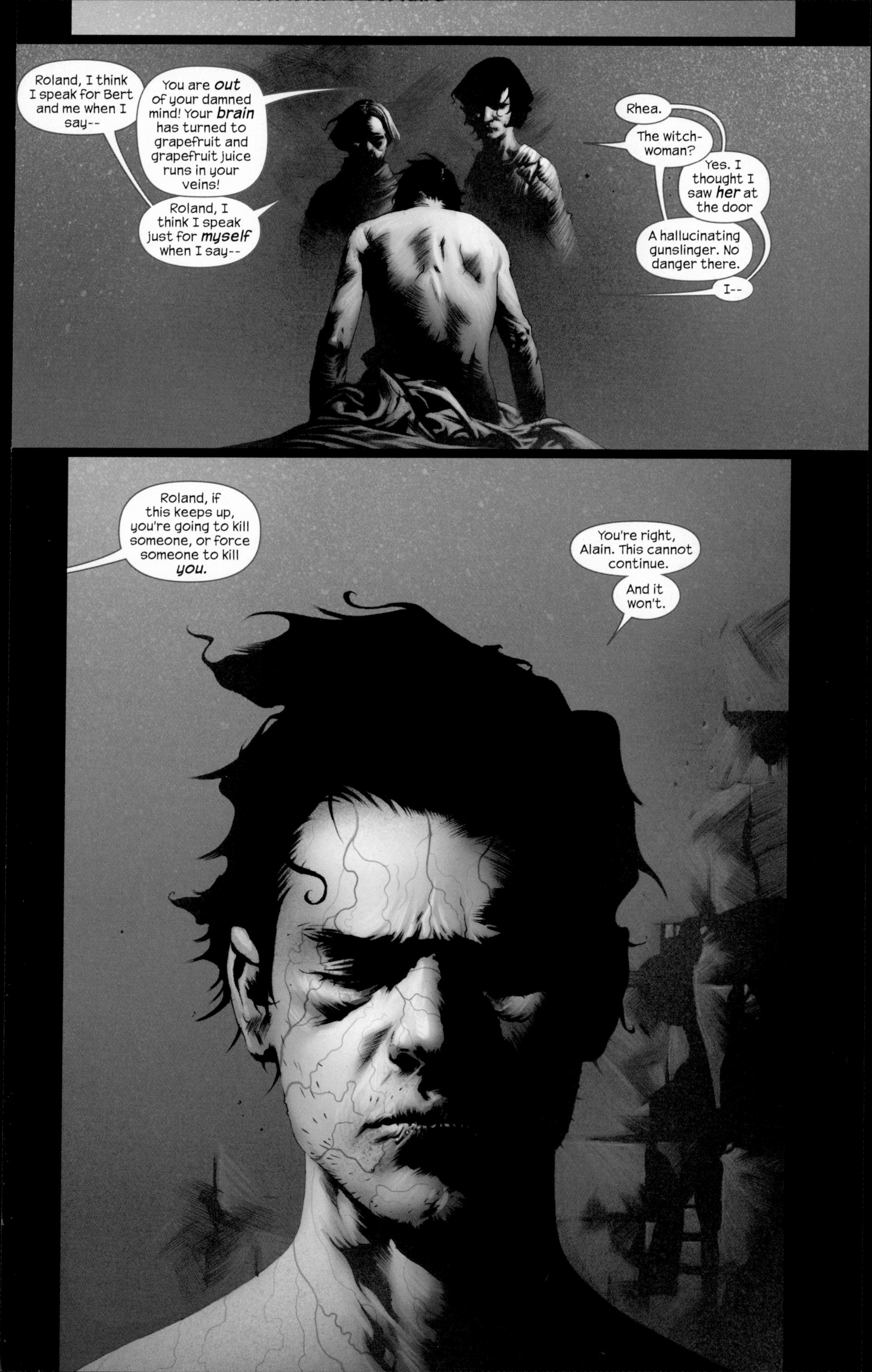
Roland, I think I speak for Bert and me when I say--
You are **out** of your damned mind! Your **brain** has turned to grapefruit and grapefruit juice runs in your veins!
Roland, I think I speak just for **myself** when I say--
Rhea.
The witch-woman?
Yes. I thought I saw **her** at the door
A hallucinating gunslinger. No danger there.
I--
Roland, if this keeps up, you're going to kill someone, or force someone to kill **you.**
You're right, Alain. This cannot continue.
And it won't.

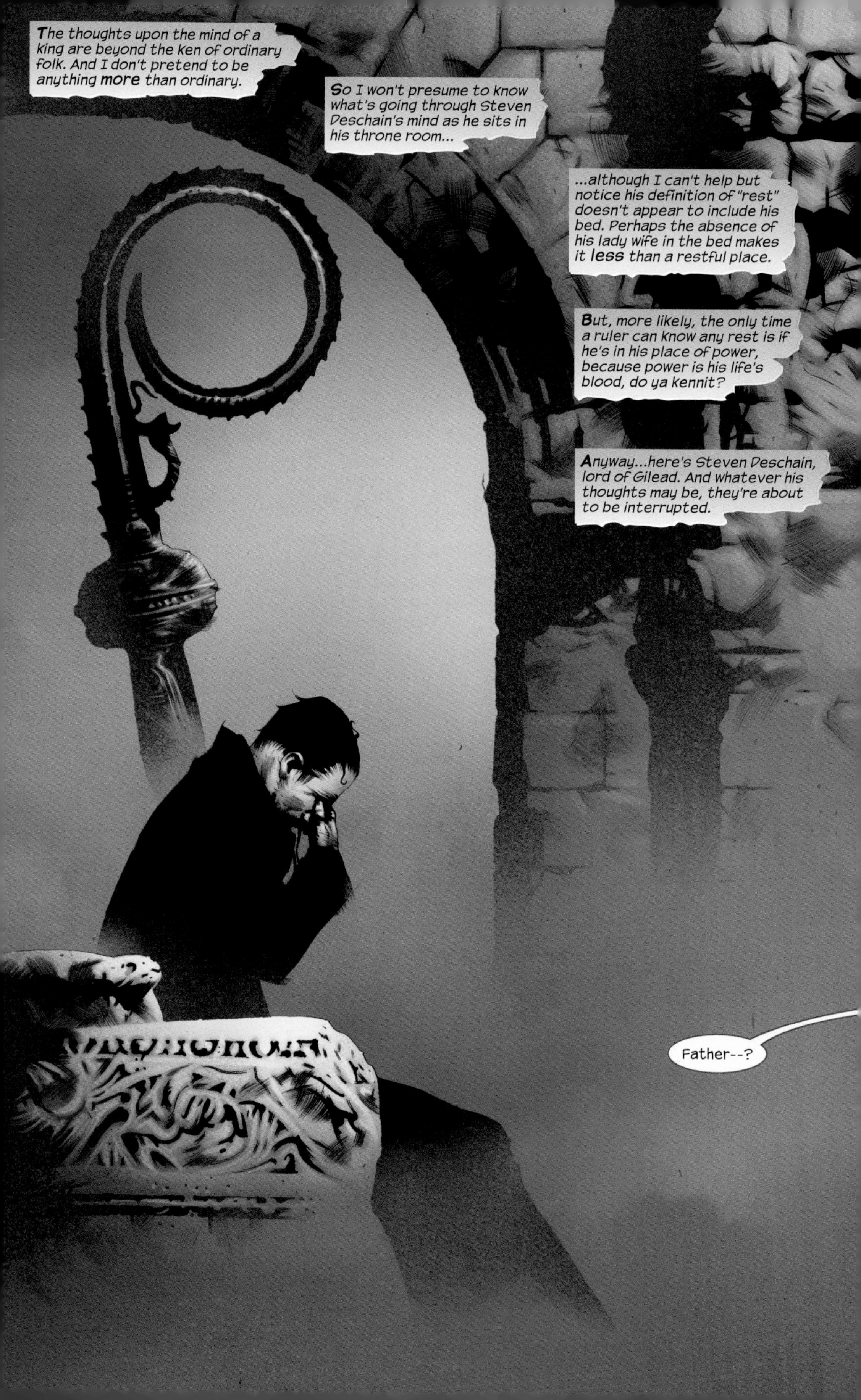
The thoughts upon the mind of a king are beyond the ken of ordinary folk. And I don't pretend to be anything **more** than ordinary.
So I won't presume to know what's going through Steven Deschain's mind as he sits in his throne room...
...although I can't help but notice his definition of "rest" doesn't appear to include his bed. Perhaps the absence of his lady wife in the bed makes it **less** than a restful place.
But, more likely, the only time a ruler can know any rest is if he's in his place of power, because power is his life's blood, do ya kennit?
Anyway...here's Steven Deschain, lord of Gilead. And whatever his thoughts may be, they're about to be interrupted.
Father--?

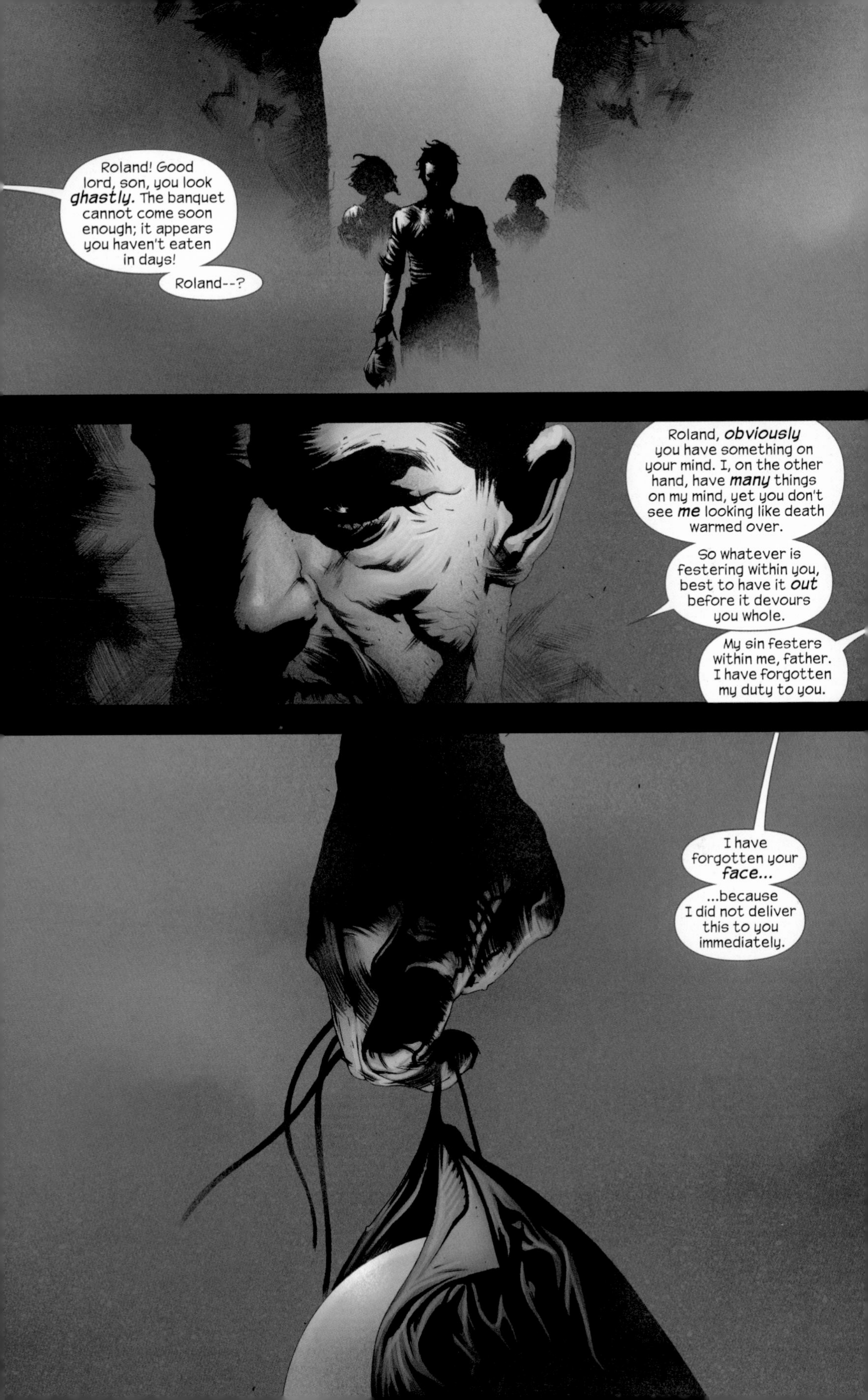
Roland! Good lord, son, you look ghastly. The banquet cannot come soon enough; it appears you haven't eaten in days!
Roland--?
Roland, obviously you have something on your mind. I, on the other hand, have many things on my mind, yet you don't see me looking like death warmed over.
So whatever is festering within you, best to have it out before it devours you whole.
My sin festers within me, father. I have forgotten my duty to you.
I have forgotten your face...
...because I did not deliver this to you immediately.

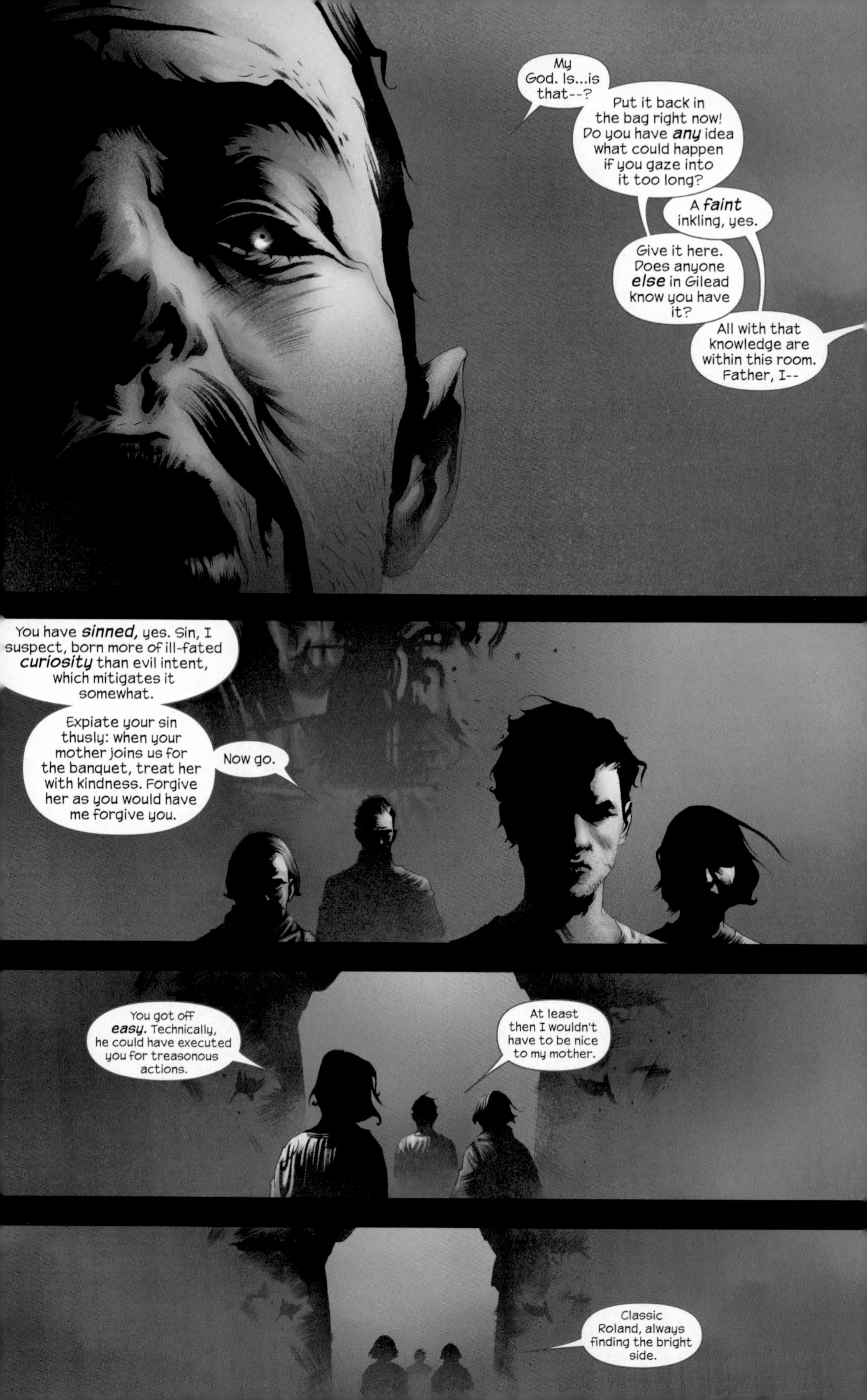

My God. Is...is that--?
Put it back in the bag right now! Do you have *any* idea what could happen if you gaze into it too long?
A *faint* inkling, yes.
Give it here. Does anyone *else* in Gilead know you have it?
All with that knowledge are within this room. Father, I--
You have *sinned,* yes. Sin, I suspect, born more of ill-fated *curiosity* than evil intent, which mitigates it somewhat.
Expiate your sin thusly: when your mother joins us for the banquet, treat her with kindness. Forgive her as you would have me forgive you.
Now go.
You got off *easy.* Technically, he could have executed you for treasonous actions.
At least then I wouldn't have to be nice to my mother.
Classic Roland, always finding the bright side.

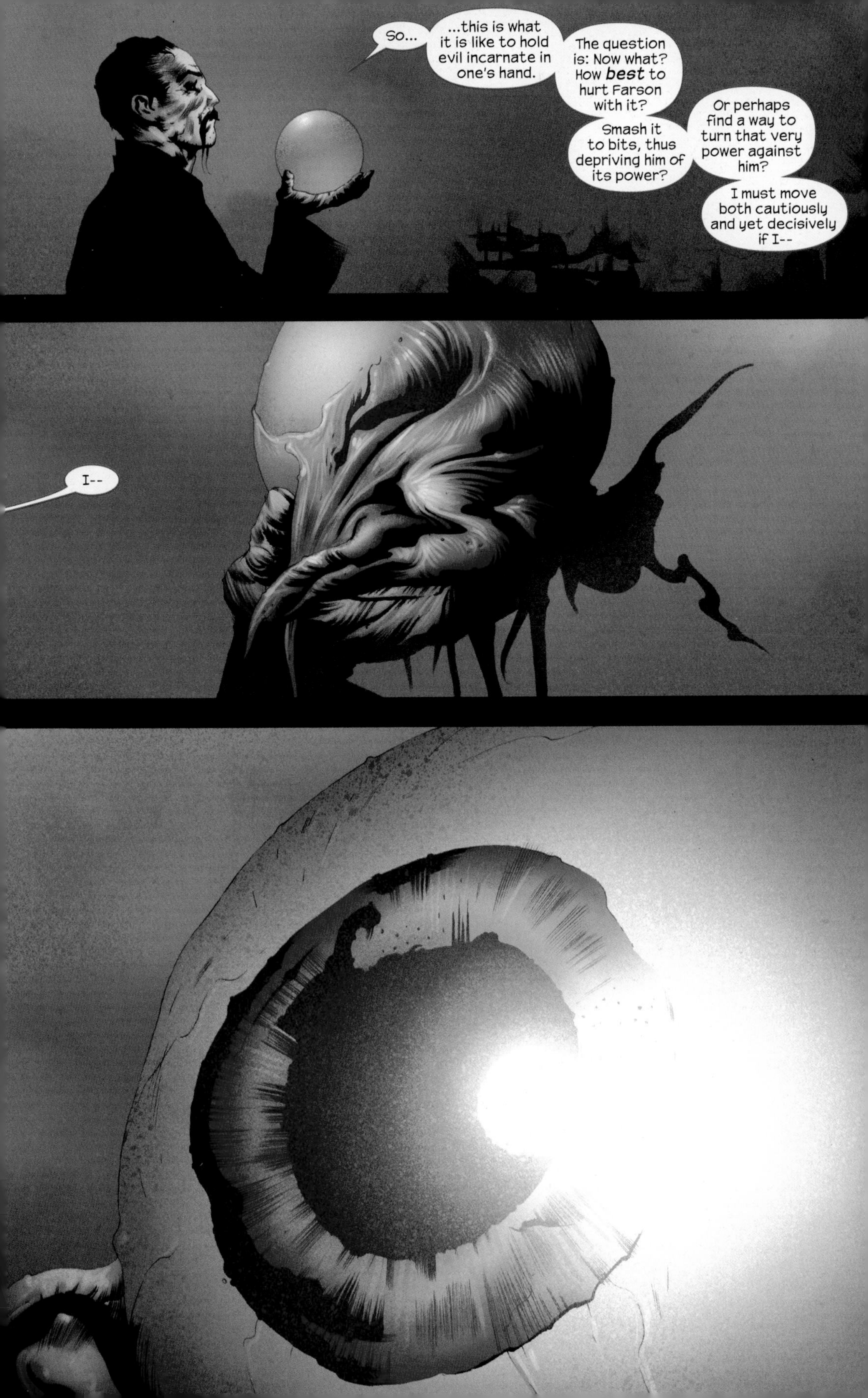
So...
...this is what it is like to hold evil incarnate in one's hand.
The question is: Now what? How **best** to hurt Farson with it?
Smash it to bits, thus depriving him of its power?
Or perhaps find a way to turn that very power against him?
I must move both cautiously and yet decisively if I--
I--

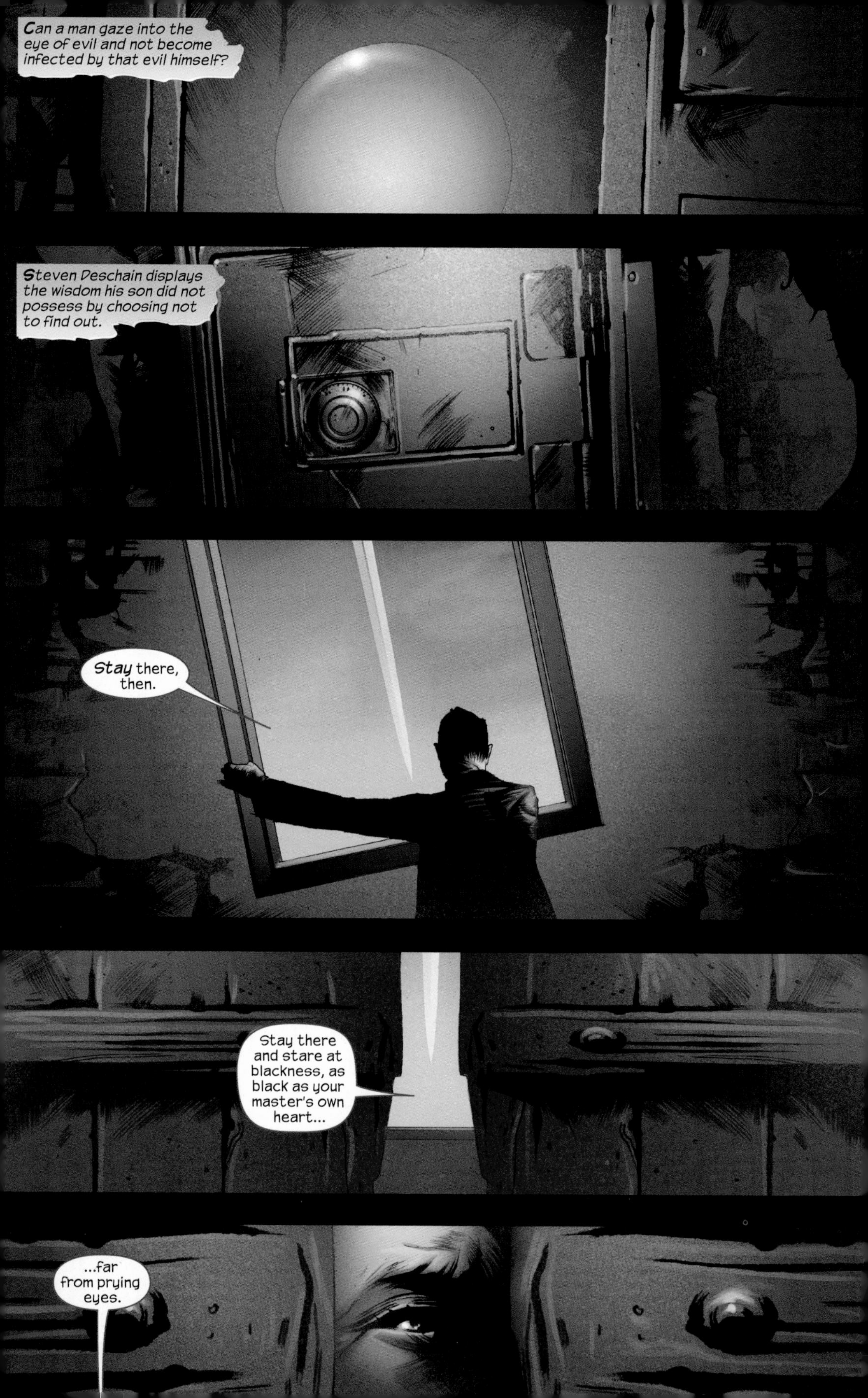

Can a man gaze into the eye of evil and not become infected by that evil himself?
Steven Deschain displays the wisdom his son did not possess by choosing not to find out.
Stay there, then.
Stay there and stare at blackness, as black as your master's own heart...
...far from prying eyes.

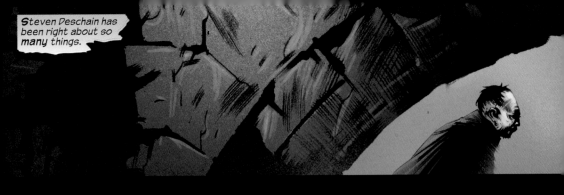

Steven Deschain has been right about so *many* things.

That there are spies and treachery everywhere.

That Maerlyn's Grapefruit is a source of great power and can be a potent weapon.

But it appears he was wrong about *one* thing:

Deschain
hAs the bALL.
meet behind
PALAce
tomorrow midnight

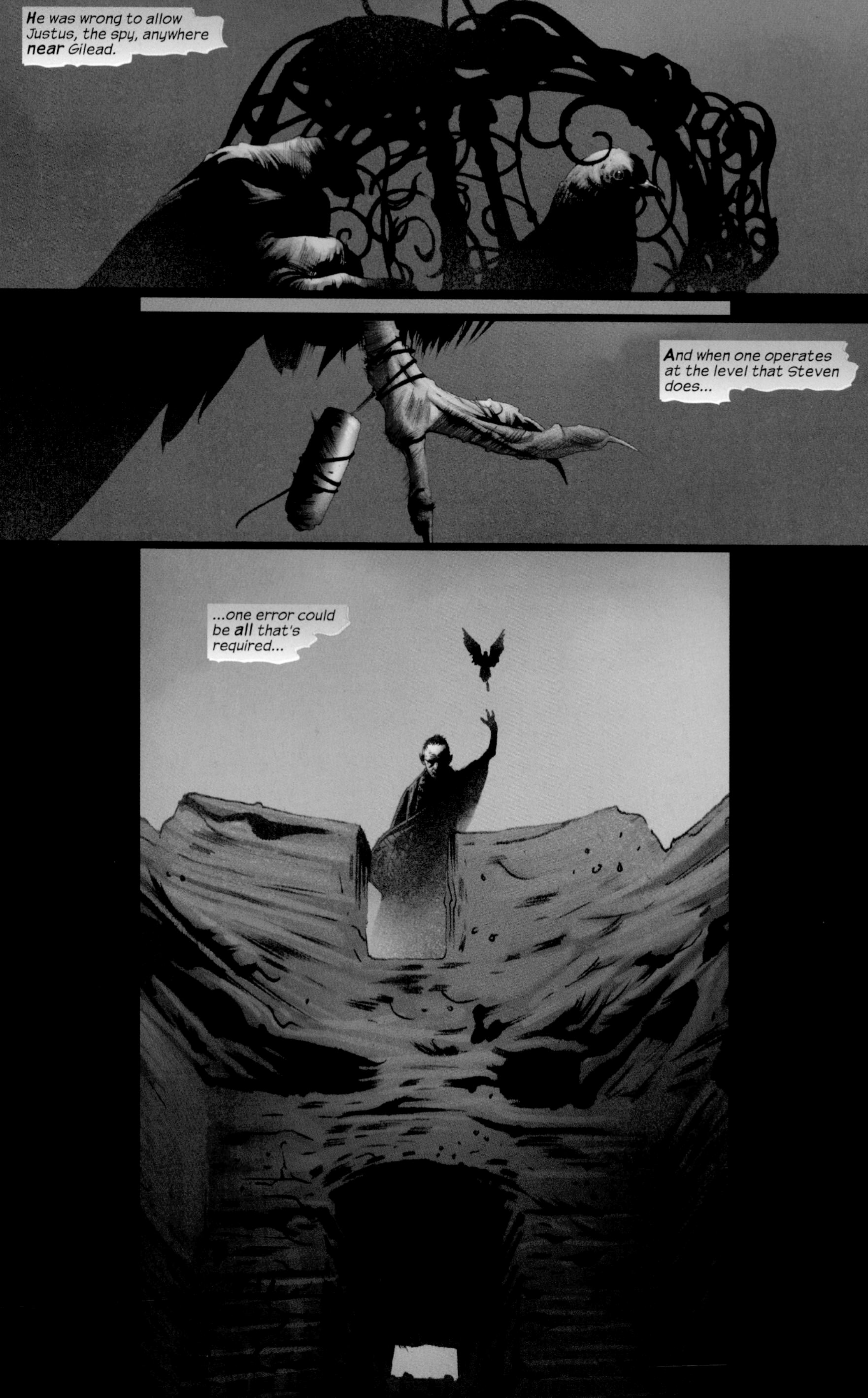
He was wrong to allow Justus, the spy, anywhere near Gilead.
And when one operates at the level that Steven does...
...one error could be all that's required...

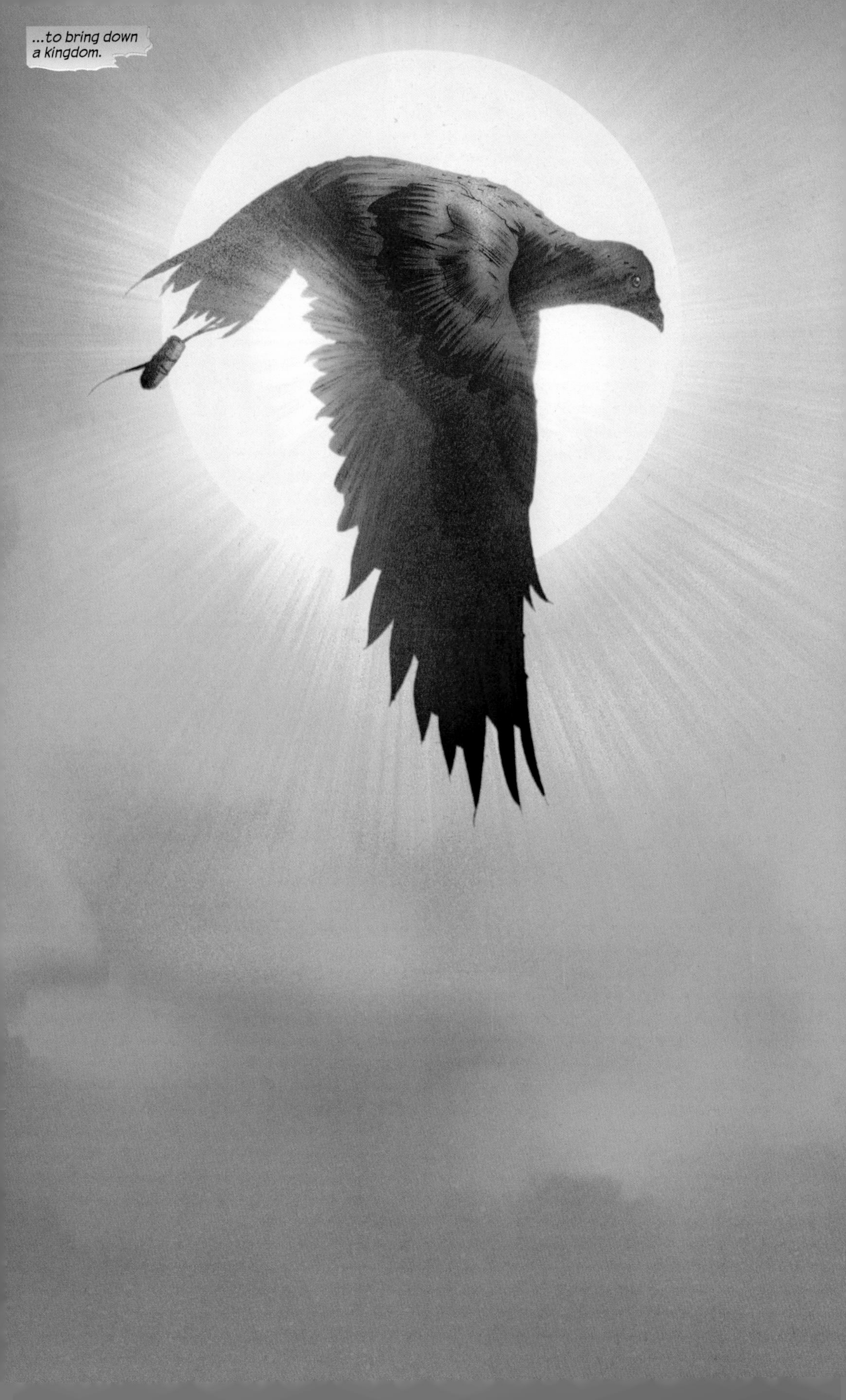
...to bring down a kingdom.

STEPHEN KING

THE DARK TOWER

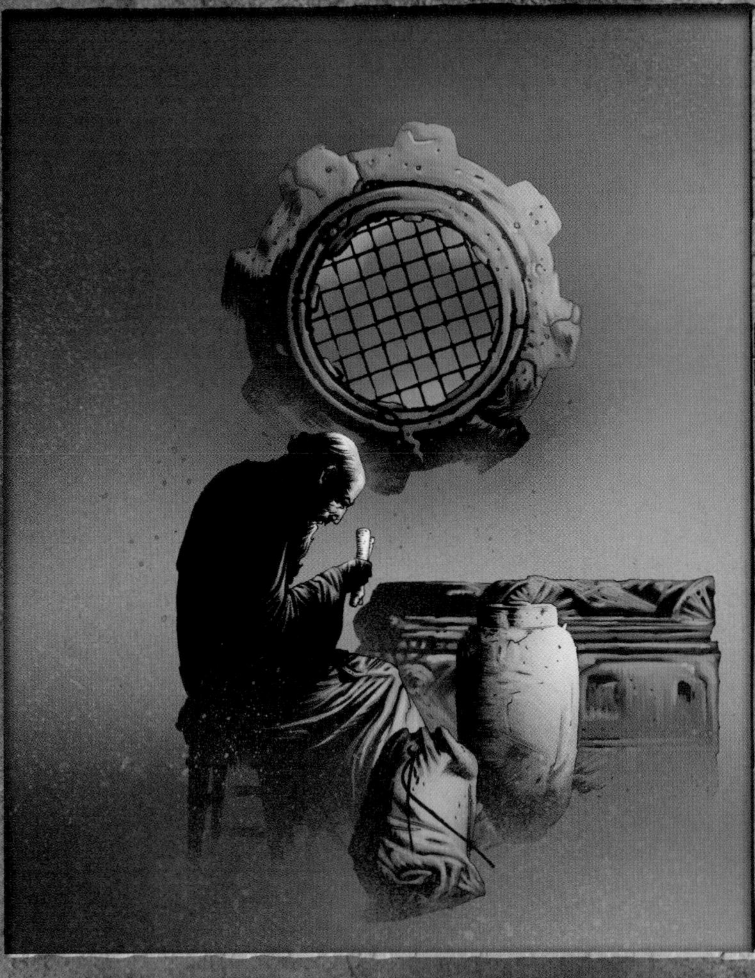

TREACHERY

CHAPTER FIVE

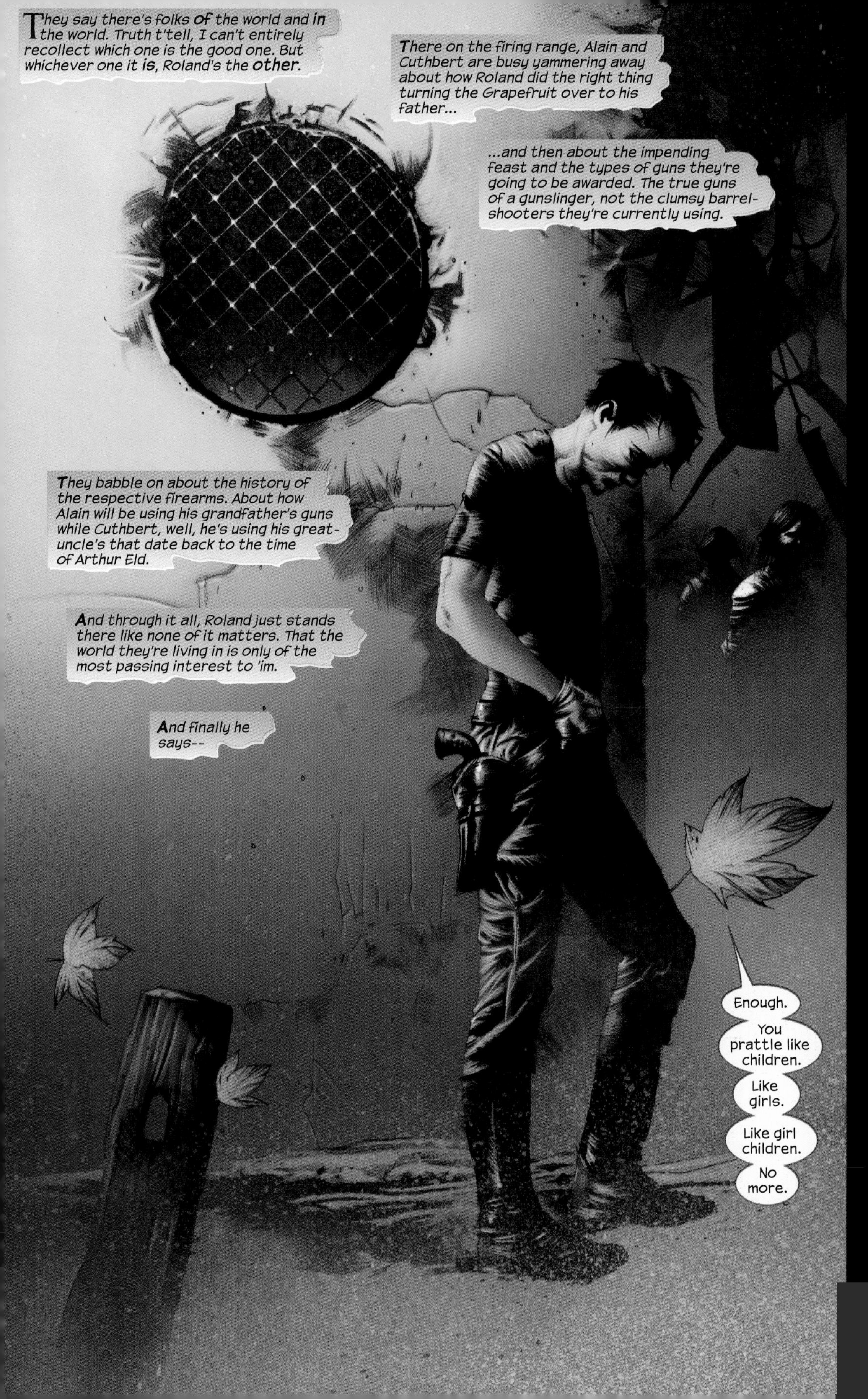
They say there's folks of the world and in the world. Truth t'tell, I can't entirely recollect which one is the good one. But whichever one it is, Roland's the other.
There on the firing range, Alain and Cuthbert are busy yammering away about how Roland did the right thing turning the Grapefruit over to his father...
...and then about the impending feast and the types of guns they're going to be awarded. The true guns of a gunslinger, not the clumsy barrel-shooters they're currently using.
They babble on about the history of the respective firearms. About how Alain will be using his grandfather's guns while Cuthbert, well, he's using his great-uncle's that date back to the time of Arthur Eld.
And through it all, Roland just stands there like none of it matters. That the world they're living in is only of the most passing interest to 'im.
And finally he says--
Enough.
You prattle like children.
Like girls.
Like girl children.
No more.

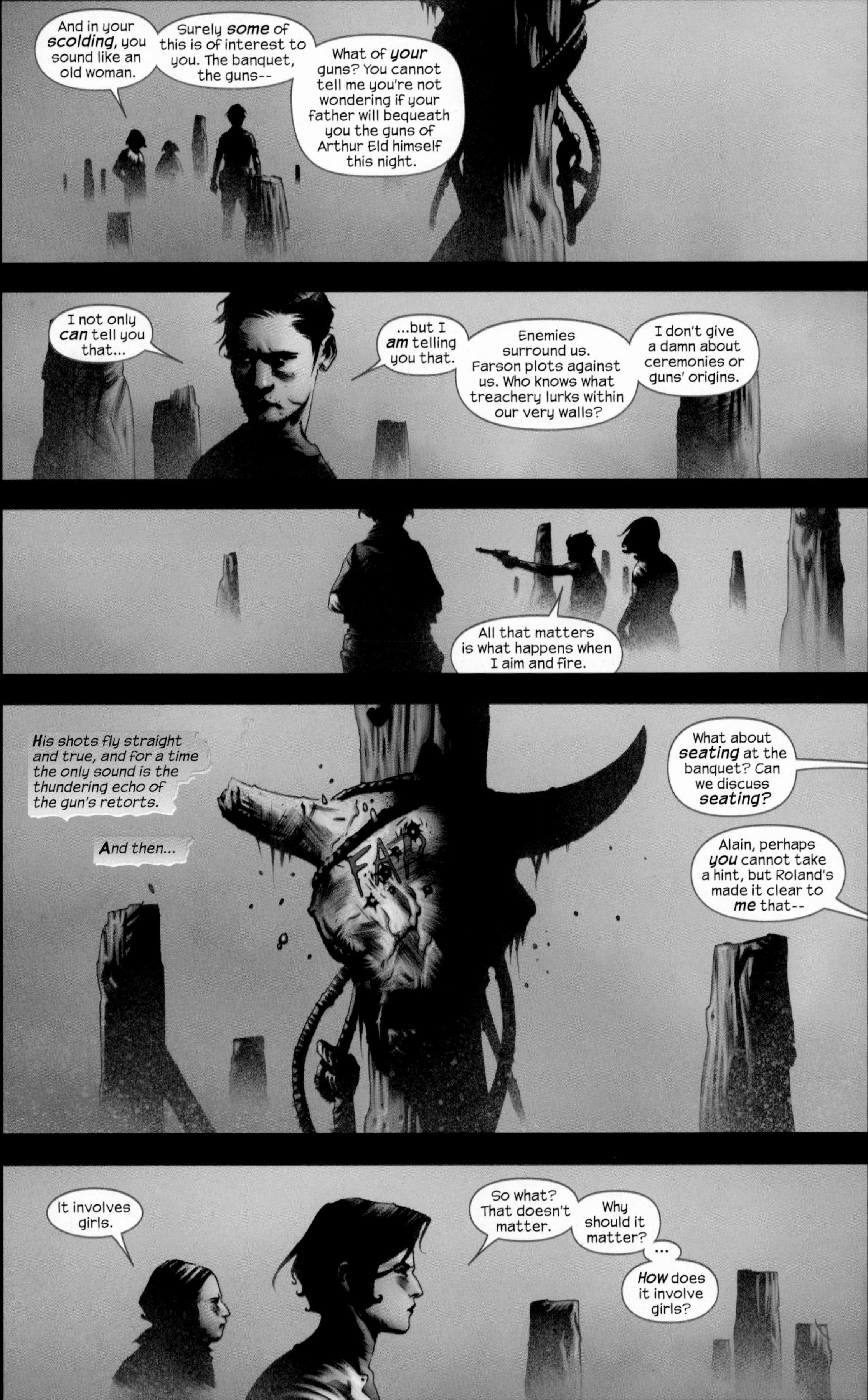

And in your scolding, you sound like an old woman.
Surely some of this is of interest to you. The banquet, the guns--
What of your guns? You cannot tell me you're not wondering if your father will bequeath you the guns of Arthur Eld himself this night.
I not only can tell you that...
...but I am telling you that.
Enemies surround us. Farson plots against us. Who knows what treachery lurks within our very walls?
I don't give a damn about ceremonies or guns' origins.
All that matters is what happens when I aim and fire.
His shots fly straight and true, and for a time the only sound is the thundering echo of the gun's retorts.
And then...
What about seating at the banquet? Can we discuss seating?
Alain, perhaps you cannot take a hint, but Roland's made it clear to me that--
It involves girls.
So what? That doesn't matter.
Why should it matter?
...
How does it involve girls?

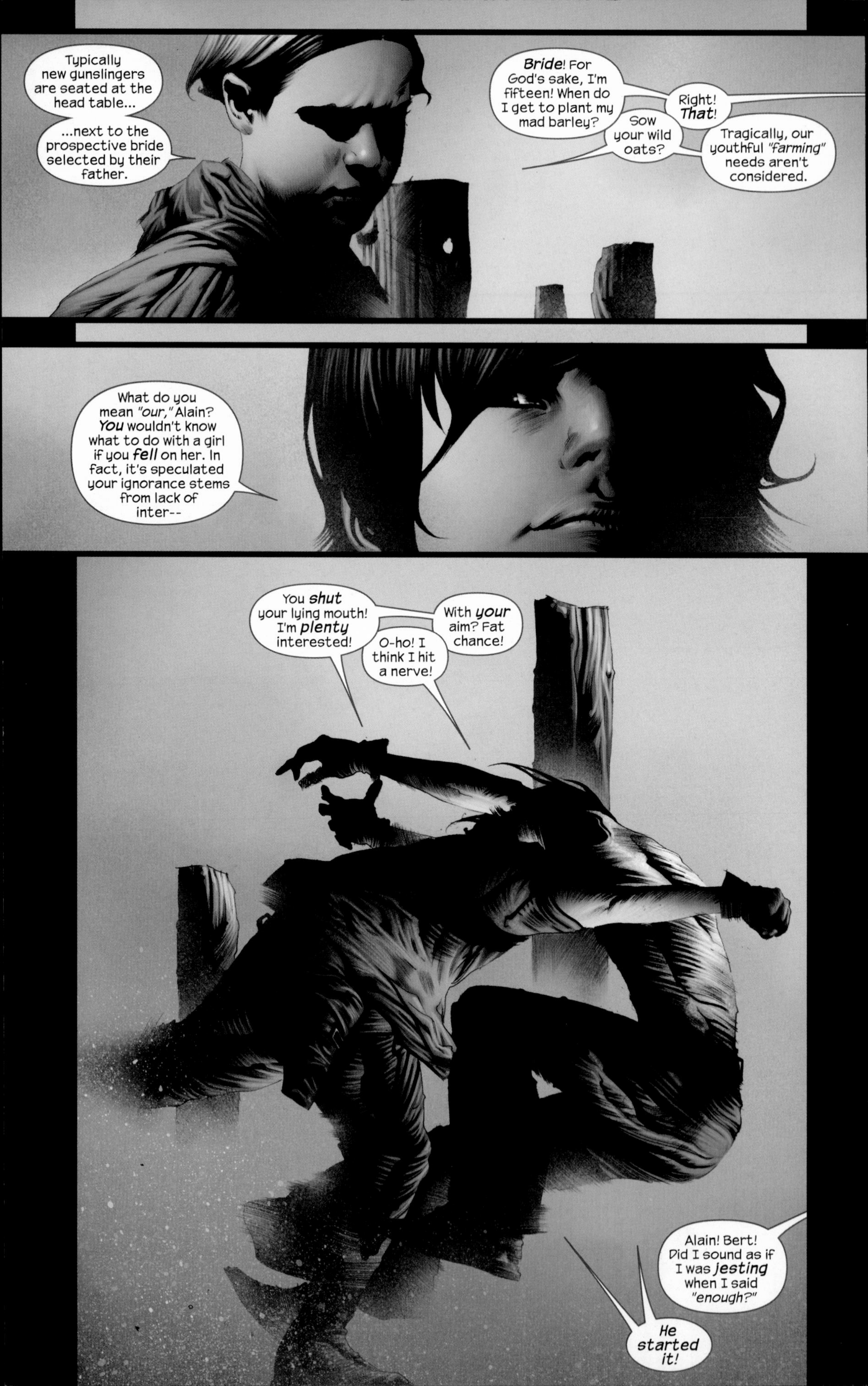
Typically new gunslingers are seated at the head table...
...next to the prospective bride selected by their father.
Bride! For God's sake, I'm fifteen! When do I get to plant my mad barley?
Sow your wild oats?
Right! That!
Tragically, our youthful "farming" needs aren't considered.
What do you mean "our," Alain? You wouldn't know what to do with a girl if you fell on her. In fact, it's speculated your ignorance stems from lack of inter--
You shut your lying mouth! I'm plenty interested!
With your aim? Fat chance!
O-ho! I think I hit a nerve!
Alain! Bert! Did I sound as if I was jesting when I said "enough?"
He started it!

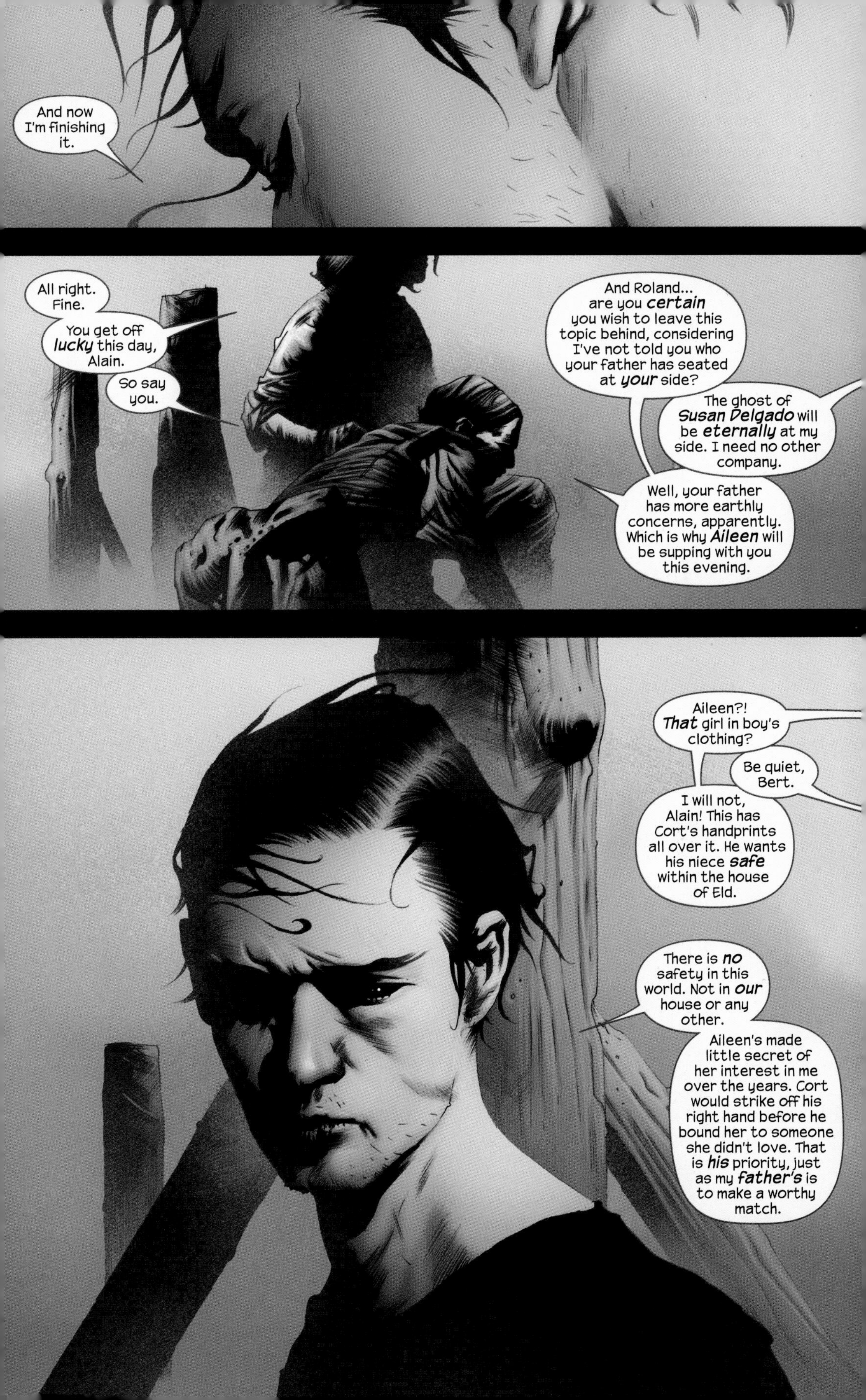
And now I'm finishing it.
All right. Fine.
You get off lucky this day, Alain.
So say you.
And Roland... are you certain you wish to leave this topic behind, considering I've not told you who your father has seated at your side?
The ghost of Susan Delgado will be eternally at my side. I need no other company.
Well, your father has more earthly concerns, apparently. Which is why Aileen will be supping with you this evening.
Aileen?! That girl in boy's clothing?
Be quiet, Bert.
I will not, Alain! This has Cort's handprints all over it. He wants his niece safe within the house of Eld.
There is no safety in this world. Not in our house or any other.
Aileen's made little secret of her interest in me over the years. Cort would strike off his right hand before he bound her to someone she didn't love. That is his priority, just as my father's is to make a worthy match.

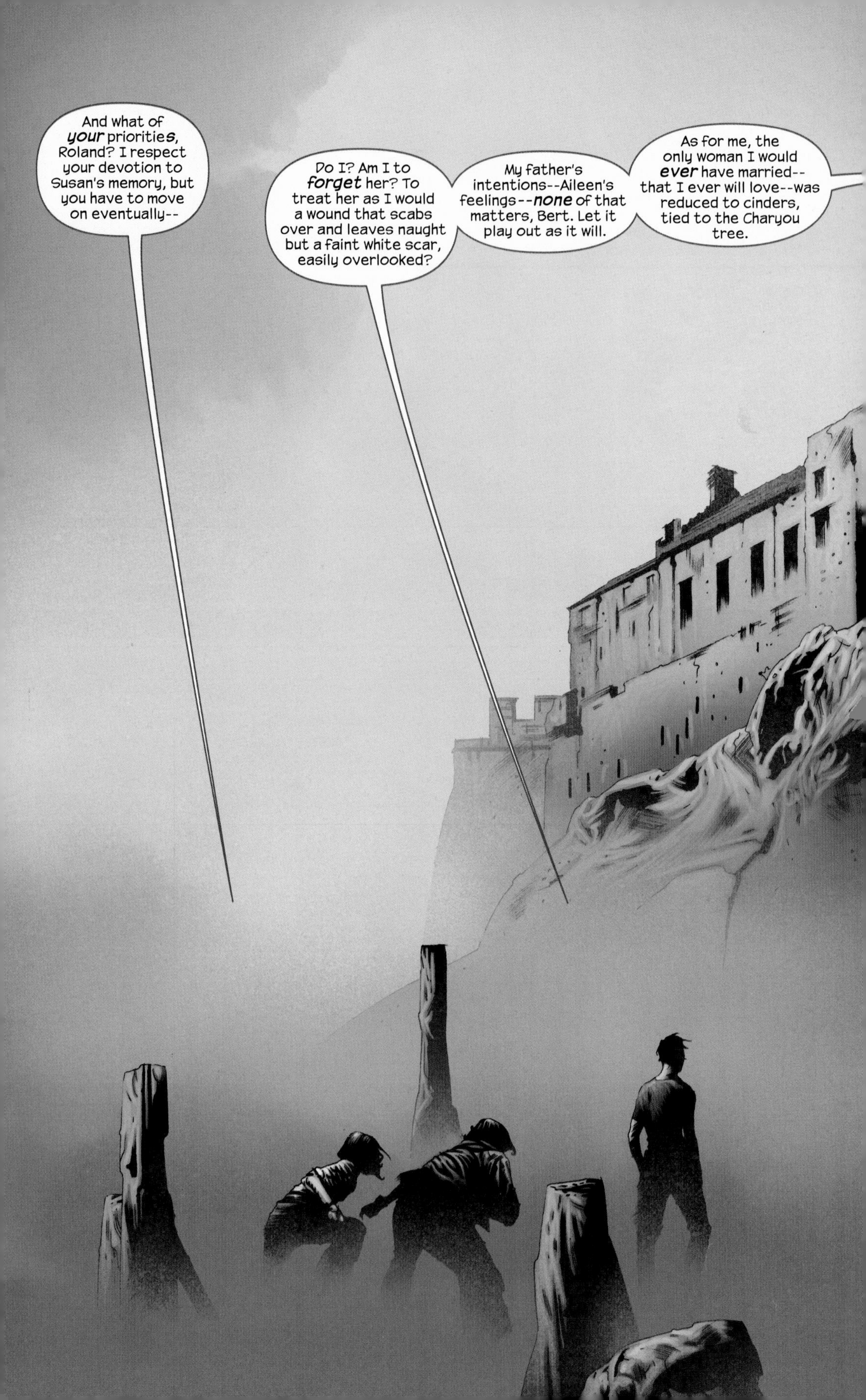
And what of your priorities, Roland? I respect your devotion to Susan's memory, but you have to move on eventually--
Do I? Am I to forget her? To treat her as I would a wound that scabs over and leaves naught but a faint white scar, easily overlooked?
My father's intentions--Aileen's feelings--none of that matters, Bert. Let it play out as it will.
As for me, the only woman I would ever have married--that I ever will love--was reduced to cinders, tied to the Charyou tree.

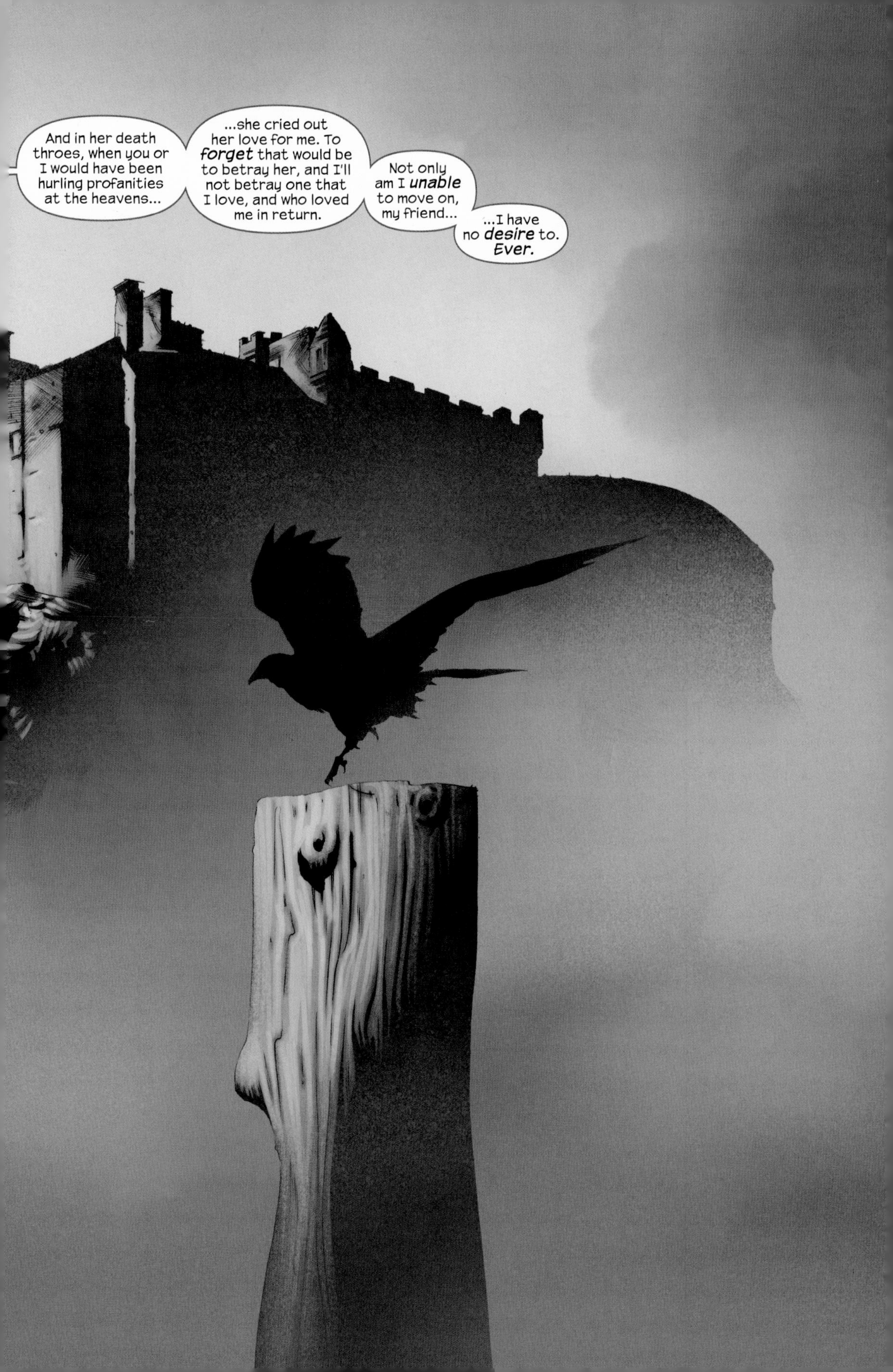
And in her death throes, when you or I would have been hurling profanities at the heavens...
...she cried out her love for me. To forget that would be to betray her, and I'll not betray one that I love, and who loved me in return.
Not only am I unable to move on, my friend...
...I have no desire to. Ever.

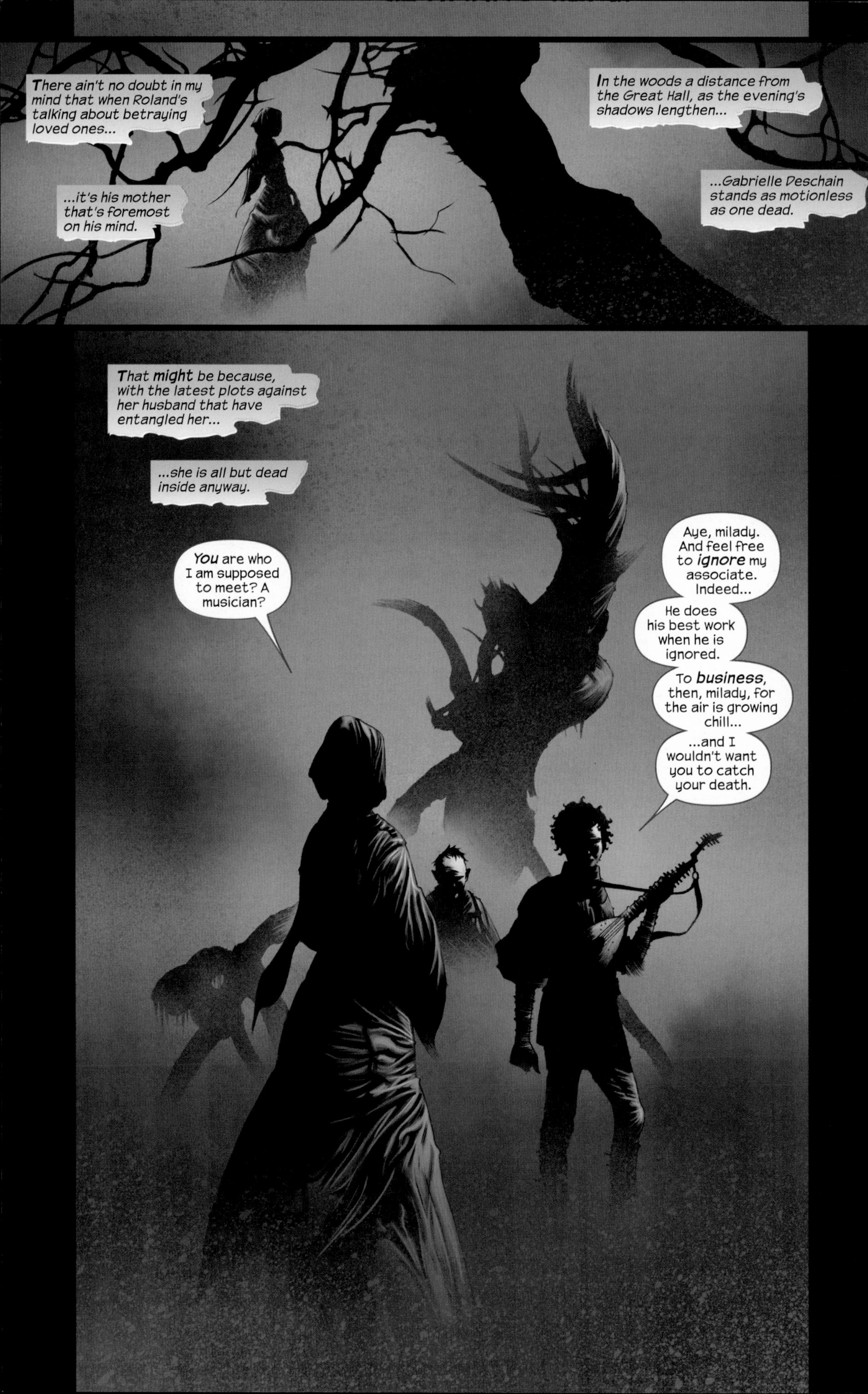

There ain't no doubt in my mind that when Roland's talking about betraying loved ones...
...it's his mother that's foremost on his mind.
In the woods a distance from the Great Hall, as the evening's shadows lengthen...
...Gabrielle Deschain stands as motionless as one dead.
That might be because, with the latest plots against her husband that have entangled her...
...she is all but dead inside anyway.
You are who I am supposed to meet? A musician?
Aye, milady. And feel free to ignore my associate. Indeed...
He does his best work when he is ignored.
To business, then, milady, for the air is growing chill...
...and I wouldn't want you to catch your death.

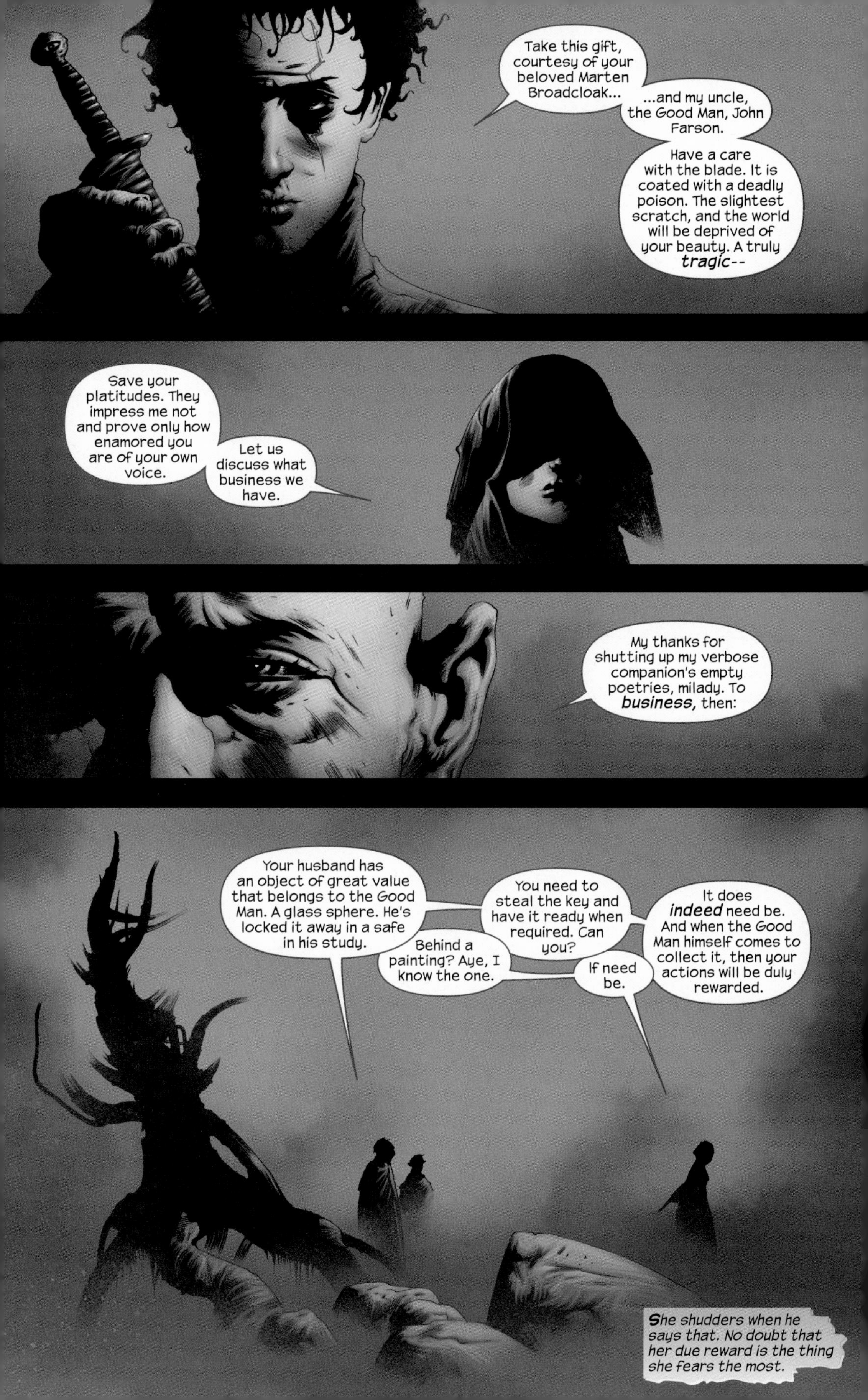
Take this gift, courtesy of your beloved Marten Broadcloak...
...and my uncle, the Good Man, John Farson.
Have a care with the blade. It is coated with a deadly poison. The slightest scratch, and the world will be deprived of your beauty. A truly *tragic*--
Save your platitudes. They impress me not and prove only how enamored you are of your own voice.
Let us discuss what business we have.
My thanks for shutting up my verbose companion's empty poetries, milady. To *business*, then:
Your husband has an object of great value that belongs to the Good Man. A glass sphere. He's locked it away in a safe in his study.
Behind a painting? Aye, I know the one.
You need to steal the key and have it ready when required. Can you?
If need be.
It does *indeed* need be. And when the Good Man himself comes to collect it, then your actions will be duly rewarded.
She shudders when he says that. No doubt that her due reward is the thing she fears the most.

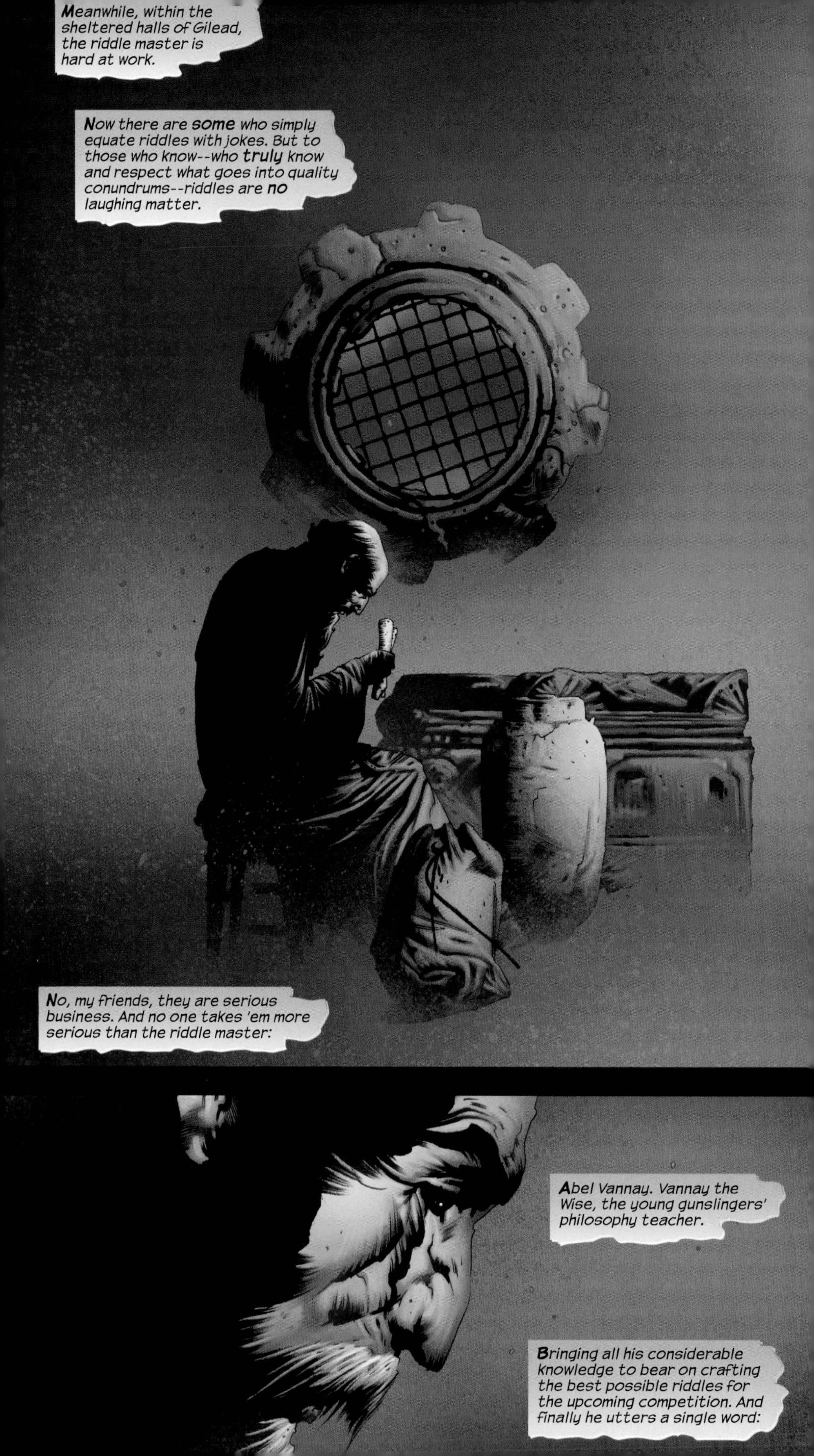
Meanwhile, within the sheltered halls of Gilead, the riddle master is hard at work.
Now there are **some** who simply equate riddles with jokes. But to those who know--who **truly** know and respect what goes into quality conundrums--riddles are **no** laughing matter.
No, my friends, they are serious business. And no one takes 'em more serious than the riddle master:
Abel Vannay. Vannay the Wise, the young gunslingers' philosophy teacher.
Bringing all his considerable knowledge to bear on crafting the best possible riddles for the upcoming competition. And finally he utters a single word:

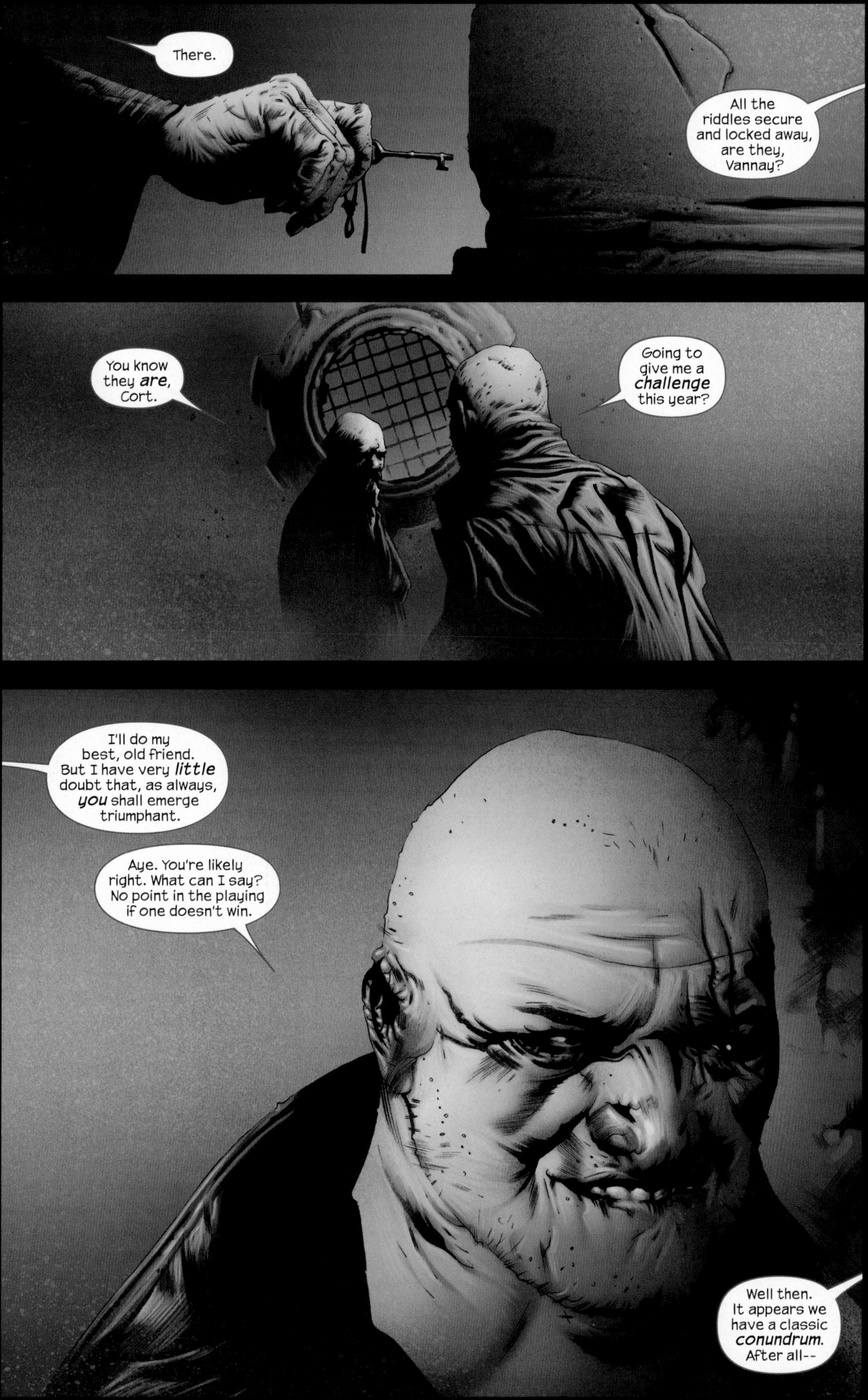
There.
All the riddles secure and locked away, are they, Vannay?
You know they *are*, Cort.
Going to give me a *challenge* this year?
I'll do my best, old friend. But I have very *little* doubt that, as always, *you* shall emerge triumphant.
Aye. You're likely right. What can I say? No point in the playing if one doesn't win.
Well then. It appears we have a classic *conundrum*. After all--

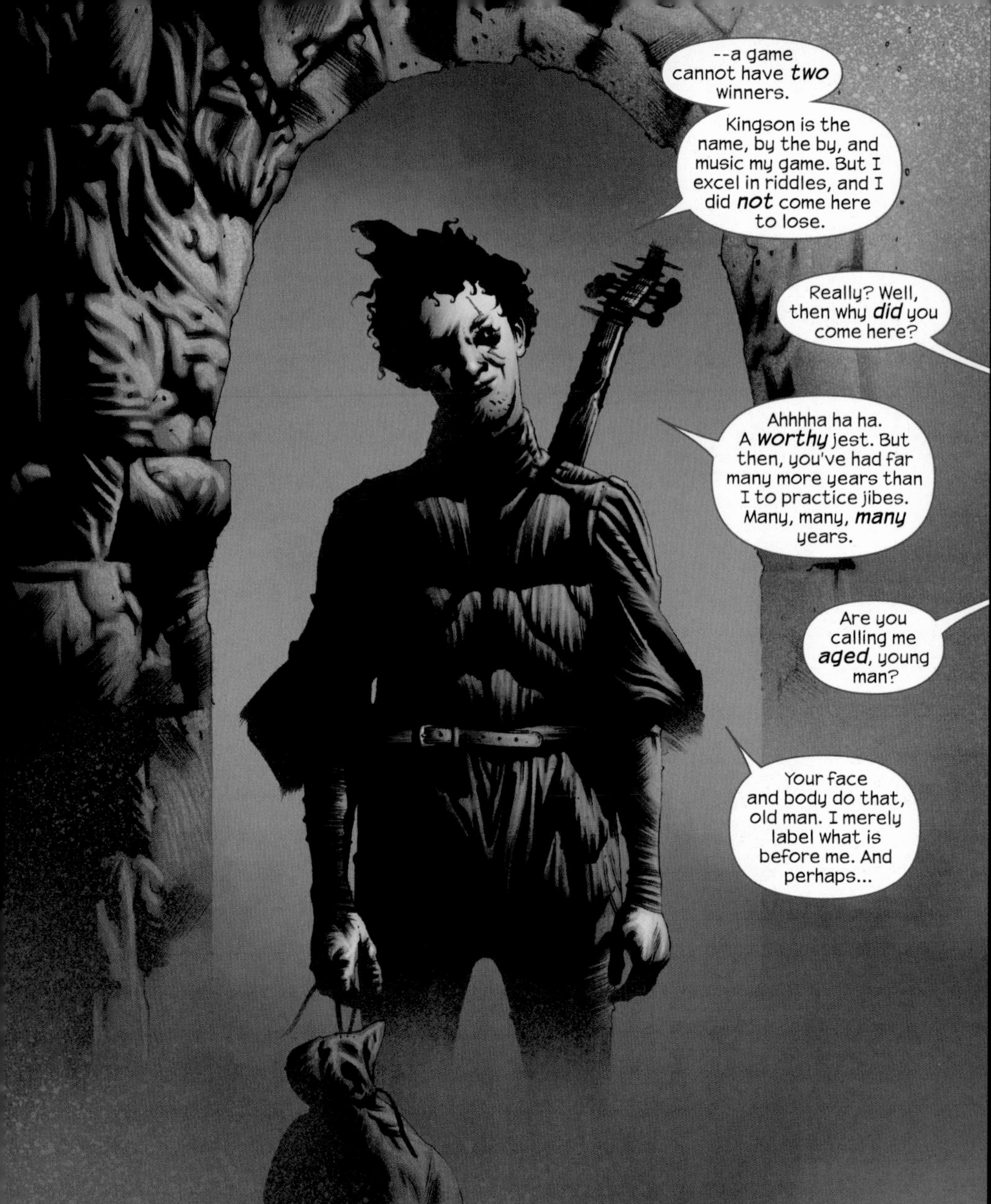
--a game cannot have *two* winners.
Kingson is the name, by the by, and music my game. But I excel in riddles, and I did *not* come here to lose.
Really? Well, then why *did* you come here?
Ahhhha ha ha. A *worthy* jest. But then, you've had far many more years than I to practice jibes. Many, many, *many* years.
Are you calling me *aged*, young man?
Your face and body do that, old man. I merely label what is before me. And perhaps...

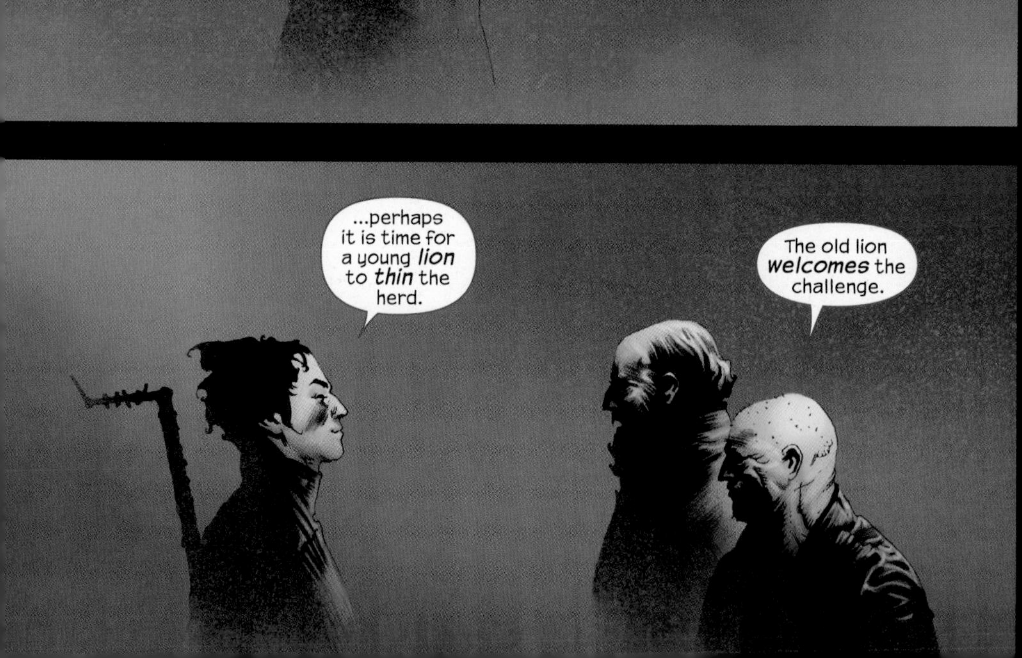
...perhaps it is time for a young *lion* to *thin* the herd.
The old lion *welcomes* the challenge.

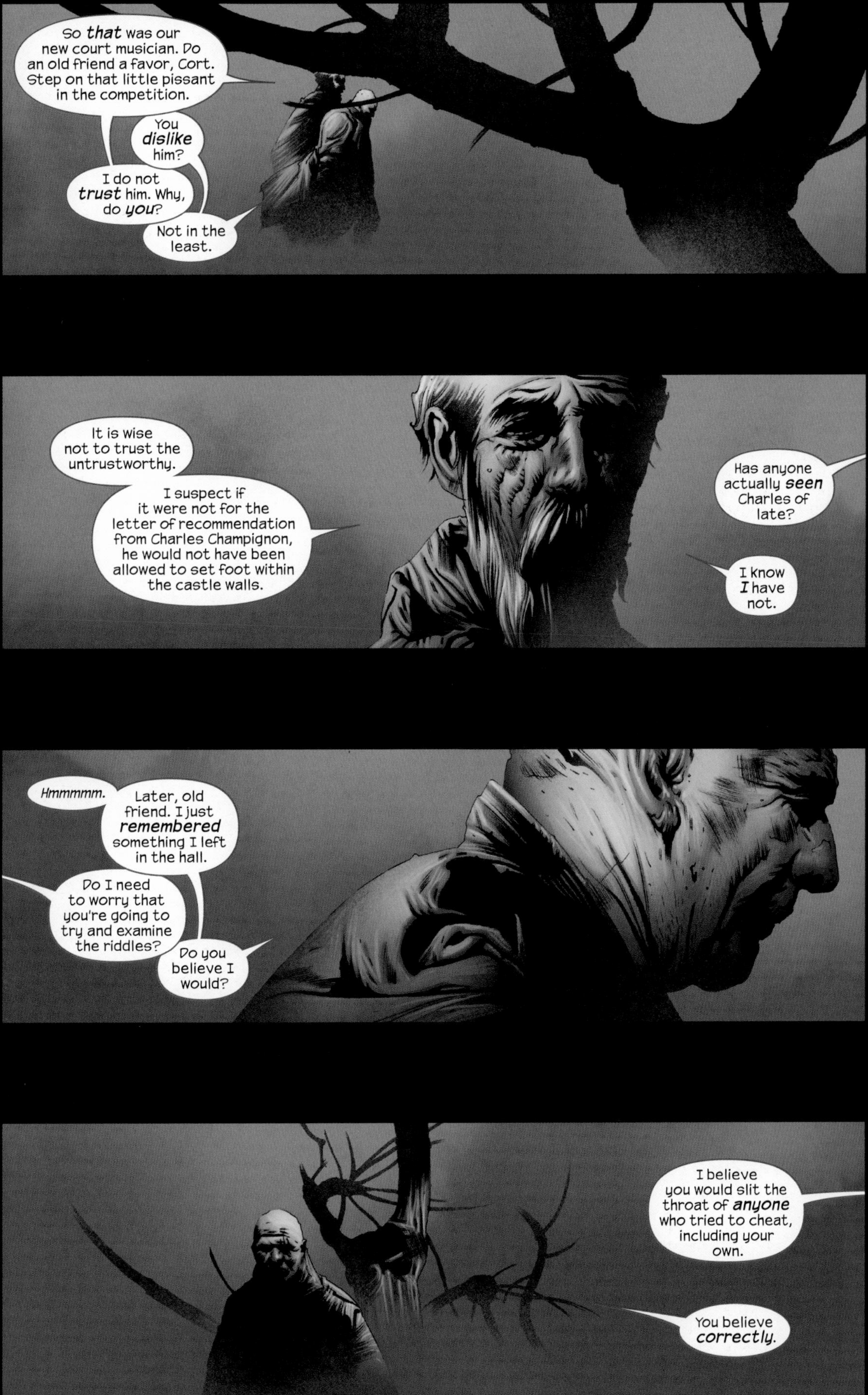
So *that* was our new court musician. Do an old friend a favor, Cort. Step on that little pissant in the competition.
You *dislike* him?
I do not *trust* him. Why, do *you*?
Not in the least.
It is wise not to trust the untrustworthy.
I suspect if it were not for the letter of recommendation from Charles Champignon, he would not have been allowed to set foot within the castle walls.
Has anyone actually *seen* Charles of late?
I know *I* have not.
Hmmmmm.
Later, old friend. I just *remembered* something I left in the hall.
Do I need to worry that you're going to try and examine the riddles?
Do you believe I would?
I believe you would slit the throat of *anyone* who tried to cheat, including your own.
You believe *correctly*.

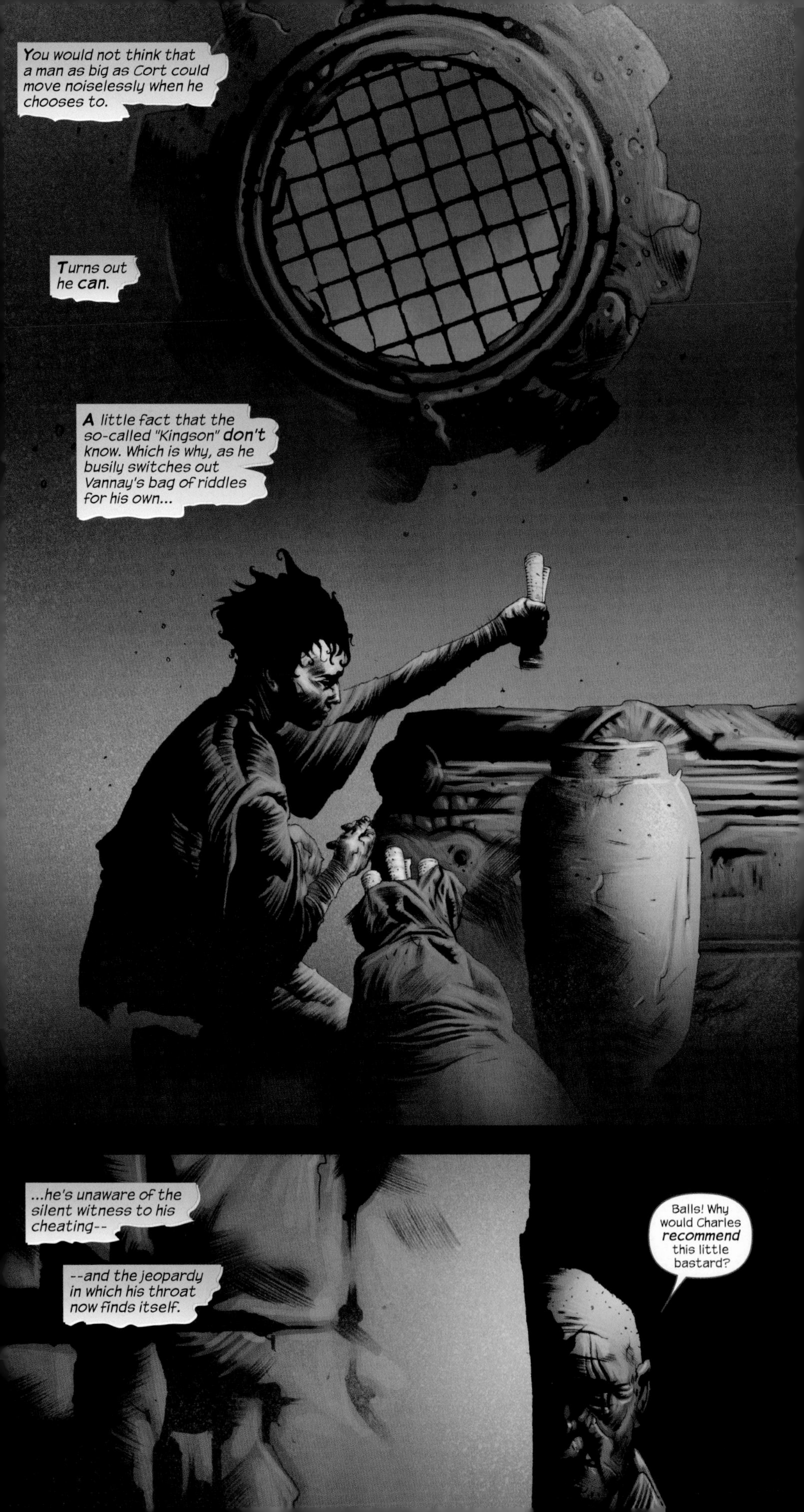
You would not think that a man as big as Cort could move noiselessly when he chooses to.
Turns out he can.
A little fact that the so-called "Kingson" don't know. Which is why, as he busily switches out Vannay's bag of riddles for his own...
...he's unaware of the silent witness to his cheating--
--and the jeopardy in which his throat now finds itself.
Balls! Why would Charles recommend this little bastard?

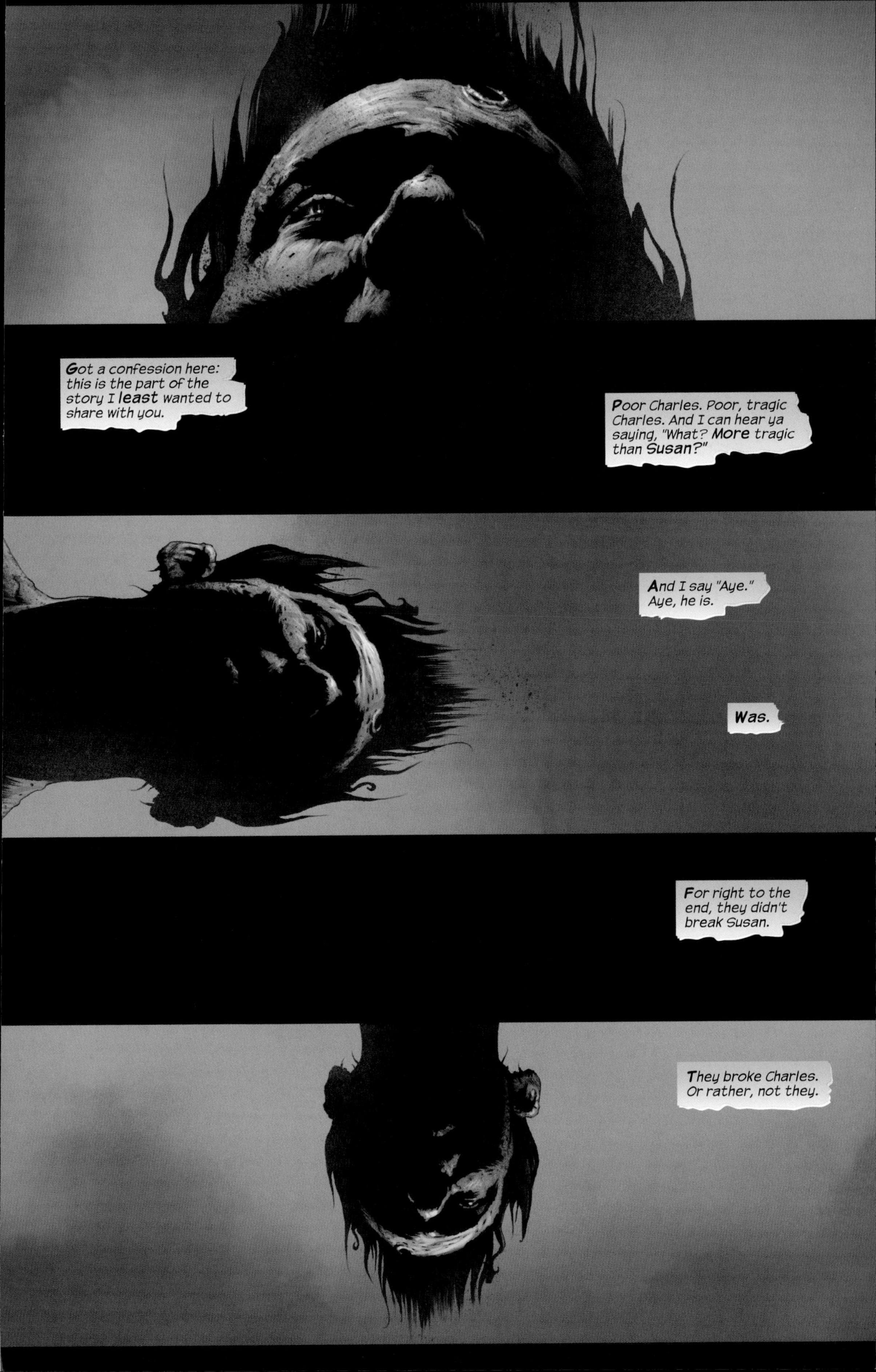

Got a confession here: this is the part of the story I **least** wanted to share with you.
Poor Charles. Poor, tragic Charles. And I can hear ya saying, "What? **More** tragic than **Susan?**"
And I say "Aye." Aye, he is.
Was.
For right to the end, they didn't break Susan.
They broke Charles. Or rather, not they.

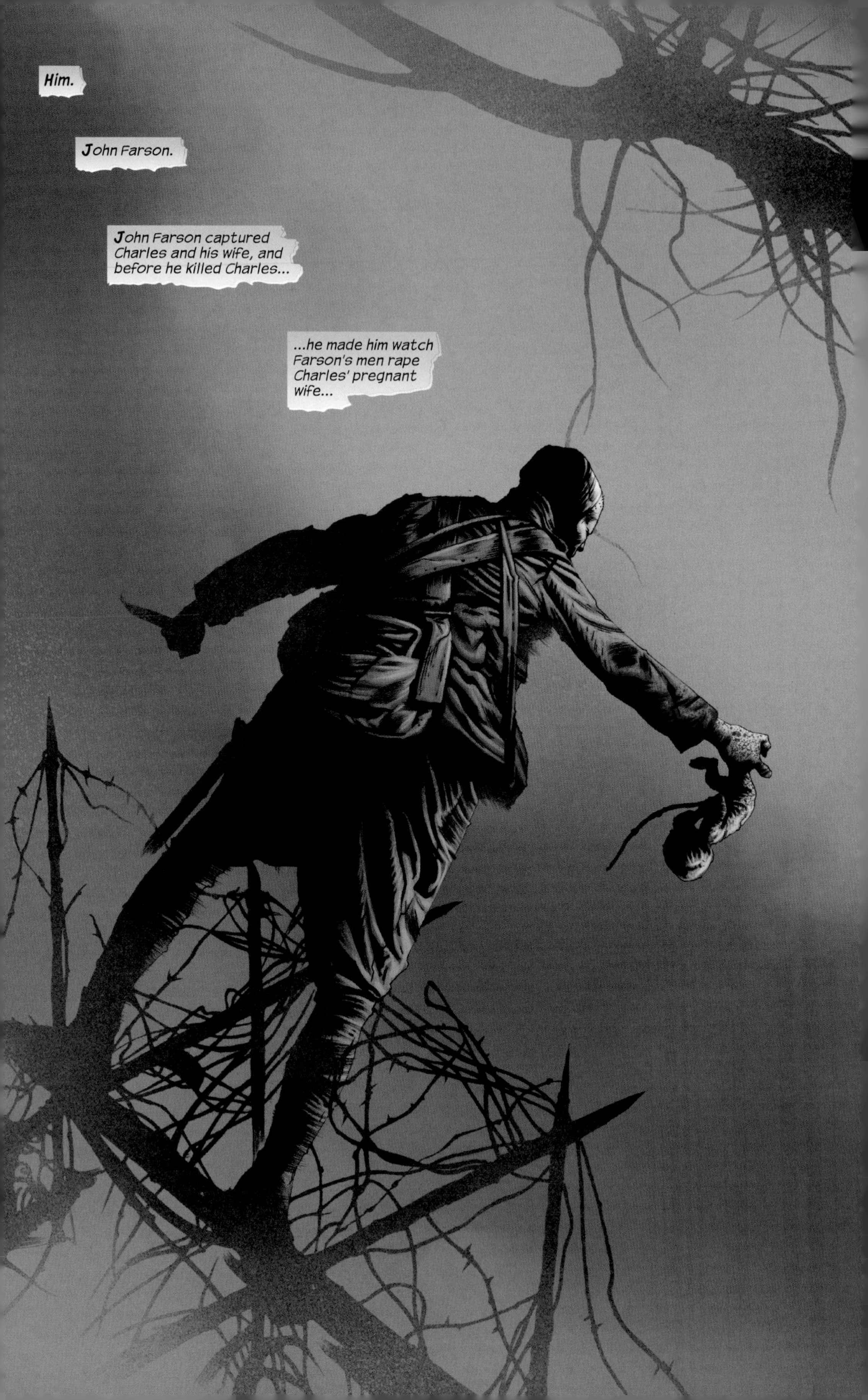
Him.
John Farson.
John Farson captured Charles and his wife, and before he killed Charles...
...he made him watch Farson's men rape Charles' pregnant wife...

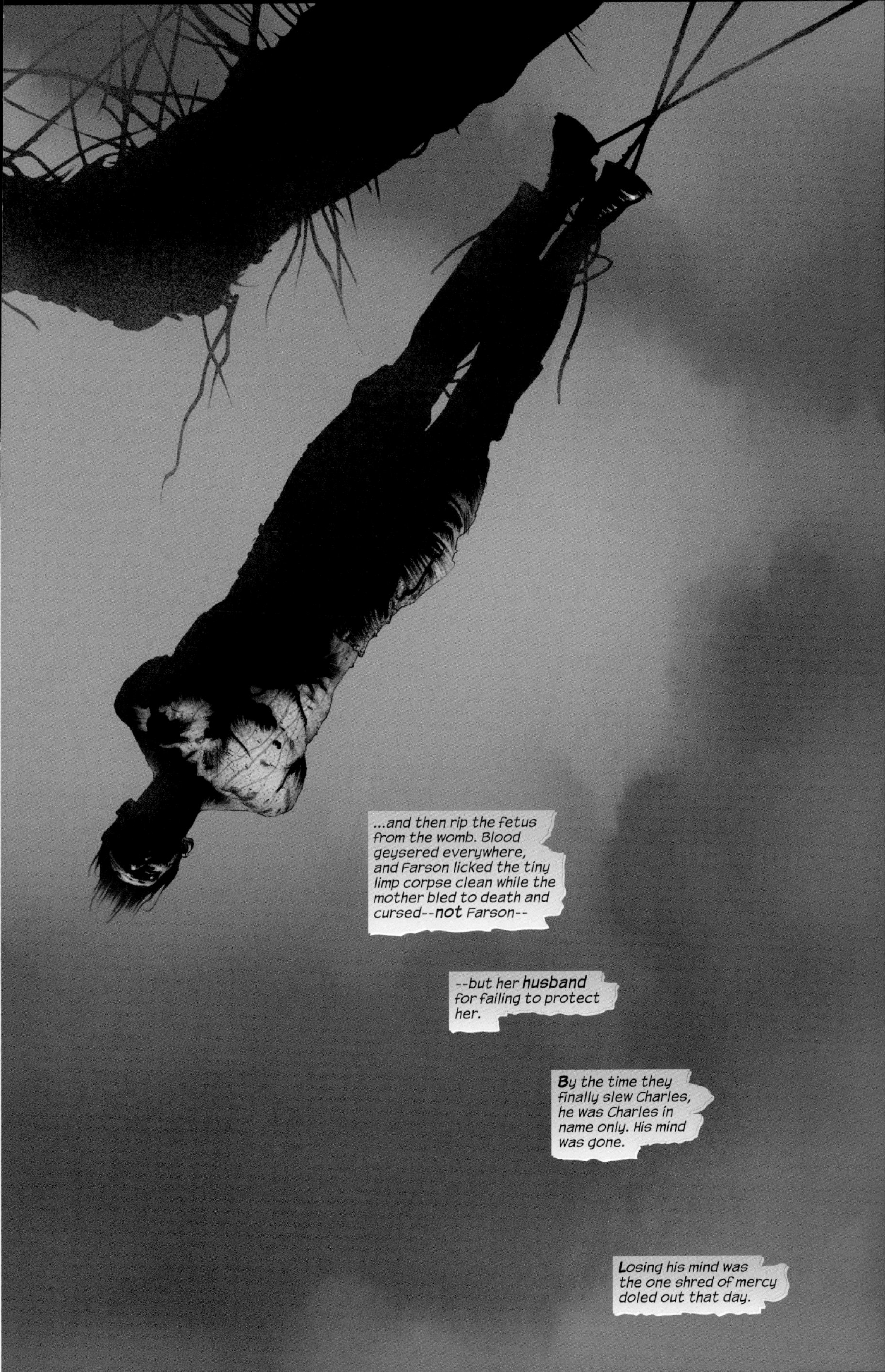
...and then rip the fetus from the womb. Blood geysered everywhere, and Farson licked the tiny limp corpse clean while the mother bled to death and cursed--not Farson--
--but her husband for failing to protect her.
By the time they finally slew Charles, he was Charles in name only. His mind was gone.
Losing his mind was the one shred of mercy doled out that day.

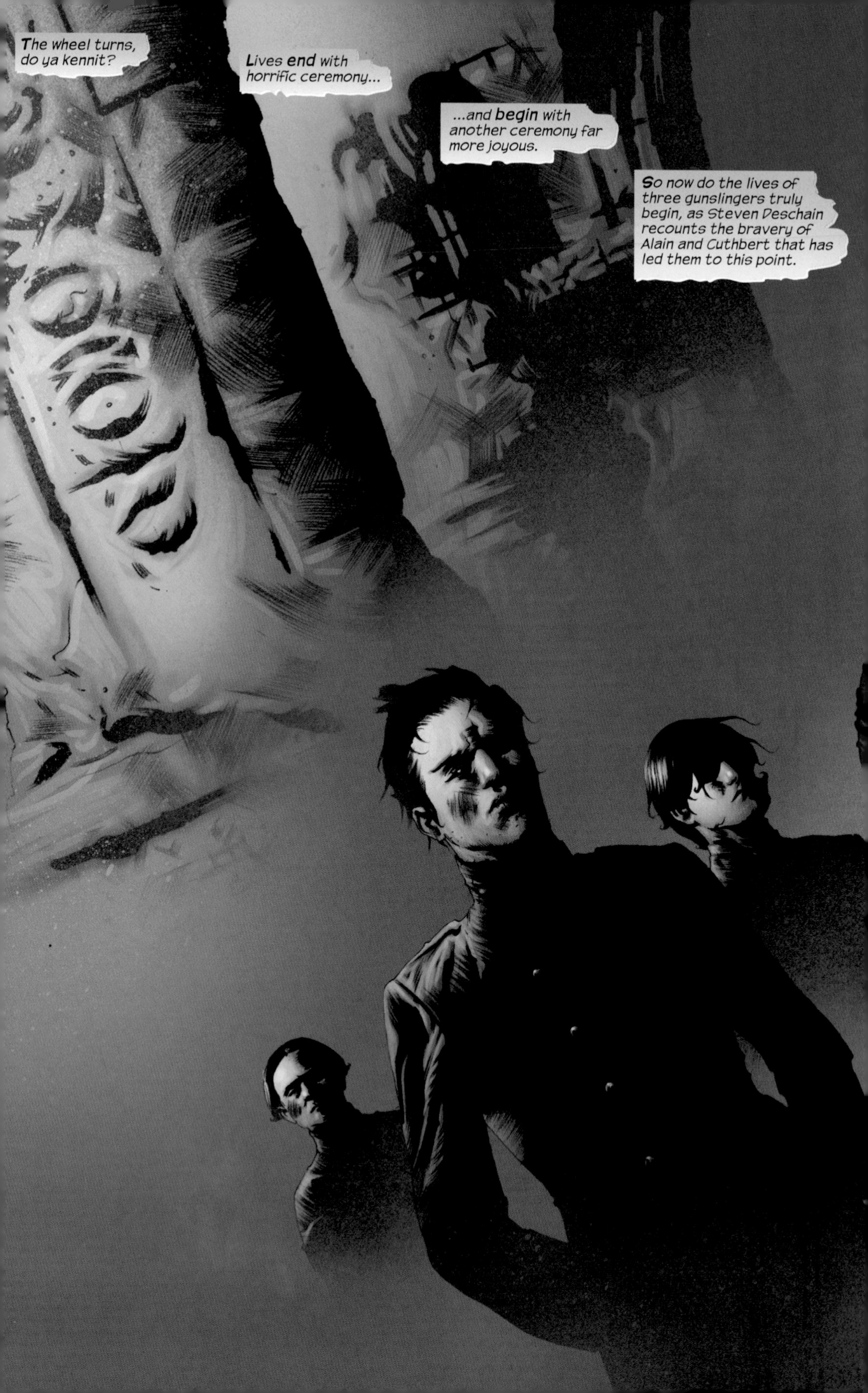
The wheel turns, do ya kennit?
Lives end with horrific ceremony...
...and begin with another ceremony far more joyous.
So now do the lives of three gunslingers truly begin, as Steven Deschain recounts the bravery of Alain and Cuthbert that has led them to this point.

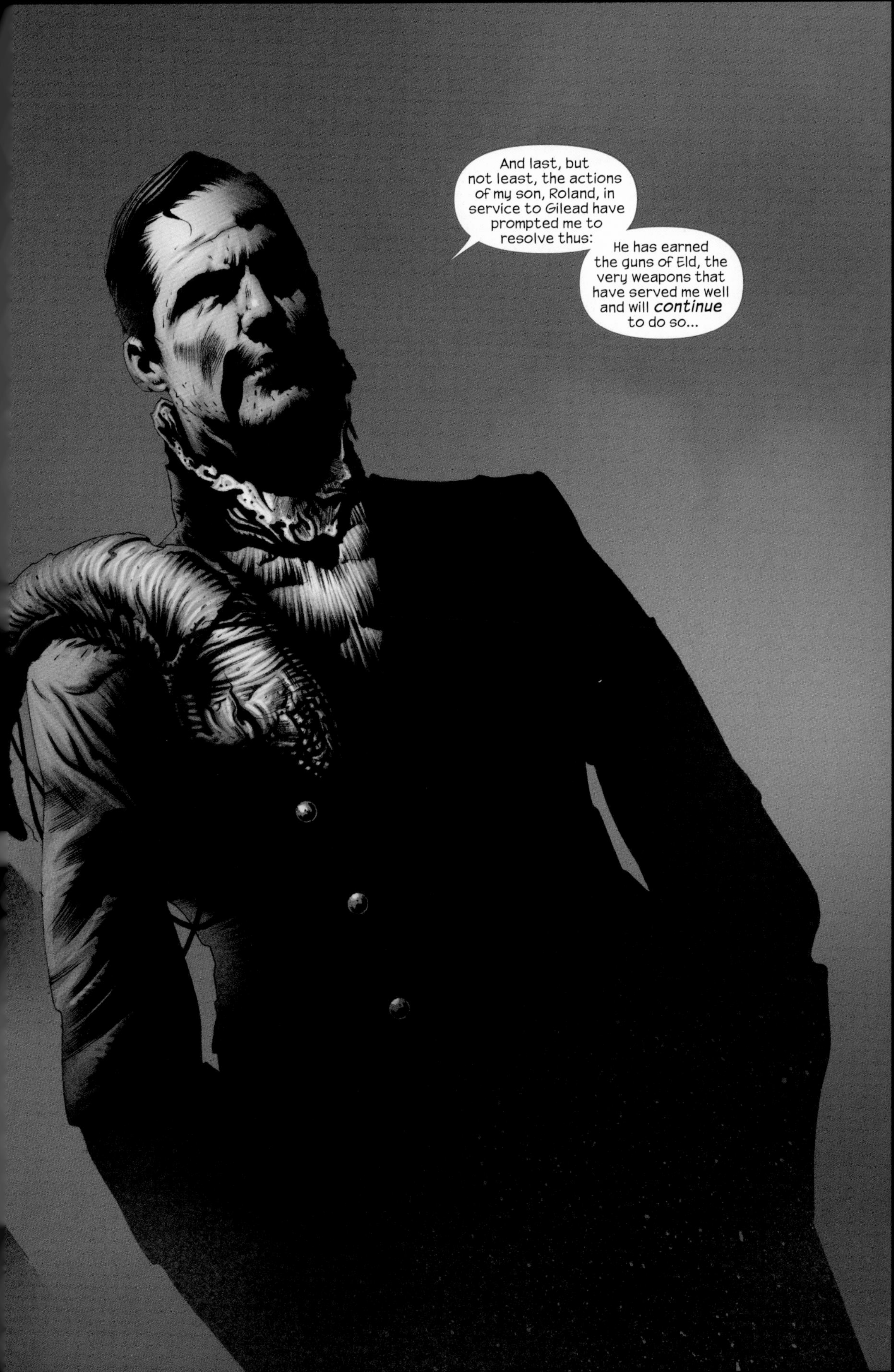
And last, but not least, the actions of my son, Roland, in service to Gilead have prompted me to resolve thus:
He has earned the guns of Eld, the very weapons that have served me well and will *continue* to do so...

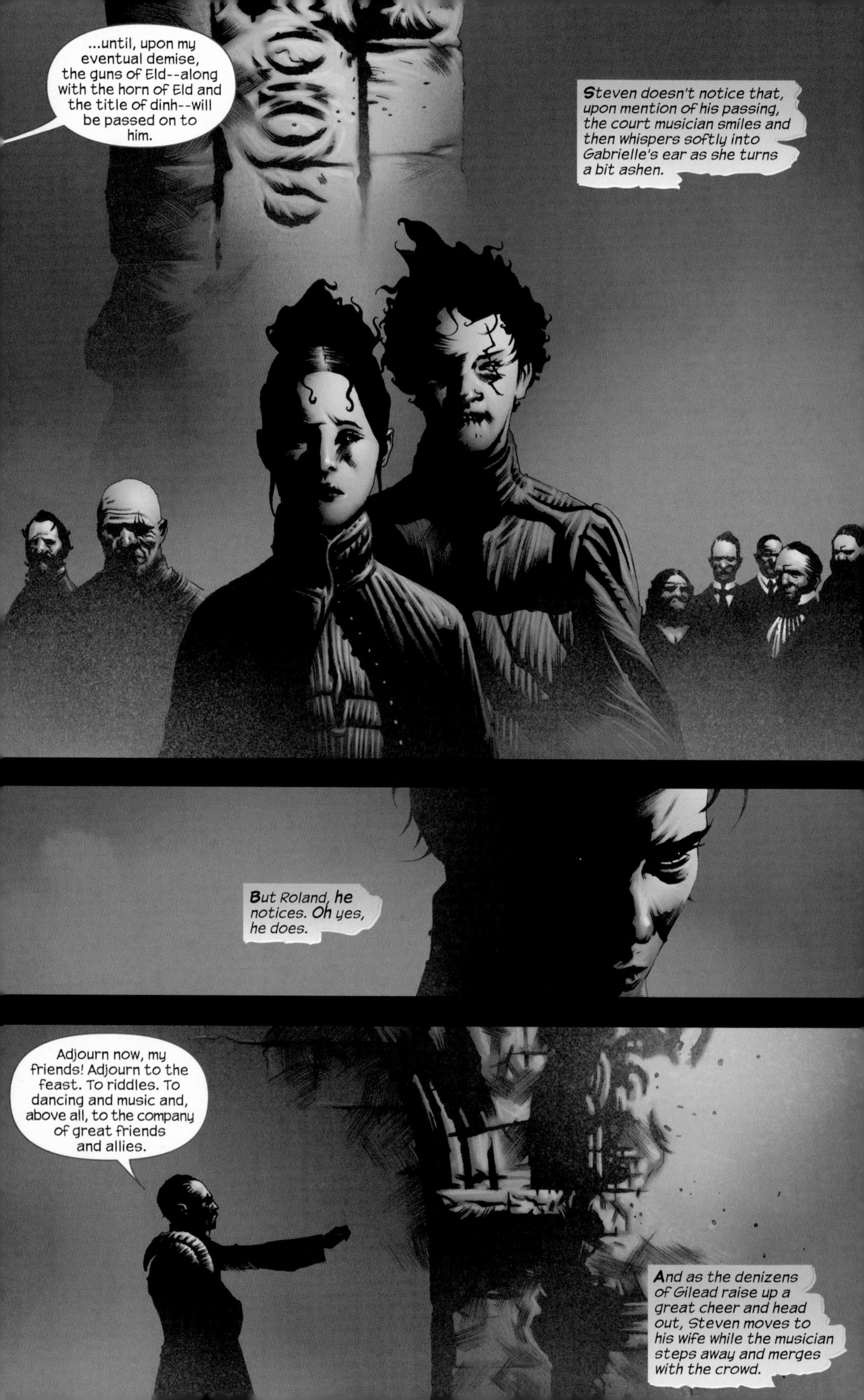
...until, upon my eventual demise, the guns of Eld--along with the horn of Eld and the title of dinh--will be passed on to him.
Steven doesn't notice that, upon mention of his passing, the court musician smiles and then whispers softly into Gabrielle's ear as she turns a bit ashen.
But Roland, he notices. Oh yes, he does.
Adjourn now, my friends! Adjourn to the feast. To riddles. To dancing and music and, above all, to the company of great friends and allies.
And as the denizens of Gilead raise up a great cheer and head out, Steven moves to his wife while the musician steps away and merges with the crowd.

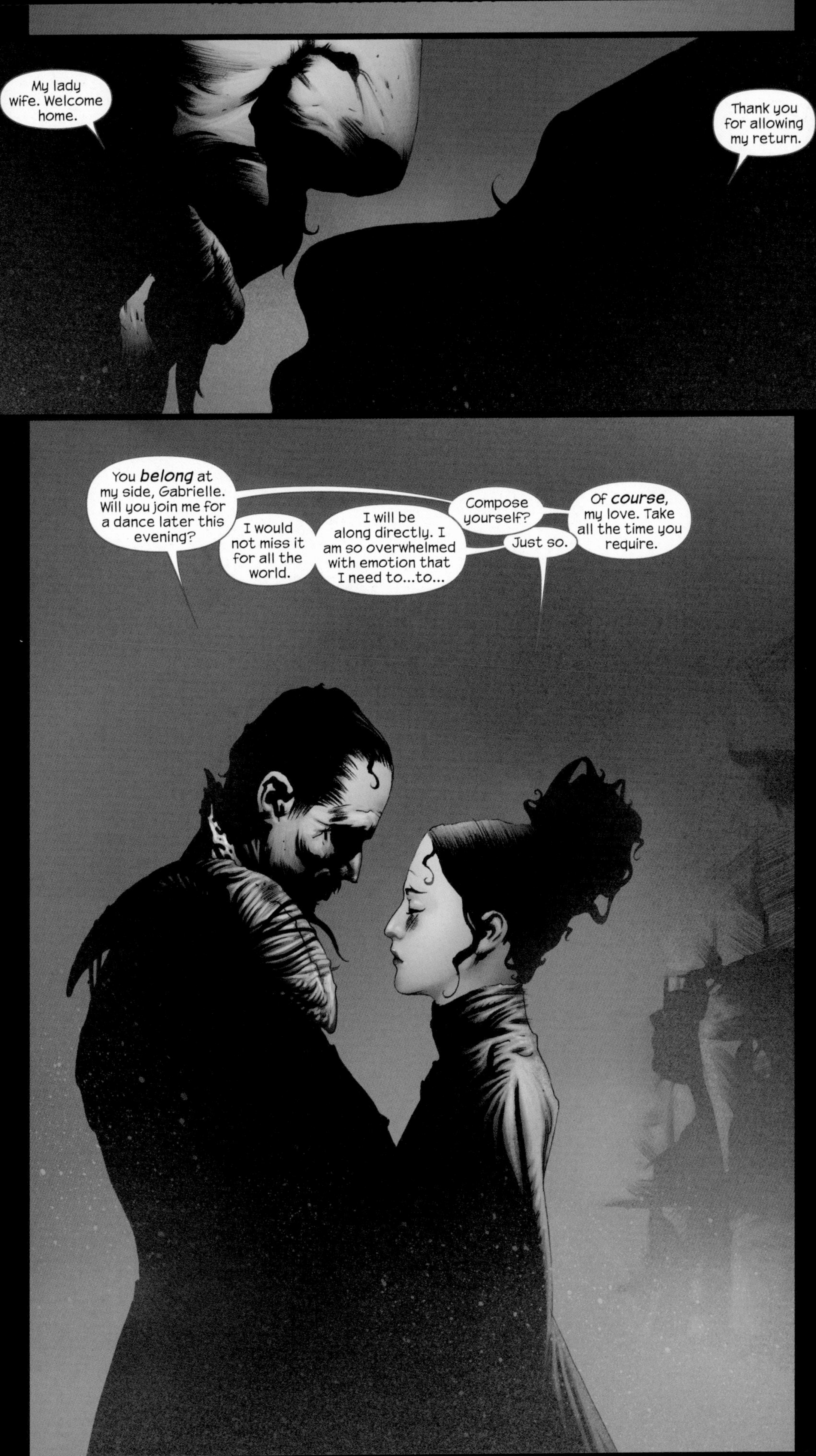
My lady wife. Welcome home.
Thank you for allowing my return.
You *belong* at my side, Gabrielle. Will you join me for a dance later this evening?
I would not miss it for all the world.
I will be along directly. I am so overwhelmed with emotion that I need to...to...
Compose yourself?
Just so.
Of *course*, my love. Take all the time you require.

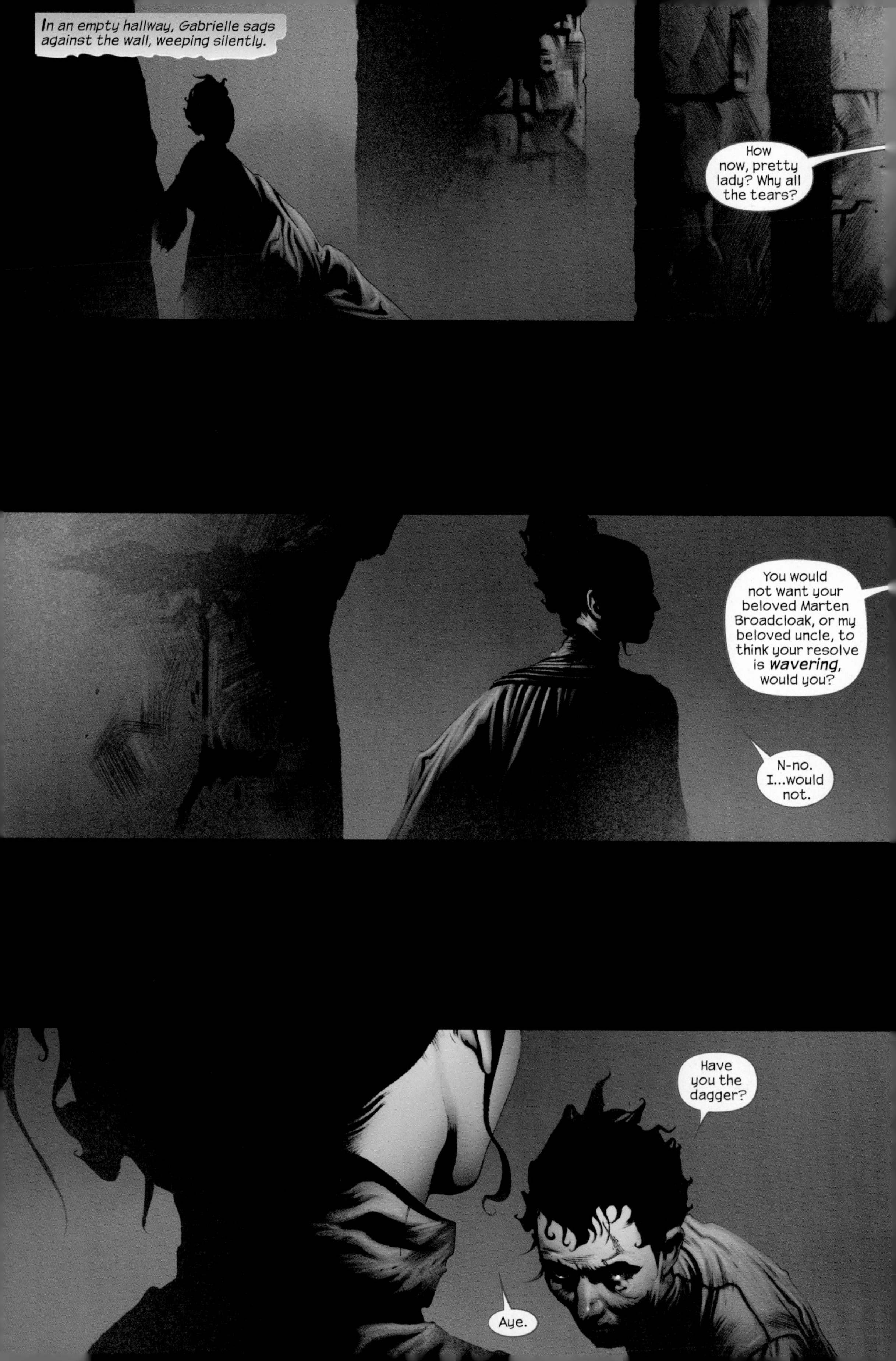

In an empty hallway, Gabrielle sags against the wall, weeping silently.
How now, pretty lady? Why all the tears?
You would not want your beloved Marten Broadcloak, or my beloved uncle, to think your resolve is *wavering*, would you?
N-no. I...would not.
Have you the dagger?
Aye.

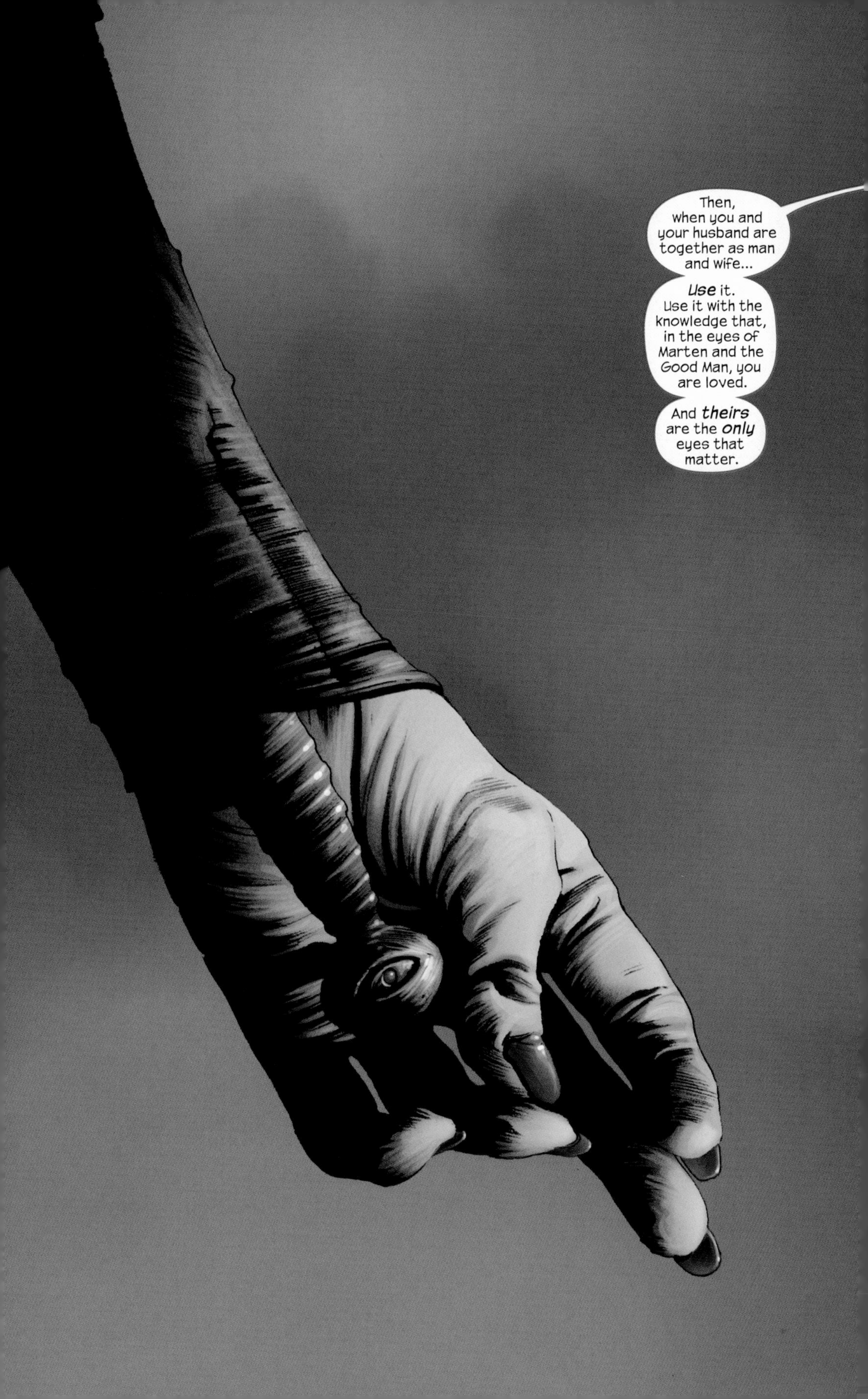
Then, when you and your husband are together as man and wife...
Use it. Use it with the knowledge that, in the eyes of Marten and the Good Man, you are loved.
And theirs are the only eyes that matter.

STEPHEN KING

THE DARK TOWER

TREACHERY

CHAPTER SIX

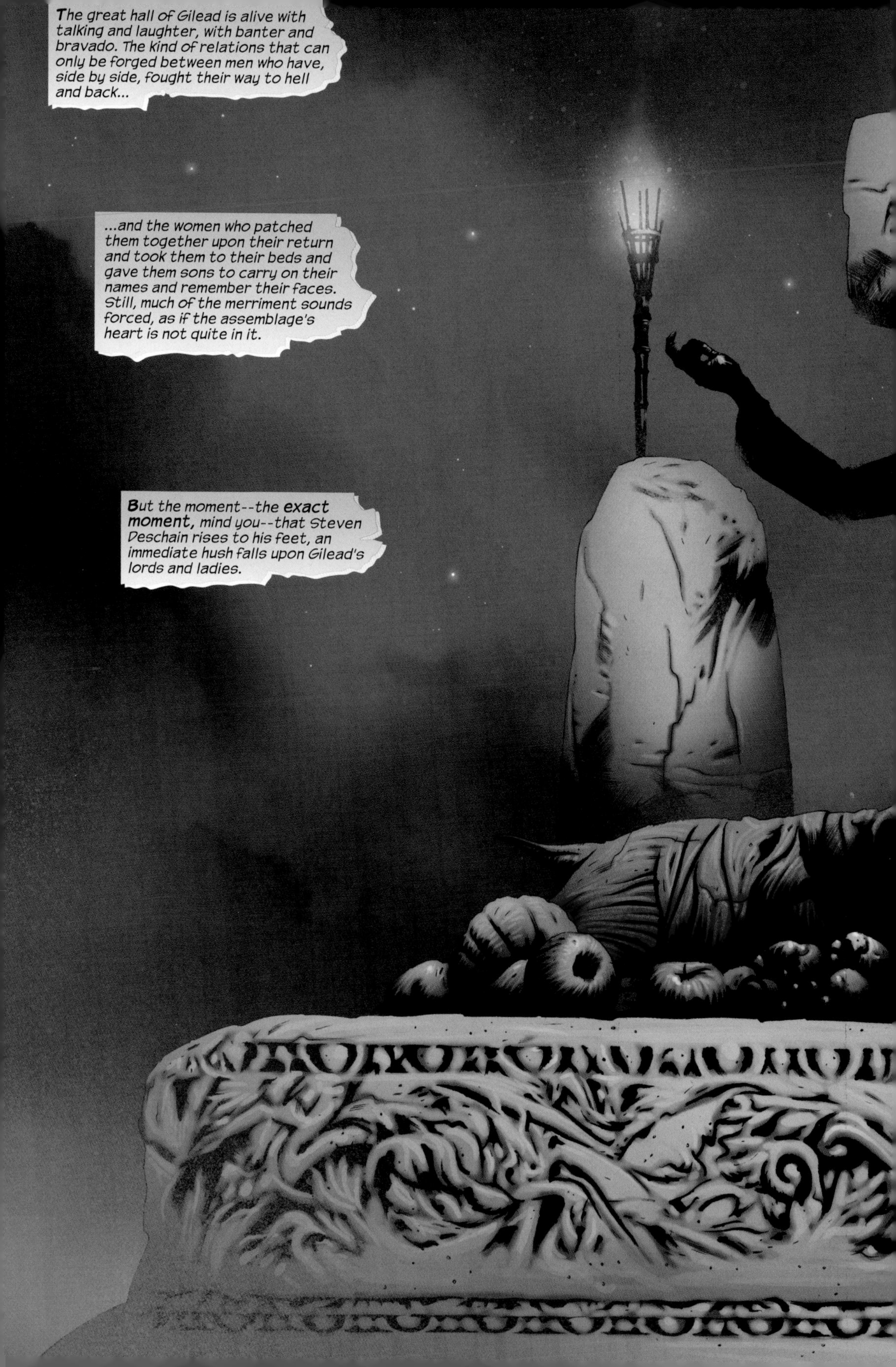
The great hall of Gilead is alive with talking and laughter, with banter and bravado. The kind of relations that can only be forged between men who have, side by side, fought their way to hell and back...
...and the women who patched them together upon their return and took them to their beds and gave them sons to carry on their names and remember their faces. Still, much of the merriment sounds forced, as if the assemblage's heart is not quite in it.
But the moment--the **exact moment,** mind you--that Steven Deschain rises to his feet, an immediate hush falls upon Gilead's lords and ladies.

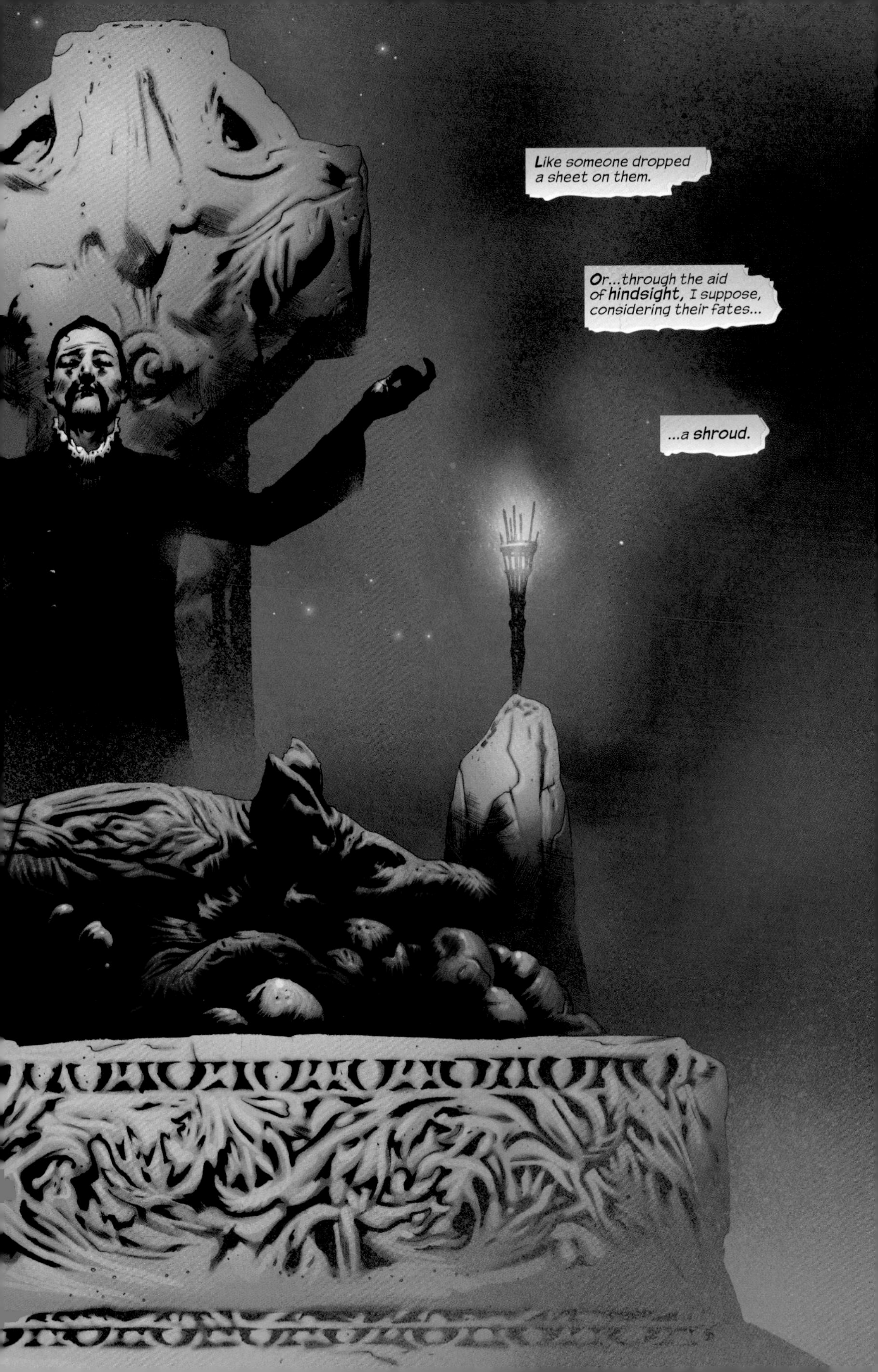
Like someone dropped a sheet on them.
Or...through the aid of hindsight, I suppose, considering their fates...
...a shroud.

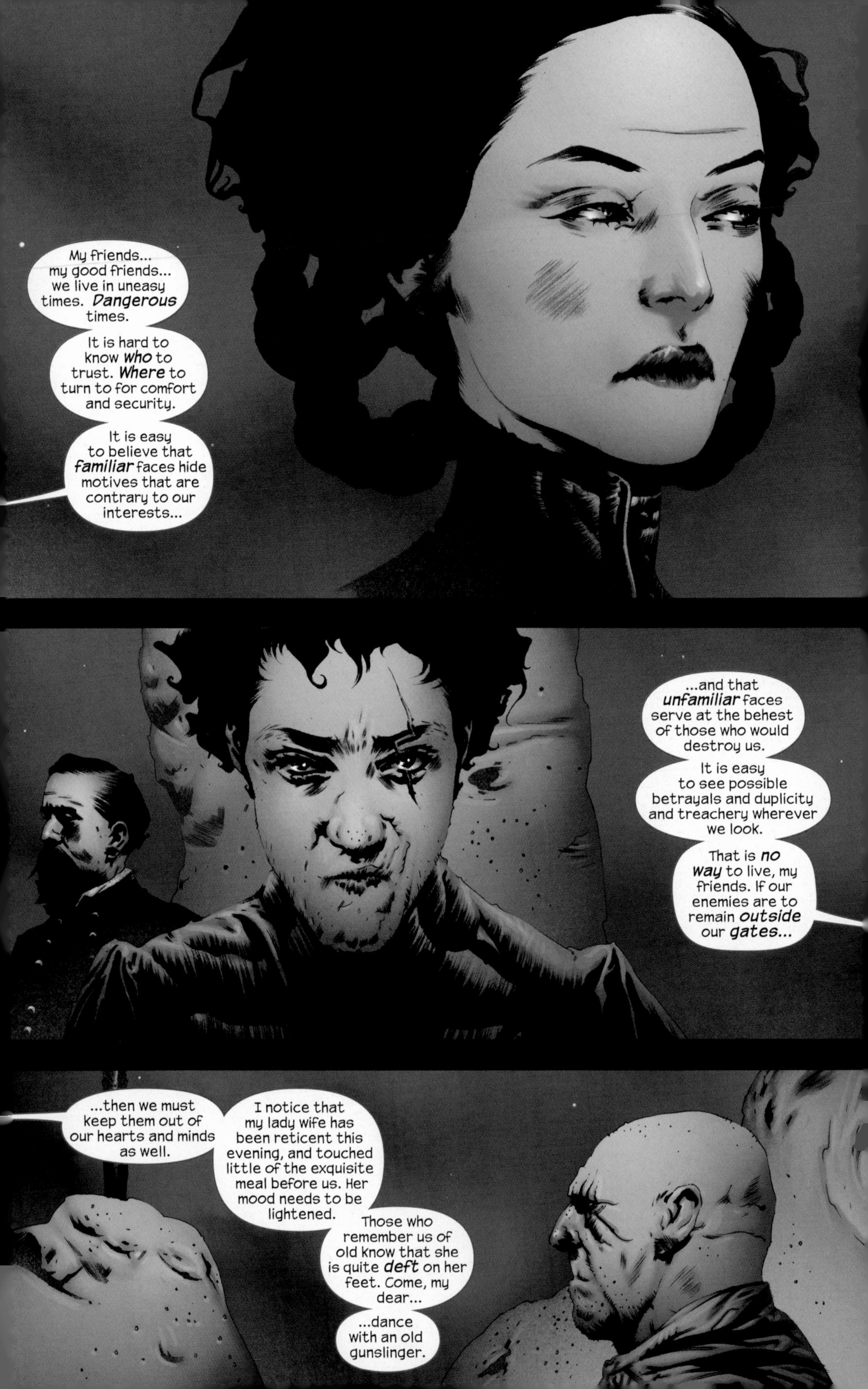
My friends... my good friends... we live in uneasy times. *Dangerous* times.
It is hard to know *who* to trust. *Where* to turn to for comfort and security.
It is easy to believe that *familiar* faces hide motives that are contrary to our interests...
...and that *unfamiliar* faces serve at the behest of those who would destroy us.
It is easy to see possible betrayals and duplicity and treachery wherever we look.
That is *no way* to live, my friends. If our enemies are to remain *outside* our *gates*...
...then we must keep them out of our hearts and minds as well.
I notice that my lady wife has been reticent this evening, and touched little of the exquisite meal before us. Her mood needs to be lightened.
Those who remember us of old know that she is quite *deft* on her feet. Come, my dear...
...dance with an old gunslinger.

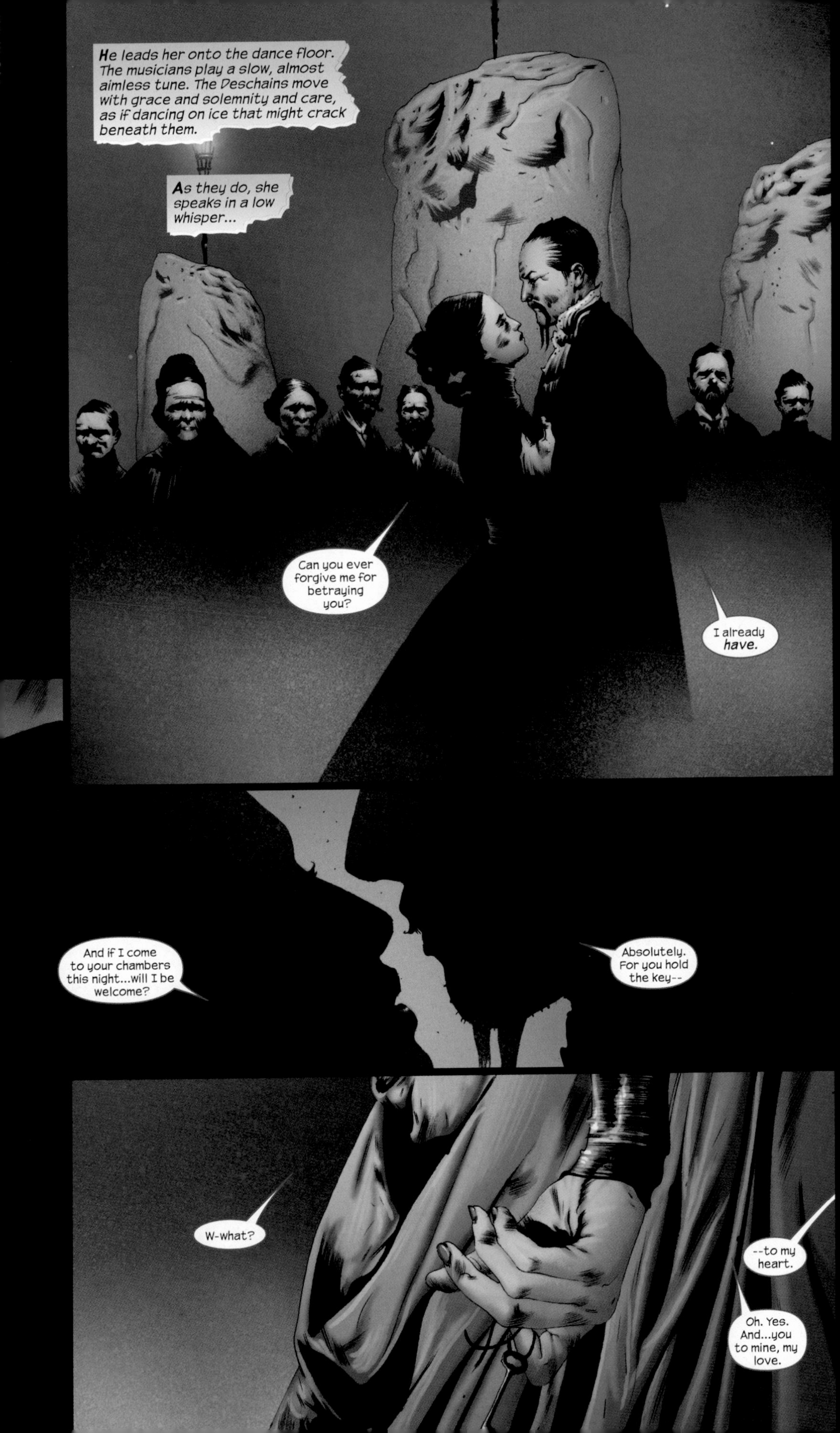
He leads her onto the dance floor. The musicians play a slow, almost aimless tune. The Deschains move with grace and solemnity and care, as if dancing on ice that might crack beneath them.
As they do, she speaks in a low whisper...
Can you ever forgive me for betraying you?
I already *have.*
And if I come to your chambers this night...will I be welcome?
Absolutely. For you hold the key--
W-what?
--to my heart.
Oh. Yes. And...you to mine, my love.

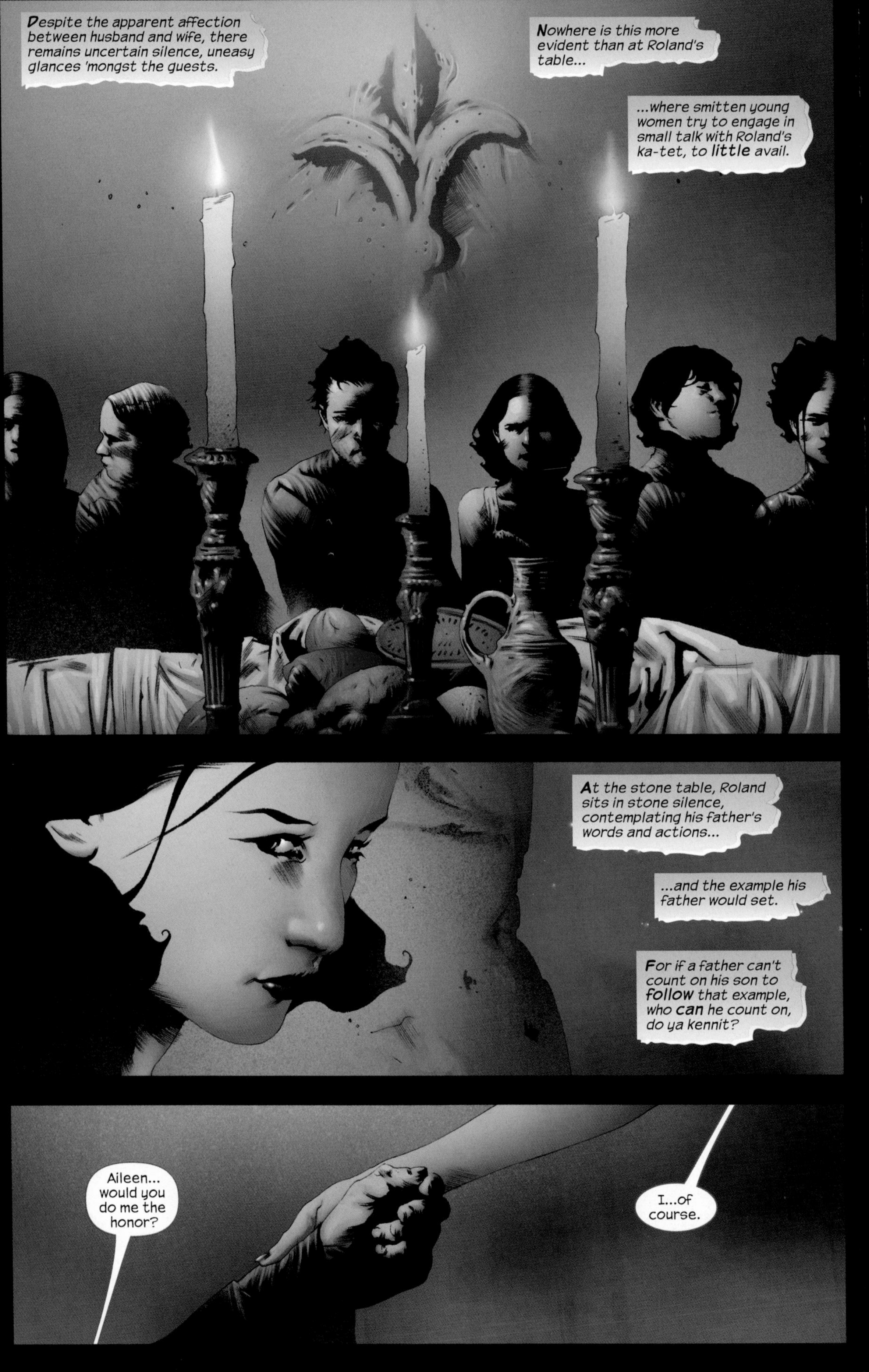
Despite the apparent affection between husband and wife, there remains uncertain silence, uneasy glances 'mongst the guests.
Nowhere is this more evident than at Roland's table...
...where smitten young women try to engage in small talk with Roland's ka-tet, to little avail.
At the stone table, Roland sits in stone silence, contemplating his father's words and actions...
...and the example his father would set.
For if a father can't count on his son to follow that example, who can he count on, do ya kennit?
Aileen... would you do me the honor?
I...of course.

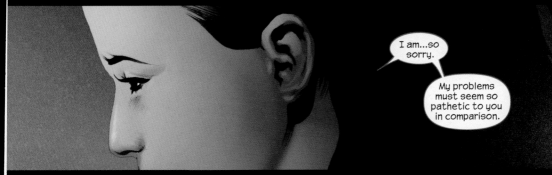

Thank you for asking. I... did not think you much *liked* me.

I dislike that others would force us together. But I like *you* well enough. I always have. Even if you *do* think your place is on the battlefield.

My life, and my people's interests, are no less precious to *me* than yours are to *you*. Why should I be less entitled to fight for them?

Fight as you did in Hambry? How *exciting* that must have been for you.

"*Exciting*." You make it sound so--

It was *bloody*, Aileen. Bloody and brutal, and the wrong people died. The wrong...*person*...died.

Who *was* she? It...*was*...a she, I take it...?

Her name was Susan. They burned her on a Charyou Tree fire.

Her last words were, "*Roland, I love thee*," screaming like a dying hawk. And in my own way, I died as well.

I am...so sorry.

My problems must seem so pathetic to you in comparison.

... Would you like to get some fresh air?

Desperately.

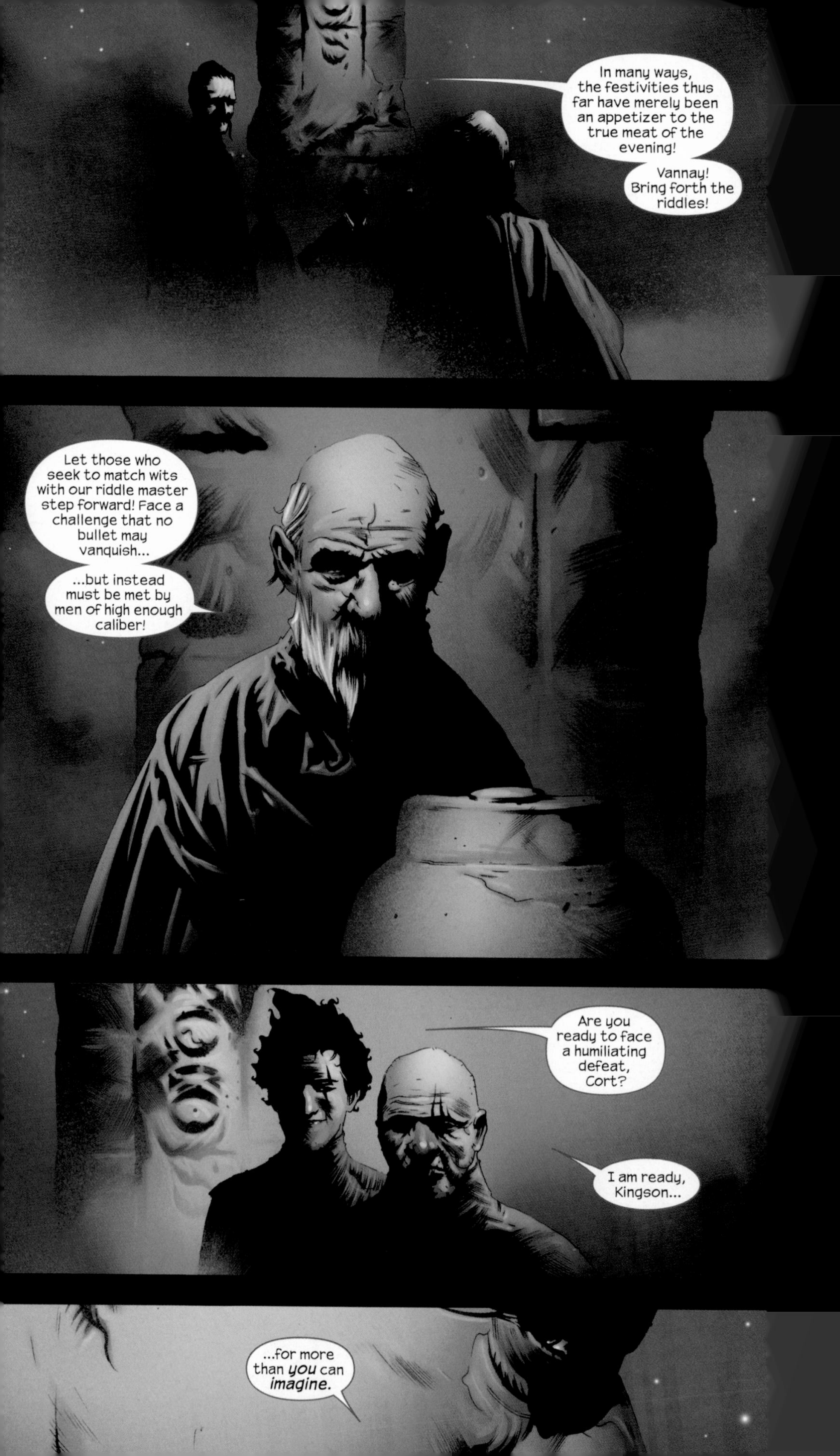

In many ways, the festivities thus far have merely been an appetizer to the true meat of the evening!
Vannay! Bring forth the riddles!
Let those who seek to match wits with our riddle master step forward! Face a challenge that no bullet may vanquish...
...but instead must be met by men of high enough caliber!
Are you ready to face a humiliating defeat, Cort?
I am ready, Kingson...
...for more than *you* can *imagine.*

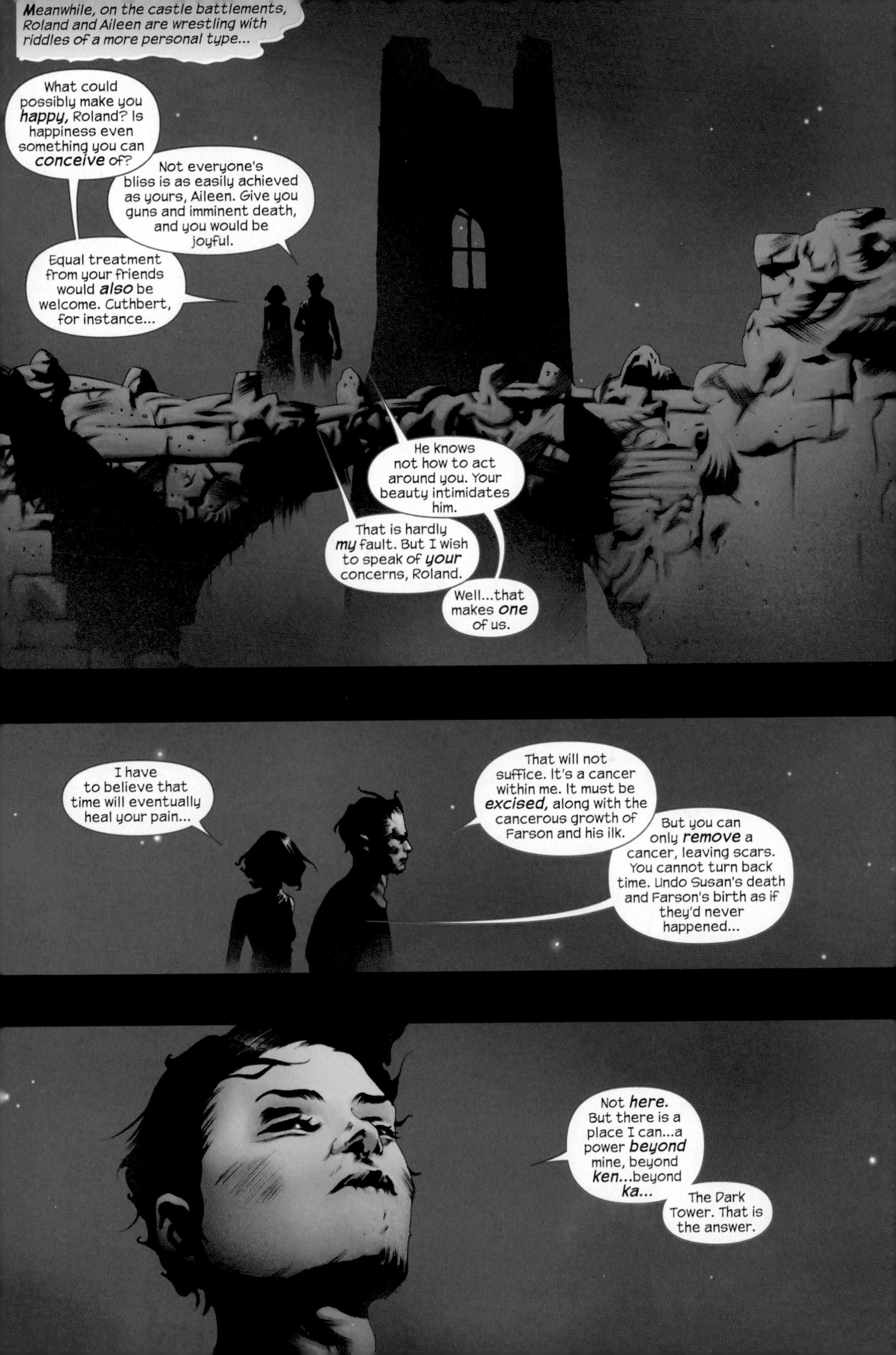
Meanwhile, on the castle battlements, Roland and Aileen are wrestling with riddles of a more personal type...
What could possibly make you happy, Roland? Is happiness even something you can conceive of?
Not everyone's bliss is as easily achieved as yours, Aileen. Give you guns and imminent death, and you would be joyful.
Equal treatment from your friends would also be welcome. Cuthbert, for instance...
He knows not how to act around you. Your beauty intimidates him.
That is hardly my fault. But I wish to speak of your concerns, Roland.
Well...that makes one of us.
I have to believe that time will eventually heal your pain...
That will not suffice. It's a cancer within me. It must be excised, along with the cancerous growth of Farson and his ilk.
But you can only remove a cancer, leaving scars. You cannot turn back time. Undo Susan's death and Farson's birth as if they'd never happened...
Not here. But there is a place I can...a power beyond mine, beyond ken...beyond ka...
The Dark Tower. That is the answer.

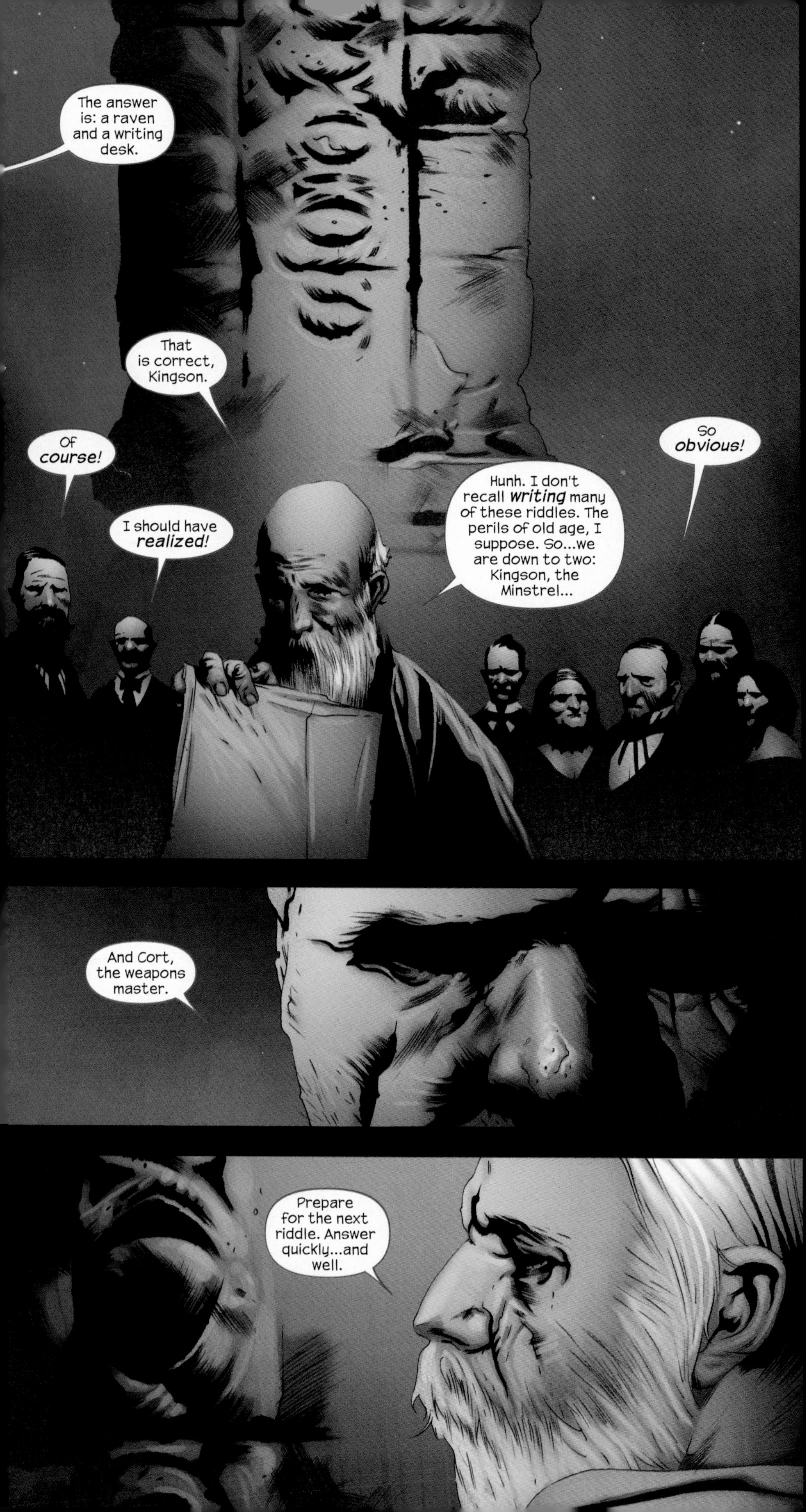

The answer is: a raven and a writing desk.
That is correct, Kingson.
Of *course!*
I should have *realized!*
Hunh. I don't recall *writing* many of these riddles. The perils of old age, I suppose. So...we are down to two: Kingson, the Minstrel...
So *obvious!*
And Cort, the weapons master.
Prepare for the next riddle. Answer quickly...and well.

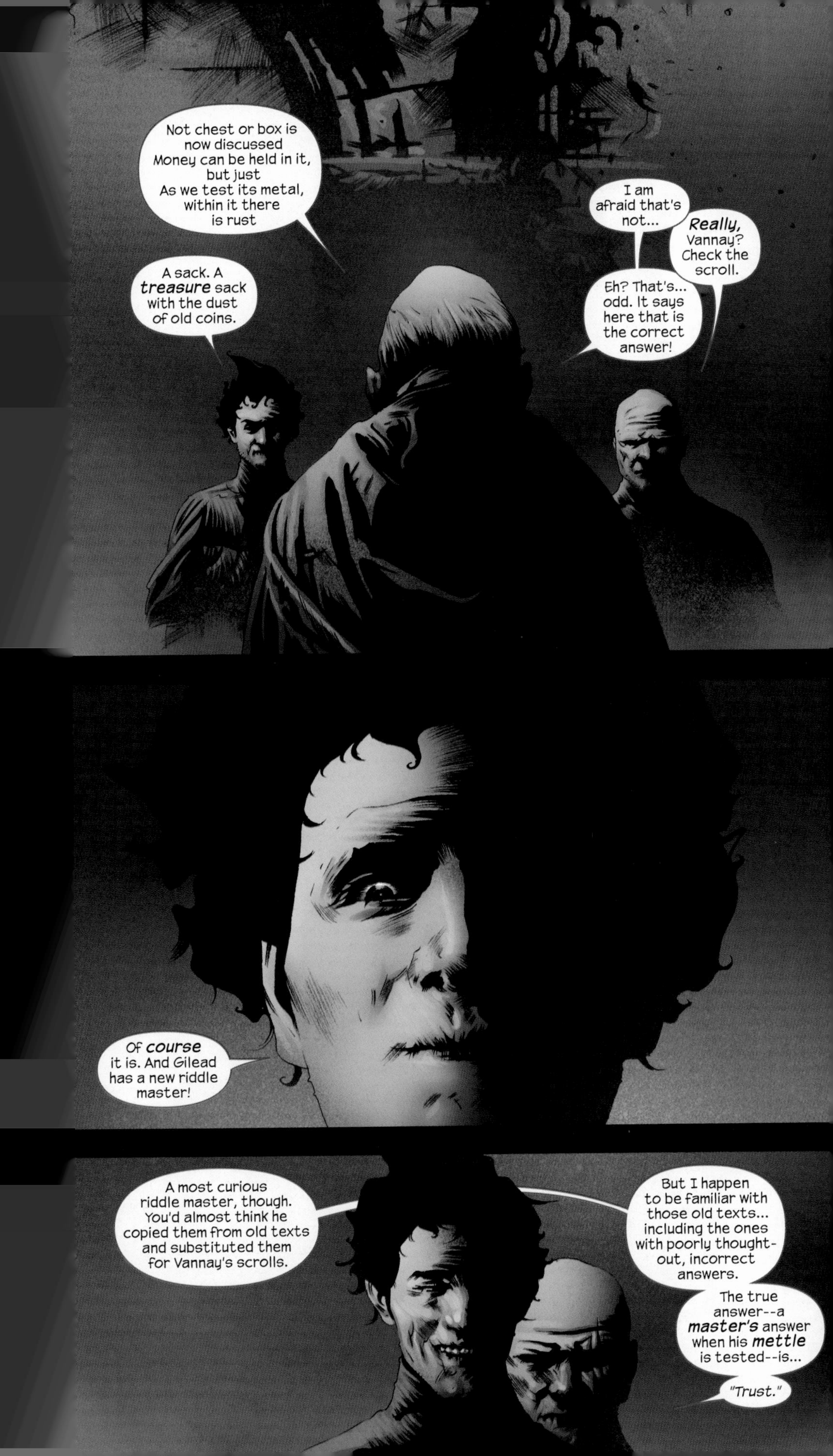
Not chest or box is now discussed Money can be held in it, but just As we test its metal, within it there is rust
A sack. A **treasure** sack with the dust of old coins.
I am afraid that's not...
Really, Vannay? Check the scroll.
Eh? That's... odd. It says here that is the correct answer!
Of **course** it is. And Gilead has a new riddle master!
A most curious riddle master, though. You'd almost think he copied them from old texts and substituted them for Vannay's scrolls.
But I happen to be familiar with those old texts... including the ones with poorly thought-out, incorrect answers.
The true answer--a **master's** answer when his **mettle** is tested--is...
"Trust."

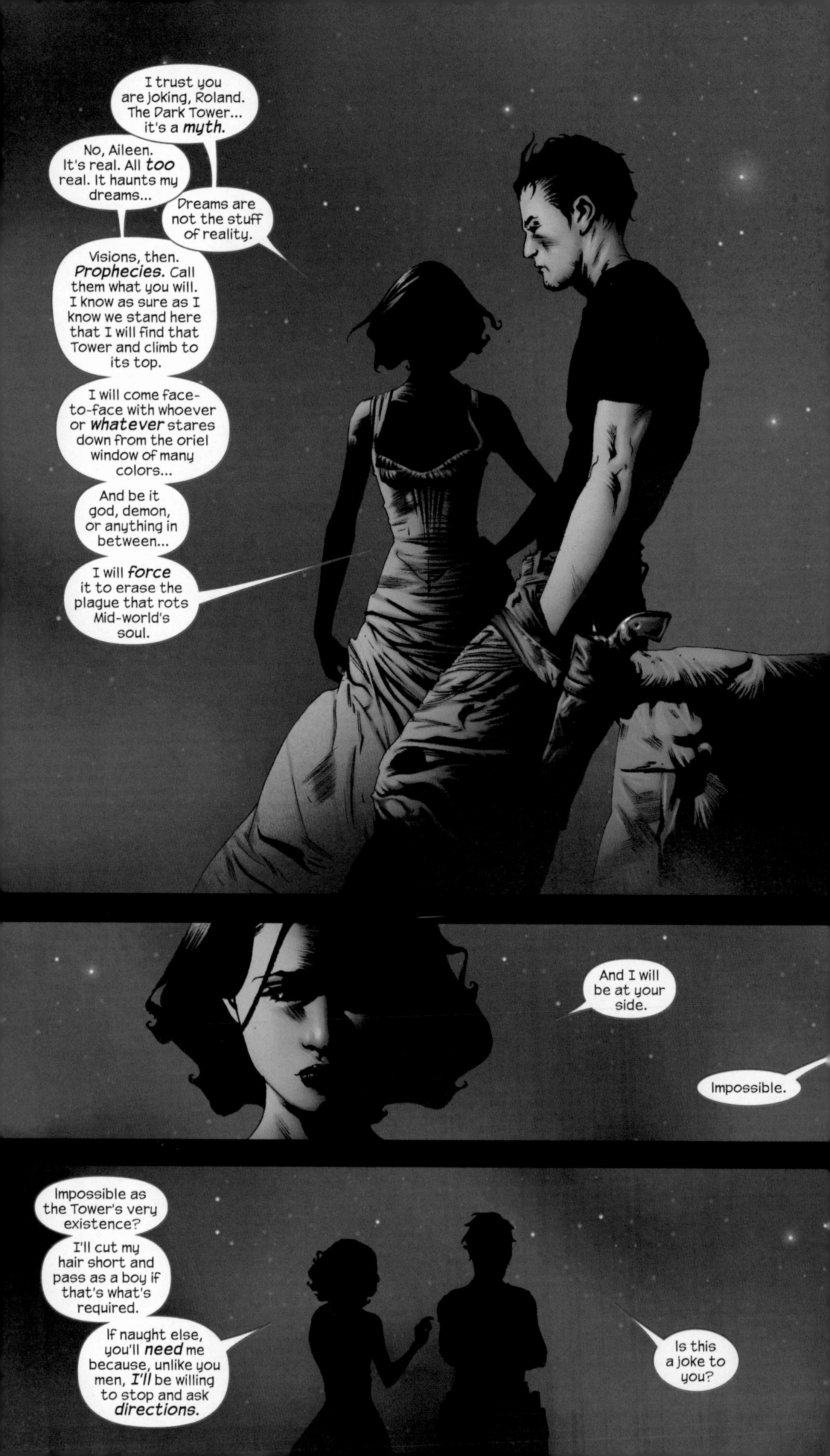

I trust you are joking, Roland. The Dark Tower... it's a *myth.*
No, Aileen. It's real. All *too* real. It haunts my dreams...
Dreams are not the stuff of reality.
Visions, then. *Prophecies.* Call them what you will. I know as sure as I know we stand here that I will find that Tower and climb to its top.
I will come face-to-face with whoever or *whatever* stares down from the oriel window of many colors...
And be it god, demon, or anything in between...
I will *force* it to erase the plague that rots Mid-world's soul.
And I will be at your side.
Impossible.
Impossible as the Tower's very existence?
I'll cut my hair short and pass as a boy if that's what's required.
If naught else, you'll *need* me because, unlike you men, *I'll* be willing to stop and ask *directions.*
Is this a joke to you?

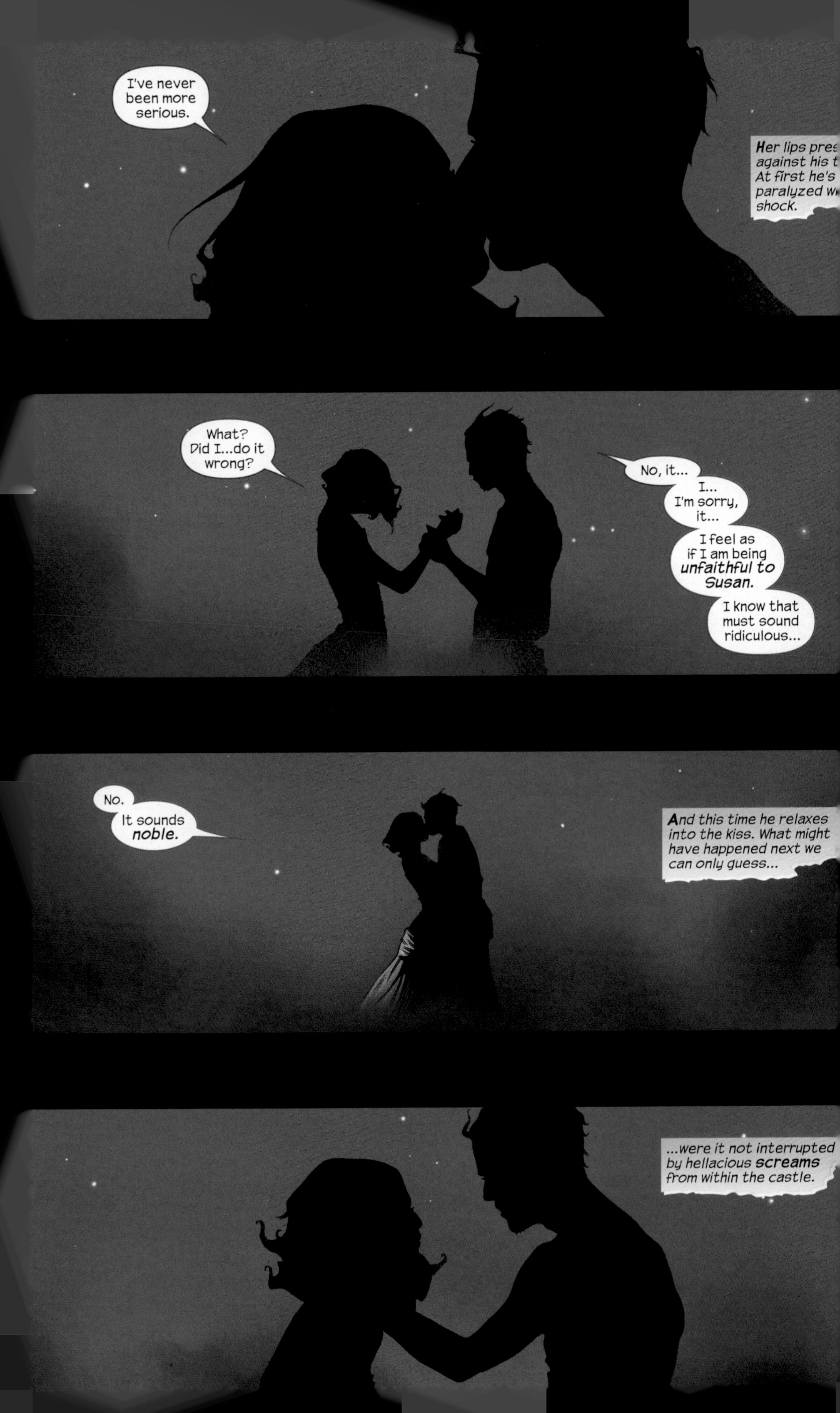
I've never been more serious.
Her lips pres against his t At first he's paralyzed w shock.
What? Did I...do it wrong?
No, it...
I... I'm sorry, it...
I feel as if I am being *unfaithful to Susan.*
I know that must sound ridiculous...
No.
It sounds *noble.*
And this time he relaxes into the kiss. What might have happened next we can only guess...
...were it not interrupted by hellacious **screams** from within the castle.

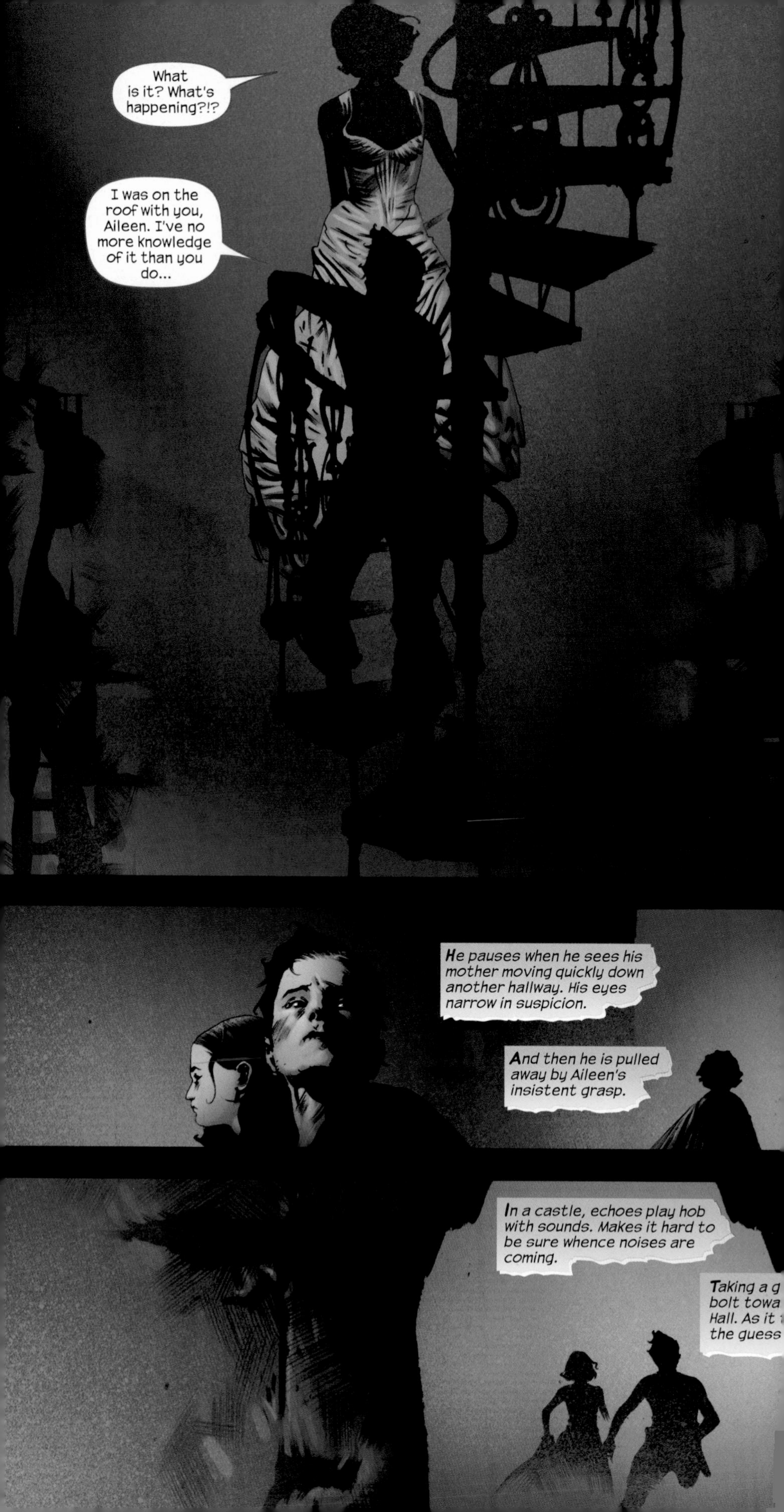
What is it? What's happening?!?
I was on the roof with you, Aileen. I've no more knowledge of it than you do...
He pauses when he sees his mother moving quickly down another hallway. His eyes narrow in suspicion.
And then he is pulled away by Aileen's insistent grasp.
In a castle, echoes play hob with sounds. Makes it hard to be sure whence noises are coming.
Taking a g
bolt towa
Hall. As it
the guess

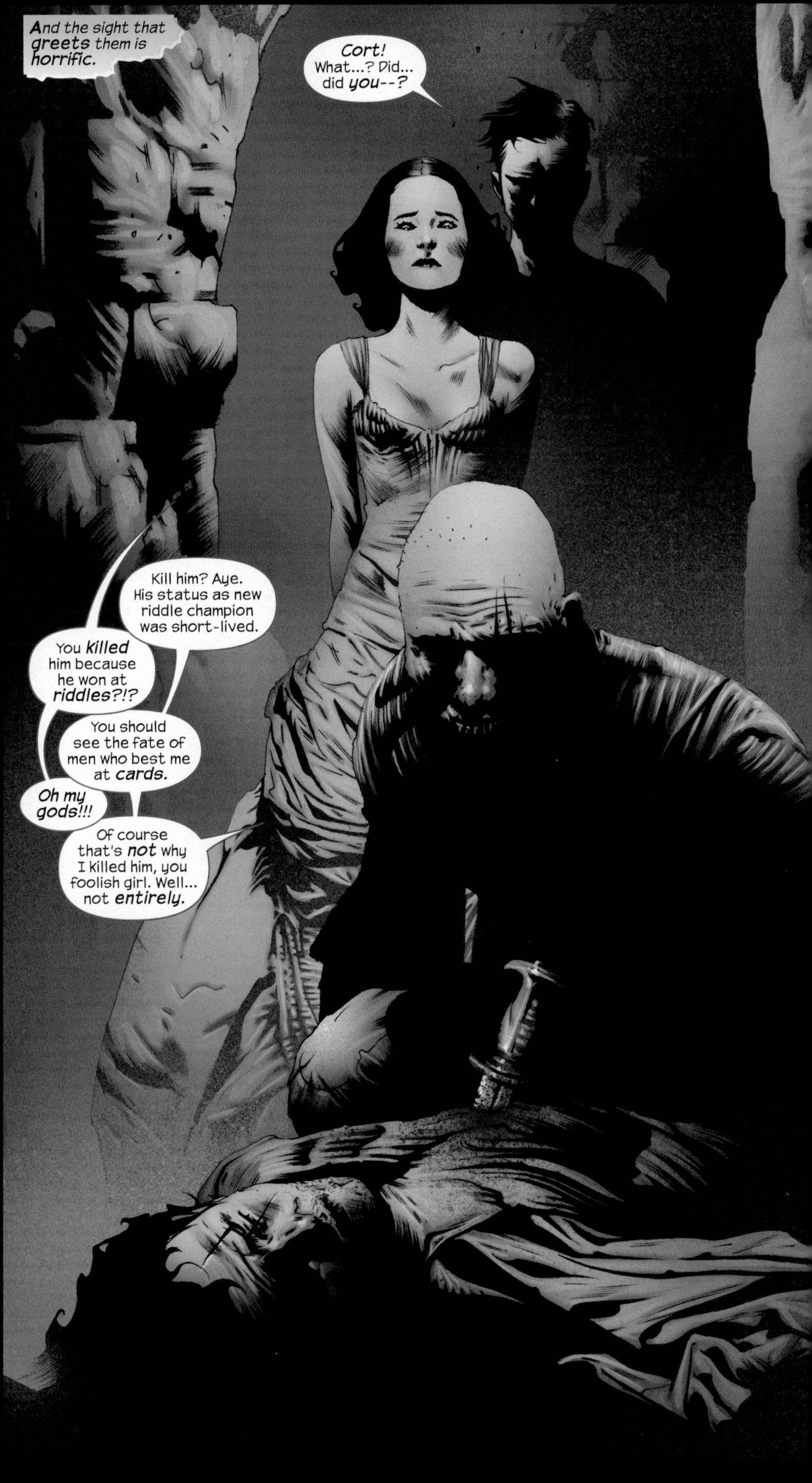
And the sight that greets them is horrific.
Cort! What...? Did... did you--?
Kill him? Aye. His status as new riddle champion was short-lived.
You killed him because he won at riddles?!?
You should see the fate of men who best me at cards.
Oh my gods!!!
Of course that's not why I killed him, you foolish girl. Well... not entirely.

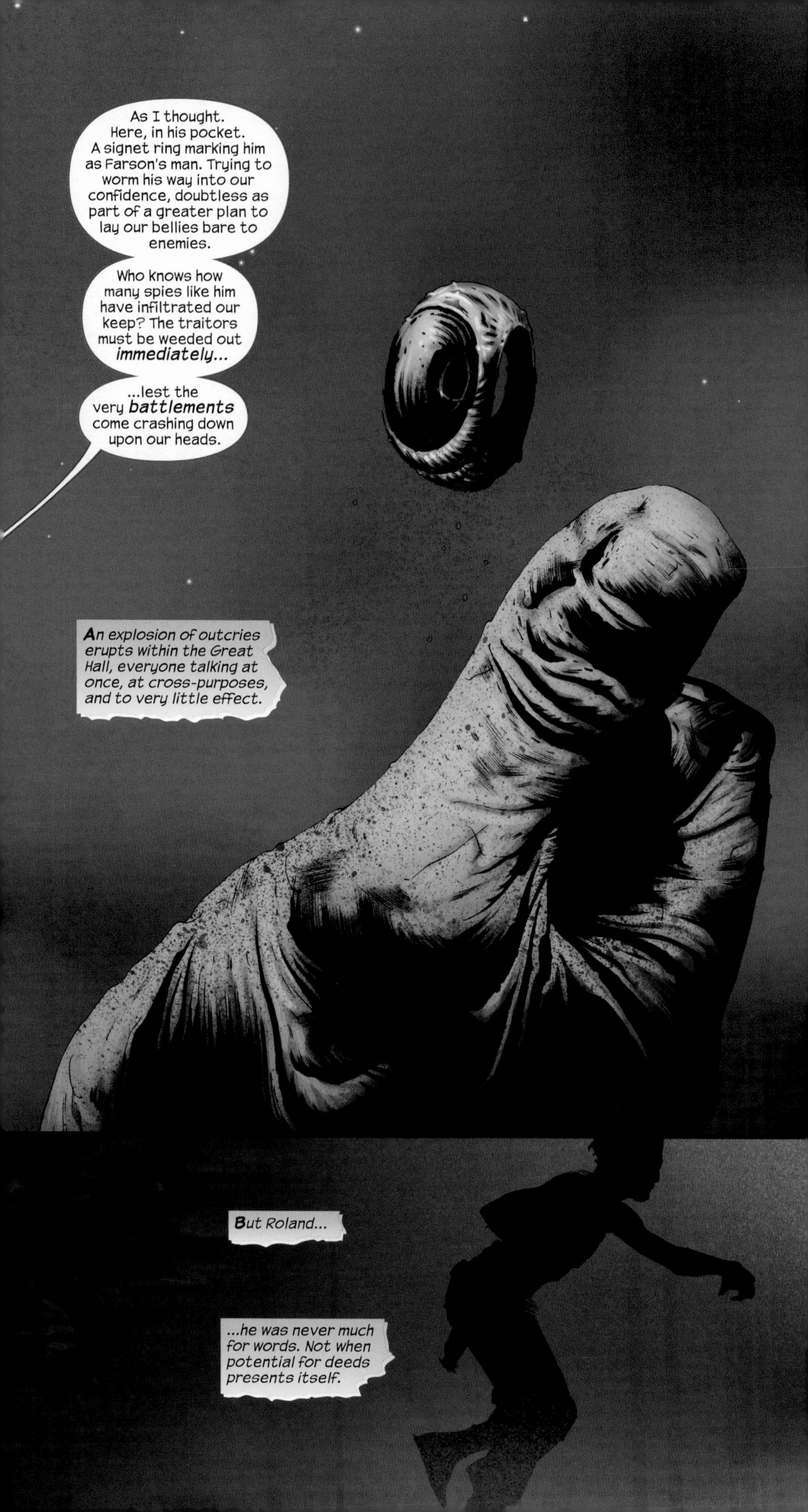
As I thought. Here, in his pocket. A signet ring marking him as Farson's man. Trying to worm his way into our confidence, doubtless as part of a greater plan to lay our bellies bare to enemies.
Who knows how many spies like him have infiltrated our keep? The traitors must be weeded out *immediately*...
...lest the very *battlements* come crashing down upon our heads.
An explosion of outcries erupts within the Great Hall, everyone talking at once, at cross-purposes, and to very little effect.
But Roland...
...he was never much for words. Not when potential for deeds presents itself.

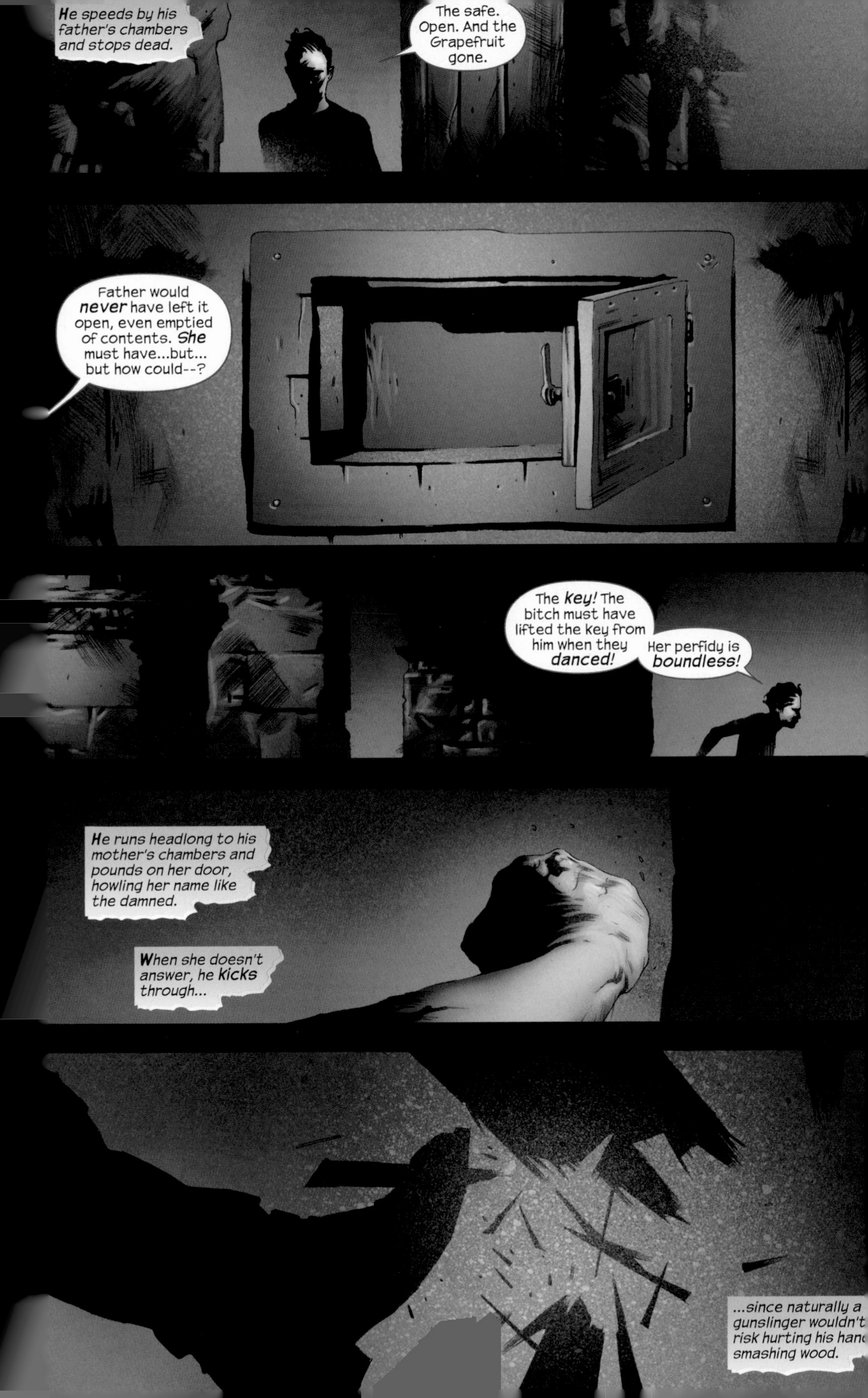
He speeds by his father's chambers and stops dead.
The safe. Open. And the Grapefruit gone.
Father would never have left it open, even emptied of contents. She must have...but... but how could--?
The key! The bitch must have lifted the key from him when they danced!
Her perfidy is boundless!
He runs headlong to his mother's chambers and pounds on her door, howling her name like the damned.
When she doesn't answer, he kicks through...
...since naturally a gunslinger wouldn't risk hurting his hand smashing wood.

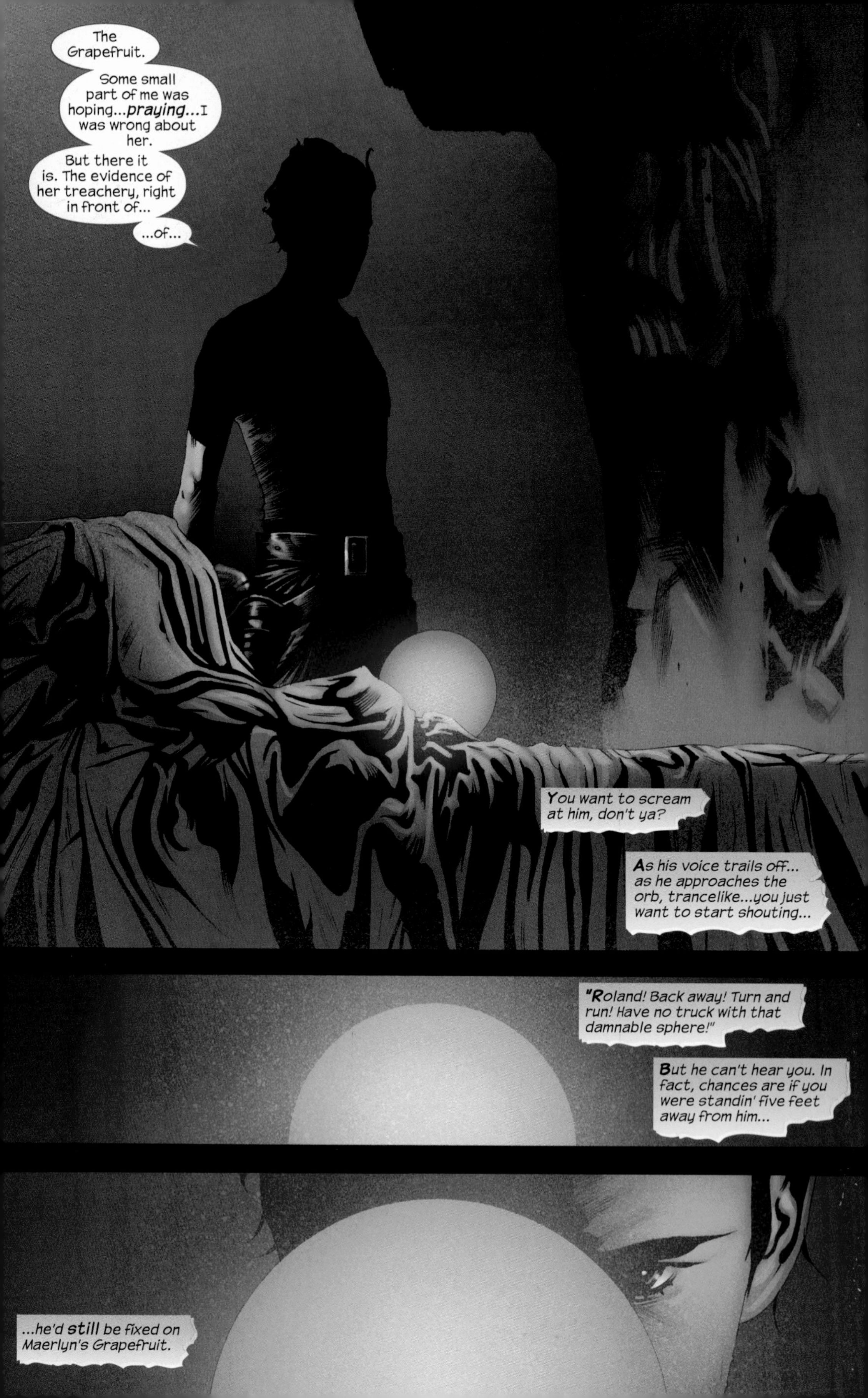
The Grapefruit.
Some small part of me was hoping...praying...I was wrong about her.
But there it is. The evidence of her treachery, right in front of...
...of...
You want to scream at him, don't ya?
As his voice trails off... as he approaches the orb, trancelike...you just want to start shouting...
"Roland! Back away! Turn and run! Have no truck with that damnable sphere!"
But he can't hear you. In fact, chances are if you were standin' five feet away from him...
...he'd still be fixed on Maerlyn's Grapefruit.

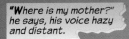

"Where is my mother?" he says, his voice hazy and distant.

The sphere provides no answer...

...but instead Roland **sees** something reflected in the sphere's surface.

Rhea of the Cöos, creeping up behind him, a garrote in her hand...

...preparing to dispatch him in the exact same way she intends to kill his father.

And the gunslinger's credo burns through his mind as if in letters of flame, and he condenses it into a defiant battlecry...

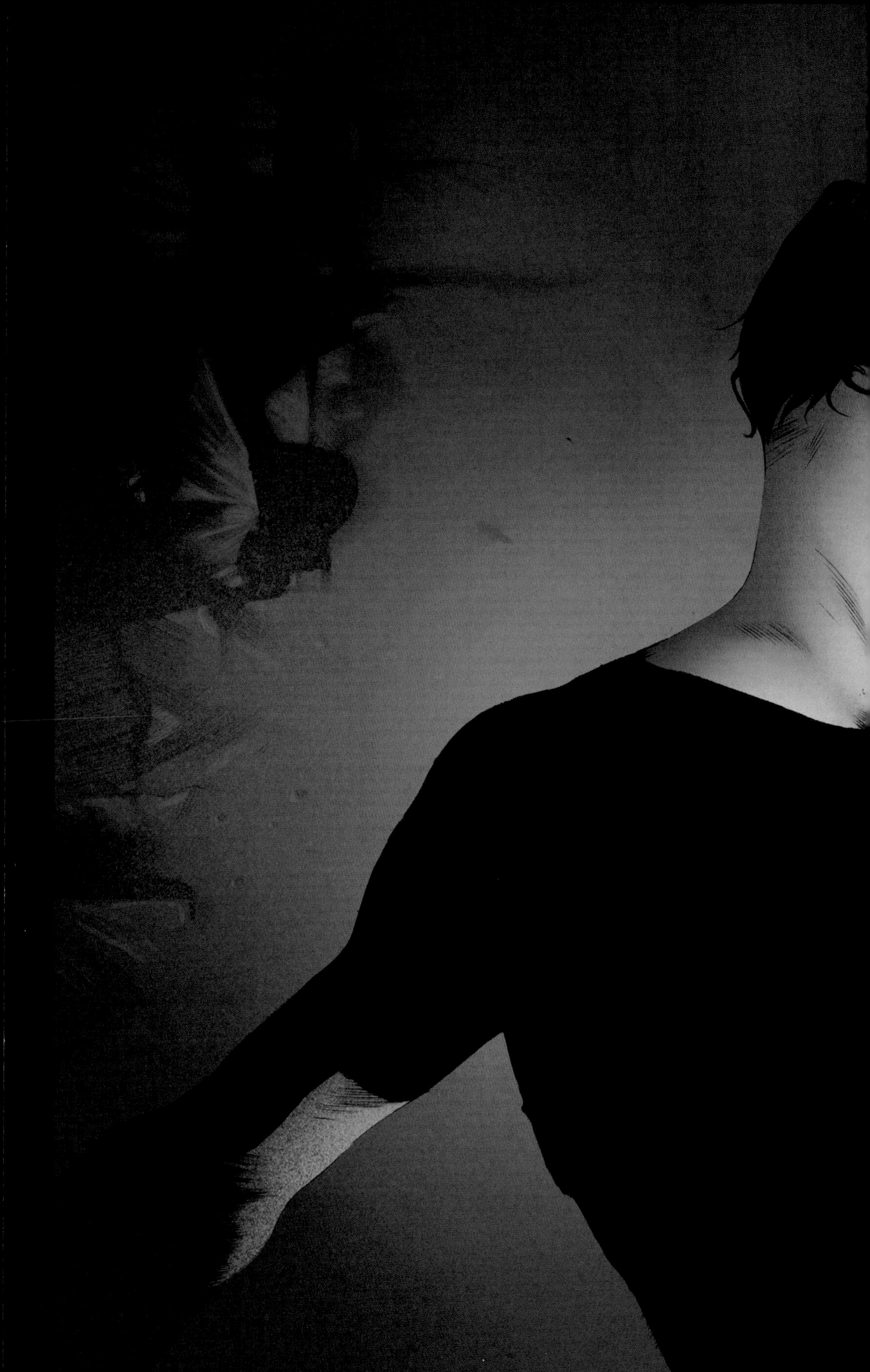

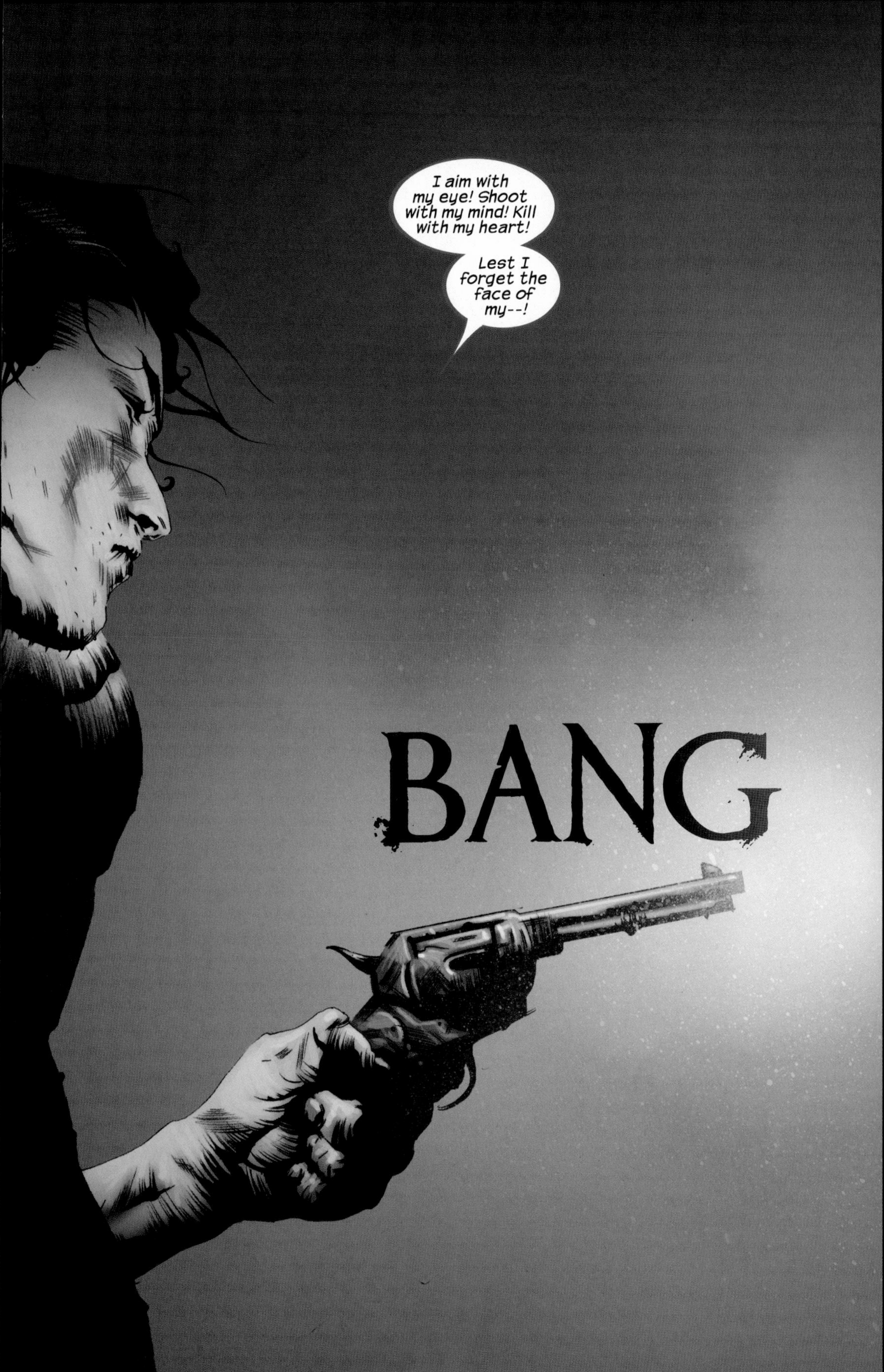
I aim with my eye! Shoot with my mind! Kill with my heart!
Lest I forget the face of my--!
BANG

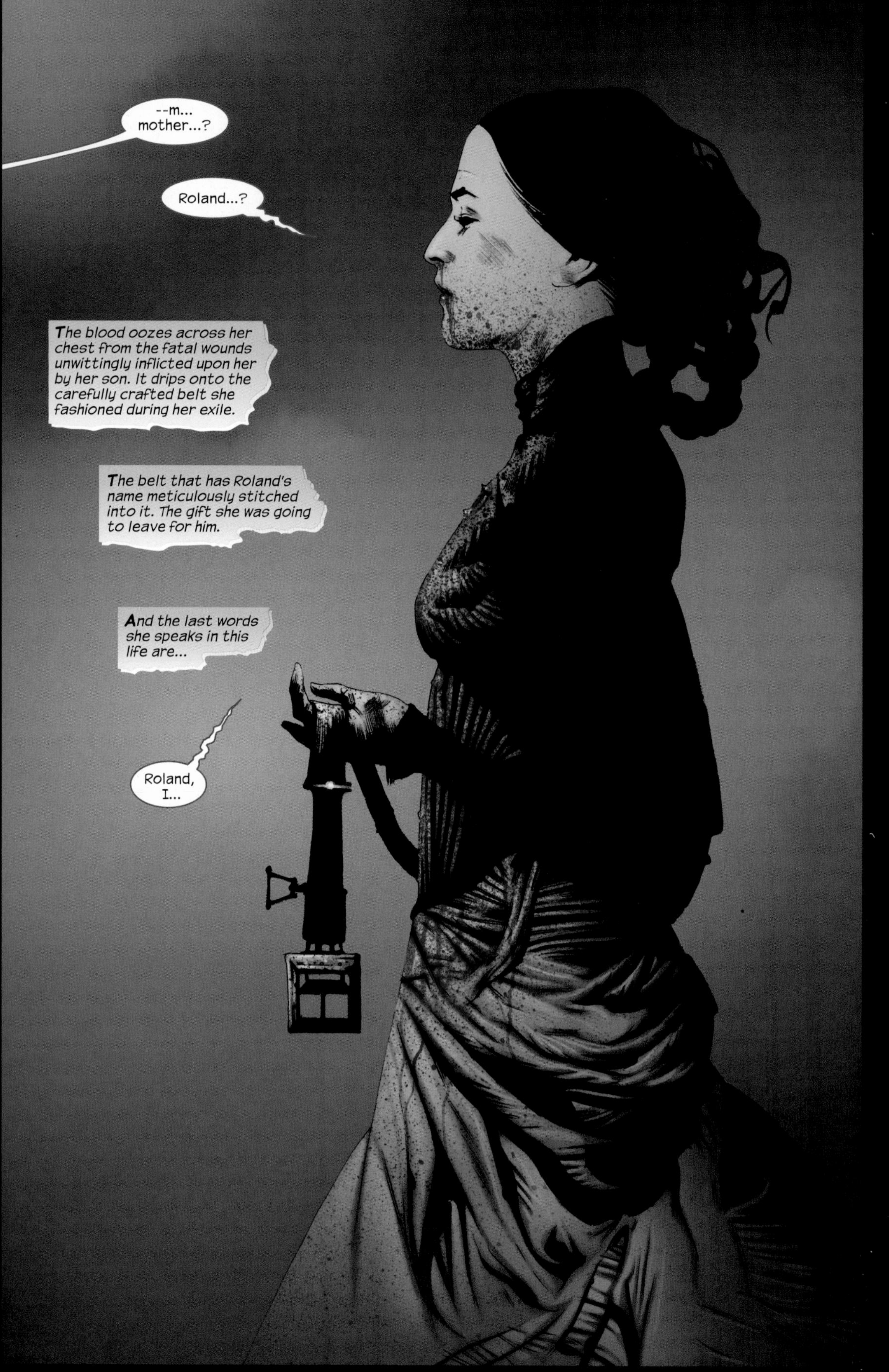
--m... mother...?
Roland...?
The blood oozes across her chest from the fatal wounds unwittingly inflicted upon her by her son. It drips onto the carefully crafted belt she fashioned during her exile.
The belt that has Roland's name meticulously stitched into it. The gift she was going to leave for him.
And the last words she speaks in this life are...
Roland, I...

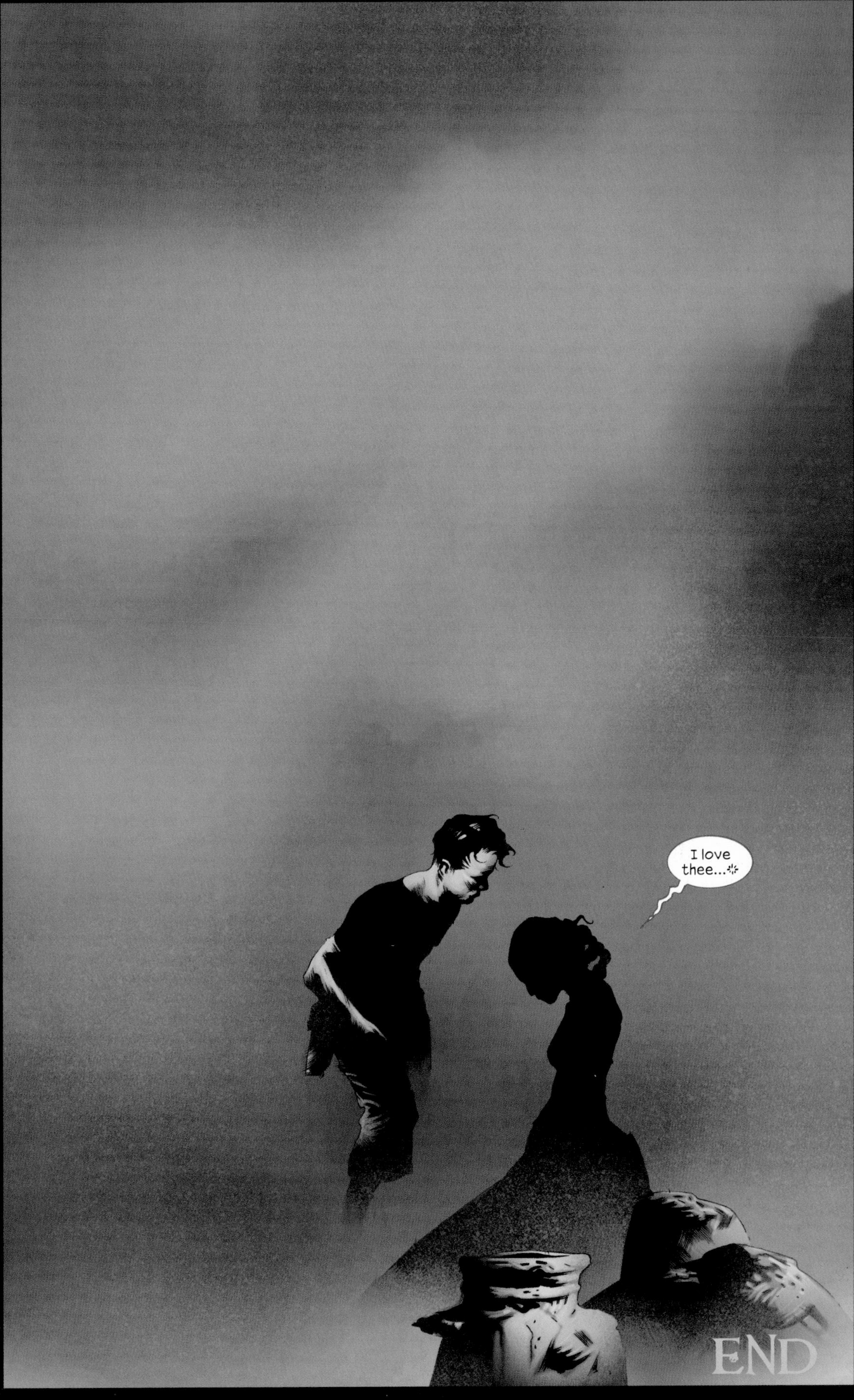
I love thee...
END

Dark Tower: Treachery #1 Variant Cover by Gabriele Dell'Otto

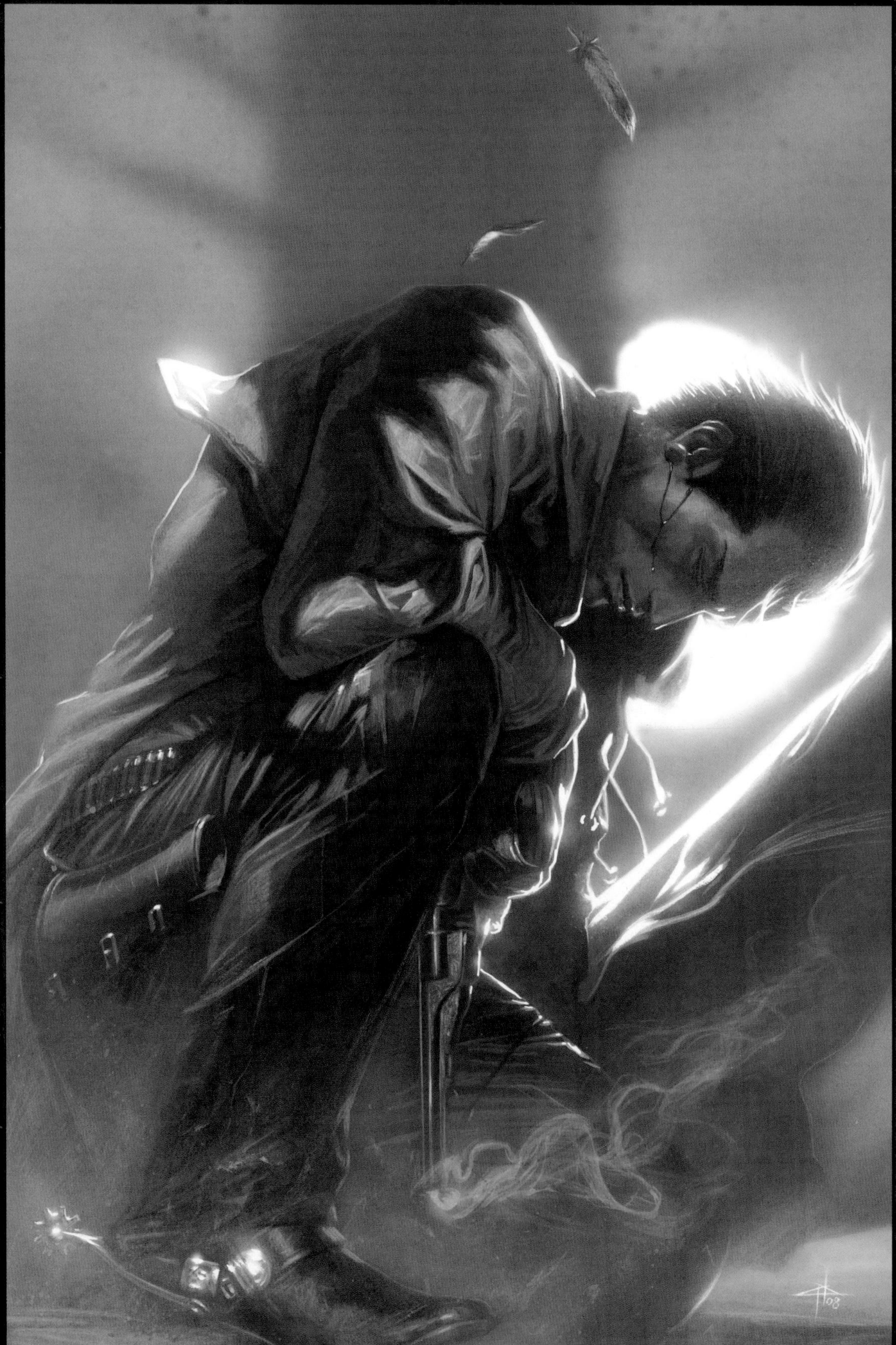

Dark Tower: Treachery **#1 Midnight Opening Gatefold Variant Cover by Emily Warren**

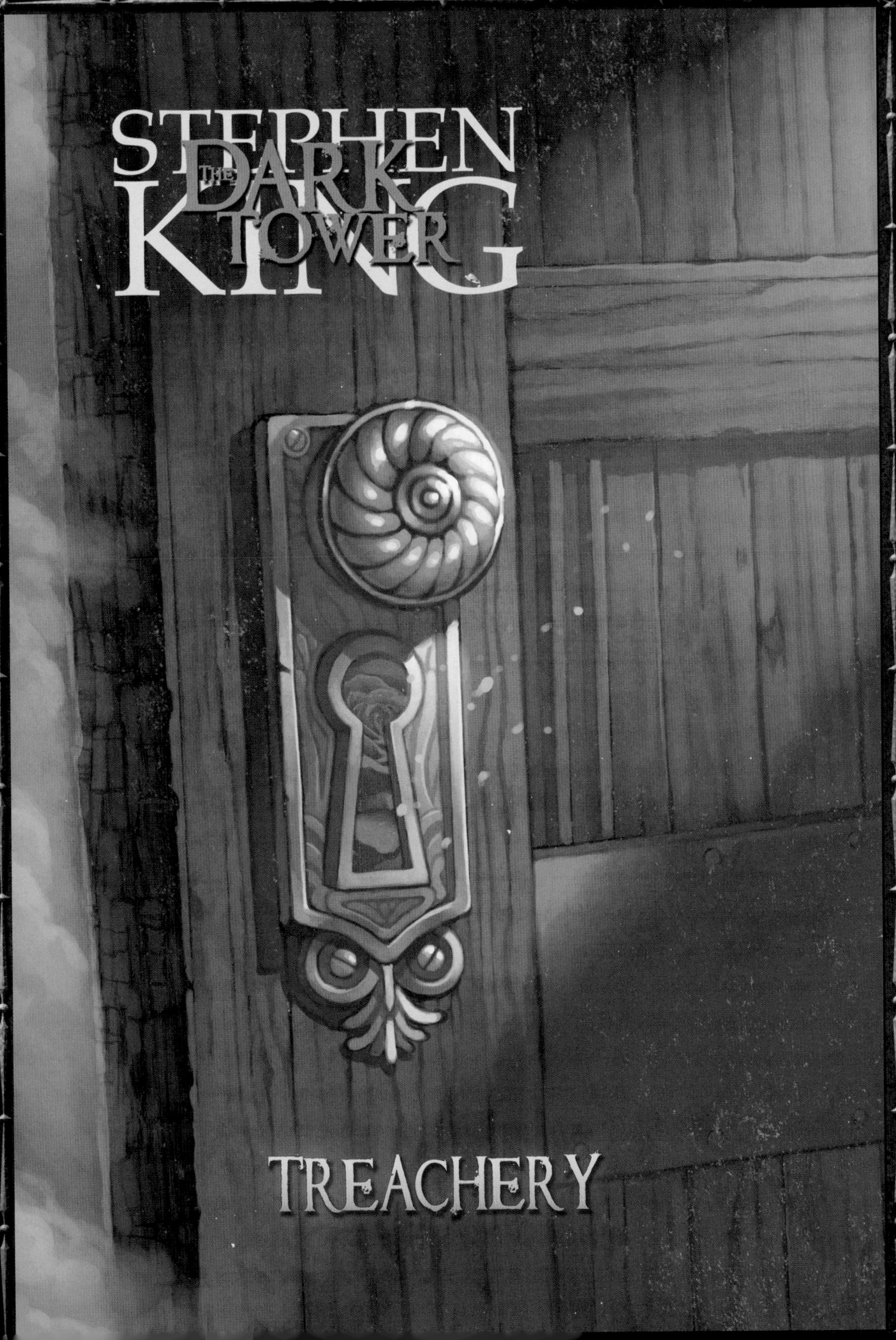
STEPHEN KING
THE DARK TOWER
TREACHERY

***Dark Tower: Treachery* #1** **Cover by Jae Lee & Richard Isanove**

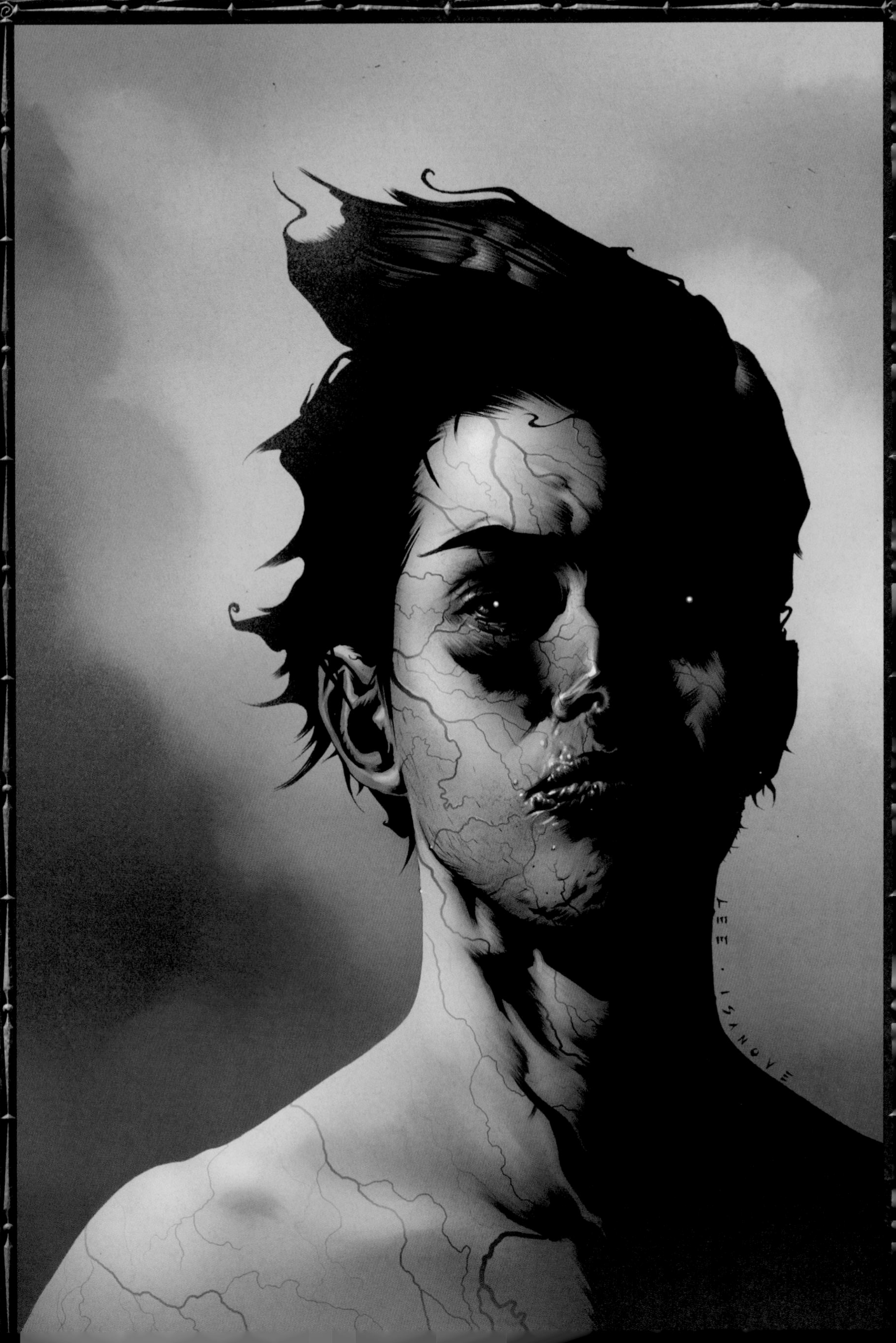
LEE · ISANOVE

Dark Tower: Treachery #1 Sketch Variant Cover by Jae Lee

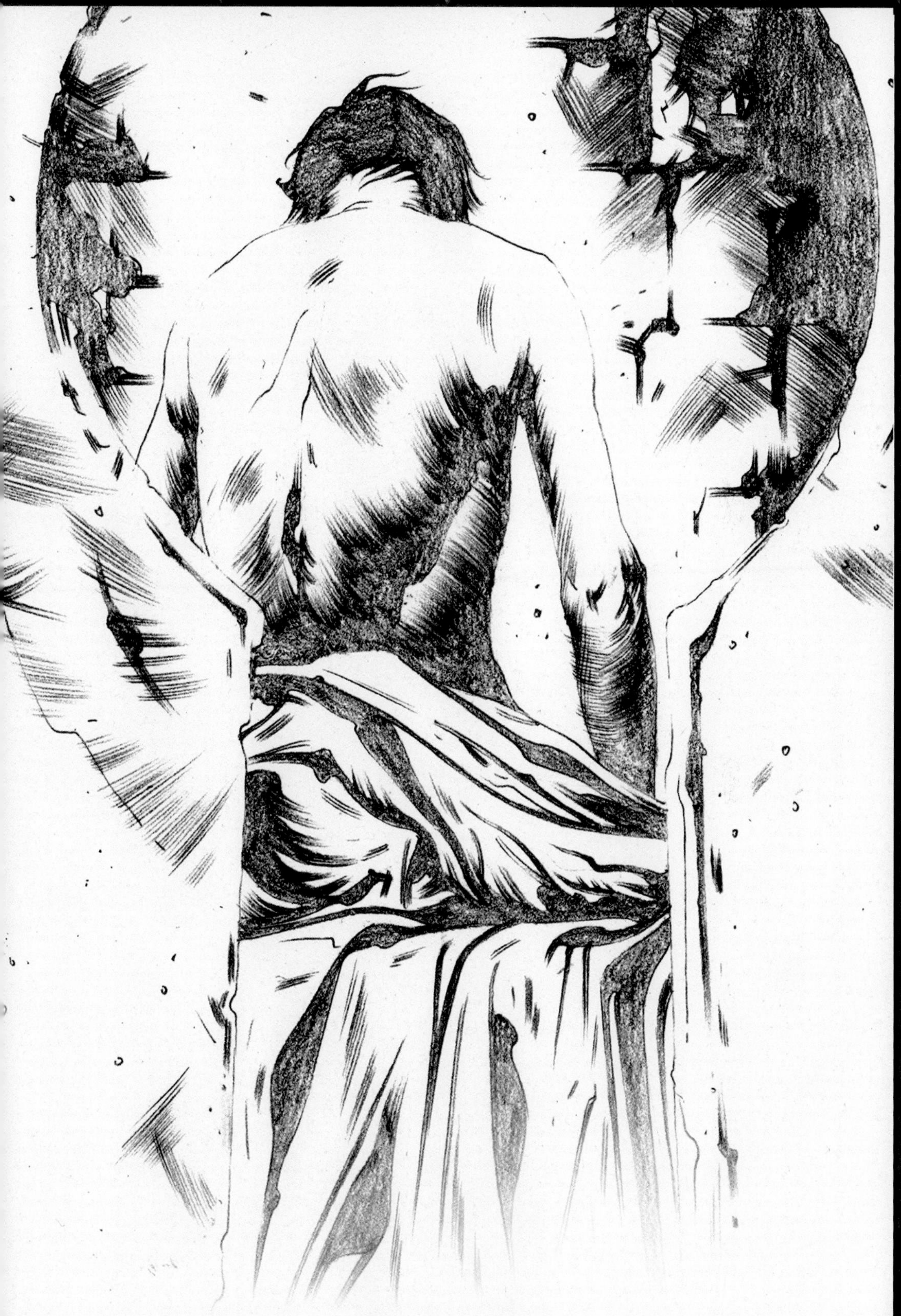

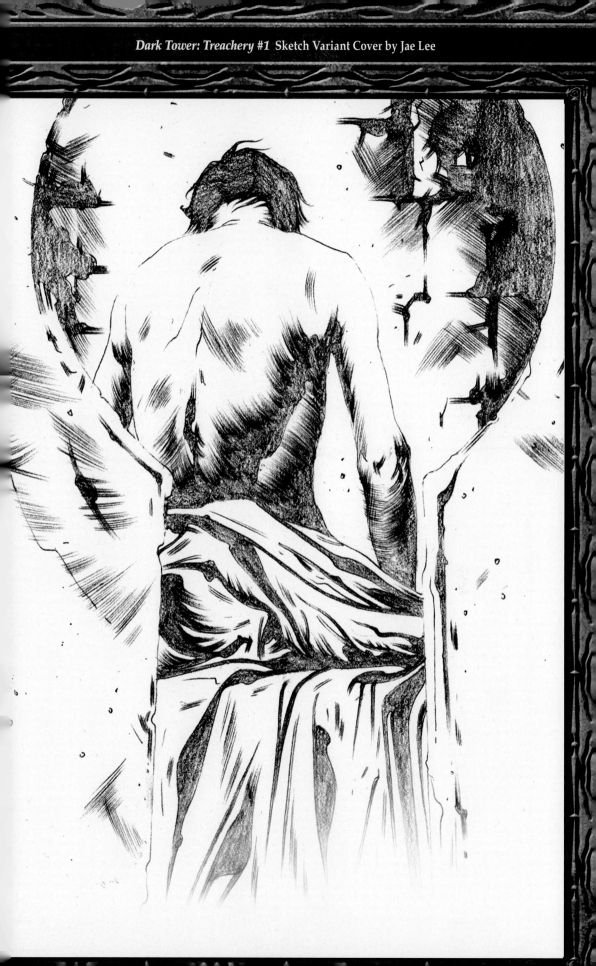

Dark Tower: Treachery #2 Cover by Jae Lee & Richard Isanove

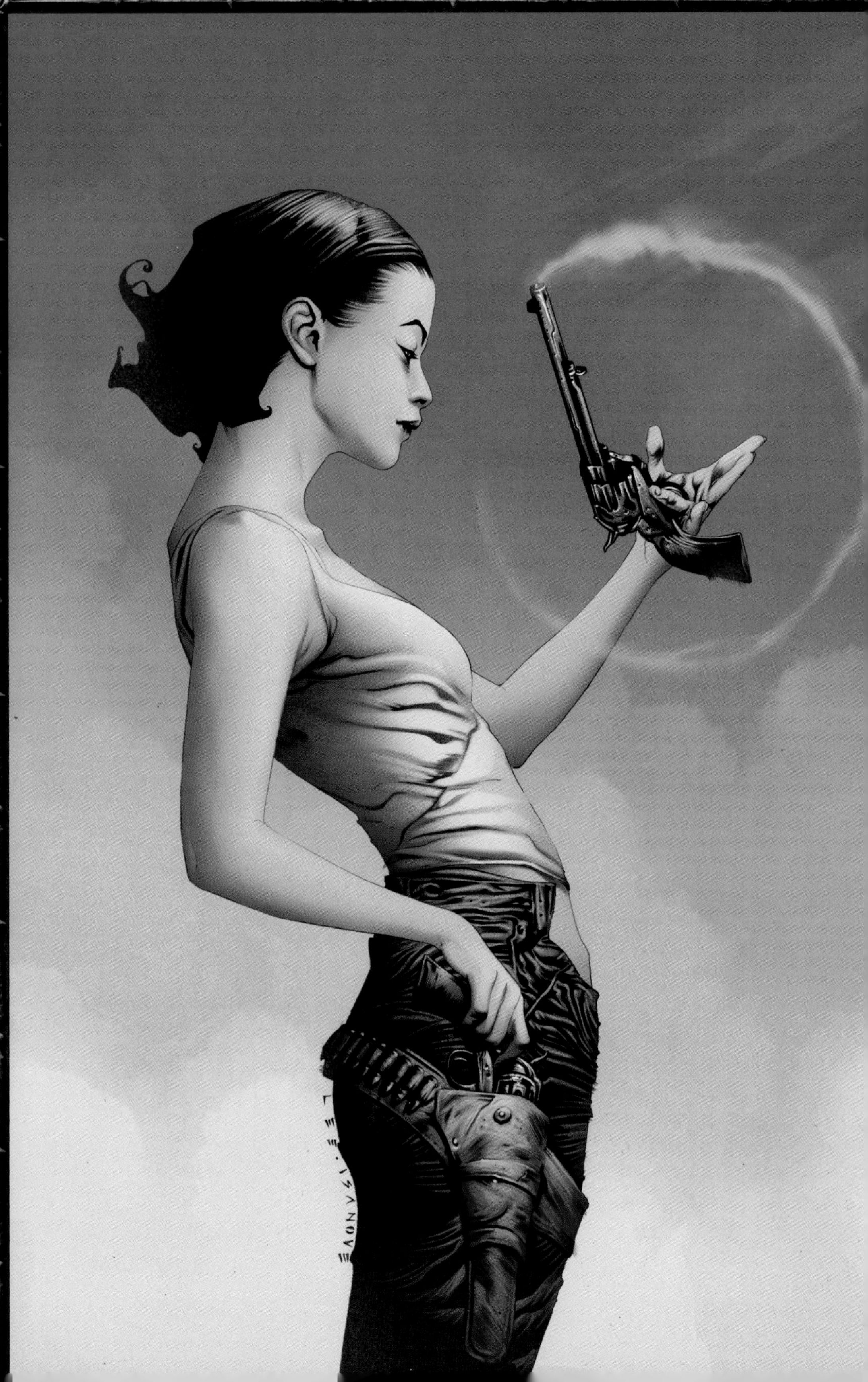

Dark Tower: Treachery #2 Sketch Variant Cover by Jae Lee

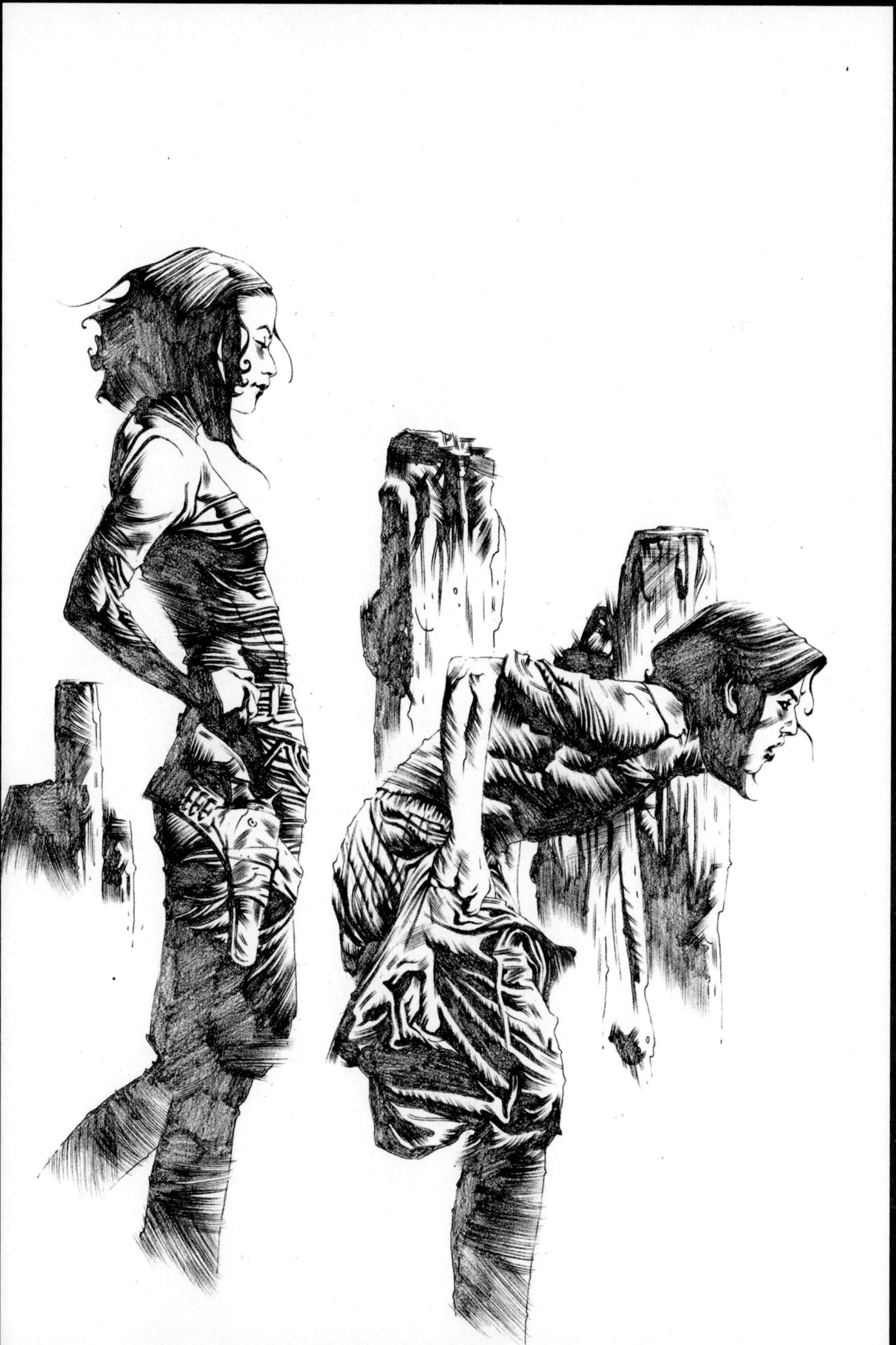

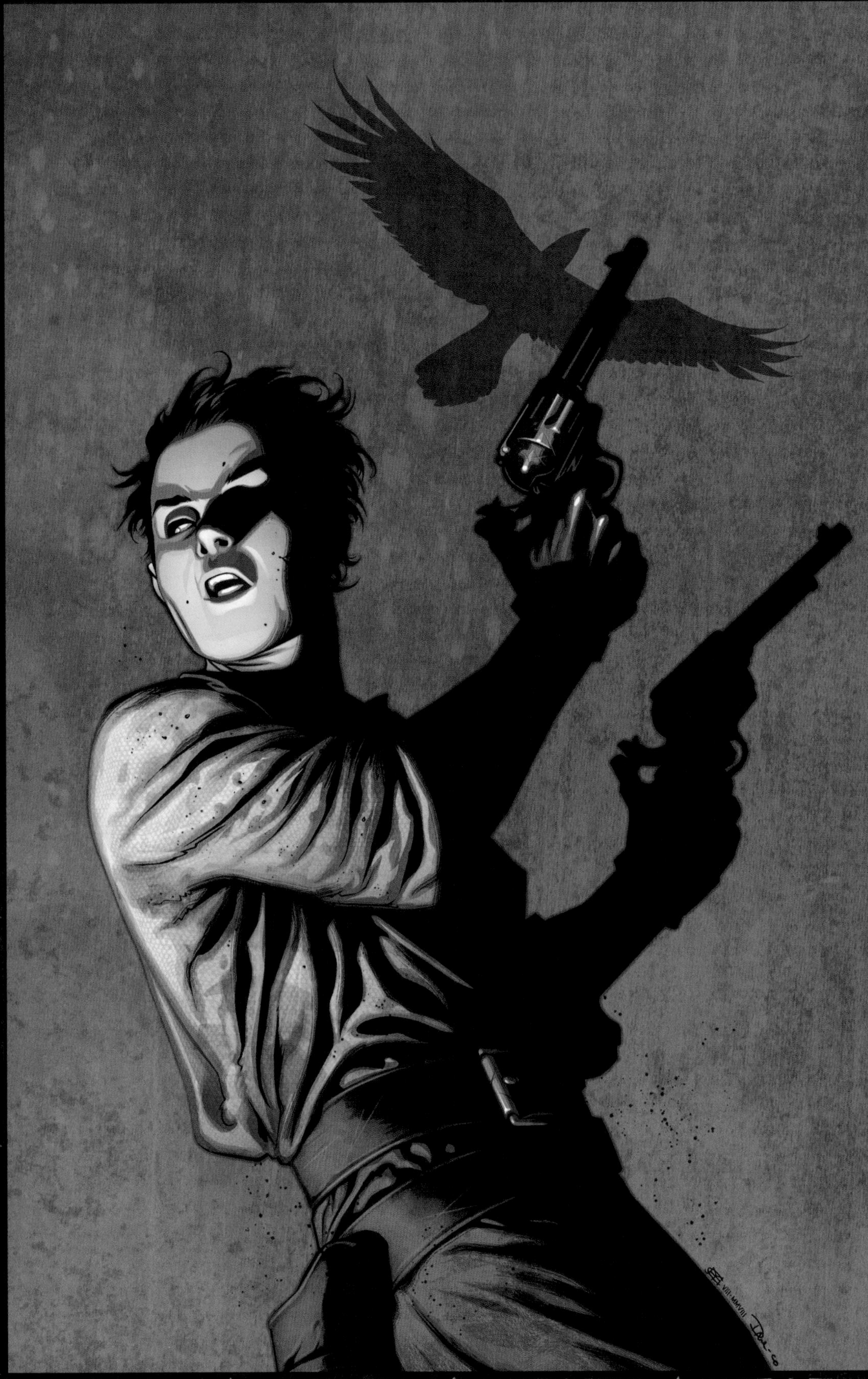

Dark Tower: Treachery **#2** Variant Cover by Jim Cheung & Dave McCaig

***Dark Tower: Treachery* #3** Variant Cover by Pasqual Ferry & Dave McCaig

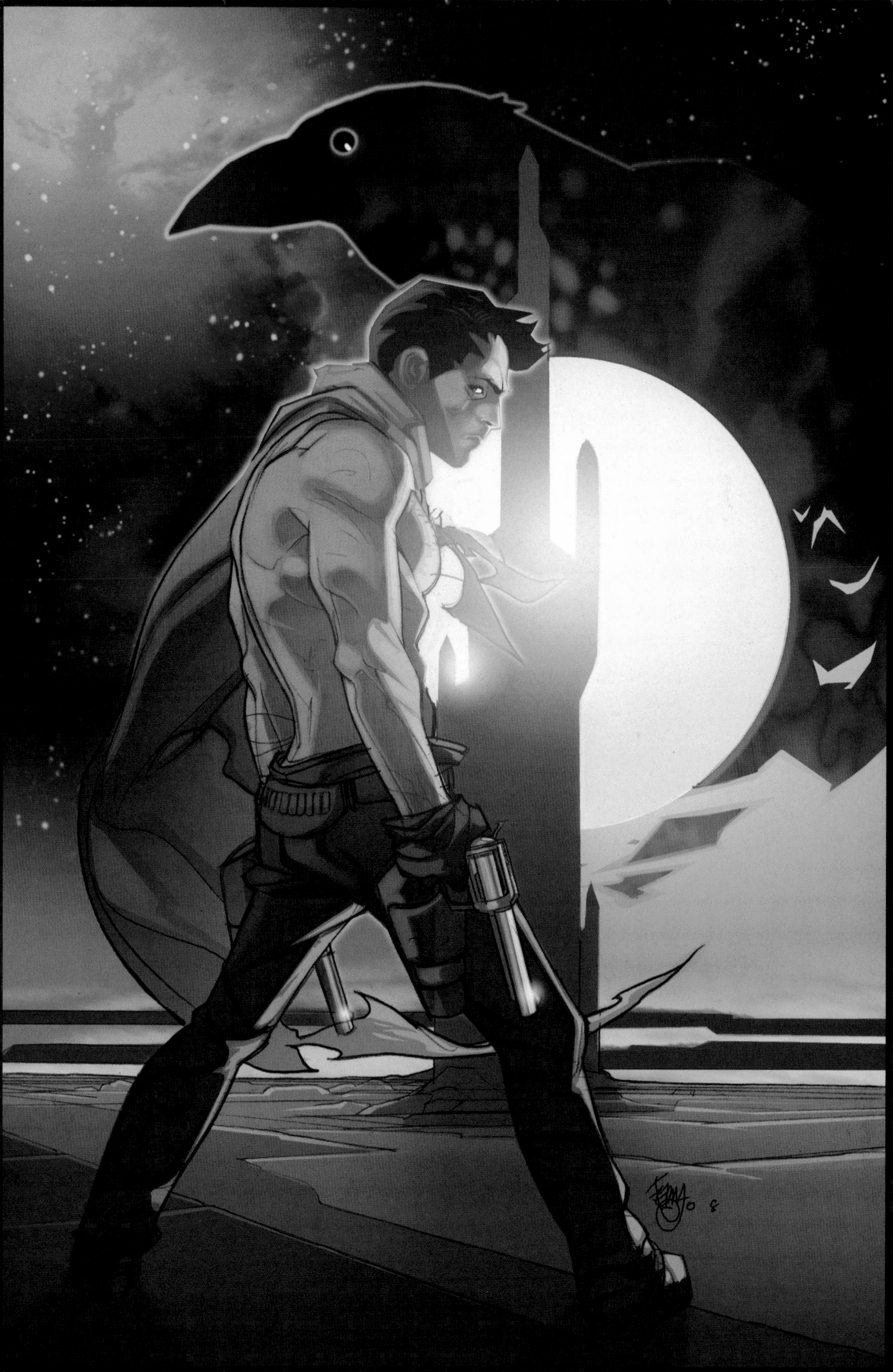

Dark Tower: Treachery #3 Cover by Jae Lee & Richard Isanove

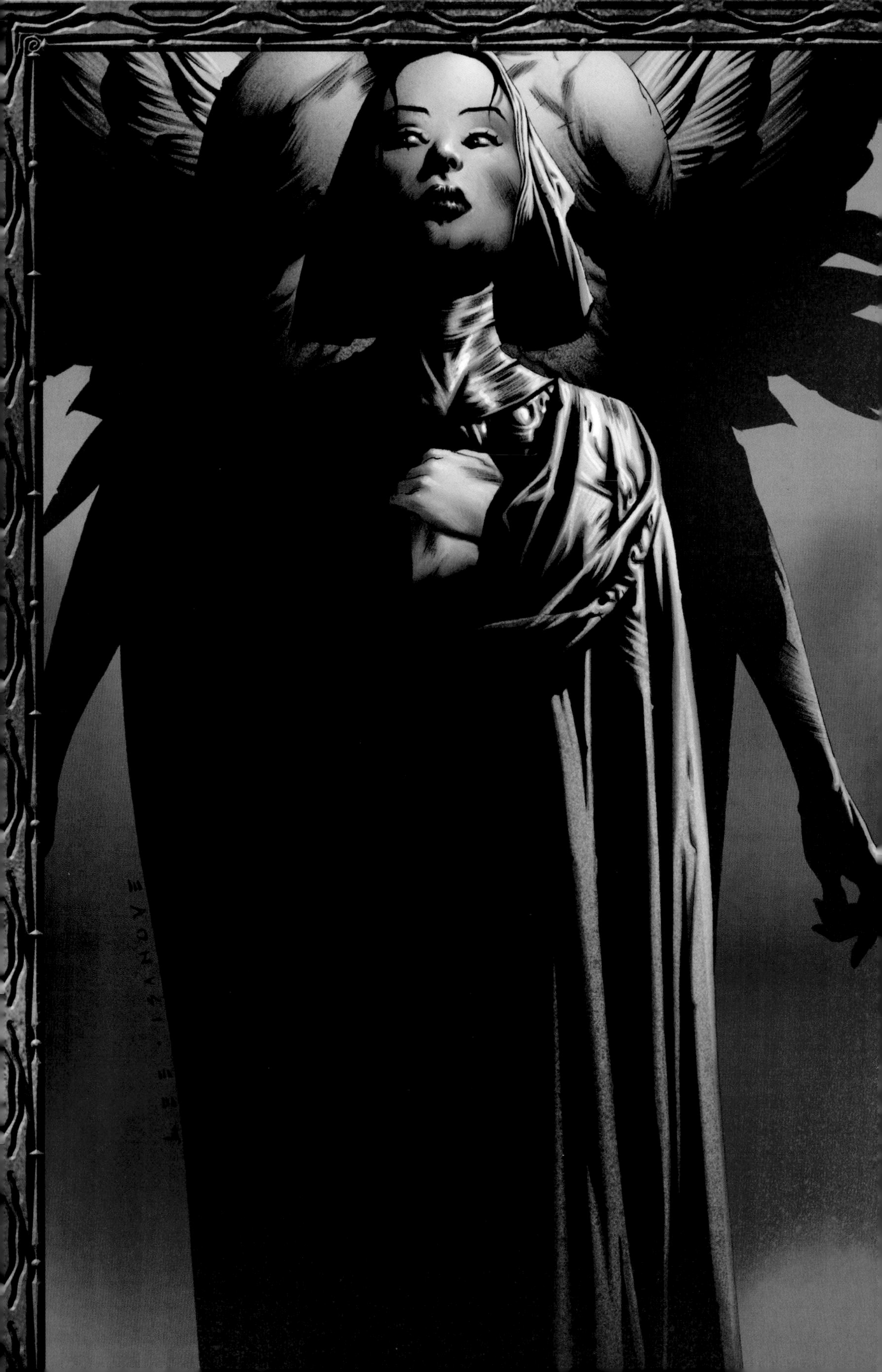

Dark Tower: Treachery #3 Sketch Variant Cover by Jae Lee

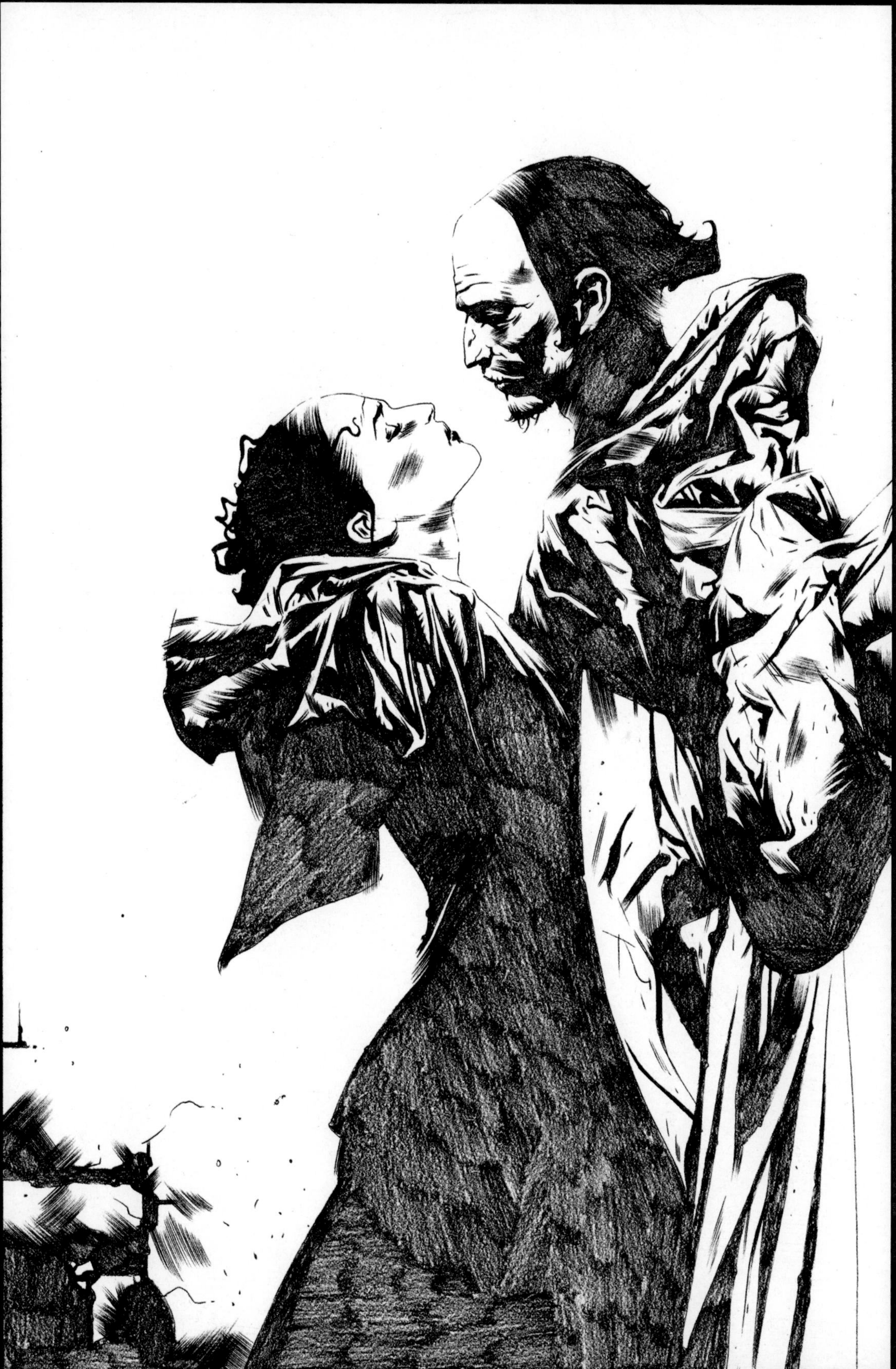

Dark Tower: Treachery #4 Cover by Jae Lee & Richard Isanove

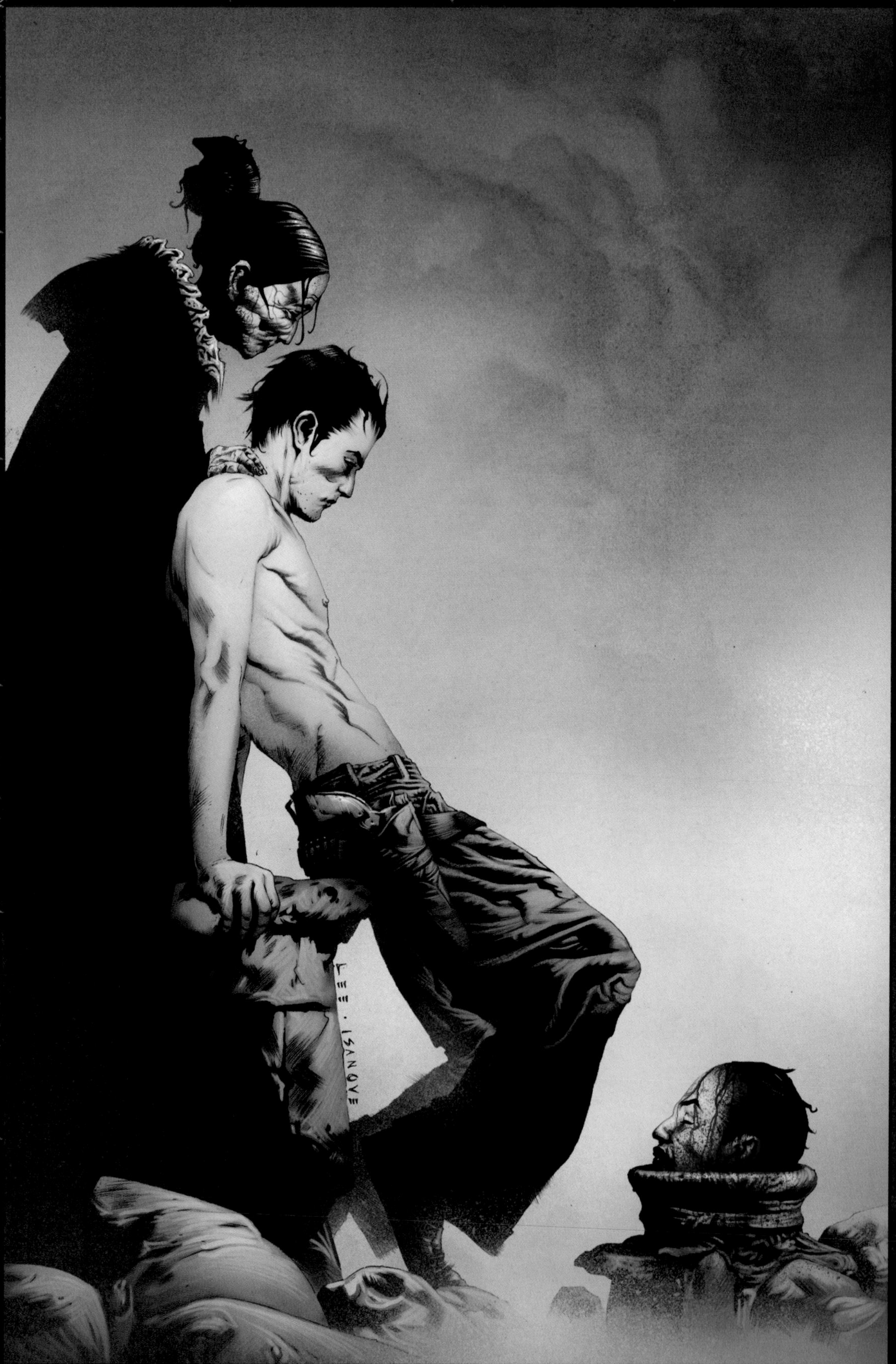
LEE · ISANOVE

Dark Tower: Treachery #4 Sketch Variant Cover by Jae Lee

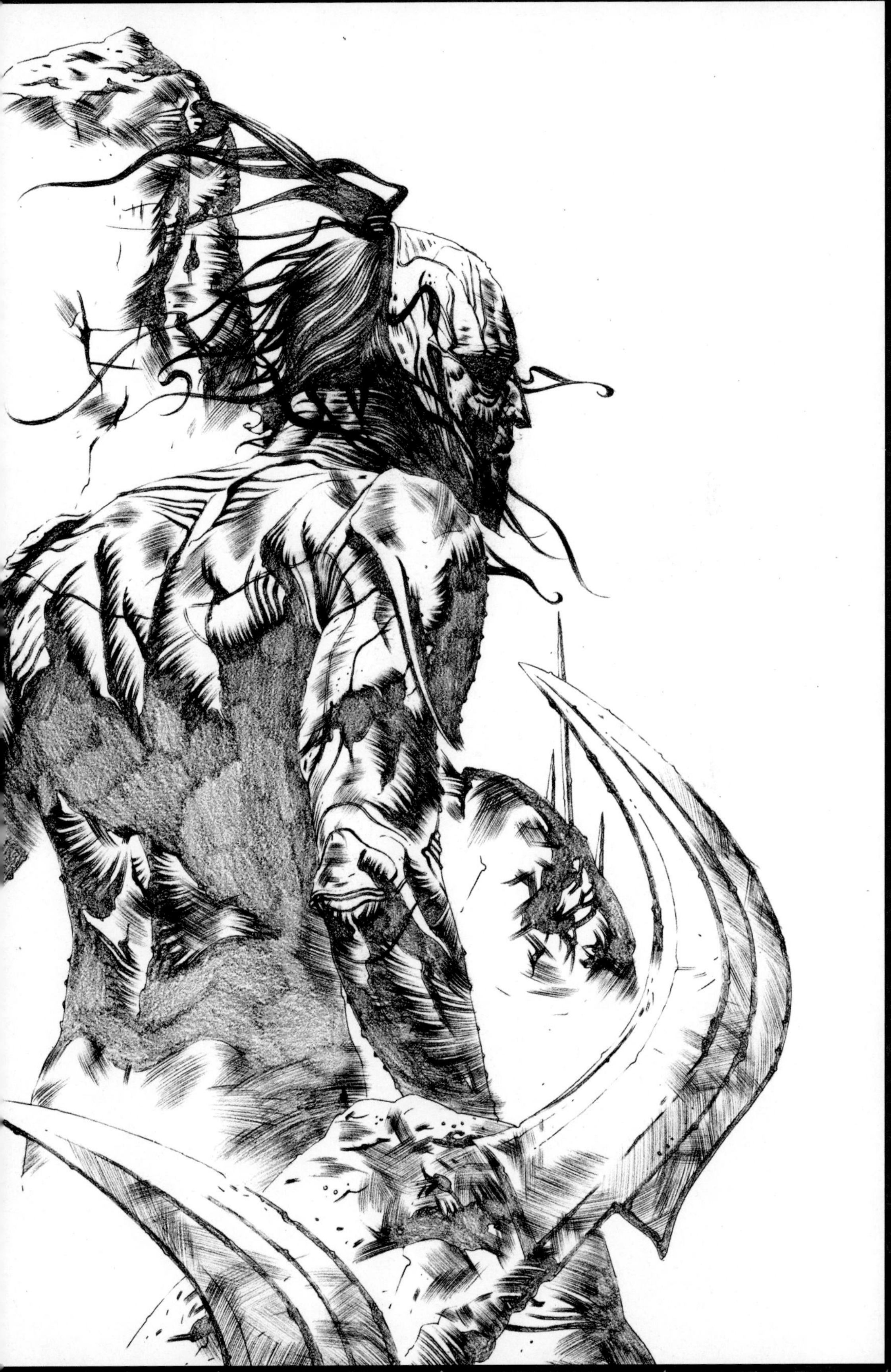

Dark Tower: Treachery #4 Variant Cover by Richard Isanove

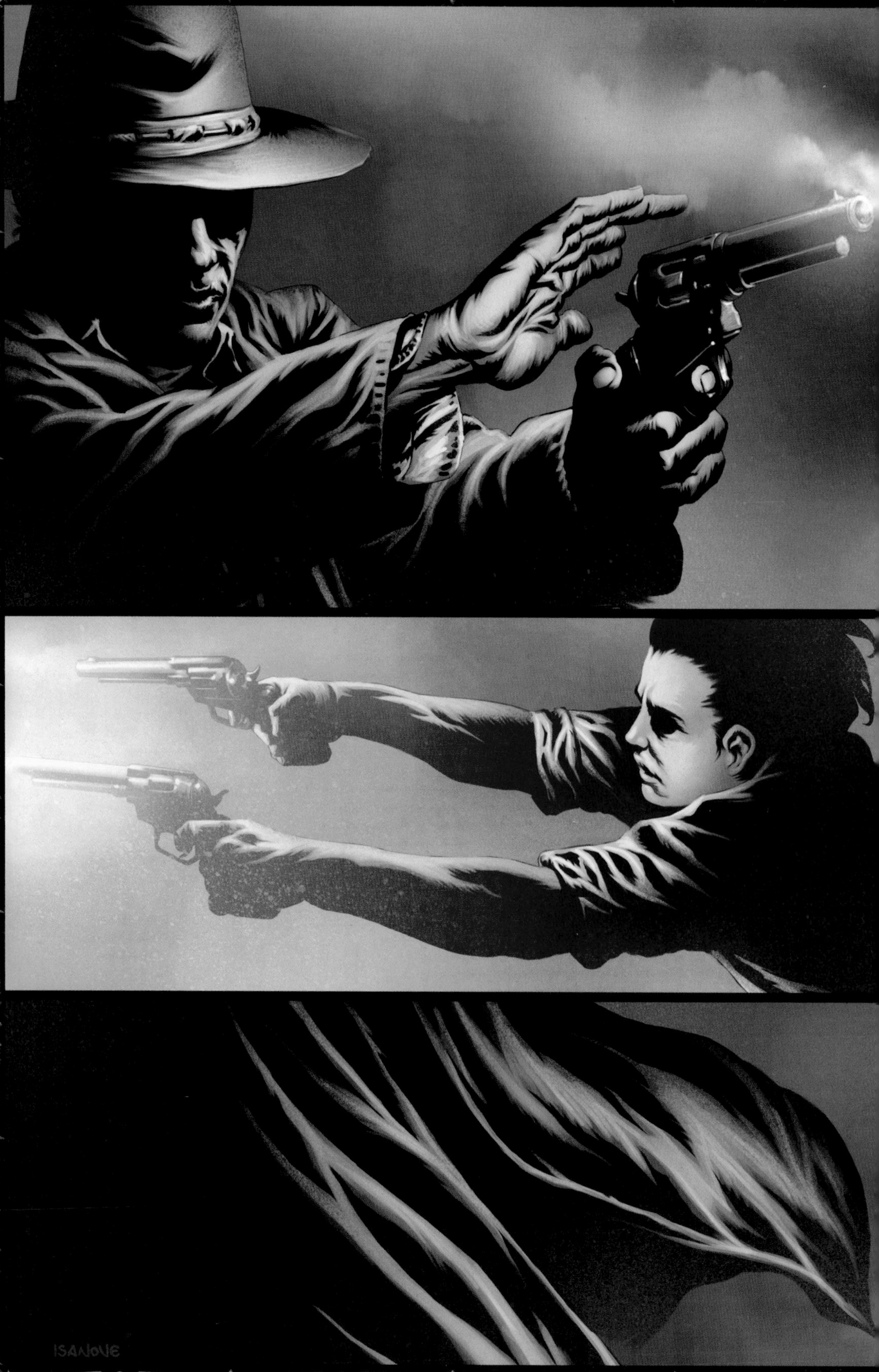
ISANOVE

Dark Tower: Treachery #5 Variant Cover by Daniel Acuña

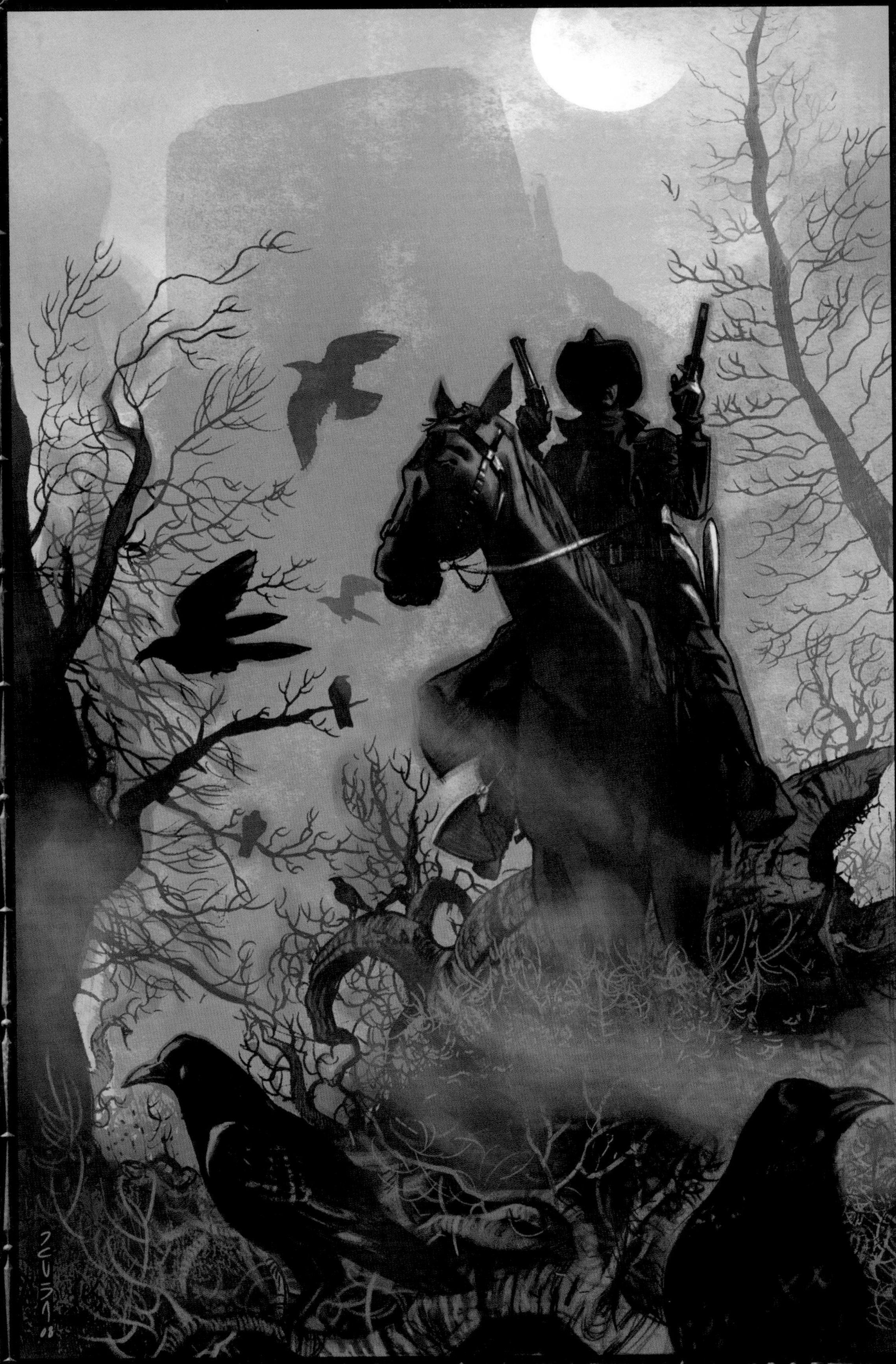

Dark Tower: Treachery **#5** Cover by Jae Lee & Richard Isanove

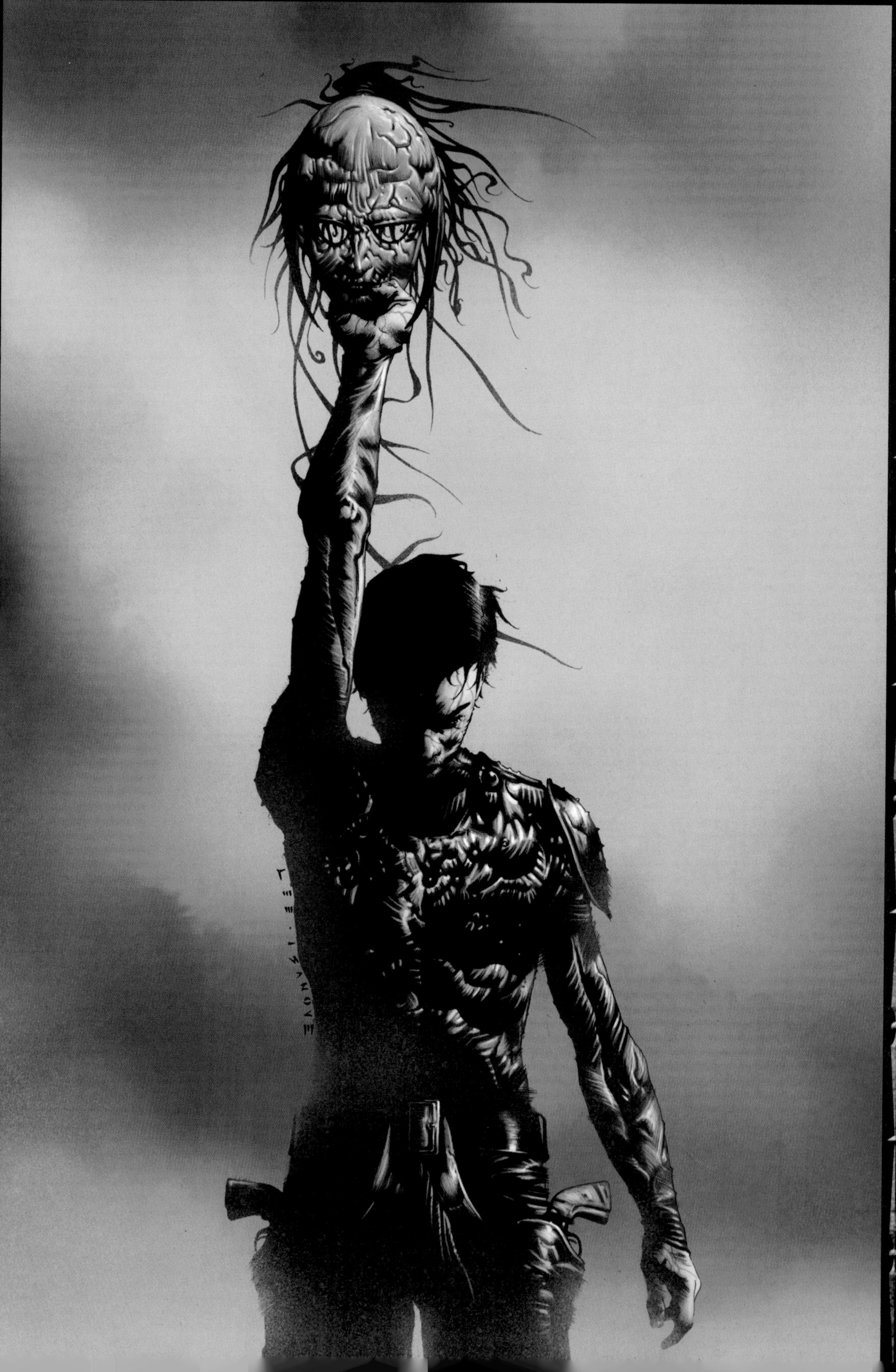

Dark Tower: Treachery #5 Sketch Variant Cover by Jae Lee

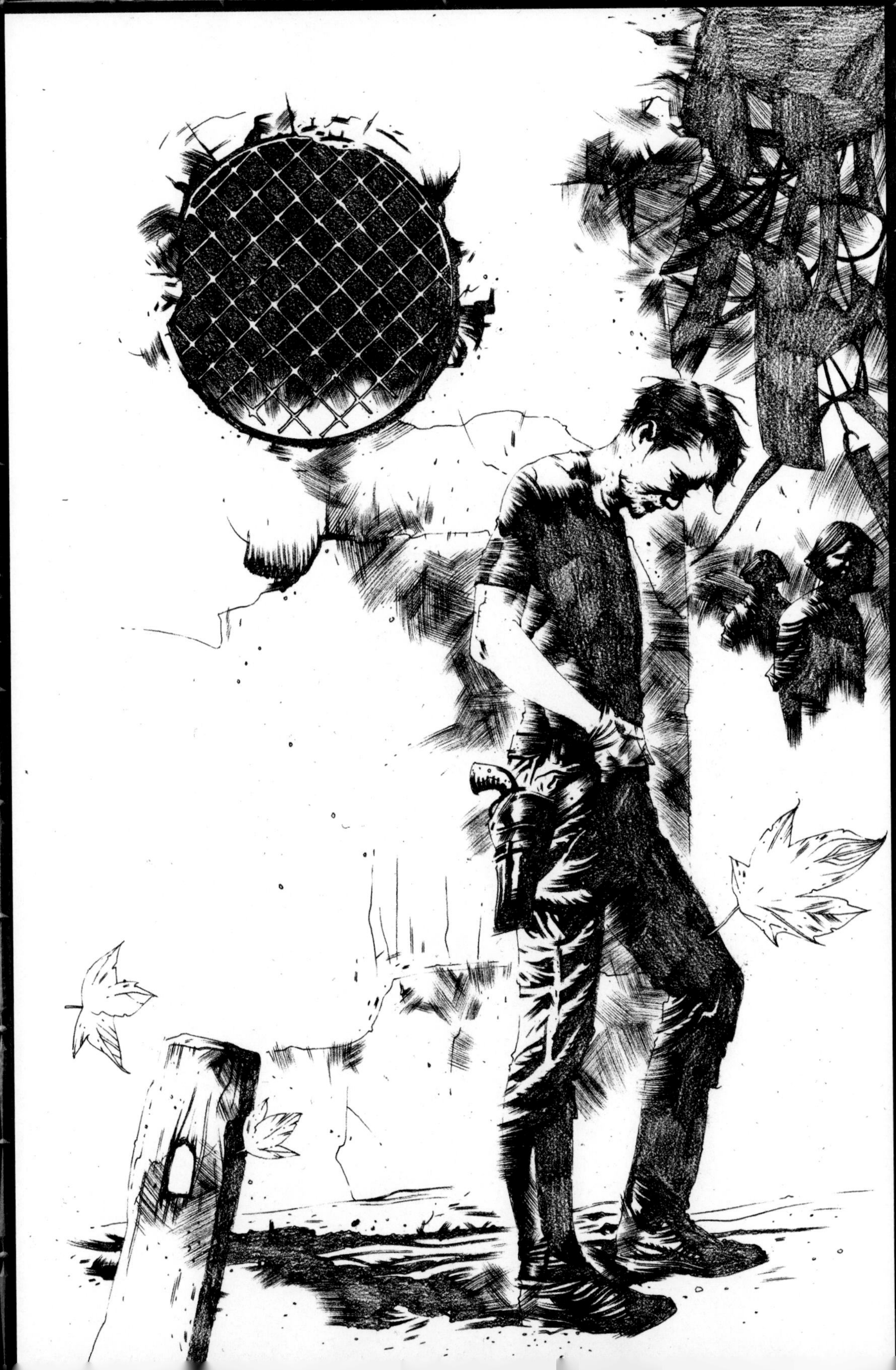

Dark Tower: Treachery #6 Cover by Jae Lee & Richard Isanove

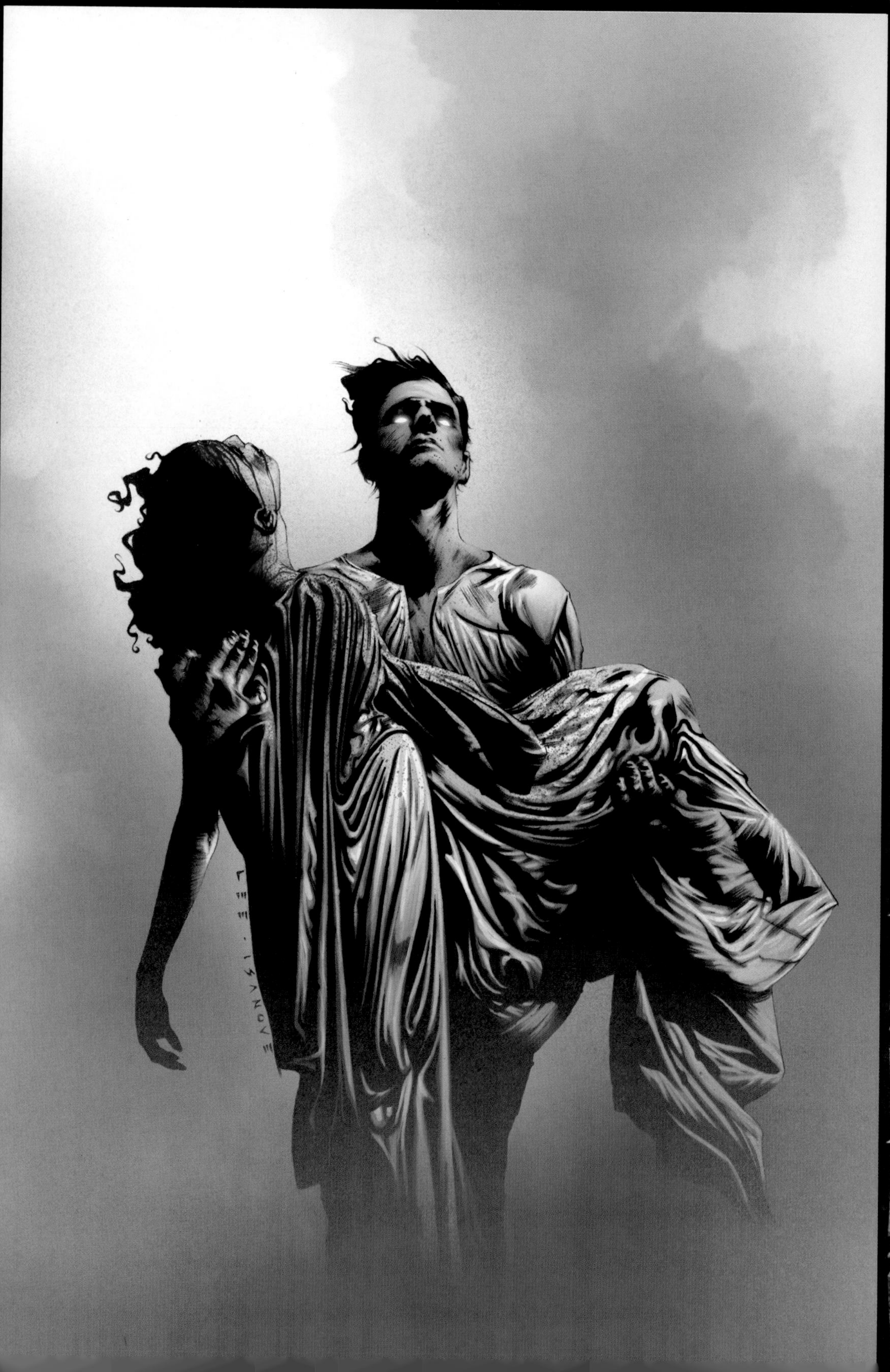

Dark Tower: Treachery #6 Sketch Variant Cover by Jae Lee

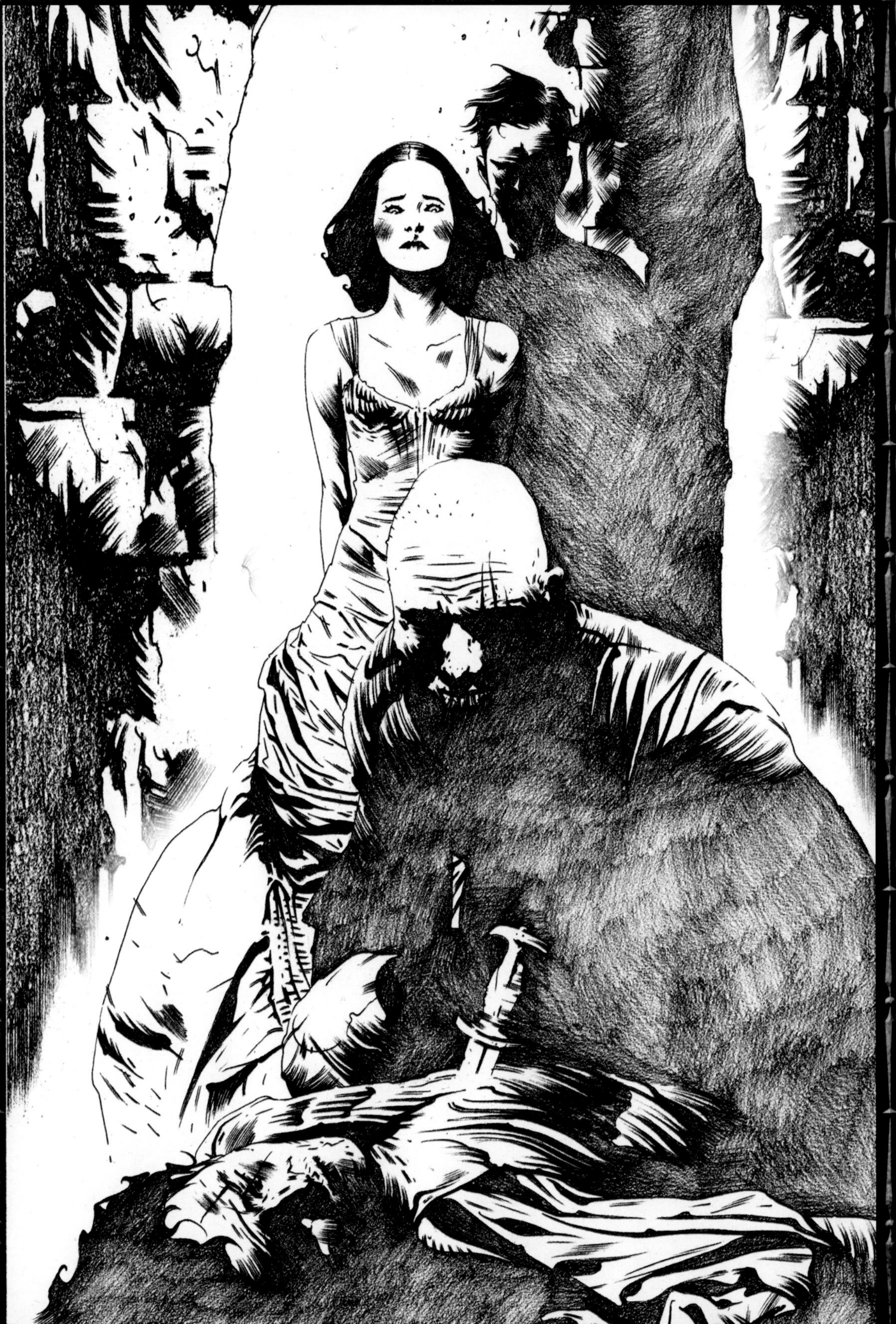

Dark Tower: Treachery #6 Variant Cover by Dennis Calero

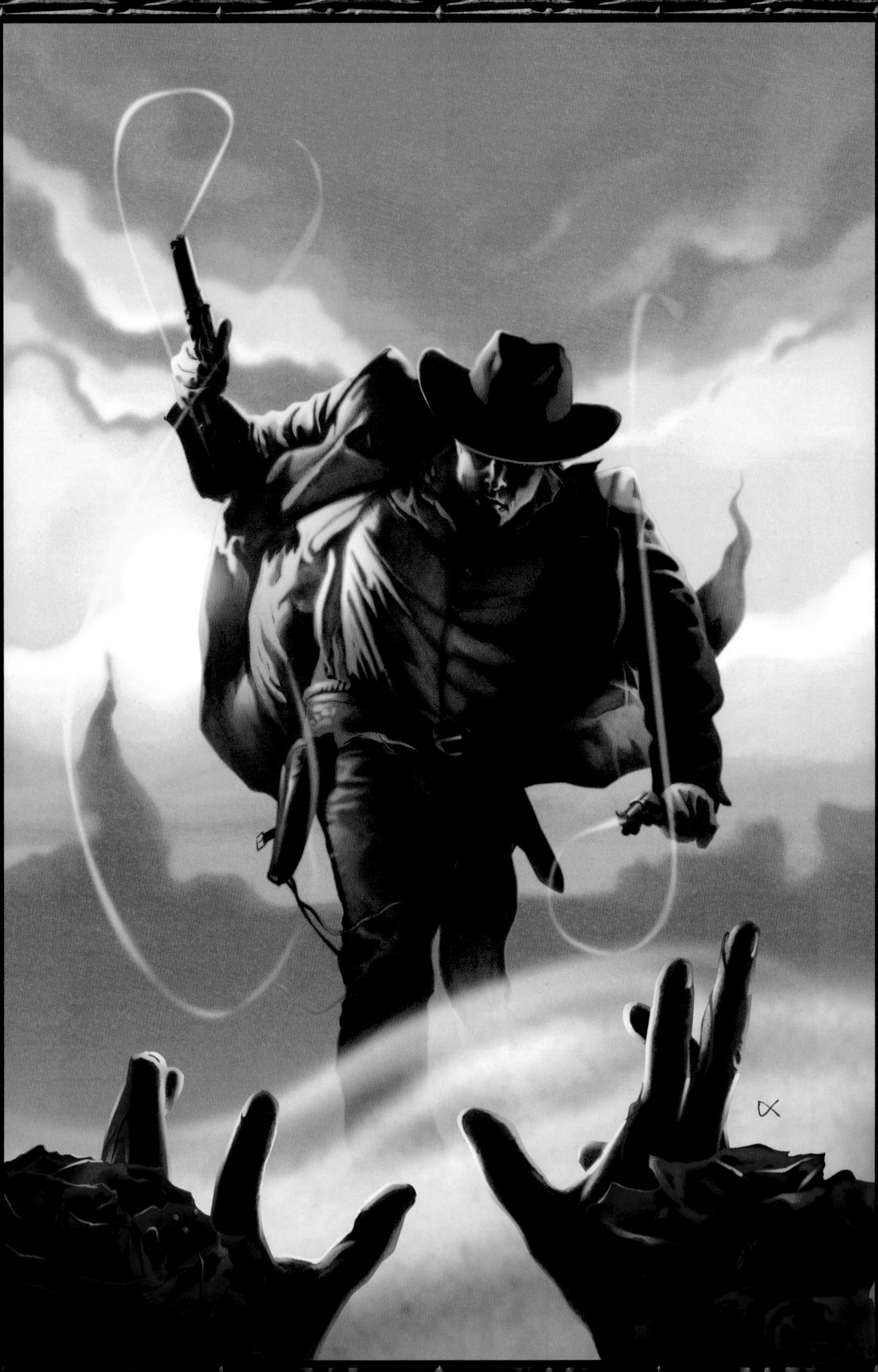

***Dark Tower: Treachery* #1** Layouts by Jae Lee

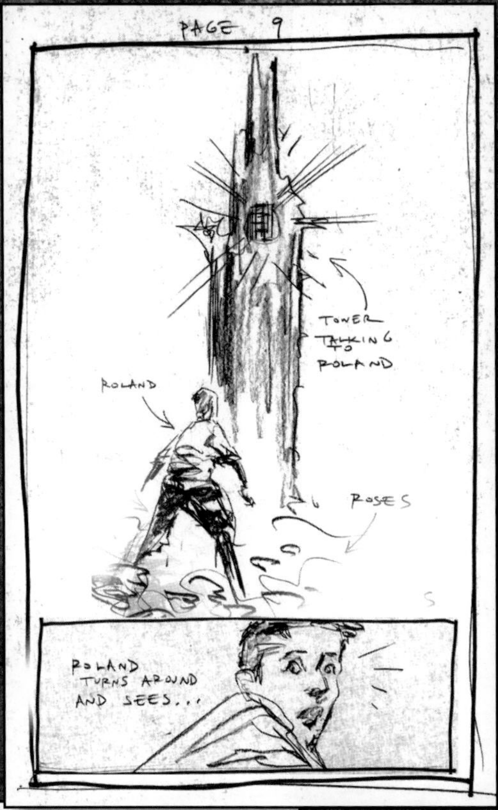

PAGE 9
TOWER TALKING TO ROLAND
ROLAND
ROSES
ROLAND TURNS AROUND AND SEES...

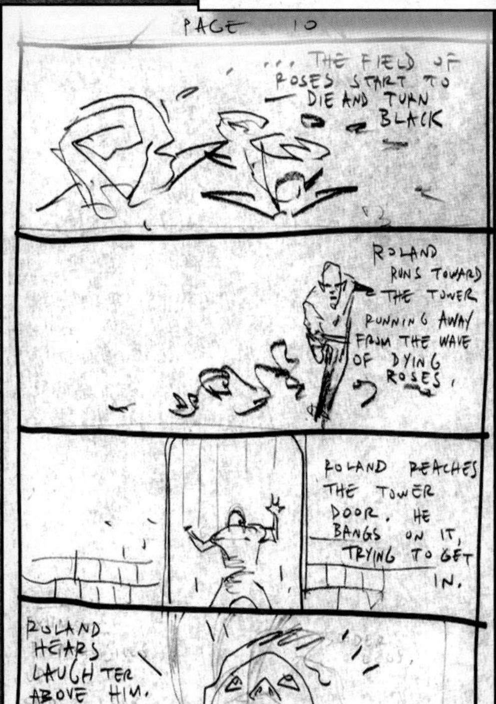

PAGE 10
... THE FIELD OF ROSES START TO DIE AND TURN BLACK
ROLAND RUNS TOWARD THE TOWER RUNNING AWAY FROM THE WAVE OF DYING ROSES.
ROLAND REACHES THE TOWER DOOR. HE BANGS ON IT, TRYING TO GET IN.
ROLAND HEARS LAUGHTER ABOVE HIM. HE LOOKS UP.

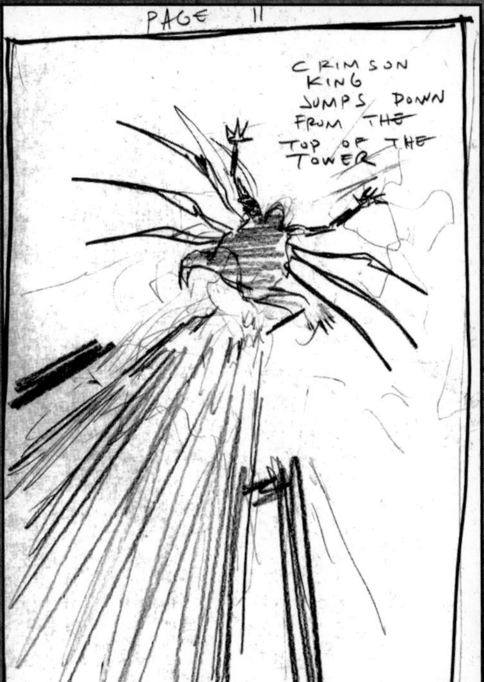

PAGE 11
CRIMSON KING JUMPS DOWN FROM THE TOP OF THE TOWER

Dark Tower: Treachery #1 Layouts by Jae Lee

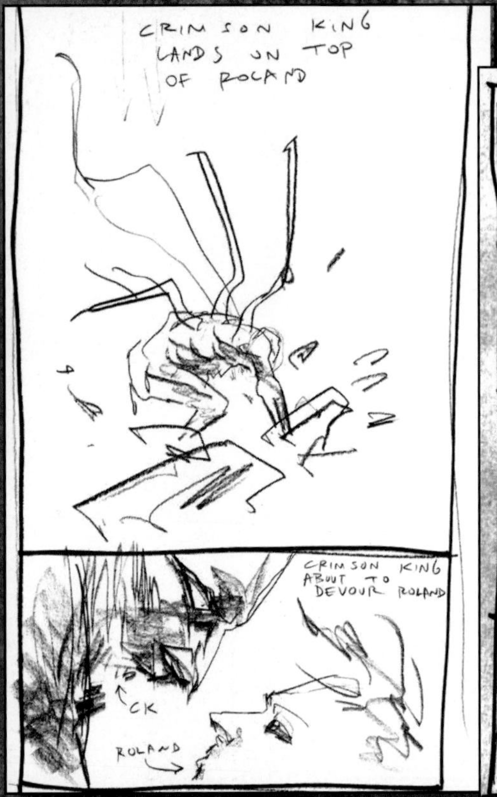
CRIMSON KING LANDS ON TOP OF ROLAND
CRIMSON KING ABOUT TO DEVOUR ROLAND
CK
ROLAND

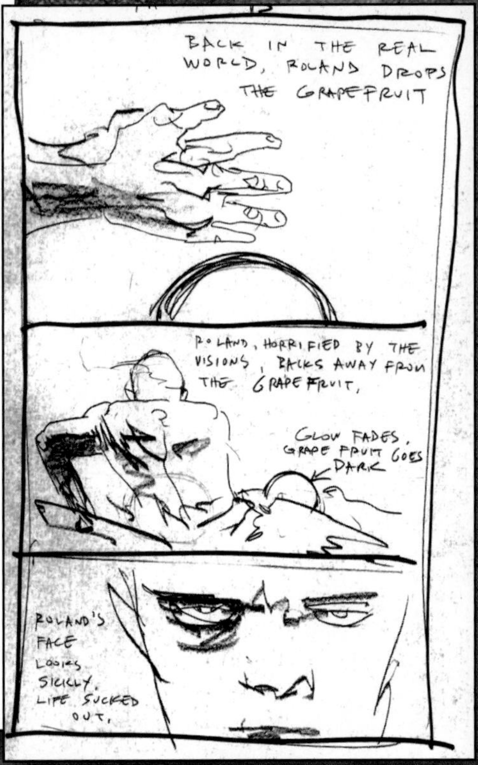
BACK IN THE REAL WORLD, ROLAND DROPS THE GRAPEFRUIT
ROLAND, HORRIFIED BY THE VISIONS, BACKS AWAY FROM THE GRAPEFRUIT,
GLOW FADES, GRAPE FRUIT GOES DARK
ROLAND'S FACE LOOKS SICKLY, LIFE SUCKED OUT,

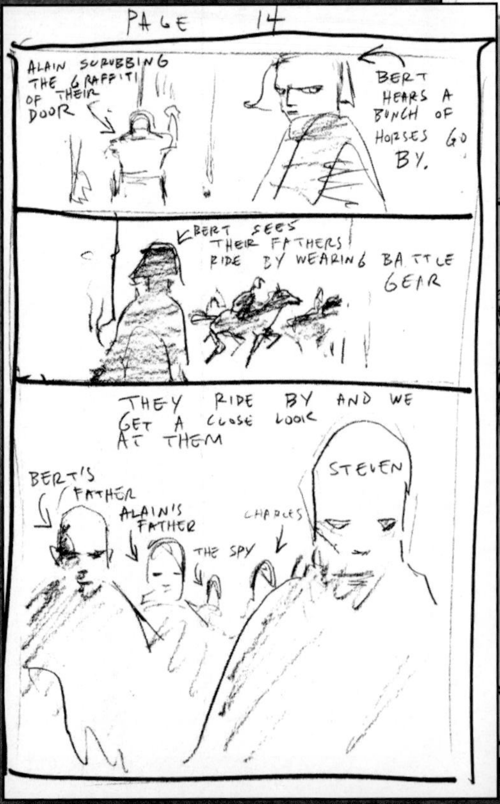
PAGE 14
ALAIN SCRUBBING THE GRAFFITI OF THEIR DOOR
BERT HEARS A BUNCH OF HORSES GO BY.
BERT SEES THEIR FATHERS RIDE BY WEARING BATTLE GEAR
THEY RIDE BY AND WE GET A CLOSE LOOK AT THEM
BERT'S FATHER
ALAIN'S FATHER
THE SPY
CHARLES
STEVEN

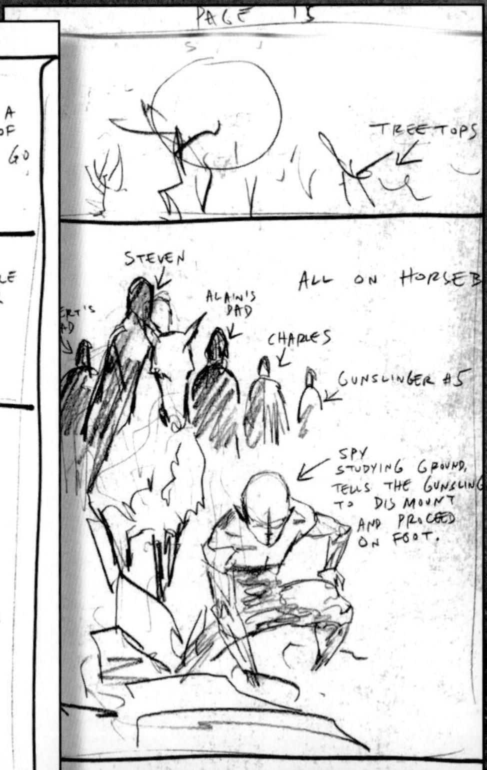
PAGE 15
TREE TOPS
STEVEN
ALL ON HORSEB
ALAIN'S DAD
CHARLES
GUNSLINGER #5
SPY STUDYING GROUND, TELLS THE GUNSLING TO DISMOUNT AND PROCEED ON FOOT.

Dark Tower: Treachery #1 Layouts by Jae Lee

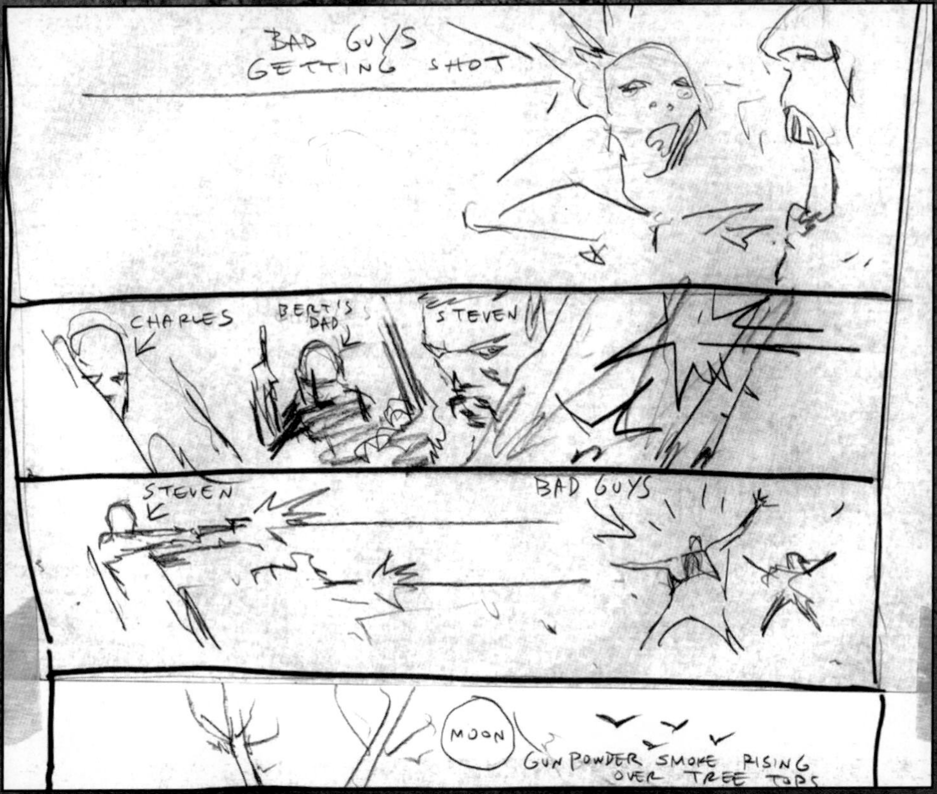
BAD GUYS GETTING SHOT
CHARLES
BERT'S DAD
STEVEN
STEVEN
BAD GUYS
MOON
GUNPOWDER SMOKE RISING OVER TREE TOPS

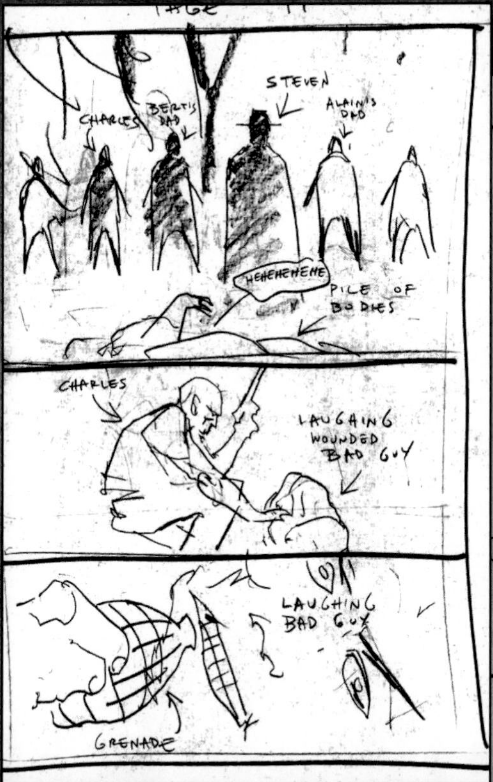
STEVEN
CHARLES
BERT'S DAD
ALAIN'S DAD
HEHEHEHEHE
PILE OF BODIES
CHARLES
LAUGHING WOUNDED BAD GUY
LAUGHING BAD GUY
GRENADE

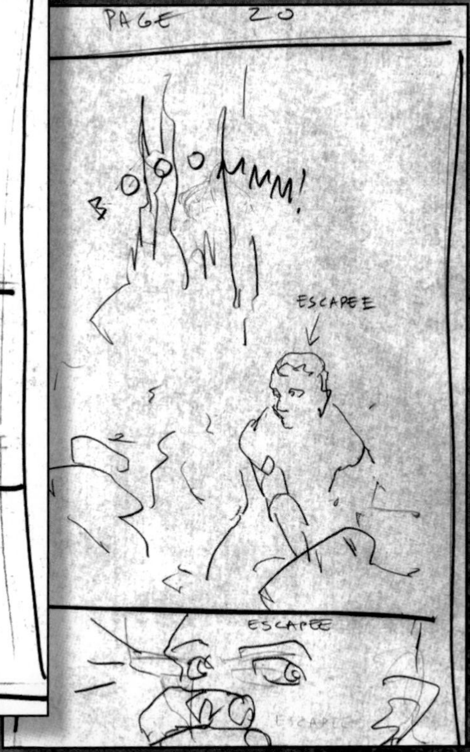
PAGE 20
BOOOOMMM!
ESCAPEE
ESCAPEE

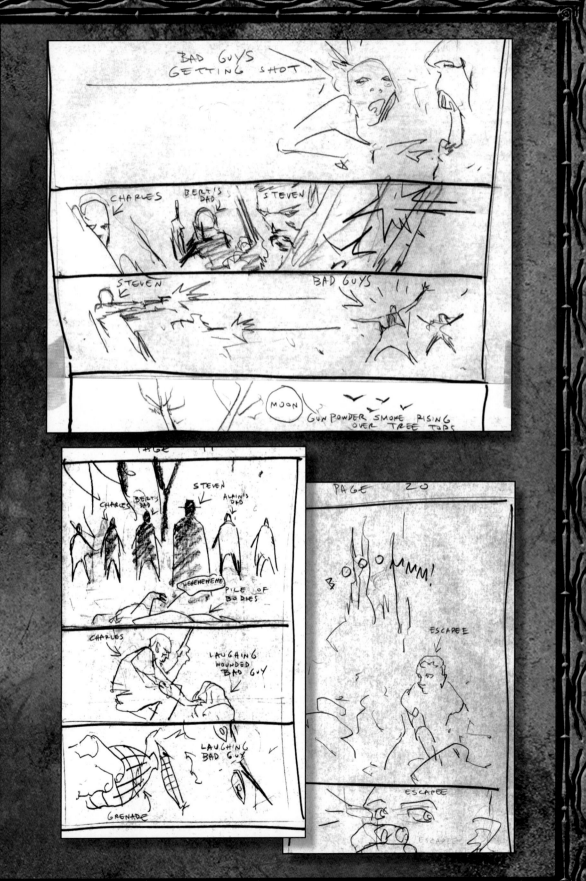

PAGE 13
ALAIN
ON TOP OF
BERT
ROLAND
ROLAND
ALAIN GETTING OFF OF
BERT

PAGE
ALAIN
BERT
ROLAND
ROLAND

PAGE 15
STEVEN LOOKING SOMBER ON HIS THRONE

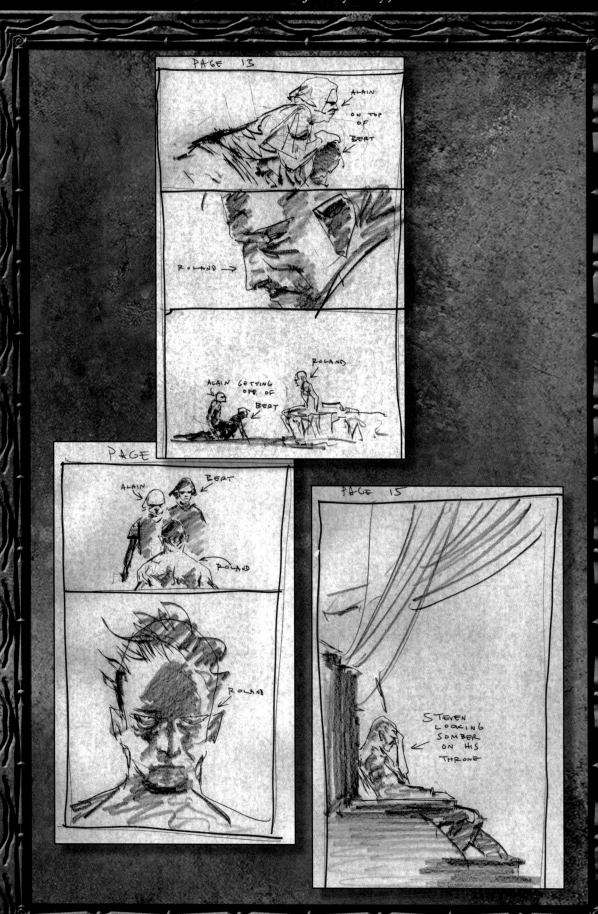

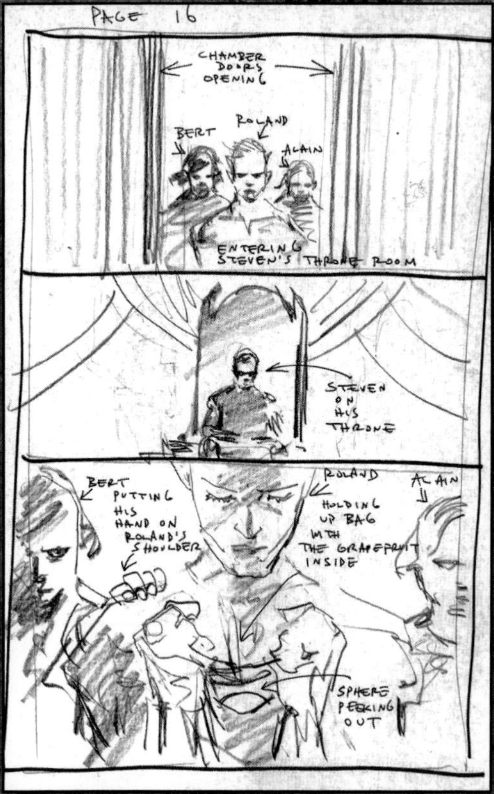
PAGE 16
CHAMBER DOORS OPENING
BERT
ROLAND
ALAIN
ENTERING STEVEN'S THRONE ROOM
STEVEN ON HIS THRONE
BERT PUTTING HIS HAND ON ROLAND'S SHOULDER
ROLAND
HOLDING UP BAG WITH THE GRAPEFRUIT INSIDE
ALAIN
SPHERE PEEKING OUT

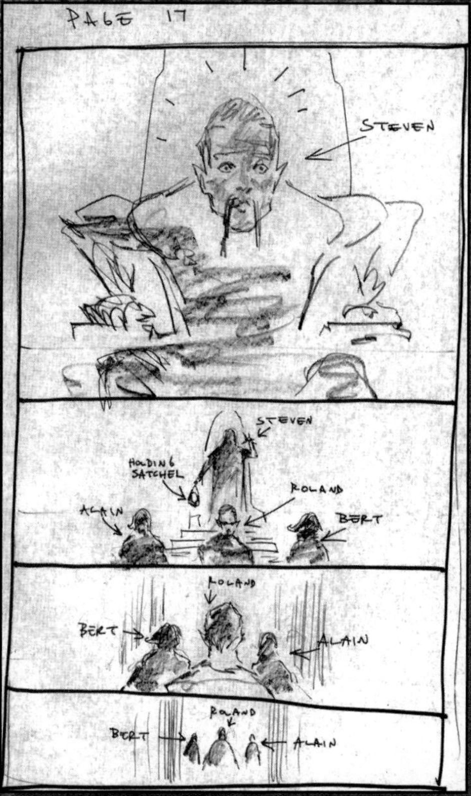
PAGE 17
STEVEN
STEVEN
HOLDING SATCHEL
ROLAND
ALAIN
BERT
ROLAND
BERT
ALAIN
ROLAND
BERT
ALAIN

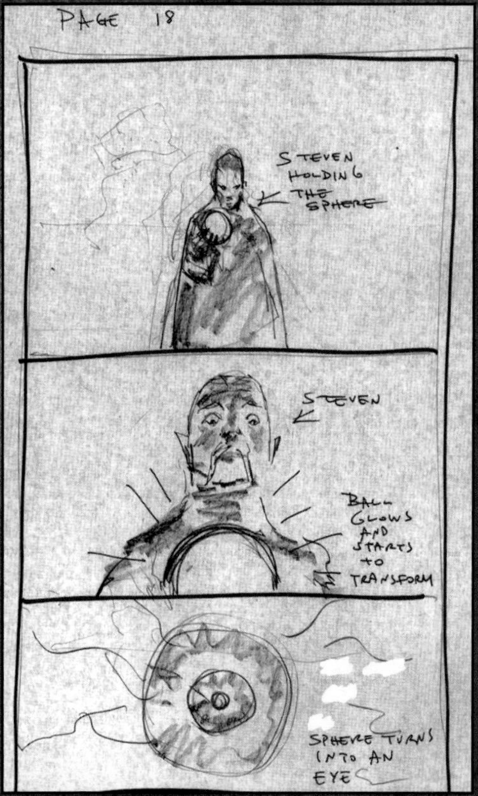
PAGE 18
STEVEN HOLDING THE SPHERE
STEVEN
BALL GLOWS AND STARTS TO TRANSFORM
SPHERE TURNS INTO AN EYE

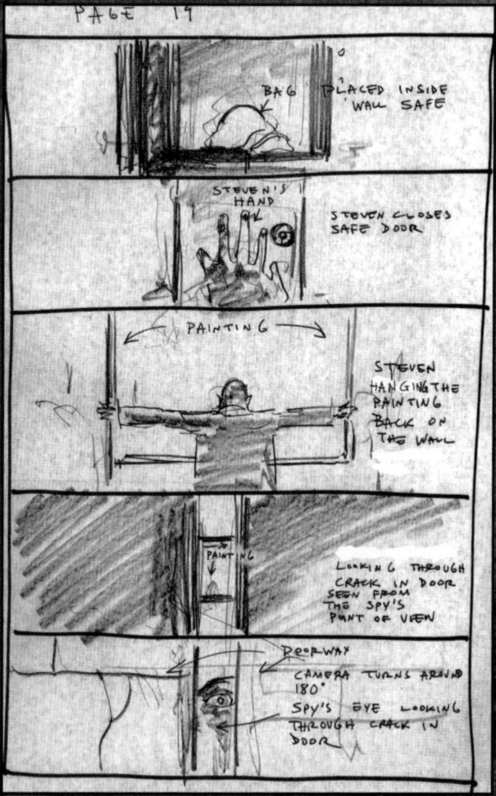
PAGE 19
BAG PLACED INSIDE WALL SAFE
STEVEN'S HAND
STEVEN CLOSES SAFE DOOR
PAINTING
STEVEN HANGING THE PAINTING BACK ON THE WALL
PAINTING
LOOKING THROUGH CRACK IN DOOR SEEN FROM THE SPY'S POINT OF VIEW
DOORWAY
CAMERA TURNS AROUND 180°
SPY'S EYE LOOKING THROUGH CRACK IN DOOR

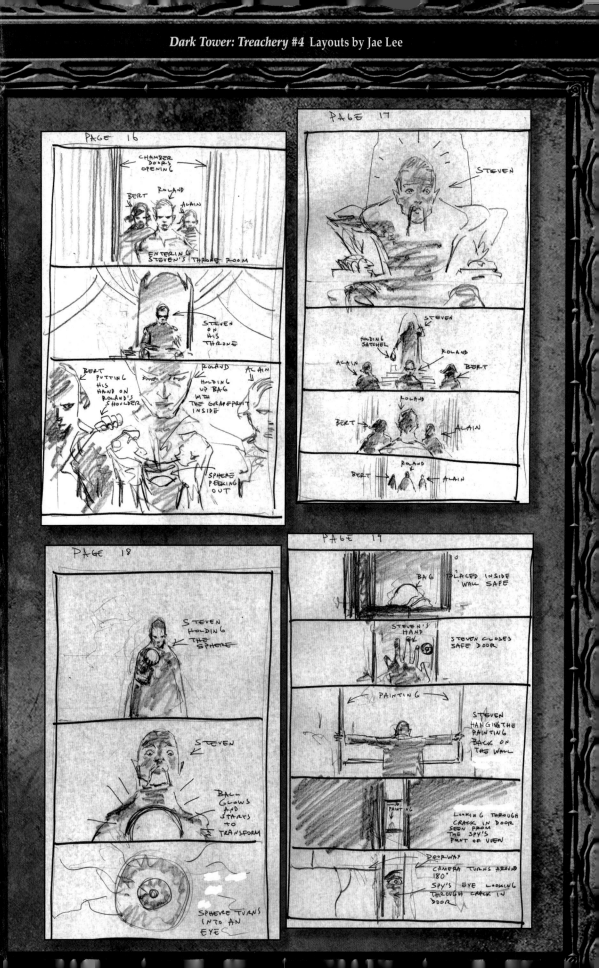

Dark Tower: Treachery #4 **Preliminary Variant Cover Art and Cover Inks by Richard Isanove**

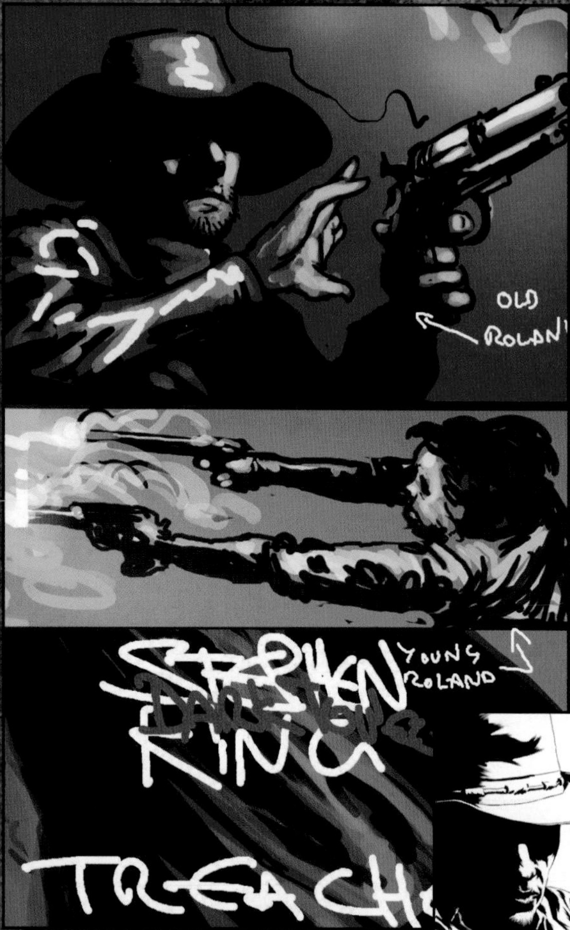
OLD
ROLAN
YOUNG
ROLAND
STEPHEN
KING
TREACH

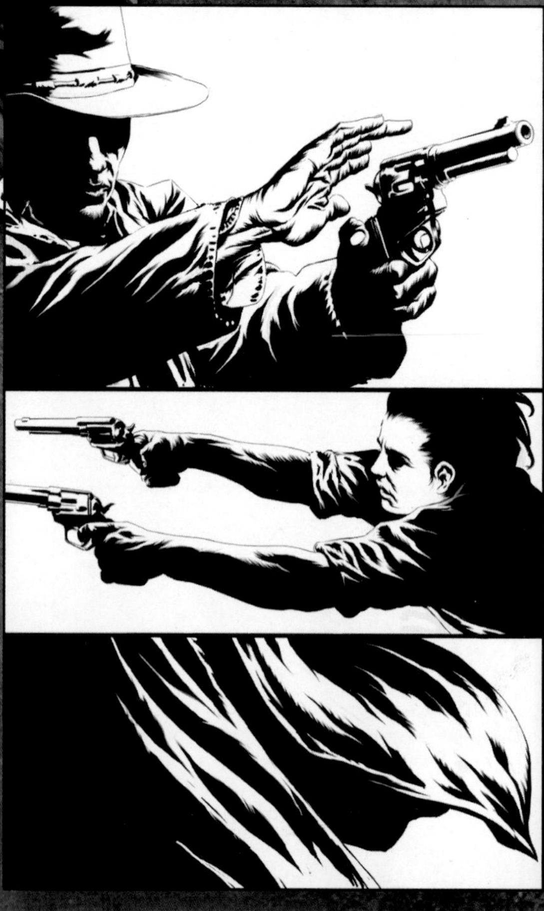